Michael Backman "really understands why business evolved the w— did in Asia" – *The Economist*

Michael Backman: A "brilliant writer on regional business strategi *Australian Financial Review*

"According to Michael Backman, an expert on the overseas Chinese (then) **Prime Minister of Singapore Goh Chok Tong**, *making ι Michael Backman in his National Day Address 1998*

"By attacking the government's media policy and urging the adopt the Western model [Michael Backman] has clearly crossed the lin engaged in our domestic politics." – **Singapore Minister for Informa... Lee Boon Yang**, *speaking to the Singapore Press Club in November 2003*

"Renowned author Michael Backman ... apt and cogent." – (then) **Malaysian Transport Minister and MCA President Ling Liong Sik**, *in a speech at Kampar, Malaysia, January 2002*

Michael Backman "raises extraordinarily important questions about the national interest ..." – **Senator Susan Knowles**, *in a speech to the Australian Senate*, Parliamentary Hansard, *April 1999*

D0696761

THE ASIAN INSIDER

Also by Michael Backman:

BIG in Asia: 25 Strategies for Business Success (with Charlotte Butler)*
Inside Knowledge: Streetwise in Asia
Asian Eclipse: Exposing the Dark Side of Business in Asia

* Published by Palgrave Macmillan

MICHAEL BACKMAN

The Asian Insider

Revised and updated

UNCONVENTIONAL WISDOM FOR ASIAN BUSINESS

© Michael Backman 2004, 2006

All rights reserved. No reproduction, copy or transmission of this publication may be made without written permission.

No paragraph of this publication may be reproduced, copied or transmitted save with written permission or in accordance with the provisions of the Copyright, Designs and Patents Act 1988, or under the terms of any licence permitting limited copying issued by the Copyright Licensing Agency, 90 Tottenham Court Road, London W1T 4LP.

Any person who does any unauthorised act in relation to this publication may be liable to criminal prosecution and civil claims for damages.

The author has asserted his right to be identified as the author of this work in accordance with the Copyright, Designs and Patents Act 1988.

First published in hardcover, 2004
First published in paperback, 2006 by
PALGRAVE MACMILLAN
Houndmills, Basingstoke, Hampshire RG21 6XS and
175 Fifth Avenue, New York, N.Y. 10010
Companies and representatives throughout the world

PALGRAVE MACMILLAN is the global academic imprint of the Palgrave Macmillan division of St. Martin's Press, LLC and of Palgrave Macmillan Ltd. Macmillan® is a registered trademark in the United States, United Kingdom and other countries. Palgrave is a registered trademark in the European Union and other countries.

ISBN-13: 978–1–4039–1657–0 hardback
ISBN-10: 1–4039–1657–8 hardback
ISBN-13: 978–0–230–00021–6 paperback
ISBN-10: 0–230–00021–5 paperback

This book is printed on paper suitable for recycling and made from fully managed and sustained forest sources.

A catalogue record for this book is available from the British Library.

The Library of Congress has cataloged the hardcover edition.

10   9   8   7   6   5   4   3   2   1
15 14 13 12 11 10 09 08 07 06

Printed and bound in Great Britain by
Creative Print & Design (Wales), Ebbw Vale

The Chinese character used on the cover and throughout is that for "Inside" or "Insider".

CONTENTS

ACKNOWLEDGEMENTS

Travel helps one to become an Asian Insider and so at times this book has a strong travel narrative component. I travel constantly – always looking, always learning. The other key component for me when it comes to understanding Asia is to have a strong network of good friends and associates who, by passing on ideas or simply supplying anecdotes in the course of conversation, help not only to deepen my understanding of Asia but to enliven it.

Among those who have provided ideas and anecdotes that I have used in this book are Charlotte Butler, Rudolf Phua, Raymond Yee, Eric Pringle, Louis Kraar, Cherie Nursalim, Yau Su Peng, Peter Hendy, Jennifer Gee, Alistair Nicholas, Jeffrey Tan, Sandra Chia, Daryl Kennedy, Sandrine Westcott, Anne Richter, Piers Brunner, Joni Djuanda, Justin Doebele, Shabanji Opukah, Gabriella Tuason Quimson, Ritchie Ramesh, Zaman Tambu, Vijya Patel, and Zhang Qiang.

And to Eddie Chin, thank you for your ideas and your insights. There's more here because of your influence than you will realize!

Thank you to Stephen Rutt, my commissioning editor at Palgrave Macmillan. Stephen thinks in terms of authors as well as products and so is always keen to know what I'm going to write next. On top of that he's gracious and unflappable, despite all my attempts to prove otherwise. Thanks also to Steve Maginn, head of Palgrave Macmillan's Hong Kong office and a true Asian Insider, for his ideas and his directness which save time, and to Regina Chan, also in Hong Kong.

Finally, thank you to the team at Aardvark Editorial for their copy-editing work. There's a lot to be said for those who know that Bodhisattva has only one "d".

Every effort has been made to trace all the copyright holders but if any have been inadvertently overlooked the publishers will be pleased to make the necessary arrangements at the first opportunity.

FACTS

- About 20 million Indians in India can afford Western-style levels of consumption. But about 100 million Chinese can.

- India has 1.1 billion people but only 22 million of them have a credit card.

- Japan's population will peak at 127.6 million by 2007 and will fall to 102 million by 2035. (So you think Japanese real estate is a good long-term investment?)

- 350 million adult Indians cannot read or write. But they can vote.

- Prostitution is illegal in Bangkok but permitted in Singapore.

- Shanghai has more than 4,000 buildings that are 18 storeys or more high.

- After the United States, the country with the biggest number of proficient English speakers is the Philippines. It is not India.

- Almost 70% of the world's Muslims live not in the Middle East but east of Karachi.

- The Dalai Lama eats meat.

Comparing Asia: who ranks where

Country or territory	Disposable income (GDP per capita: purchasing power parity basis, US$)	Population (millions)	Corruption (Perceived corruption: rank out of 158 countries; the higher the rank, the more corrupt)	Adult literacy (%)	Aging population (Median age of population, years)
Hong Kong	36,800	6.9	15	93.5	39.4
Japan	30,400	127.4	equal 21	99.0	42.6
Singapore	29,700	4.4	5	92.5	36.8
Taiwan	26,700	22.9	equal 32	86.0	34.1
Brunei	23,600	0.37	n.a.	93.9	27.0
South Korea	20,300	48.4	equal 40	97.9	34.5
Malaysia	10,400	24.0	39	88.7	23.9
Thailand	8,300	65.4	equal 59	92.6	30.9
China	6,200	1,306.0	equal 78	90.9	32.3
Philippines	5,100	87.9	equal 117	92.6	22.3
Sri Lanka	4,300	20.1	equal 78	92.3	29.4
Indonesia	3,700	242.0	equal 137	87.9	26.5
India	3,400	1,080.3	equal 88	59.5	24.7
Vietnam	3,000	83.5	equal 107	90.3	25.5
Pakistan	2,400	162.4	equal 144	48.7	19.6
Mongolia	2,200	2.8	n.a.	97.8	24.3
Bangladesh	2,100	144.3	equal 158	43.1	21.9
Cambodia	2,100	13.6	equal 130	73.6	19.9
Laos	1,900	6.2	77	66.4	18.7
Myanmar (Burma)	1,800	42.9	equal 155	85.3	26.1
North Korea	1,800	22.9	n.a.	99.0	31.7
Nepal	1,500	27.7	equal 117	45.2	20.1
Bhutan	1,400	2.2	n.a.	42.2	20.3
East Timor	400	1.0	n.a.	58.6	20.4
***	***	***	***	***	***
United States	41,800	295.7	17	97.0	36.3
Australia	32,000	20.1	9	100.0	36.0
United Kingdom	30,900	60.4	equal 11	99.0	39.0

Sources: CIA Factbook, 2006; Transparency International, www.transparencyinternational.org.

Chapter 1

THE ASIAN INSIDER: AN INTRODUCTION

"Knowledge itself is power."

(Francis Bacon, 1597, *Meditationes Sacrae*)

It was a warm, humid Hong Kong day. I'd just given a speech on corporate governance practices among Asian firms at a conference in the Marriott Hotel. I had lingered too long over the question and answer session and now I was in a mad rush to get to the airport. I half ran along the pavement beneath the Mandarin Oriental Hotel in Hong Kong's central district to catch the train to Chek Lap Kok Airport. I only just made the flight. But within a few hours I was in Kuala Lumpur, and having dinner with a local Chinese friend. We sat at a table on the pavement outside Devi's Corner, a *Mamak* or Muslim Indian restaurant in Bangsar. My friend's mobile phone rang. He looked titillated. "What's up?" I asked. "Someone has died", he said.

That someone turned out to be Cantonese film and pop star Leslie Cheung. He had thrown himself from a window on the 24th floor of Hong Kong's Mandarin Oriental Hotel. He landed right where I had walked earlier that day. I sank into my chair, took a long sip of my iced lime juice and imagined the odd possibility that Leslie Cheung might have killed me.

My friend's phone rang again. Then he received an SMS. Then a few more calls. The world's overseas Chinese community was becoming energized before my eyes. Soon, everyone knew the news. Or at least everyone who is Chinese. Text messages flew around the world to announce what had happened and all before official confirmation that the victim was indeed the Hong Kong singer and actor.

I was at another Kuala Lumpur restaurant the following evening. A large Chinese family dined nearby. They spoke loudly and in Cantonese. All the way through their boisterous conversation I could hear the words

Gor Gor, which in the Hong Kong dialect means elder brother, the nickname by which Leslie Cheung was known.

I was in Singapore the following day. A color photograph of Leslie Cheung was splashed across the *Straits Times*. A week later I was in London's Chinatown where the Chinese language *Sing Tao* newspaper had rushed out a full-color commemorative booklet with pictures of the star's Hong Kong funeral. A suitably morose picture of Cheung had been chosen for the cover and so his mournful face stared from windows across Soho, from the windows of dim sum places run by Cantonese from Hong Kong and Chinese supermarkets owned by Teochiu from Bangkok.

The death of Leslie Cheung captured the attention of the world's overseas Chinese communities. Briefly, they were united by one thing: they all wanted to know more about Cheung's death. Meanwhile, the rest of the world was largely ignorant. "Leslie who?" might have been its collective response. How circles move within circles.

But then does it matter? Does it matter not to know these things: Asia's personalities, the nuances for which it is unique and, in essence, all its details? The answer is yes, it does matter, particularly if you want to succeed in Asia. It is, after all, details such as these that make Asia Asia.

But then what is Asia? Culturally, it is not a series of discrete parcels that match the borders of countries. For centuries, influences that pay scant regard to where one country ends and another begins have washed through the region. Centers of defined culture exist but they blur at their margins, thanks to migration and population drift. And so Asia is both nuanced and interconnected.

Look at the food. Malaysia's *laksa lemak*, a coconut-based noodle soup that's served with prawns and the buds of fresh ginger, is known as *kao soi* in Thailand where it's served with pork or chicken. In Myanmar it is known as *ohnokaukswe* where it's made with chicken and thickened with chickpea flour, a consequence of a shared border with India. All along, it's the same soup but with local variations.

Asia is like that. It's one big regional marketplace and always has been. Chinese junks have long traded with Southeast Asia. And so too did Arab traders. Some scholars have even suggested that King Solomon's Temple was embellished with materials sourced either from peninsular Malaysia or the east coast of Sumatra and carried to the Middle East via India aboard Arab dhows, judging by descriptions of its interior in the Old Testament. In any event, when it came to trade, the South China Sea functioned as the Mediterranean of the East.

Most of Asia's countries have significant commercial ethnic Chinese minorities. The connections and common interests between them act to pull the region together and, in turn, the region to the rest of the world. Chinese cultural and economic space knows no borders. But so it is with the many Asians of Arab or Indian descent.

So much happens in Asia, particularly in business, that can be explained by the backgrounds, family relationships and cultural histories of the players involved. These cultural and other differences need to be understood if one also intends to be a player. Understanding them is essential to becoming an Asian Insider.

Those in business in Asia need to know about Asian politics because Asia's politicians and governments typically are highly intrusive in business. They need to know about family structures and behavior in Asia because families run most Asian business. They need to know about imperfections in the law because the rule of law is weak in many parts of Asia. And they need to know about what interests the locals because nowhere do people and personalities count in business more than they do in Asia. Business in the West might be about companies and corporations. But in Asia it is about individuals and families. In the West the demarcation between the business and non-business worlds tends to be well defined. In Asia it's not. And so doing well in business in Asia means not just understanding Asian business but understanding Asia.

As for businesspeople who are from Asia, it should never be assumed that, because they are Singaporean, from Hong Kong or are Malaysian, they know all there is to know about Asia. After all, what American knows everything about America? And yet Asia is far more diverse. So this is as much a book for a Singaporean, or a Malaysian or someone from Hong Kong as it is for anyone else.

But is it possible to be an Insider when one comes from outside? I believe so. Because the condition of being inside comes not from birth or ethnicity, but from knowledge. Similarly, how much of an Insider are those who are from Asia but who know little of their heritage? Proximity need not mean familiarity. What this means is that coming ethnically from outside Asia need not mean that one is frozen out. Conversely, being ethnically from Asia need not mean that one is frozen in.

This is why travel is so important. With travel comes knowledge. And with knowledge comes opportunity. It is how Southeast Asia's ethnic Chinese minorities came to be so disproportionately successful in business and trade. Like other commercial migrant minorities, they had traversed borders and markets. Knowledge of product and commodity deficiencies in one market could be matched with excesses in another. This put them at enormous commercial advantage compared with indigenous people who by and large hadn't traveled or been migrants and so were less able to unite markets with their knowledge.

I've written elsewhere (most notably in *Asian Eclipse: Exposing the Dark Side of Business in Asia* and *Big in Asia: 25 Strategies for Business Success* with Charlotte Butler) on the machinations of Asia's corporate world. This book and its companion book, *Inside Knowledge: Streetwise in Asia* take the next step, the journey to the inside: to delve into the all-important context. It is not crafted from an academic viewpoint, with chapters included for the sake of completeness and academic argument. Rather, it is crafted from the point of view of those who are likely to read it, their locations and in what are they likely to be interested. It includes several chapters on Islam in Asia. It's a subject that will only grow in importance and one that has a business dimension in addition to the more obvious political and religious dimensions. There are chapters on India and China, including a new chapter on China as a consumer market. It is a book that has been written not just to be bought, but to be read. It makes no claim to be comprehensive, but then how could it? And the mix of chapters is eclectic. But then so is Asia.

Part I
HOW ASIA REALLY WORKS

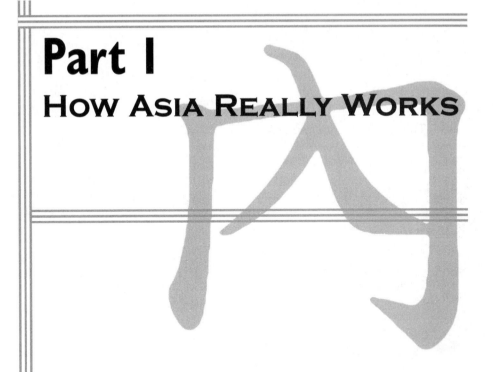

It is companies in the West that are well known, and not the people behind them. Everyone has heard of Coca-Cola, Siemens and General Motors. But who can name their CEOs? Or their largest shareholders? Indeed the only time that Western executives become household names seems to be when they are arrested or convicted of some extravagant white-collar crime. Who among the general public would have heard of Kenneth Lay if not for his arrest in the aftermath of the collapse of Enron?

In Asia, it's different. Companies are less important. It is the people behind them who really matter. Generally, they and their families are the founders, owners and managers. It is the families who define the companies and not the other way around. And so the number one attribute to being an Asian Insider is recognizing the centrality of the people behind Asia's companies, rather than the companies themselves: knowing their names, understanding them, their backgrounds, their families and their links with other business families. This section provides an introduction to the Asian corporate landscape. There is a chapter about families. The third chapter looks at the consequences of all this for corporate governance.

Chapter 2

ASIAN FAMILY CONNECTIONS

I visited the Hong Kong offices of Kerry Investments (part of the Kuok Group) some time back in the mid-1990s. There, a fund manager told me of the advantages of the group's Marco Polo Dynasty Fund. It was a mutual fund that invested in stocks listed in Singapore, Thailand, Malaysia, the Philippines and Hong Kong and then only if they were controlled by Asian founding families.

The intriguing reasoning was that such stocks outperformed the indices of the region's bourses. And for a time that was true. How could this be so, I asked? "Oh, we ring up Chye Kuok [Robert Kuok's nephew]. He knows all the families; all the players. He finds out what's going on and we then know which stocks to buy." That seemed to be about the extent of the fund's research, but then those were the days of the Asian "miracle", when real research wasn't necessary. Even a mutual fund could operate on the basis of *guanxi*.

Times have changed. The idea now that a mutual fund could market itself by claiming to invest only in firms that are connected to conglomerates, embedded in a sea of related-party transactions, often with privately held companies, and in which there is little or no separation between management and ownership seems almost comical. But it did and the Marco Polo Dynasty Fund raised millions of dollars on that basis.

Nonetheless, Asian business is still family business. A recent World Bank study analysed almost 3,000 publicly traded companies in Hong Kong, Indonesia, Japan, Korea, Malaysia, the Philippines, Singapore, Taiwan and Thailand. It focused on the largest public companies in these countries.[1] It found that outside Japan, families controlled on average at least 60% of the large listed companies. Separation of ownership from family control was also found to be rare. And that is for listed companies. Family control of unlisted companies is much higher. For many, the family and the firm are synonymous concepts. And that is key to understanding how business in much of Asia works.

Old Ways

Genes connect people across borders and across time. Geneticists have estimated, for example, that some 16 million men, mostly living in China, bear Y chromosomes that are characteristic of the Mongol ruling house. It means that they can claim to be descendants of Genghis Khan.[2] It's also been estimated that each of us alive today would have had more than 1.1 million ancestors living in 1066, assuming that there was no intermarriage among them. And yet back then the world's population could not have been more than 200 million.[3] So the chance that any two people alive today shared a common ancestor a thousand years ago is roughly one in two hundred. "We're all one family" literally is (almost) true.

Marrying within the family is common in contemporary Asia. Partly this happens to preserve family wealth. Excessive marriage within families was an explicit criticism of Malay culture that former Malaysian Prime Minister Mahathir Mohamad made in his book *The Malay Dilemma*. Even today, marriage between cousins and second cousins persists among Malays. "She comes from a good family" goes the refrain. Well, one would hope that she would. But inbreeding can also derive from the problem of small numbers. Such is the case among Bangkok's Indian Sikh community and Mumbai's Parsee community. But it's a practice that's not unique to Asia. Researchers have estimated that in the Arab world, on average, 45% of married couples are related.[4] And in Iraq it's estimated that almost half of all married couples are either first or second cousins.[5] Family trees in such instances are more like family thickets.

Polygamy is another aspect of some Asian cultures. The region's Muslim men are permitted as many as four wives. Hamzah Haz, Indonesia's vice president between 2001 and 2004, has three wives. The third wife he married while he served as vice president. Former Malaysian Finance Minister Daim Zainuddin has two wives and so too did the Sultan of Brunei until he divorced one in early 2003. The Sultan and his principal wife celebrated their fortieth wedding anniversary on July 25, 2005. And then a month later at a ceremony in Kuala Lumpar, he married a 26-year-old Malaysian woman, a former newsreader. So the Sultan once more has two wives. Polygamy is also permissible in some Himalayan cultures. Jigme Singye Wangchuk, the King of Bhutan since 1972, is married to four sisters and has children by each of them. He married all four during a ceremony in 1988. A brother of the four sisters serves as Bhutan's health and education minister. A cousin until recently served as the justice minister, and so on. Polygamy is common in Nepal, although legally a man can only take a second wife if after 10 years of marriage there are no living children. In Thailand, the practice of politicians and big businessmen keeping a "minor" wife is common. A study in 2001 estimated that as many as a quarter of Thai men aged between 30 and 50 keep a "minor" wife.[6]

And among the Chinese, the system of concubinage persists, especially among the big, traditional Chinese businessmen in Hong Kong and Southeast Asia, even though bigamy is illegal in most Asian countries other than for Muslims. "One man is best suited to four women, as a teapot is best suited to four cups" is the graphic adage that some traditional Chinese men adhere to.[7]

It was common for Chinese émigrés to leave a wife behind in China but then to take another wife in their adopted country. Liem Sioe Liong, the founder of Indonesia's Salim Group, did this. In British-ruled Hong Kong, the practice of polygamy was outlawed by the colony's Legislative Council in 1971, when concubinage became bigamy and thus illegal.[8] But the practice still occurs. Hong Kong businessman and Macau casino partner Henry Fok has at least 3 wives and at least 10 children.[9] His partner in the Macau casino business, Stanley Ho, has at least 3 wives and 17 children.[10]

Elsewhere, Chew Choo Keng, the founder of Singapore's Khong Guan biscuits, had 5 wives and 23 children. Thaworn Phornpapha, the founder of Thailand's Siam Motors had 3 wives and 13 children. Eka Tjipta Widjaja, the founder of Indonesia's Sinar Mas Group which controls the Singapore-based and Nasdaq-listed Asian Pulp & Paper, has at least 8 wives and more than 40 children. Tiang Chirathivat, the founder of Thailand's Central Group has several wives and 26 children. Aw Boon Haw and Aw Boon Par, the founders of the Tiger Balm empire, had 4 and 3 wives respectively.[11] C.Y. Bao, the founder of Taiwan's Chung Shing Textiles had 3 concurrent wives.[12] And Chin Sophonpanich, the founder of Bangkok Bank, had 2 wives.

Singaporean Chew Choo Keng explained once that his polygamy was necessary because as a Chinese, "the greatest act of being unfilial is to have no descendant".[13] This is one of the greatest fears of most traditional Chinese men – not to have a son. And so, some of the region's ethnic Chinese business families are extraordinarily large and complex. Srisakdi

Charmonman, the head of Thailand's KSC Group, has 31 brothers and sisters, for example. With their children, they now account for an extended family of more than 300. Given that most businesses in Asia are owned and run by families, complex families can make for complex business arrangements. And complex families also are conducive to plenty of family infighting that also tends to spill over into the business arena.

Alliances and Coalitions Among Asia's Big Families

But it's the interconnectedness of the big business families in Asia that is especially fascinating. In many instances, the interconnectedness spreads across borders, so the families behind some of the biggest business groups in Asia are related. Politicians too are wrapped into these family networks. How does Asia really work? Here's how:

- Quek Leng Chan, head of Malaysia's massive Hong Leong Group, is a cousin of Kwek Leng Beng, head of Singapore's Hong Leong Group. (The two groups are separate but share the same name. *Hong* means good and plentiful; *leong* means great prosperity.) Kwek is a shareholder in Hotel Properties, controlled by Ong Beng Seng. Ong was a substantial shareholder of NatSteel until 2005, when it was acquired by Tata Steel, part of India's Tata Group. David Fu, Ong's brother-in-law, served as a director. Fu's cousin, David Ban, the co-owner of the worldwide franchise rights for Japanese fast-food chain Genki Sushi outside Japan, Taiwan and Hawaii, also served as a director. Lee Suan Yew is a past director of Hotel Properties. His brother is Lee Kuan Yew, Singapore's former prime minister. Their brother Freddy Lee is a former chairman of Vickers Ballas of which Ong was a major shareholder.

  Dennis Lee, the chairman of Singapore food company Cerebos Pacific up until his death in 2003, was another of Lee Kuan Yew's brothers. Dennis's wife, Gloria Lee, is the founder of one of Singapore's most prominent stockbrokerages, Kim Eng Securities.

  Lee Kuan Yew's mother, Lee Chin Koon, was a cousin of Wee Kim Wee, Singapore's former ambassador to Malaysia and later a president of the Republic of Singapore. His son Lee Hsien Yang heads up Singapore Telecom, which is controlled by Temasek Holdings. This in turn is headed by Ho Ching, wife of Lee Hsien Loong, Hsien Yang's brother.
- Temasek Holdings bought, in January 2006, almost half of Shin Corp, the company founded by the Thai Prime Minister Thaksin Shinawatra. Monthatip, a sister of Thaksin, is married into the Kovitcharoenkul family.

Yaowapa, another Thaksin sister, is married into the Wongsawat family. And the Kovitcharoenkuls and the Wongsawats jointly own M Link Asia Corp which, like Shin Corp, is a Thai telecommunications company.

- Thailand's Vilailuck family also had a stake in Shin Corp. In turn, they control another Thai telecommunications company called Samart. Telekom Malaysia owns 44% of Samart. Telekom Malaysia and India's Tata Group joined a consortium that acquired control of IDEA Cellular in December 2004, a leading mobile telephone company in India.

- Tata is headed by Ratan Tata. Pallonji Shapoorji Mistry, the largest individual shareholder in Tata Sons, is the father-in-law of Ratan Tata's half-brother Noel Tata. Ratan is very close to Nuslia Wadia, chairman of the massive Bombay Dyeing and Manufacturing Company. In turn, Wadia is the son of Dina Wadia, the only daughter of Mohammad Ali Jinnah, the founder of Pakistan. Tata controls Tata Consulting Services (TCS), India's biggest software company. The wife of Narayana Murthy, chairman of Infosys, one of TCS' main competitors, is the sister of the wife of Gururaj Deshpande, founder of Sycamore Networks.

- Ferry Santosa is the founder of Indonesia's Ometraco Group. One of his daughters married a nephew of the wife of Sjamsul Nursalim, founder of another Indonesian conglomerate, the Gadjah Tunggal Group. Nursalim is related to Singapore's Goh family that founded the Tat Lee Bank (which later merged with Keppel Bank and then with Overseas Chinese Banking Corporation). Dennis Lee (Lee Kuan Yew's brother) was a former director of Tat Lee.

- The sister of Indonesia's Gunawan brothers, the founders of Panin Bank, is Suryawaty Lidya. She married Mochtar Riady, the founder of Lippo Group. Hari Darmawan, the founder of Indonesia's Matahari department store chain (now owned by Mochtar Riady) is related by marriage to Ong Tjoe Kim, the owner of Singapore's Metro department store chain.

- The founder of Indonesia's Bank Harapan, the late Hendra Rahardja, was related to Eddie Tansil, the fugitive founder of the collapsed Golden Key Group. (Rahardja too became a fugitive and died in Australia in 2002.) Tansil's sister is married to Paulus Tumewu, the owner of Indonesia's Ramayana department store chain.

- Listed Singapore companies Van der Horst and L&M are controlled by Indonesia's Edward Soeryadjaya. Edward is married to Atilah Rapatriarti, whose brother is married to Sukmawati, a sister of Indonesia's former President Megawati Sukarnoputri. His late first wife also was the adopted daughter of Megawati's father's third wife. L&M director Bambang Sukmonohadi is the father-in-law of Megawati's only daughter.

- Peter Woo, the head of Hong Kong's Wharf Holdings, and Edgar Cheng, the head of Singapore's Wing Tai Holdings, are both married to sisters. The sisters' father was Pao Yue Kong, who founded the shipping and hotel group, World International.
- Sue Kuok, the daughter of Hong Kong-based Robert Kuok, the owner of the Shangri-La Hotel chain and Hong Kong's leading English daily, the *South China Morning Post*, married Malaysia's Rashid Hussain, who founded RHB Bank. *Ming Pao,* another Hong Kong newspaper, is owned by Tiong Hiew King, the billionaire owner of Malaysia's Rimbunan Hijau Group. He is the nephew of Wong Tuong Kwang, the owner of the WTK Group. Kuok, Tiong and Wong are all of the comparatively rare Fuzhou Chinese dialect.
- Tony Tan, who built up Singapore's Parkway Holdings, is a nephew of Malaysia's Tan Chin Nam who controls Malaysia's IGB Group.
- A daughter of Singapore's late Lim Kah Ngam who founded the Lim Kah Ngam property group is married to Malaysia's Mohamed Rahmat, a former information minister and secretary general of Malaysia's ruling Barisan Nasional coalition. And on it goes.

Alliances such as these help to tie Asia's economies together. They also help to explain why some business mergers and joint ventures happen and why others don't. Rarely is business in Asia simply about profits or fighting for market share. How can it be when most companies are owned and managed by families and many of those families, and hence their companies, are related?

What are Asian Family Firms for?

Typically, Western firms aim for one of two things – profits or market share. Asian family firms may be interested in these things too. But they might also exist for other reasons – things that work against conventional notions of corporate governance.

So what are some of the other aims of Asian family firms? The companies of Asia's business families mean everything to the families. Witness the number of Asian families that fight to keep their companies long after they should have sold out had they wanted to keep their wealth intact. For many, the company is synonymous with the family. Direction and management may be determined more by emotion than by principles of sound governance.

Apart from the provision of a source of income, the Asian family firm also exists:[14]

- to give family members a job
- to hold the family together
- to honor the ancestral founders of the firm
- for the family's prestige and honor.

These are things that most Asian business families care deeply about. They are motivations not cared for by most outside partners and investors or regulators. Each motivation has nothing to do with enhancing the firm's productive capacity and improving rates of return on invested equity.

For example, a corporate structure that is highly complex and lacking in transparency might be that way in order to make it harder for individual family members to split off and go their separate ways, taking their equity with them. Appeals for reform based on efficiency, transparency, and better corporate governance in general are likely to fall on deaf ears in such cases.

Similarly, return on capital may not be much of a motivator. Some Asian family-run business groups are not profitable at all. They are not required to be. Some groups have become large and complex because the families behind them have become large and complex. Agility and flexibility have been sacrificed to keep the family working together. Sometimes this reaches the point when returns are so low that working in the family business is the only way that individual family members are able to profit from it. If everyone is together and has a job then why change? Even if they wanted to change, many families cannot because their ownership structures are too complex, precisely to stop meddling with the structure.

Some Chinese business families do anything to avoid bankruptcy or shedding companies when they should. They do this to avoid the loss of prestige and "face" in the local business community. But it is also to uphold the honor of the family's ancestors. Many Asian business families would see it as unfilial to sell or liquidate a company that a grandfather or great-grandfather had founded. It's another important motivator in corporate Asia that almost certainly will be at odds with the interests of outsiders, such as minority shareholders, bankers and bondholders.

The desire to keep companies under family control can mean that many families do not raise capital and bring in outside investors when their companies need it. Sometimes companies are pushed to the point of insolvency before their controlling families are ready to accept other shareholders.

Furthermore, many of Asia's business families prefer to borrow rather than issue new shares that might see a dilution of their control. This pushes their gearing ratios beyond what is optimal, making them vulnerable at times of crisis. The desire to preserve family control is an indulgence that can mean that bondholders, creditors, minority shareholders and joint venture partners are forced to bear greater risk than they should.

But families bring other problems too. Founding patriarchs who drive the family firm do not live forever. Unless they are replaced by a similarly driven successor, the family's firm can become rudderless. This can be compounded with the joint stock nature of family ownership, whereby families control companies through a trust arrangement. Equity is not readily ascribed to individual family members and family members receive dividends according to their needs rather than in a manner that necessarily reflects their share of the family's equity. This lessens the interest they have to ensure sound governance and an adequate return on their invested capital. After all, how can they make an assessment of the rate of return when they don't know what their equity is in the first place?

Understanding the nature of Asia's business families is essential to becoming an Asian Insider. Families have a very great impact on the quality of corporate governance in Asia. There are cultural considerations too. This is the subject of the next chapter.

Chapter 3

WHY IS CORPORATE GOVERNANCE SO BAD IN ASIA?

Corporate governance was the new buzz phrase in the aftermath of the 1997 Asian economic crisis. Conferences were held on it, new laws were passed, and everyone was talking about it. Why? Probably not because Asia's companies actually wanted better corporate governance. What they wanted was investment funds from outside Asia to return. It became clear that the best way to attract back investment was to have better corporate governance. Or at least to acquire some of the trappings of it.

But as growth has returned to Asia, the desire for reform, and certainly its imperative, has slowed. But it remains the case that corporate governance in much of Asia is still terrible. Things have improved. But they have not improved enough.

Even in Singapore, the commitment to better corporate governance remains a little too superficial. There is not a culture of transparency. There is no natural inclination toward openness either in government or in the corporate sector, and corporate governance is still something that is done by ticking boxes. A genuine culture of good corporate governance is yet to evolve.

This is clear, particularly from where portfolio investors choose to invest their money. Or to be more accurate choose not to invest. *Asiamoney* magazine noted in late 2005 that the typical global fund manager allocates around 4–5% of his or her portfolio to Asia, other than Japan, even though Asia minus Japan makes up 23% of the world economy on a purchasing power parity (PPP) basis.[1] And if you take out Asian-based funds from this, such as those operated by the Government of Singapore Investment Corporation and Malaysia's Khazanah, then the 4–5% figure falls even more. Some fund managers even make up their Asia quota by buying Australian stocks.

Why then don't global funds want to invest in Asia? The main problem is that strong economic growth in Asia often does not translate into good investment returns.

By 2005 China, for example, achieved almost 10% economic growth but its stock markets hit eight-year lows. Not only that, but China's mutual fund industry incurred an aggregate loss of US$741 million in the first half of that year.[2] Why is that? The answer is that by and large the companies listed on China's stock markets are either in terrible shape, or have very poor transparency or terrible corporate governance or a mixture of all three. Many have been listed not because they are good and need cash to expand but because the Chinese state wants to get rid of them. Many are subsidiaries of state-owned enterprises which use the stock market to raise cash which is then passed back to their parent companies via highly questionable related-party transactions.

But then this, in varying degrees, is similar to what has happened on many of Asia's stock markets. Listing is often used as an exit strategy. The view of Asia's business families is best summed up by: "what is profitable is mine, and what is not can be yours."

Rarely do Asia's founding families list their holding companies. Typically they list only the outer reaches of their empires. Hong Kong-based Malaysian billionaire Robert Kuok, for example, hasn't listed his holding company or his reputedly highly profitable international sugar trading business but he's happy for you to have a share in his Shangri-la Group, which is involved in the highly cyclical and costly hotel business.

So the gap between a 4–5% portfolio share and 23% GDP (on a PPP basis) could be called the corporate governance gap. This is the cost to Asia of its very poor record on corporate governance. Of course another reason why funds underweight Asia and Asian stocks is because many Asian stocks do not have sufficient liquidity. But then this too is part of the corporate governance problem: many Asian companies that are listed have only a very tiny proportion of their shares available for the general public, say 10 or 20%. The rest of the stock typically is owned, or at least controlled, by the family. One reason for listing in this event is simply for the family to get a market valuation of its holdings. With a market value, their stake can then be used as collateral to get bank loans. So once again, the motive for listing has little to do with having outsiders take sizable and profitable stakes in the companies concerned.

Indeed even among those funds that do invest in Asian stocks, many see it not as an equity play but as a currency bet. They are betting that most of their gain will come not from share price growth and income but simply from a valuation effect; from the appreciation of Asia's currencies.

This is not to say that all companies in Asia are bad at governance. But it does say there's a perception that, on average, they are bad. One way for outside investors to be exposed to Asia's growth but not its poor corporate governance is to invest in Western firms that have a lot of Asian exposure: firms such as Australia's BHP-Billiton or Germany's Volkswagen.

Western Corporate Governance

Asia does not have a monopoly on poor corporate governance. The mature economies of the West certainly do not have uniform and perfect corporate governance. One of the most appalling instances of governance abuse in the US today, for example, relates to the pay that many CEOs of listed companies get. There is no statutory requirement in the US that shareholders must be allowed to vote on executive pay of listed companies.

The gap between what managers do and what shareholders want is known as an "agency problem" and many CEOs and other senior managers are able to exploit this gap by awarding themselves obscene amounts of pay in what amounts to legalized theft.

Fortune magazine showed that in 1970 the compensation for America's top 100 CEOs averaged US$1.3 million or about 39 times that of an average worker.[3] By the end of the 1990s, the average was US$37.5 million or about 1,000 times that of an average worker.

There have been some truly extraordinary outcomes. In 2001, Larry Ellison of Oracle took home US$706 million in pay and benefits just for that year. The following year Alfred Lerner of MBNA Bank took home US$195 million for the year.[4]

But what about the really big scandals to have hit corporate America in recent years: Enron, WorldCom and Tyco? Here things are a little more promising. The point about these instances is that no economy has perfect corporate governance. But some have far better governance than others. And besides it's not that corporate frauds occur that is the real concern but what happens next. Are the perpetrators punished? Well increasingly, in the US they are.

In the US, Dennis Kozlowski, former CEO of Tyco, was given a 25-year prison term and a fine of US$167 million. Mark Swartz, his deputy, was given the same sentence and ordered to pay US$72 million. Andrew Fastow, CFO of Enron, was given a 10-year jail term and surrendered almost US$24 million. Bernard Ebbers of WorldCom received a 25-year jail term. John Rigas of Adelphia Communications got 15 years. Alfred Taubman of Sotheby's got a year in jail and a US$7.5 million fine for price fixing. Weston Smith of HealthSouth got 27 months in jail and a fine of US$1.7 million. The list of high-flying, convicted, white-collar criminals is growing. And they are not being given just mere slaps on the wrist.

But rarely do white-collar criminals go to jail in Asia even though Asia is home to some of the world's worst corporate governance. Asia's biggest single corporate disaster has been Asia Pulp and Paper (APP), a Singapore company with operations based largely in Indonesia. Up until Enron, it was the world's single biggest corporate defaulter. Among the questionable transactions was the transfer of around a billion dollars to five British Virgin Island companies linked to APP's controlling shareholders, which accounted for almost a third of APP's sales in 1999 alone.[5]

Singapore's Commercial Affairs Department investigated APP, but the results of any such investigation have not been made public. Nor have there been any charges or jailings. This is not an isolated case and of course elsewhere in Asia, the situation is much worse.

So why does Asia have persistent bad corporate governance a decade after the Asian economic crisis? What follows, in no particular order, is a list of ten enemies of good corporate governance in Asia.

Enemy 1: Asia Hype

Billions of dollars in direct investment are pouring into Asia, particularly China, and to a lesser extent, India. Such investment tends to suggest to governments that they are doing enough on corporate regulation and fighting corruption.

In some respects, the view is who needs good governance when so much money is pouring in? China's banks are a case in point. They have not been run as conventional banks but more as welfare agencies delivering grants dressed up as loans to state-owned enterprises, often on the basis of due orders of Communist Party officials rather than on risk analysis. And so all too often banks continue to lend to enterprises on the verge of collapse so that local officials don't have to cope with the unemployment consequences.

Not surprisingly, the system has accrued billions in bad loans that routinely have had to be cut out of the system. And yet by 2006, more than US$13 billion in foreign direct investment (FDI) had flowed into China's banking system, with billions more promised. But the governance of China's banks has been particularly terrible, so presumably the investment is all on the basis of China having a large population and what that might mean for the future.

More generally, in 2003, China actually exceeded the US for the first time as the world's biggest destination for FDI, taking in US$53 billion compared with the US's US$40 billion. Who needs good corporate governance, sound regulation and institutions not marred by corruption? Clearly not China, given this vote of confidence. So will corporate governance improve markedly in China over the next decade? Probably not. Corporate governance in China must be about the worst in the world. And yet China is the world's hottest destination for FDI. So why change?

Enemy 2: Confucianism

Confucianism was developed in China 2,500 years ago. The trouble is, a lot has changed since then. But the basic tenets of Confucianism haven't. The tenets of Confucianism are very good for running a village, or even a country that comprises a collection of villages, and they might even present some fairly decent rules for ordering a society, but they have no place at all in a modern company or a modern economy.

Above all, Confucianism preaches loyalty, particularly to one's seniors and family. It places huge importance on order and hierarchy. Authority flows down from the emperor or ruler who issues rules but then is not subject to them. Loyalty and obedience are valued over merit and productivity.

Now think of each Asian firm, especially each Asian family firm, as a little kingdom. There is a king and there are his servants. The king rules by decree. What he says goes. He is the law. He does not share his power with some rule book. Employees are exquisitely sensitive to the bosses' demands and wishes. And so everything is as it should be according to Confucian sentiment.

In such an environment, is such a thing as an Asian whistleblower even possible? Whistleblowers have a hard time even in the US, but how much harder is blowing the whistle on fraud or corruption committed by your boss or your colleagues if you live in a Confucian society?

Harmony and dislike of confrontation are other typically Confucian traits. Many in Asia do not like confrontation and criticism. It's for that reason that Western-style adversarial legal systems either do not exist in much of Asia or have been watered down. And yet, corporate governance by its very nature is adversarial: it is about challenge and accountability. "If you do not want problems, then do not look for them" is an attitude commonly heard in Asia. But how can a truly independent audit, for example, be conducted in that sort of environment, where everyone has to preserve face, harmony must be maintained, and open criticism is best avoided?

Also, Confucius was very good at defining relationships between rulers and the ruled, fathers and sons, and so on. But he did not define relationships very well between strangers. And that is a problem today, because joint stock companies are basically groups of strangers. Minority shareholders are usually strangers to the majority shareholders. They are outside the Confucian five cardinal relationships and that is another reason why they tend to get ripped off.

Enemy 3: Staff Loyalty

Employees in Asia tend to be too loyal. They follow orders. Management is not participative. And so it allows staff to adopt the Nuremberg defense: "Oh, I was only following orders."

Promotions in Asia often are not linked so much to merit as to the personal relationships that junior staff might have with their superiors. Scaling the corporate ladder is a sign of one's trustworthiness; not necessarily of one's inherent productivity. All too often, subservience and sycophancy are rewarded; and initiative, which by definition demonstrates a lack of dependence on senior staff, is not.

Similarly, shareholders are too timid at annual general meetings (AGMs). They're too afraid to speak up and hold directors accountable. Instead, some AGMs, in Malaysia for example, have become a farce – individuals obtain proxies from real shareholders and then turn up solely to consume free food and drink. The rush to the buffet has become so obscene that it is routinely reported in local newspapers. Listed food and beverage companies such as Fraser & Neave are particular targets. Some attendees even bring food containers so they can take away free food. The biggest complaint at some Malaysian AGMs now is not that directors are paid too much or there are too many questionable related-party transactions but that not enough free food is provided at meetings.

Enemy 4: Lack of Employee Empowerment

Many employees in Asia are shy, timid, don't want to stand out, don't want to rock the boat, just want to keep their heads down, be low profile, and above all be seen as loyal. That is no way to run a proactive system of internal controls for good corporate governance. Part and parcel of demonstrating loyalty means not questioning the boss.

Also, because many Asian firms operate without written internal rules and guidelines and instead largely rely on the whims and orders of the boss, many staff are unsure of exactly what their roles are and where their responsibilities start and end.

Consequently, many do little more than follow orders. They are unwilling to extend themselves and to take responsibility for things because that means accepting risk. Corporate governance problems might be noticed but no-one wants to say anything.

No-one wants to be seen to outshine their boss; nor does anyone want to deliver bad news to their boss. So bad governance often continues, even when staff are aware of the problem and have an idea for a solution.

Enemy 5: Inadequate Staff Training

Companies across Asia tend to underinvest in staff training, like they tend to underinvest in all intangibles and services. Staff are expected to be completely loyal but then little is invested in them. So it is not surprising that many staff know little about corporate governance, what it is for, and why they have a stake in it.

Enemy 6: Face

"Face" is a very Asian and particularly a very Chinese concept, but it is an inefficient characteristic and nowhere more so than in the workplace. Face causes no end of problems. It leads to terrible cover-ups and lies as everyone tries to preserve face rather than admit to a mistake or concede that there is a problem.

The problem is also particularly extreme in Japan, where officials sometimes kill themselves rather than stay around to fix a problem they've caused. And in Southeast Asia, face induces businesspeople to buy luxury imported European cars they don't need, offices that are way too flash, and even unnecessary corporate jets.

Within companies it causes problems to be papered over rather than fixed. It means that bad news doesn't travel up and so managers are only given good news, which is a terrible basis on which to run a company. Staff feel unable to offer even constructive criticism of one another in meetings for fear of turning work colleagues into enemies.

Enemy 7: Families

Families are the most important building blocks for any society. But they are a disaster for corporate governance. And that's a pity because most companies in Asia are owned and run by families, including listed companies.

Good corporate governance involves internal checks and balances. It means not treating the head of the company as a feudal lord or demigod but rather as someone to be monitored and challenged. Loyalty must not be given solely to the controlling shareholder but also to the other shareholders, the minority shareholders.

Given this, corporate governance is not so much a difficulty for many Asian family firms as an anathema. Asian families typically see checks and balances as an affront; a challenge to their authority and a loss of face before their employees. "It's my firm and I'll do what I like with it" seems to be a common viewpoint.

The companies of Asia's business families mean everything to the families. Witness the number of Asian families that fight to keep their companies long after they should have sold out had they wanted to keep their wealth intact. For many, the company is synonymous with the family. Direction and management may be determined more by emotion than by principles of sound governance.

But even if Asia's founding families do have the capacity for world-class corporate governance, many don't want it because they won't benefit from it. It all comes down to what Asian family firms are for. Chapter 2 looked at some of the motives, other than market share or profit maximization, that many Asian business families consider important but which are detrimental to transparency and the interests of other stakeholders.

A corporate structure that is highly complex and lacking in transparency might be that way in order to make it harder for individual family members to split off and go their separate ways, taking their equity with them. Appeals for reform that are based on efficiency, transparency, and better corporate governance in general are likely to fall on deaf ears in such cases.

Similarly, return on capital may not be much of a motivator. Some Asian family-run business groups are not profitable at all. They are not required to be. Some groups have become large and complex because the families behind them have become large and complex. Agility and flexibility have been sacrificed to keep the family working together. Sometimes this reaches the point when returns are so low that working in the family business is the only way that individual family members are able to profit from it. If everyone is together and has a job then why change?

Having said all this, family-run companies are hardly restricted to Asia, but what does seem less peculiar to Asia is the degree to which companies are owned and run by families.

Family firms pose governance problems everywhere. The collapse of the Robert Maxwell-owned Mirror Group Newspapers in the UK is a case in point. The UK Government report into the collapse, released in 2001, highlighted a range of problems in the group that had as its source the group's family control. Maxwell's son Kevin was quoted in the British media at the time as saying that no-one should work for a family business. The temptation to flout the law to save the family empire is substantial.

Kevin Maxwell said

> In family-run businesses, the conflicts of interest with outside shareholders are so deep and so impossible to deal with that I don't think it is either safe or fair for family relations to be exposed to those types of pressures.

> If you are brought up in a family business, you view the continuity of that business as almost sacred, as a duty. You do everything you can to save it and you lose sight that you are just a manager, no different from the hired gun who you pay a large sum to … one's sense of duty to the family overrides everything.[6]

And that is a huge problem in Asia.

Enemy 8: Asia's Governments

What else in Asia works against good corporate governance? Other big culprits are Asia's governments themselves. How can Asia's companies be expected to have good governance when Asia's governments don't?

Witness the case of the administration of vehicle import licenses in Malaysia. The system was exposed in 2005 as a shambles. Former Prime Minister Mahathir complained that so many licenses had been awarded that it was now hurting Proton, Malaysia's locally assembled national car.

The responsible minister Rafidah Aziz claimed that in fact she wasn't responsible; that the permits had always been granted with the prime minister's knowledge. Next Rafidah held a press conference at which she burst into tears and swore on the Koran that she had nothing to do with any license holders.

Then it was revealed that in fact the single biggest holder of licenses for the year was a former senior official in Rafidah's own ministry. Not only that, but her niece and her niece's husband had been given more than a thousand licenses in the past two years.

Then the customs director general tried to explain publicly how the licenses were allocated. But how they were really allocated became clear when it was revealed that a company owned by his own son had been awarded licenses.

Many called for Rafidah's resignation. But Rafidah isn't the world's longest serving trade minister for nothing. She then released the names of all the politicians who had taken up a license, and there were 337 in all.

When you consider that this sort of administrative sloppiness is replicated across ministries in Malaysia, and in governments across Asia more generally, how can companies be expected to operate with prudence and good governance? Where is the openness and accountability in how Asia's governments manage their own houses?

Singapore provides something of an exception. At least Singapore is an exception to the extent that we are allowed to know. Singapore does well on auditing and corruption measures but lets itself down when it comes to transparency and openness.

The Singapore Government's two main holding companies, Temasek Holdings and the Government of Singapore Investment Corporation (GIC), manage at least US$300 billion in wealth on behalf of all Singaporeans. But what are the GIC's total assets? What does the GIC earn each year? Who decides in what it should invest and what guidelines are used? None of this information is made public. Temasek started to release an annual account of itself in 2004, but it is not an annual report. It prefers to style them as annual "reviews". Under Singapore law it remains an exempt private company and is not required to publish its audited financial statements.

How can Asia's governments demand that companies have transparency and openness when they themselves don't? How can governments that waste billions of dollars then charge managers in a company for wasting just a few million?

Leadership by example is not something that Asia's governments seem to want, particularly when it comes to sound governance and transparency.

Enemy 9: Fear of Disclosure

The ninth enemy of good governance in Asia is the very great fear of openness, transparency and disclosure that many companies and their owners have.

It's often very difficult to get good information on Asian companies.

They err on the side of withholding information which anywhere else is publicly available.

Recently I contacted a prominent local chain of coffee shops in South-east Asia to find out who owned it. I was told by the staff that that information was "confidential". How can something that basic be confidential? Of course it's not – it's just that the staff don't feel empowered to give out any information. They don't want to take responsibility for it. And the result is that such organizations look shady and weak.

Enemy 10: Timid Media

An essential player in the fight for better governance is the media. But across Asia the media is hamstrung by government with censorship and excessive control (often with the self-serving idea that the media must do as the government says in the name of nation building), and by companies that wish to avoid exposure.

Given the success of its government in building a dynamic state with excellent infrastructure and a satisfied and well-catered-for citizenry, Singapore ought to have the freest and most dynamic media in all of Asia. Instead it has one of the most cowering.

Bad news stories are managed and they tend to disappear altogether from Singapore newspapers around August, because that is the month in which National Day is held and the government wants its citizens to feel particularly happy to be Singaporean. But that is no good for governance.

Journalists are very valuable for exposing problems – a great deal of the Enron scandal was exposed by journalists doing their job, for example. But in this regard Singapore has been left naked. Also, most of Singapore's media outlets are controlled by shareholders who are linked to Singapore government-linked companies. So how is a Singapore journalist ever going to go about investigating Temasek's finances, for example?

The media in China is similarly circumspect. The government routinely issues directives as to how things are to be reported or, in some cases, not reported at all. There is a long list of data that comes under the rubric of "state secrets", which cannot be reported. The true condition of China's banking system is one of these.

The increasing use of defamation threats by companies is another problem in Asia. In Russia, business writers have been murdered for trying to uncover the truth about big businesspeople. But in Asia, there is a growing tendency by some big businessmen to personally name journalists in defamation actions. Recent examples have occurred in Thailand, Indonesia, Malaysia and in Singapore where local journalist Catherine Ong was named as a defendant in a defamation case brought by a wealthy local businessman against her and her then newspaper, *The Business Times*.

Some businesspeople in the region do not seem to be interested in using defamation or the threat of defamation to seek compensation but rather to intimidate writers, and to get a name for being litigious so that journalists will know to back off writing about such people.

Asia's business leaders can shoot all the messengers they like but it won't make their companies any better governed or any more desirable to investors.

Culture and the Speed of Glaciers

So why are genuine improvements in corporate governance in Asia so slow to take hold? Because many of the impediments are cultural. And changing culture does not happen overnight. What are the solutions? There are no easy answers, particularly as the obstacles to corporate governance are many, varied and multidimensional. But what is important is to keep promoting the benefits of sound corporate governance, not for economic growth per se but for *sustainable* economic growth. Sure, China is growing, for example, but without good public and private sector governance, China's economic growth is not sustainable and a devastating economic correction is inevitable. That goes for all economies, anywhere.

Part II

GOVERNMENT, THE RULE OF LAW AND DEMOCRACY IN ASIA

Governments like to govern. Which means they like to intrude. And the one place where they like to intrude most is in the economy and in business. So understanding government is essential to understanding business, not just in Asia but anywhere.

How governments are installed matters to business. Political processes can be strengthening or destructive to the local business environment. Democracy has been foisted on most countries in Asia. But are most ready for it? Chapter 4 considers this.

And what about the rule of law? The efforts of most governments in Asia are subverted to varying degrees by corruption. Officials' poor pay is a key cause. So there's a chapter on that.

The consequences of corruption in Thailand's police force are examined in the next chapter. The chapter is illustrative, in that it could have been based on the situation in Indonesia, Vietnam, China or the Philippines, for example.

The ultimate sanction of government against the individual is the death penalty. But even here the application of the rule of law is not as it should be. So there is a chapter that looks at legal and illegal executions by governments in Asia. After all, the ethical setting will matter to businesspeople more and more. Look at the decision of Calpers, the massive Californian public sector employees' pension fund, to pull out of various Southeast Asian markets in 2002, largely on account of ethical considerations.

Business needs reliable statistics and mostly government statistics agencies are relied upon. But how reliable are they in Asia? A chapter looks at this too.

Politicians' families being in business is a recurring theme in Asia, so there is a chapter on this.

Finally, what happens when government is so weak that it is not only unable to uphold the rule of law but also barely able to hold the country together? So the final chapter in this section is on Indonesia.

Chapter 4

IS DEMOCRACY ALWAYS GOOD?

India is a democracy, respects human rights and has a free media. And in relative terms, it is an economic backwater, despite its success in the software and business process outsourcing sectors. China is a totalitarian dictatorship, contemptuously disregards human rights and has a media that is shackled and journalists who are jailed. And it's the biggest destination for foreign investment in the world today, has economic growth rates that are probably unprecedented and is the economy in which all multinationals want to have a presence. Yet China is at a relative disadvantage when one looks at its scant natural resources. Look at cultivable land, for example. China has just 0.08 hectares (0.2 acres) of such land per person, while India has 0.2 hectares (0.5 acres) per person.[1]

India is a democracy and China isn't. Is unfettered democracy always unambiguously a good thing? Is the US right to export it to developing countries around the world as a condition for trade deals and other favors? The answer in both cases is no.

Indonesia has moved closer to being an unfettered democracy since the resignation of its long-term dictator, President Soeharto, in 1998. Political parties have proliferated and so too has the number of media outlets. Of course the US has applauded each step. But to what end? Politicking in Indonesia is about as sophisticated as following one's favorite sports team. Colors identify the main parties and many Indonesians support a color more than a party. And as for the media, it's not clear that responsible political reporting is available to the masses any more now than in the Soeharto era. Instead, many of the new publications are sensationalist, gossipy and, with Indonesia's vague laws on defamation, libelous. Mainstream opinion now has more of a voice, but so too does extreme opinion.

Megawati Sukarnoputri received the highest number of votes in the 1999 elections (although not the majority) and later became president after the impeachment of President Abdurrahman Wahid. But how many Indonesians who voted for her actually did so because they had even the vaguest understanding of what her policy platform was? Did Megawati even know what her policy platform was? What was important was that she was the daughter of Indonesia's charismatic first President Sukarno. And for many, and probably most, a vote for her was somehow a vote for him, long-dead though he was.

Megawati was an appalling flop as president. She had been a Jakarta housewife until political opportunists decided that mileage could be had from exploiting her parentage. Managerially and intellectually, she was poorly equipped for the job. Nor did she grow into it. By 2004, having served as president for three years, a newspaper report of a public appearance in Jakarta went thus:[2]

> Although she did appear before journalists, the President appeared chronically shy, giggling and waving and only attempting one question herself before refering others to her new deputy. Although Mr Muzardi [the deputy] had only been her running mate for a few moments, she even called on him to take a question about the shape of the new cabinet.

This from the president of the world's fourth most populous country.

Things were much improved by the 2004 presidential elections when Megawati lost to Susilo Bambang Yudhoyono. He is widely seen as a good choice for president. But to what degree is that a happy accident? Electioneering was still a relative shambles, particularly for the Indonesian Parliament for which separate elections were held. The 24 parties spent enormous sums on hiring people to attend rallies. Thousands of people were paid in cash to turn up at rallies. Others received gifts such as T-shirts, bottled water, sweets, cigarettes, and even jars of ointment. Others were induced with free rock concerts. Local companies received orders for millions of party T-shirts, jackets and caps. The bigger parties, such as Megawati's PDI-P, placed massive orders for such gear with clothing manufacturers in China. Streets of almost every town and city in Indonesia were plastered with thousands of tonnes of the various parties' bunting, so much so that it was more an urban environmental catastrophe than an election campaign.

Star power remains a huge factor in Philippines' politics too. President

Joseph Estrada, who was removed from office in 2001 amid allegations of corruption and other wrongdoing, was elected largely because he'd been a film star. The main challenger to the incumbent Gloria Arroyo in the 2004 presidential elections was Fernando Poe Jr. A high school dropout who had never held public office, Poe presented the electorate with almost no policies. But he had appeared in almost 300 films. He almost won. The election result was so close it took more than a month to confirm that Mrs Arroyo had been reelected.

She Can't Read but She Can Vote

India is a democracy, spectacularly so. But India also has the world's largest population of illiterates. Just 59.5% of the population aged 15 or more is deemed to be able to read and write. That means about 280 million adult Indians are illiterate. Illiteracy among Indian women is especially appalling – 51.7% – but they can vote. In neighboring Nepal the figure is 72.4%.

Literally, there are hundreds of millions of voters in India who cannot so much as read a newspaper. This means that about half of all India's eligible voters will cast their votes on the basis of something other than the news of current affairs as it's written. And so illiteracy makes vote-buying so much easier, for example.

How useful is it giving people a full vote in a fully fledged democratic system when they cannot even read? Television and film stars and anyone else of public note are likely to get elected. Elections then become not so much a vote to determine who should run the country but a general vote of approval for the past career choices of the candidates. This is how the "Bandit Queen" Phoolan Devi was elected to the state Parliament of Uttar Pradesh (see Chapter 29). And how former movie star Joseph Estrada was elected president of the Philippines only to be impeached and then charged in 2001 for allegedly embezzling more than US$80 million. Of course, rich countries like the US have elected former movie stars as political leaders and presidents but that is not why they were elected. Few Americans who voted for Ronald Reagan had ever seen *Bedtime for Bonzo,* for example, the movie in which Reagan's co-star was a chimpanzee.

Do as I Say, Not as I Do

The West pushes democracy as the perfect accompaniment for the market economy. Political freedoms and economic freedoms go hand in hand, is the thinking. Well, they don't. Democracy in fact dooms many market economies to failure.

It is instructive to examine at what point in their economic development Western democracies extended the franchise to all adults. Indeed, universal suffrage (the right to vote) is something that has only come to the West comparatively recently. For centuries it was thought that the danger of class conflict made universal suffrage irreconcilable with a market economy. Nineteenth-century intellectuals rightly realized the danger to the market and the economy that giving the impoverished majority the vote would entail: they would use it to impose acts of expropriation and confiscation on the rich minority. The whole system of property rights would be undermined and with it the basis for trade and markets. And all this was in the context of populations that were relatively ethnically homogeneous. And so to protect private property, typically suffrage was granted only to those who owned property. In the UK and the US, men could only vote if they owned property. The right to vote in local council elections in Australia, for example, has only relatively recently been extended to all residents aged over 18 in the local council jurisdiction. Prior to that only men and women who owned ratable properties were entitled to vote. Renters were not. Let the poor vote and they will elect politicians who will expropriate from the rich and undermine the economy. And so it was only when the economies of the West developed and their citizens converged into one giant middle class that everyone was given the right to vote.

But what does the West, and most particularly the US, insist upon now? That every adult in, say, India, Indonesia or the Philippines, the vast majority of whom are unlikely ever to own any property of real significance, should have the right to vote in unfettered elections, a situation that almost never happened in their own countries.

It is ideology and ignorance that drives the US to be so insistent on political freedoms in countries that simply are not ready for them, not practical considerations. It is short-sighted and self-defeating. But this is not to say that democracy is wrong for these countries, rather it needs to be constrained. It is not possible to have a mature political system when most voters are not mature as voters themselves. Democracy yes, but not a free-for-all. Countries like Malaysia have had the right approach: blunt the knife of the ballot box until those who wield it have become skilled at its use. Blunt it but don't bury it. This is how democracy works in Malaysia: voters can send their politicians a message and yet the government is still able to operate and take hard decisions without the fear of being thrown from government by just a few hundred voters in marginal seats who are unhappy. Malapportionment among electorates is one means by which Malaysia blunts the knife.

Voting to Get Even

But perhaps the most dangerous mix of all is unfettered democracy with an impoverished majority and a successful minority that are drawn from different and distinct ethnic groups. Think of Germany in the 1930s. Adolf Hitler was *elected* to office. Germany and Austria's Jews were a successful minority and Hitler was elected to office on the understanding that "something" would be done about the so-called Jewish problem. He had a mandate from the people to do *something* and, as we all know, he did.

Indonesia's wealthy but minority Chinese population was protected under the dictatorship of President Soeharto. But that protection has now been stripped away. Instead, there is democracy. Over the coming years, the ballot box is likely to achieve what rioters and looters have to date been unable to when it comes to constraining Indonesia's Chinese and expropriating their wealth. It is simply a matter of time.

Aligning massive commercial interests with one small ethnic minority is nearly always a recipe for disaster. Inexplicably, this is precisely what has happened in post-Soviet Russia. In the aftermath of the collapse of the Soviet Union, Roman Abramovich, Pyotr Aven, Boris Berezovsky, Mikhail Friedman, Vladimir Gusinsky, Mikhail Khodorkovsky and Vladimir Potanin became the seven richest men in Russia, thanks mostly to privatizations of formerly state-owned assets. The first six are Jewish.[3] This in a country that has a history of devastating anti-Jewish pogroms. It's almost as if the conditions were being set up to result in more such pogroms. Russian President Putin's attacks on the "oligarchs" are often portrayed in the Western media as a grab for power himself. A more benevolent take is that he is attempting to break the nexus in Russia between super-wealth and Russia's Jews, a move that counterintuitively is likely to help rather than harm Russian Jewry.

Amy Chua, a Harvard law lecturer, has written about the risks associated with unconstrained democracy in the presence of a wealth–ethnicity imbalance in her book, *World on Fire*.[4] "In countries with a market-dominant minority and a poor 'indigenous' majority, the forces of democratization and marketization directly collide", she writes.[5] "Markets concentrate wealth, often spectacularly in the hands of the market-dominant ethnic minority, while democracy increases the political power of the impoverished majority."[6] And that, she says, is an explosive imbalance.

Rarely have market-dominant minorities existed in the West to the degree that they do in the developing world, contends Chua, and so the West does not have the familiarity with the problems that can be caused by imposing free-for-all democracy in this sort of context. Societies with a market-dominant minority face two problems instead of one: ethnic conflict in addition to the more usual class or income conflict. "The rich are not just rich", says Chua, "but members of a hated, outsider ethnic group."[7]

Chua also observes that at no point did any Western country ever implement aggressive market capitalism and overnight universal suffrage at the same time, "the precise formula of free market democracy currently being pressed on developing countries around the world".[8]

Chua knows what it is like to be from a wealthy minority that is the subject of ethnic hatred. She is a Filipino of Chinese descent. The opening paragraph of her book establishes her credentials on the topic:

> One beautiful blue morning in September 1994, I received a call from my mother in California. In a hushed voice, she told me that my aunt Leona, my father's twin sister, had been murdered in her home town in the Philippines, her throat slit by her chauffeur.[9]

The killing had been planned and done with the knowledge and assistance of Chua's aunt's two maids. Hundreds of Chinese are kidnapped each year in the Philippines. Many are murdered. The perpetrators are invariably ethnic Filipinos. Does democracy provide a non-violent outlet for these sorts of ethnic grievances? The answer is no. Too often it legitimizes, unveils and perpetrates them. Siding with the majority to punish a minority is simply good politics if one wishes to get elected. The democratic process gives voice to such grievances. And it provides willing listeners. They listen. They promise. They get elected. And then they have a mandate to act; an obligation even.

Democracy is a good thing when the electorate is homogeneous, that is, the voters are roughly equal in wealth and education status. It's why democracy is a roaring success in countries like Australia, the US and Britain. They are uniformly middle class. However, democracy is far less successful in countries like India or Indonesia.

In such countries, democracy isn't the means to determine who should govern and between competing policy sets. Instead it is the means for revenge and getting even. Ill-educated and impoverished majorities can wreak havoc on an educated elite via the ballot box, ruining the economy in the process.

Life under Pressure

It really is pathetic to see what a successful minority can be reduced to in the face of an impoverished majority that is beginning to flex its muscles. Nowhere is this more clear than with the case of Indonesia's Chinese.

I was once standing at an entrance to the shopping mall Plaza Senayan in Jakarta. A black Mercedes pulled up. A back door swung open and out jumped a small, balding, elderly Chinese man with thick, black rimmed spectacles. He made his way up the steps to the Plaza. But at the last moment he detoured, almost lunging at someone he'd just noticed. I turned to watch. The target of his attentions was Indonesia's then minister for investment, who stood at the top of the stairs while he waited for his own car. The little Chinese man opened his arms with all the ebullience he could manage. He seized the minister's hand, shaking it and bowing. Rather than be embarrassed by this extravagance, the minister showed obvious delight. The superficiality of the scene – the effusive greeting between client and patron – was alarming. But which one was which?

The family of an Indonesian Chinese friend of mine owns a super-market in north Sumatra. The family's daily existence is another textbook example of what Indonesia's Chinese must do in order to survive. In their efforts to run their business, which employs a considerable number of indigenous Indonesians, they must pay a heavy regime of unofficial levies, bribes and other imposts.

Some food items for the supermarket are imported from Penang in nearby Malaysia. And so immigration and customs officials want their cut. The local *bupati* (mayor) wants his share, normally by way of free grocery items, and at Idul Fitri (the name given in Indonesia to the celebration at the end of Ramadan, the Islamic fasting month) the police and the local military call around to "remind" the family of the expense of the holiday season and what's expected of them.

If shoplifters are caught, there's no point having them arrested because the police will demand bribes to prosecute. On one occasion, the staff saw a customer's motorcycle being stolen from outside the front of the shop. The theft was reported to the police but the police then demanded the presence of the staff for endless interviews and statements. This low-grade harassment of the witnesses was a means by which the police could extract payments from the witnesses' employer – my friend's family – so that the harassment would stop.

And finally, the family's income tax must be negotiated with income tax officials. Of course this amounts to paying bribes to the officials to ensure that they will pay less tax than they otherwise should. "But why should we pay tax, when the government does nothing to protect us and only ever wants to harass us? Why should we pay for something that we never get?" my friend said to me. It's not an unreasonable position.

Other than the negotiated income tax, all these imposts add significantly to the family's costs of doing business. They face them because they are Chinese. Being Chinese means that they are assumed to have money and that the protection afforded them by the law is ambivalent. Officials know that they can harass the family and they have little recourse. So not only do the unofficial levies and bribes amount to an informal wealth tax, they also amount to a tax on the family's ethnicity.

Unfettered democracy in Indonesia will give, and is giving, Indonesia's Chinese a political voice. But will that stop the sort of harassment just described? Probably it will exacerbate and extend it. Politicians will find that there are votes in appealing to the prejudices of the majority.

The Asian Paradox

So which places in Asia are ready for greater democracy? Which jurisdictions can handle the robustness of open political debate without it erupting into ethnic violence or where the ballot box will not become the new means of oppression of a privileged minority? The answer is those that have populations that are relatively homogeneous in terms of economic opportunity; those preferably with overwhelmingly middle-class populations. Singapore and Hong Kong fit this bill.

But in Asia, the very places that are now ready for unfettered democracy – Hong Kong and Singapore – are not getting it. And the countries that are nowhere near ready for it – Indonesia, India, the Philippines, and Thailand – now have it.

Of all countries in Asia perhaps China has it the most right. "Markets first and democracy later" appears to be the thinking of the elite. Electoral and political reforms have been made but economic reforms occurred first. As the distribution of wealth in China broadens and deepens, political reforms are being made to match. It's a gradual process. How can it be otherwise? Why should countries do overnight what took the West hundreds of years?

So what really matters? The answer is, as ever, the rule of law. Indeed, Singapore's success in withstanding the 1997–98 Asian economic crisis and its high living standards demonstrate the importance of the rule of law for generating prosperity. After all, democracy without the rule of law simply provides the means to periodically change one nepotistic leader for another – to change the lineup of snouts at the same trough. Democracy without the rule of law simply gives democracy a bad name.

Singapore is a democracy but not an unfettered one. So Singapore also demonstrates the relative lack of importance of a free-for-all US-style democracy in moving from poverty to prosperity. But where a free-for-all US-style democracy really matters, where it is really useful, is in helping countries that have attained broad and widespread wealth to stay that way. That is the transition that Asia's wealthy and relatively homogeneous countries such as Singapore and Hong Kong now need to make. Taiwan has made the transition and so too has South Korea.

The free market is about competition among producers of goods and services. Democracy is about competition among the producers of ideas. Mature economies need both. Playing economic catch-up often is what fuels economic growth in immature economies. But in mature economies it is ideas and innovation that keep the economy growing.

In mature economies, people have the right to be wrong. Advancing ideas is like being an inventor. Inventions often don't work but the process of creation and invention should not be stifled because of the risk of failure. Similarly, if the consequences of presenting ideas that are deemed to be "wrong" are too drastic, then people naturally respond by presenting no ideas at all. And that is not good for business, the economy and growth.

Chapter 5

PAYING PEANUTS: POLITICIANS' PAY IN ASIA

The reasons for paying ministers, MPs, judges and other senior members of any government administration well are incontrovertible and obvious. Low pay equals high corruption. So, it is extraordinary that most of Asia's governments do not pay their senior officials decently and that international aid and lending bodies such as the International Monetary Fund (IMF) and the World Bank do not insist upon it as part of their reform agenda for countries seeking assistance from them.

The adage that if you pay peanuts you get monkeys is well known. But it's only half right. The more accurate version should be that if you pay peanuts you get corrupt monkeys.

Government officials and politicians have a good excuse for accepting bribes and other corrupt payments if they are poorly paid. Well-paid officials do not. Paying people as if they are professionals does not guarantee that they will behave professionally but it does make it easier to weed out those who are not.

Removing the excuse from officials to behave corruptly perhaps is the most important reform in Asia that needs to be made. First-rate economies cannot be built on a legal system that is patchy and poorly enforced. No country in the history of the world has ever delivered to its citizens broad and deep wealth off the back of widespread official corruption, favoritism and nepotism. Look at Italy. The further south you go, the more corrupt it gets. And the poorer it gets.

Remuneration for officials, and especially politicians, needs to have two components. There must be a competitive and adequate monthly or annual salary. And there must be retirement benefits that are generous to the point that political leaders feel able to retire with grace when they have outlived their usefulness. If leaving office means poverty, then who would want to leave?

Who Gets What

Which governments in Asia pay their officials best? It should come as no surprise that it's those that are among the more clean and free of corruption. Among the leaders it is Hong Kong's chief executive who usually is Asia's highest paid, although that position is on occasion overtaken by Singapore's prime minister.

An excellent study by the reporters at AFP's Singapore bureau in mid-2002 found that the political leaders of Singapore, Hong Kong, Japan, and Taiwan were among the highest paid in the region. Some are paid even more highly than their Western counterparts.[1]

AFP found that Goh Chok Tong, then the prime minister of Singapore, earned more than US$1 million in 2000. But his salary, like the salaries of his ministers, is linked to the performance of Singapore's economy. And so his salary was cut in subsequent years.[2] By 2002 he still earned more than US$600,000 in basic salary plus variable bonuses.

The president of the US, by comparison, earns around US$400,000 annually. The prime minister of the UK is the EU's best-paid leader but earns less than his US counterpart, earning around US$317,000 annually. Does this mean that Singapore's prime minister is overpaid? No. It means that his counterparts in North America and Europe are underpaid.

The salaries of Singapore's prime minister and ministers are linked also to equivalent private sector salaries. In 2002, the chief executive of tax company Comfort Group received S$1.431 million (US$814,000), for example. And the CEO of Singapore Telecom received S$1.42 million (US$807,000).[3] But the head of government-linked company Keppel Corporation received S$3.75–4.0 million (US$2.13–2.27 million) in 2002 and the CEO of Venture Corp was paid S$9–9.25 million (US$5.12–5.26 million).[4] Even so, the Singapore prime minister's salary might still be too low if true relativity is to be maintained with private sector remuneration. That is because many firms in Singapore are managed by their owners or part owners. The chairman of United Overseas Bank Wee Cho Yaw received S$6.5–6.75 million (US$3.7–3.84 million) in 2002 but, owning a significant part of the bank that he helped to found, he also would have received a huge dividend payout, something that the prime minister and his ministers cannot receive.

The Hong Kong chief executive is another big earner in Asia. He is paid around US$800,000 annually, while his top-level secretaries (who function as ministers) earn around US$500,000. Many in Hong Kong might argue that such salaries have not bought quality decision-making to the local government but no-one would say that the administration of Hong Kong is particularly corrupt. In fact, it's one of the cleanest in the world.

The salaries for the prime minister of Japan and his ministers do not appear to be disclosed. But instead, their total incomes are published. AFP said that the Japanese prime minister reported an income of about US$307,000 for the year to March 2002. His finance minister reported US$415,000, the chief cabinet secretary US$282,750 and the minister for economy, trade and industry US$273,000.

The president of Taiwan earns around US$180,000 and the prime minister receives US$121,500. Ministers earn around US$72,000.

The Malaysian prime minister earns far less, but it is a livable salary. He is paid around US$65,000 annually. His ministers earn around US$43,000. Salaries like these are not too far below private sector equivalents in Malaysia. (Malaysia's chief justice is paid the same salary as the prime minister, and judges of the Supreme Court the same salary as ministers.)

And then there is the rest of Asia. Here is where the real problems start. Politicians earn relatively little and historically the administrations in these countries are notoriously corrupt.

The president of the Philippines receives an annual salary of US$24,000. Cabinet ministers receive an annual salary of US$9,600. They also receive discretionary funds but these are supposed to be used for electoral purposes.

The Indonesian president is believed to earn around US$30,000 annually. Ministers earn significantly less. A minister supposedly complained to Soeharto when Soeharto was president that his ministerial salary was too low and he could not possibly survive on it. Soeharto is said to have responded with incredulity, saying something like, "You've been a minister for five years! What have you been doing? Surely you don't still need a salary?" For its part, the Soeharto family had significant stakes in at least 1,251 Indonesian companies at the time of Soeharto's resignation from the presidency in March 1998.[5] Members of Indonesia's Parliament earn around US$19,200 annually.

The prime minister of Thailand receives an annual salary of around US$32,200 and his ministers receive around US$30,000. Parliamentarians voted themselves big pay increases in mid-2003 but ministers and deputy ministers did not receive similar rises. Pay relativities were then distorted so that deputy ministers were left earning less than ordinary MPs. The government criticized the Parliament but such protests are populist. The reality is that all politicians in Thailand should be paid much more. Then any that are tainted with even a whiff of corruption should be fired on the spot.

Cambodian ministers receive a token amount of less than US$1,000 a year for their services. But MPs receive around US$24,000 a year. Accordingly, ministers who are also MPs are considerably better paid than those who are not. Once again, it is a ridiculous state of affairs.

The president of Vietnam receives US$1,650 annually. The prime minister receives US$1,640 and ministers around US$1,350. Not surprisingly Vietnam's administration is one of the most corrupt in Asia, indeed, in the world.

And the Rest

The problem of poor pay for those in public administration goes way beyond the matter of lawmakers. Those charged with administration of the law from police, to prosecutors, to judges are absurdly underpaid in many parts of Asia. It does not require rocket science to determine that when a judge is paid less than US$300 a month, as many are in Indonesia for example (many expatriates pay their local drivers more than that in Jakarta), the inevitable result is corruption.

One of my favorite exchanges on this matter occurred in 1997. A retiring Supreme Court judge, Asikin Kusumaatmadja, claimed that "half" of Indonesia's judges were corrupt. "Rubbish" replied the chairman of the Indonesian Barristers Association. The real figure, he claimed, was more like 90%.[6]

The Malaysian civil service is relatively free of corruption compared with, say, Thailand or Indonesia, but the one significant blackspot remains its police force. Police salaries and allowances were raised on 1 January 2004 but the monthly starting salary for a constable was still only M$690 (US$181) plus a M$80 service allowance. The salary range for a chief inspector was M$2,063 (US$543) to M$2,956 (US$778). Why does Malaysia have such difficulty in enforcing intellectual property laws such that pirated DVDs are routinely available even in major shopping centers such as Kuala Lumpur's Sungei Wang Plaza? Those police salaries are why.

Central banks, statistics-collecting agencies, state-owned enterprises, taxation collection agencies, customs agencies, immigration offices, even embassies and consulates abroad are all subject to corruption, be it high order or petty. The appointments secretary of one former head of Indonesia's central bank would routinely accept expensive presents purchased from Cartier and so on in return for slotting her boss into speaking spots at conferences. Essentially, she was renting him out, unbeknownst to him.

Police are poorly paid throughout much of Asia. And it shows. The culture of corruption that poor pay induces means that some of Asia's lowest paid police are also its richest. A newly commissioned officer in Thailand makes a little over Bt6,000 (US$180) a month. Poor police chasing rich criminals just isn't a sensible equation. The other consequence of poor pay is that positions that are potentially lucrative with regard to bribery become the subject of "auctions" and are awarded to the highest bidder. Junior officers allocated to them must pay commissions to senior officers if they are to retain such positions. Soldiers too, are poorly paid in much of Asia. Many earn extra after hours by operating as private security guards. A private soldier in the Philippines receives just P5,775 (US$106) a month, for example.

I once asked a friend whose father had served as a Philippines' ambassador to the UK why her father had accepted the appointment when in fact he was a businessman and came from a business family. She said:

> The government doesn't pay our ambassadors much money and it is very expensive to be an ambassador, with all the representational work and so on that is expected of them. And so the government normally only appoints rich men as ambassadors to important countries where there will be a lot of expenses. And when you're asked to do this for national service, normally it's hard to refuse.

Too Simplistic?

Corruption is not ended by paying lawmakers such as politicians and law enforcers such as judges higher salaries. But it helps. The excuse for corruption must first be removed. Then a system of greater vigilance and punishments must be enacted. So the approach needs these two important elements.

Similarly, paying salaries at the higher end of private sector equivalent salaries need not be necessary, at least not in the battle against corruption. (Paying at such levels is justified more with the need to attract top-level talent into public administration.) What is necessary is to pay a decent, livable salary. Parliamentarians in New Zealand do not receive enormous salaries, for example. Regular MPs are paid little more than US$40,000 annually. Ministers earn around US$75,000 and the prime minister receives US$120,000. These are not high salaries by top-level private sector standards. And yet New Zealand is one of the world's most corruption-free countries. The consequences of low pay and low vigilance are made clear in the following chapter. It looks at the role of Thailand's police force.

Chapter 6

POLICE CORRUPTION AND THE RULE OF LAW IN THAILAND

Thailand is the "land of smiles". It is a Buddhist society in which friends "wai" each other with clasped hands, and where tolerance and peace are valued above all else. At least that is the Thailand promoted by the Tourism Authority of Thailand. Another side of Thailand is that it is a place of godfathers and contract killings, gun culture, all-pervasive corruption and flexible social and moral values.

You don't need to be caught in any one of Thailand's regular shoot-outs to witness Thailand's gun culture. Just visit any night market outside Bangkok and you will find a startling selection of rifles, pistols and knives on sale. The night markets of the southern town of Hat Yai are a case in point. Among the pirated DVDs and CDs, one can find makeshift shops that specialize in a big range of handguns. Curiously those same shops often have an even bigger range of battery operated sex toys, although only Freud might recognize the synergies in such a pairing.

The police in Thailand, as in most other Asian countries, are poorly paid. But as mentioned in the previous chapter, that does not mean that they are poor. The Hong Kong-based Political and Economic Risk Consultancy has said that the Thai legal system has deteriorated to the point where only Indonesia's is worse in Asia. "The failure of successive governments to raise performance and ethics of the police force has become a national scandal", the consultancy has said. The police are undereducated and underpaid and have almost no forensic experts but drive around in expensive European cars.[1] Thai police are involved in everything from massage parlours to gunrunning. In July 2003, there was a large protest by taxi motorcyclists at Bangkok's City Hall at the government's inability to halt protection rackets organized by police. More than 100,000 taxi motorcyclists operate in Bangkok. Probably most are required to pay some sort of protection to police or groups backed by the police or they face constant harassment such as fines and inspections.[2] The rule of law remains a challenge for Thailand, to say the least.

At any one time in Thailand, there seem to be at least several or more major corruption scandals playing out in the public arena. One such example was the Suvarnabhumi Airport X-ray machine scandal in 2005. A unit of General Electric in the US was fined by US regulators under the US Foreign Corrupt Practices Act in relation to its bid to secure the contract to supply scanners to Bangkok's new international airport. Also, the price of the scanners almost doubled as the deal passed through various intermediaries. And yet Thai policy-makers refused to accept that any corruption had been involved in tendering out the contracts for the equipment.[3] An earlier scandal involved the Phuket Land Office in 2003. Phuket is a resort island in southern Thailand. The scandal involved corruption, false claims, missing documents and the murder of a Phuket land official sent to investigate the legality of titles. It might be imagined that the rights to what is some of the most valuable land in Thailand would be carefully administered. But as one local land official was quoted as saying: "Believe me, it is a real mess here. There is no system for us to go by at all."[4]

Even Thailand's diplomats are not immune from the culture of corruption that pervades the country. In 1999, Suseree Tavedikul, Thailand's then ambassador to The Hague, actually sold his country's embassy to a local developer. He did this without authorization from Bangkok. He claimed that he was duped into it, but that didn't explain why his signature appeared on the contract of sale and his initials on each of its 15 pages. The Thai Foreign Ministry was not impressed, especially when the Dutch "buyer" filed a lawsuit against the Thai Government for breach of contract. It dismissed Suseree from the Civil Service.[5] It also faced a lawsuit from another Dutch businessman who was contracted by the then ambassador to organize an expensive party to celebrate the Thai king's birthday. The businessman was not paid for his services.[6] (Suseree, like many Thais caught in a tight spot, later changed his name, presumably to one considered more "lucky".)

In 2003, another Thai ambassador was investigated for inappropriate conduct. This time it was the former ambassador to the Philippines. Allegedly, he had removed furniture from the ambassadorial residence for his own use and so was investigated for misappropriating state property.[7]

"Godfathers"

Mafia-like "godfathers" are common in Thai politics. Most Thai politicians are believed to maintain links to them. They help provide cash to buy votes, an essential part of the Thai electoral process. In return, politicians supply protection. Some godfathers are believed to have cut out the middleman and entered politics themselves, or they have their sons, brothers or some other close male relative elected to Parliament as a proxy.

The families of these godfathers dominate certain electorates, running them as their own feudal empires, dispensing largesse, buying votes and vetting all major local appointments. The Asavahame clan has long been dominant in Samut Prakan municipal politics, for example. The family did split though, in municipal elections in 2003. Chonsawat Asavahame, former mayor and son of a former deputy interior minister, led one group of candidates. Prasan Silpipat, his uncle, led another competing group. Chonsawat was elected in 1999 amid "widespread claims of poll fraud, including ballot boxes being allegedly stuffed with fake ballots".[8]

Thaksin's Tourism and Sports Minister Sonthaya Khunpluem is the son of Somchai Khunpluem who is typically described in the Thai media as the "eastern godfather". Evidently the family is powerful. No less than three past prime ministers and current Prime Minister Thaksin Shinawatra attended Sonthaya's January 2003 wedding in Pattaya. Hundreds of other VIPs attended as well. The Thai media has noted that whenever the performance of Thaksin's ministers is questioned in Parliament or subjected to a censure motion, Sonthaya is always excluded from those targeted. Maybe too much should not be drawn from this. Perhaps he is actually good at his job.

Hired Guns

There are many hindrances to the effective enforcement of the law in Thailand. One problem is that off-duty policemen and soldiers hire themselves out to businessmen, godfathers and anyone else with cash as security guards, hitmen or even private militia. What follows is one example of this. It describes the organized destruction of a Bangkok shopping plaza as part of a dispute over property rights.

A more than 300-strong group of men raided Sukhumvit Square in central Bangkok early one morning in early 2003. They smashed its shops and bars and completely flattened the site. Sukhumvit Square, on

Sukhumvit Road, was perhaps euphemistically best described as a "mixed use" site. It comprised about 50 souvenir shops, beer bars and eateries. It had also become home to freelance prostitutes and at least one male-to-male escort service. But this hardly marks it out as unique in Bangkok.

It is, after all, in the heart of the Sukhumvit night strip area that takes in the infamous Nana Plaza, Soi Cowboy and Thermae massage parlor and nightclub spots. With cheap beer, cheap sex and cheap souvenirs, the strip had developed as an alternative to the famous Patpong nightlife area. Foreigners (and Thais) frequent it, which made the raid all the more brazen.

Shopkeepers received no warning. They were told to leave immediately. Many lost even their personal possessions. The attack left about 500 people unemployed. Thugs initially smashed things up. Heavy machinery and cranes then completed their work. The well-organized attack lasted four hours.

Prime Minister Thaksin Shinawatra visited the site the next morning. "Barbaric" and the work of "anarchists" was his description of what had taken place. Well, anarchists not quite. Unfortunately, it turned out that members of Thaksin's own military and police force were the main perpetrators. A total of 140 people were arrested and detained at four police stations around Bangkok. Included were 15 men said to be from the Second and Fourth Cavalry Regiments.

The government later named five senior army officers as suspects behind the raid. Included were a staff officer at the Defense Ministry, the chief-of-staff of the Eleventh Infantry Regiment and a colonel attached to army headquarters.

Lt-Col Himalai Phiewphan, an officer in the Supreme Command, was named as the attack's leader. The government knew all this from a piece of paper that outlined the plan for the raid. Conveniently, it just happened to have been found at the raid site.

Himalai had been moonlighting as an "adviser" to a private security company owned by a retired senior military officer. In turn, Himalai had his own private security company, General Guard Co. He hit back at the allegations by claiming to have been framed. He presented a report to the Prime Minister in which he said that men from his private security company were innocent bystanders, all 150 of them. The real perpetrators, he claimed, were traffic police assisted by 191 anti-riot and emergency-response officers. The anti-riot police had arrived with batons at the square at 4.30am and forced the tenants out on to the street. The traffic police then arrived with more than 100 demolition workers. A police superintendent had overseen the demolition work, according to Himalai. And so the military and the police had been "rented" by the hour, as it were.

Some of the other men arrested were reported to be moonlighting security guards from UK retailer Tesco's Bangkok stores. (In 2001, a bomb exploded in one Tesco-Lotus supermarket, a hand grenade was thrown at another, another was sprayed with machine gun fire and a fourth in central Bangkok was hit with an M72 anti-tank rocket. Hence the need for the security guards. It was all a dispute about contracts.)

Further confusion about who flattened Sukhumvit Square arose when a sign appeared on the metal fence that was erected around the site. It declared that the demolition was part of the Ministry of the Interior's "social order policy". But the reality is that a dispute over land was at the heart of the raid. A company called Saen Pinyo had owned the land. It leased the site to another company called BTR Holding. But BTR then developed the site and subleased spaces to small traders. Saen Pinyo then sold or forfeited the site to a finance company called Tisco. BTR's lease came up for renewal and Tisco refused to renew it. BTR claimed that Saen Pinyo had assured it of a 10-year lease.

Tisco later sold the site to a company called Sukhumvit Silver Star. BTR continued to demand and receive rent from the small traders. Unable to clear the site, Sukhumvit Silver Star leased it to yet another company, Nickel. This company also demanded rent from the small traders, raising complaints from them that they were now expected to pay rent twice over.

Himalai is believed to be "close" to former deputy supreme commander General Akradej Sasiprapa. And Akradej is said to be "close" to a former beauty queen who is said to own Nickel. It's a very Thai twist.

Meanwhile, by the end of the week, one of the suspects arrested for destroying Sukhumvit Square was dead. An autopsy showed that the 30-year-old had died while in custody of head injuries and severe bruising. The bruising was extensive to the point of taking in his lower groin and everything attached to it, complained his wife to journalists.

Massage parlor operator Chuwit Komolvisit was then arrested for directing the raid on Sukhumvit Square. He was outraged. He had, he claimed, been paying bribes to the police for years, and after all his largesse, he still faced arrest.[9] The injustice of it all!

"Mafia" or Military?

Thaksin complained that he does not want "mafia" groups operating in Thailand. But as the Sukhumvit Square fiasco shows, it's common practice in Thailand (and also in Indonesia and the Philippines) for military and police personnel to hire themselves out after hours to clear land of squatters and pursue business vendettas. The real problem though is not mafia groups but an inadequate legal system that forces businesspeople to take extra-legal measures to solve contractual disputes. It's a situation that's aided and abetted by poor pay for military and police personnel, which makes it both necessary and acceptable for them to seek outside employment opportunities in addition to their soldiering and police work. Once again, the false economy in paying government employees poorly should be apparent to all.

Chapter 7

EXECUTIONS AND EXTRAJUDICIAL KILLINGS

Every country in Asia has the death penalty on its statute books except one: Cambodia. Evidently, Cambodia lost the taste for state-sponsored killing after the Pol Pot years and his notorious killing fields. Asia's governments are active executioners too, accounting for as much as 80% of all the world's judicial executions. Grim as these facts are, they contribute to a more complete picture of Asia, which is essential for those intent on committing funds to the region.

China routinely executes hundreds and sometimes thousands of its citizens each year. There were 27,120 death sentences reported in China's official media in the 1990s and more than 18,000 confirmed executions. There are more than 50 crimes punishable by death.[1] Famously, relatives of the executed are invoiced for the cost of the bullets used to kill their wayward relative. Economic crimes have featured increasingly as reasons for defendants being put to death. Lai Changxing, head of China's Yuanhua Group, evaded corruption charges and a possible death sentence by fleeing China for Canada in 1999. China's then Premier Zhu Rongji said at the time in a television interview that "he should be killed three times over and even that wouldn't be enough".[2] Zhu made no mention of a trial. Lai's guilt had been determined already.

Several Asian countries such as Singapore and Malaysia impose a mandatory death penalty for certain offences, typically those relating to drug possession. But in those countries, such as all EU member countries, which have abolished the death penalty as being contrary to the strictures of a civil society, mandatory death penalties are regarded as particularly pernicious. Such penalties are contrary to the rule of law because they do not recognize the notion of judicial discretion in sentencing or proportionality between crime and punishment which lies at the heart of all just judicial systems.

On a per capita basis, Singapore is a world leader in execution. The annual average number of executions in Singapore in recent years is almost 35. But in absolute numbers Singapore even beat the US, 76 to 31, in 1991, although its population is around 4 million compared with the US with 265 million. More than 400 people are known to have been executed in Singapore since 1991.[3] But then most of those who Singapore executes are not Singaporeans.[4] Typically they are Thai or Malaysian. The first Westerner to be hanged in Singapore was Johannes van Damme, a Dutch national who was executed in 1994 for drug trafficking. In December 2005, Singapore hanged Nguyen Tuong Van, a young Australian of ethnic Vietnamese descent who'd been born in a refugee camp in Hong Kong. He was convicted of trafficking less than 400 grams of heroin. Importantly he was arrested at Singapore's Changi Airport while in transit from Vietnam to Australia. He had not even legally entered Singapore. In any event, if killing criminals is supposed to be a deterrent, in Singapore it appears not to be working.

Most are executed for drug offences. Possession of half a kilo of cannabis in Singapore is defined as narcotics trafficking for which the mandatory penalty is death. In the Netherlands it would define you as a small businessman or perhaps a café owner. (According to the Dutch Justice Ministry, there are 782 coffee shops in the Netherlands that legally sell marijuana and hashish along with coffee.[5] If in Singapore, their owners would face execution.) Executions in Singapore take place on a Friday, before dawn, at Changi prison, using the "drop" method, as opposed to the "hoisting" method. There have been mornings when as many as seven people were hanged together.

The Methods of Dispatch

The Singapore Government hangs people. But how do other Asian governments kill those who they condemn to death? The Philippines uses lethal injection. China also occasionally uses lethal injection, but the more usual method is shooting, as in Taiwan and Vietnam. But Chinese executions are carried out by a single bullet to the back of the head. Vietnam, Indonesia, and Taiwan use conventional firing squads. Vietnam uses them a lot. And often in public.

Thailand probably was alone in the world with its use of a lone executioner equipped with a machine gun until legislation was promulgated in

September 2002 to replace the machine gun with lethal injection. At that time in Thailand, 950 prisoners faced the death sentence after having exhausted all court appeal procedures. They could look forward to three injections: one to induce unconsciousness, a second to induce muscular paralysis and a third to stop the heart.[6] All executions in Thailand take place at Bangkok's Bang Kwang maximum security prison.

Chaowarate Jarubun, an executioner, had mixed feelings about the change. He'd shot dead 55 people in his nineteen-year career. "It wasn't difficult but I was happy to stop", he said. His first killing was in 1984. "The first one was exciting, a little bit scary", he said. "Normally I fired about 10 of my 15 bullets. People may think it too much, but this helped prisoners die more quickly." And how did he cope with the moral issues? "I just made my mind clear and relaxed, and I held within me Buddha's teachings."[7]

Hanging is used in Japan, Malaysia, India and Pakistan. India passes the death penalty but then rarely carries it out. Usually it's commuted to life imprisonment. However, an execution was carried out in the state of West Bengal in August 2004. That ended an unofficial moratorium on executions that had been in force since 1989 when one of Prime Minister Indira Gandhi's assassins was hanged. People are sometimes hanged in groups in South Korea: on 30 December 1997, a total of 23 people were hanged for various offences. But no executions took place in South Korea from early 1998 to early 2003, the time during which Kim Dae-jung was president. Kim, a former political dissident, had after all been on death row himself.

In Japan, prisoners are informed of their executions only on the morning on which they are to take place. The thinking is that this is more humane, but possibly it's not. Condemned prisoners are prone to wonder if each day might be their last. And the short notice effectively denies them the right to see relatives or consult their lawyers. Sometimes there is not time even for a farewell telephone call to family. Publicly, Japan's Justice Ministry simply announces that an execution has taken place. It does not indicate who has been executed. It does though inform the immediate family, and the identity of the executed only becomes public knowledge if the family then informs the media.

Singapore has used the same executioner for almost 50 years.[8] Darshan Singh has personally hanged 850 people in his career, including Nguyen Tuong Van in late 2005. "I am going to send you to a better place than this. God bless you", whispers Singh to each of the condemned as he places the rope around their necks. Singh has officially retired but as of 2006, the Singapore Government still had not found a replacement to do its killing. To mark his 500th execution several years ago, several former colleagues reportedly turned up to his Housing Development Board flat close to Singapore's northern border, with a bottle of Chivas Regal. On the day of an execution, a government car picks up Singh from his HDB flat and arrives at the prison at 2am. Singh prepares the gallows and shortly before 6am, he collects the condemned prisoner from his or her cell for the final walk to the gallows, a short walk from the cell. What attracted Singh into this line of work? The money apparently. Singh reportedly receives a S$400 fee for each execution. He also used to deliver strokes of the *rotan* for which his fee was 50 cents per stroke. In the 1960s, he single-handedly executed 18 men on one day: a good day's work and no doubt a profitable one.

The Police as Judges and Executioners

The death penalty is in force in 83 countries, but few countries actively use it. Asia, however, is unusually bloodthirsty and all the more so when extra-judicial killings are taken into account.

Indonesia does not rank high in the list of countries around the world that resort to the death penalty. But ironically that's only because such league tables only take into account legal killings. The death penalty is in force in Indonesia. It's not often carried out but that seems to be changing, given the number of drug convictions being made in Indonesia – both locals and foreigners – and the frequency with which prosecutors now ask for the death penalty, as in the case of Schapelle Corby, a young Australian who was convicted of importing marijuana into Indonesia in 2005. In August 2004, Indonesia staged its first execution in three years of a 67-year-old Indian national who was convicted of involvement in importing 12 kilograms of heroin into Indonesia. He was executed by firing squad in the Sumatran city of Medan at 2.30 in the morning.[9] In any event, there hasn't been much need to carry out the death penalty in Indonesia. Suspected criminals often die long before there's a chance of a trial let alone a conviction.

During 1982–83, the *Petrus* campaign was underway in Jakarta. *Petrus* came from the words *penembak* or "shooting" and *misterius* or "mysterious". Perhaps 5,000 corpses of street youths appeared on the streets of Jakarta.[10] Most were shot with silencers with which only the security forces were legally equipped. The bodies were left during the night in open places for members of the public to find the next day. But there was no mystery to the shootings. It was a deliberate policy of the government to clean up Jakarta's streets by having street hoodlums murdered.

Soeharto admitted in his autobiography *My Thoughts, Words and Deeds*, published in Indonesia in Indonesian while he was still president, that the killings were orchestrated by the government and approved by him. They were necessary because of the "persistent" problem of street hoodlums and petty criminals. "But that firmness did not mean shooting, bang! bang! Just like that. But those who resisted, sure, like it or not, had to be shot."[11]

But even since, alleged criminals are frequently murdered by the police in Indonesia. Usually they are shot while "resisting" arrest. Curiously, almost never are they merely wounded. Hundreds and maybe thousands of separatist rebels and their relatives in Aceh and Irian Jaya have been slain by Indonesia's security forces in extrajudicial killings over the years.

In China many people die while in police custody. In recent years, almost 800 have been Falun Gong members. A fair proportion of these can be considered extrajudicial executions. But a far greater number are shot while resisting or fleeing arrest. Usually they are suspected petty criminals. The numbers are enormous and possibly amount to more than 10,000 people a year.[12]

Extrajudicial executions are common in the Philippines too, particularly of criminal suspects. In Mindanao many such killings, including those of minors, have been attributed in recent years to the so-called "Davao Death Squad" vigilante group, which appears to have the tacit approval of local authorities. Local officials in some areas are believed to advocate a "shoot to kill" policy with respect to criminal suspects who resist arrest.[13]

Even Malaysia does not have a clean record on extrajudicial killings. In the late 1990s, the police in Malaysia appeared to have adopted a "take no prisoners" approach. Scores of suspected criminals were shot dead while allegedly resisting arrest. Once again, rarely were suspected criminals merely wounded by the police. If the police chose to shoot, the criminals almost always ended up dead. Occasionally, these sorts of killings still occur in Malaysia but in nowhere near the numbers as occur in, say, Thailand, Indonesia or the Philippines.[14] Of course, extrajudicial killing is not unique to Asia, although some Asian countries do appear to rely on it heavily to get rid of troublesome members of its population. Police in Rio de Janeiro, for example, killed a record 132 people in the month of October 2003. Most of the deaths were attributed to gun clashes with the police (so said the police). "If someone should die in clashes between officers and bandits, then it should be the criminals", commented Rio's state security minister.[15] But how to tell them apart?

There's another aspect to all this. That's when the killing is done even before the alleged criminals are in the hands of the police, usually by bystanders who take matters into their own hands by beating and often killing alleged wrongdoers. Comparative figures on these sorts of killings don't exist, but such killings appear to be most common in Indonesia. Typically, someone is allegedly caught thieving red-handed and then neighbors and anyone else around at the time combine to beat the alleged offender, usually to death. One of countless examples of this occurred in Tangerang, near the outskirts of Jakarta in September 2003, when local residents set upon two men who had allegedly sought to steal a motorcycle. The motorcycle's owner yelled for help, a crowd quickly formed and the two would-be thieves were stoned and stabbed. Police arrived but after they cleared the crowd, the two men were found to be already dead.[16] Such killings occur with sickening regularity across Indonesia. Sometimes crowds even break into police stations, drag out alleged criminals and kill them. It is a phenomenon borne out of a general lack of confidence in the criminal justice system.

Thailand's "War" on Drugs

The government of Prime Minister Thaksin Shinawatra showed very clearly how seriously it approaches the rule of law and due process in 2003 with its so-called "war on drugs". The police and the Interior Ministry compiled lists of drug traffickers, drug kingpins and users. The government then set as its target the elimination of all the people on these so-called "blacklists" in their capacity as drug traffickers or users by the end of a three-month period. The interior minister threatened provincial governors and police and district chiefs with demotion if they did not meet their targets.

They took him at his word. By the time the three-month period expired at the end of April 2003, 50,000 arrests had been made and 2,274 people on the drug lists were dead. The police admitted to killing just 42 of these for "resisting arrest". The rest, the police said, were killed by other drug traffickers to ensure their silence. It was preposterous nonsense. Almost certainly many, and probably most, were killed by the police or those acting on their behalf. Conveniently, rarely were there witnesses to the killings, while little packages of drugs – invariably methamphetamine pills – helpfully were found alongside many of the bodies and the bodies usually were removed without autopsies being performed.

In any event, few doctors wanted to visit the crime scenes – they did not want to have problems with the police. The previous administration under Prime Minister Chuan Leekpai had amended autopsy laws to try to counter the problem of extrajudicial killings by requiring on-site examinations of bodies by pathologists. But now the acting director of Thailand's Forensic Science Institute complained that before the war on drugs started the Institute examined "one to two" extrajudicial killings a day (a number that is instructive in itself) but once the drug war started this number had dropped to zero.[17] Chuan's administration had attempted to stop extrajudicial killings but under Thaksin, they had become a matter of policy.

One victim was a nine-year-old boy. His father was arrested while attempting to sell 6,000 pills. His mother tried to flee in the family's Honda sedan with the boy in the back. Undercover police fired on the vehicle, not so much to stop it but to kill its occupants. The car was riddled with bullet holes. The boy was hit twice. On another occasion, the Prime Minister was confronted by a tearful assistant cameraman from state-run Channel 11 who said that both his parents had been shot dead on their way back from a police station. His stepfather had earlier been arrested for marijuana use and had claimed that the police had tried to persuade him to admit that he held methamphetamine pills.[18]

The then Interior Minister Wan Muhamad Nor Matha, who had taken personal charge of the campaign, put it like this in respect of those named on the blacklists: "They will be put behind bars or even vanish without a trace. Who cares? They are destroying our country."[19] The Prime Minister picked up the theme. "In this war, drug dealers must die. But we do not kill them. It is a matter of the bad guys killing the bad guys", he said.[20] The government identified from within its own ranks 710 officials suspected of having an involvement with the drugs trade, including 209 police, 42 soldiers and 233 village heads.[21]

Inevitably, the blacklists were used to settle old scores. Once on a list, the only way off was to bribe the police or surrender at a police station. But that carried its own risks. Many, and possibly most, of those killed were shot on their way back from having reported to the police. They tended to be small-time traffickers and even reformed traffickers who were known to the police. Some had even entered government drug rehabilitation programs. But the police were required to meet their quotas and so in some districts reformed addicts and traffickers made easy targets. "The program application forms are like death warrants", remarked a woman whose husband had just been shot dead even though he'd been attending a government drug rehabilitation program for the past two years and submitting monthly urine samples to prove that he was clean.[22] Meanwhile, the drug bosses were able to pay the right people to ensure that their names were removed. They are still selling drugs in Thailand today.

It was all reminiscent of Stalin's Soviet Union when, in 1937, the Politburo assigned quotas of arrests and executions of "enemies of the people" to regional officials. The Ukraine, for example, was required to meet a quota of 35,000 arrests and 5,000 liquidations. It was incumbent on the Communist Party hierarchy in the Ukraine to go out and find these people, whether they existed or not. Thousands were arrested and died unnecessarily.

Pradit Chareonthaitawee, head of Thailand's human rights commission, said that "People are living in fear all over the kingdom." He was right and shortly after making these remarks he became one of them for he received several death threats.[23]

Once the war on drugs had been declared a success, the government busied itself by compiling lists of hired gunmen and gangsters. There was to be another war, this time, a war against "dark influence". A list of 800 names was compiled and the police were to get to work. But this time the government was rated less likely to succeed. After all, most of Thailand's major political parties have links to gangsters and regional godfathers. But it would be an excellent opportunity for another round of settling scores and removing rivals.

It's Everyone's Business

Perhaps a chapter on executions and extrajudicial killings is not what you'd expect in a conventional business book. But no longer is it enough for businesspeople to concern themselves only with what has traditionally been defined as "business". Increasingly, it is the total picture of an operating environment that is relevant to business, particularly in the face of growing pressure from activist shareholders, legislators and the media. Corporate social responsibility is the catchphrase that is now in vogue. In any event, executions and extrajudicial killings tell something of a country's legal system and how the law is applied. And that is something that should be of interest to all businesspeople, even those who resolutely stick to narrower definitions of what constitutes "business".

Chapter 8

GOVERNMENT STATISTICS AND OTHER LIES

What does it mean that China's exports rose 6.2% or that Indonesia's economic growth in the quarter rose 1.3%? Are these countries' statistics agencies so well funded, so expertly managed, computerized, efficient, independent, and professional that such numbers actually matter? Sure they might be indicative of broad trends but should we care about quarter-on-quarter changes? Should multibillion dollar investment decisions be based on them?

Everyone agrees that civil servants in China, Indonesia, India, Vietnam, Myanmar, the Philippines, and Thailand are, by and large, corrupt. They're paid so poorly that they have little choice. They're undertrained too. Why do we implicitly assume that statistics collecting agencies are any different, which is what we are doing when we accept official statistics at face value?

Statistics are treated with great reverence by most governments in mature economies. Vast sums are spent in compiling them and ensuring their integrity. The UK even has a well-funded, independent statistics watchdog, the Statistics Commission, which has overseen the work of the Office for National Statistics since 2000. Mistakes are still made. But that is not the point. A great deal of effort is spent attempting to minimize them and minimize the risk of political interference.

Government statistics in most Asian countries are unreliable. Typically, they err on the side of the positive. Governments like good statistics. Bureaucrats who collate statistics are poorly paid. It's not difficult to work out what happens next. This is particularly the case as Asia's countries have moved toward being democracies, making good statistics even more imperative. Look at the case of Thailand: a billionaire, autocratic prime minister and government statistics that just keep getting better. Consider this: for the first seven months of 2002, foreign direct investment (FDI) in Thailand fell 93% to just US$143 million over the same period the year before.[1] And yet, the Bank of Thailand's index of private investment for the same period rose 22%. And then by the end of the year, FDI was way down, exports were down but, somehow, the government's forecast of GDP growth of 4–4.5% was met! Too often in Asia the forecast tail wags the statistics dog.

Sometimes Asia's governments are caught red-handed. The Philippines in 2003 had to admit that it had grossly overstated its current account surplus in 2000. The published figure was US$9.19 billion. The real figure was almost 40% less at US$5.87 billion. The figure for 2001 was overstated too. It was revised from US$4.03 billion to just US$305 million, which means that the Philippines had overstated it by an even more preposterous factor of more than 13. The figure for 2002 showed a surplus. The real figure was likely to have been a deficit. The Philippines was found out after the IMF had questioned the data. It didn't believe the figures and said so, forcing an embarrassing recalculation.[2]

The investment bank UBS Warburg then issued a report that questioned the veracity of the Philippines Government's economic statistics. This was not unreasonable given the revelations that had just come to light. And its reward? The Philippines Government banned it from raising or managing government funds and from various trading activities in the country.[3] And so UBS Warburg was shown what was expected of it in future as was the rest of the international investment banking community.

The government of Myanmar produces copious statistics but mostly they are believed to be unreliable and in some cases outright lies. The government said that the economy grew by 12.6% in 2004. But the IMF estimated growth at around zero. Others felt that Myanmar's economy probably shrank during the course of the year. The truth is that almost nothing is known with any certainty about Myanmar's economy.[4] Part of the reason is the enormity of the black economy. Another reason derives from how prices and exchange rates are calculated. The official exchange rate for the Burmese kyat (pronounced "chat") is 6 to the US dollar. Government banks offer visiting foreigners a rate of around 450 kyats. And in recent years the market rate has been closer to 1,000.

Statistics on non-performing loans (NPLs) in the banking system are another area typically fudged. Many countries in Asia adopt their own rather unique criteria to determine whether a loan is being serviced or not. Official statistics in India, for example, suggest that NPLs account for around 10% of all loans. But if India adopted internationally accepted criteria, the figure for NPLs rises to well over 20%.

Japan has a similar problem. Companies that are hopelessly in debt are allowed to limp along because creditor banks prefer to roll over their loans and reduce their interest obligations rather than have the loans declared "bad". And so the loans are not defined as non-performing although effectively they are. Consequently, Japan's banks have one of the lowest returns to equity in the developed world, as low as 3% on net equity, when banks in the UK, the US and Australia routinely generate returns of five to six times that.[5]

Statistics are not always misleading because of poor practices and deliberate intent. Tax incentives can distort investment data. Country source data for FDI in India is very misleading. Mauritius accounts for at least half of India's FDI as recorded in official government statistics but only because Mauritius has signed a favorable taxation treaty with India. So many foreign investors route their investment via shell companies in Mauritius. Singapore government holding company Temasek Holdings is one such example. It uses a wholly owned subsidiary called Aranda Investments (Mauritius) to buy assets in India, including, for example, a 10% stake in Indian logistics company Gateway Distriparks in late 2004, a stake that cost almost US$5 million but which almost certainly would have appeared in India's national statistics as investment sourced from Mauritius and not Singapore.[6]

Similarly, Hong Kong's investment in mainland China is misleading. The figures are overexaggerated because many non-Hong Kong firms that intend to invest in China establish a shell company in Hong Kong first and then use that as the vehicle through which the investment takes place. The investment is recorded as having come from Hong Kong when in fact the real source of the funds might be the US, Canada, Taiwan, or even China itself, in which case the investment is not foreign at all.

But then country source data for foreign investment is misleading everywhere. The United Nations Conference on Trade and Development (UNCTAD) releases FDI figures for most countries each year. Why it bothers isn't clear. The figures released in 2003 (in respect of the previous year) announced that Luxembourg was the world's second biggest source of FDI (after the US) and that among developing countries the biggest recipients of FDI in 2002 were Bermuda (ranked at 5) and the Cayman Islands (coming in at 9).[7] Hong Kong came in as the developing world's third biggest destination for FDI at US$14 billion which, like all the other figures, is nonsense. Common sense says that most of the money "destined" for Hong Kong was really destined for China.

The black economy is another source of distortion. In mid-2003, an odd spat occurred between the governments of Indonesia and Singapore. For the previous 29 years, the Singapore Government had not published its annual data on trade between Indonesia and Singapore but instead had quietly handed it over to the Indonesian Government. The unstated reason was because Singapore's figures bore little relationship to the numbers compiled by the Indonesian Government. In 2002, for example, Singapore recorded non-oil exports to Indonesia of US$5.25 billion. Indonesia's Central Bureau of Statistics (BPS) reported imports from Singapore of just US$2.44 billion. Singapore put its non-oil imports from Indonesia at US$7.41 billion. But the BPS put the figure at US$4.6 billion.[8]

Incompetence in statistics gathering might account for at least some of the difference. But the real reason is smuggling. Smuggling in and out of Indonesia is rife. Part of the problem is that various provincial governments in Indonesia have a hand in the smuggling, as no doubt do elements in Indonesia's military, and particularly its navy. But then sometimes the operations of the Indonesian navy cut across smuggling operations of other arms of the Indonesian state. It was reported in mid-2004 that the Indonesian navy had impounded a boat carrying more than 1,000 cubic meters of undocumented logs off the east coast of Sumatra. It was later determined that the boat was linked to Indonesia's police force.[9]

Singapore's government had been doing Indonesia a favor, although ministers in Indonesia's new regime appeared no longer to appreciate Singapore's gesture. Singapore first withheld the figures from publication in 1974, a sop to Indonesia's then President Soeharto. Smuggling was something with which Soeharto himself had more than a passing acquaintance. In the 1950s, Colonel Soeharto, as he was then, was in charge of the army's Diponegoro division. Smuggling was one means by which he supplemented his army income and that of his fellow officers.[10] But by 1974, much of the smuggling was thought to be in the hands of the emerging cronies of the President.

Ultimately, the mid-2003 spat between Singapore and Indonesia revealed that all Indonesia's trading partners record very different trade data with Indonesia compared with what Indonesia reports. The biggest data gaps relate to Indonesia's trade with Singapore, China, Germany, Japan, Malaysia and the US.[11] The difference suggests that Indonesia's smuggling problem runs to many billions of dollars each year. And what this means is not only that Indonesia's trade data with these countries is a nonsense but also Indonesia's trade data overall is next to worthless. Recorded imports might, for example, show a dramatic increase in any given year when in fact there has been no such increase. It might be simply that Indonesian customs became less inefficient for that year and detected more smuggling than previously.

Smuggling was again in the headlines in 2005 with record nominal oil prices. Subsidies in Asia for petroleum products served to exacerbate the difference between consumer prices across countries and thus the incentive for smuggling. Both Malaysia and Indonesia subsidize the price that consumers face for gasoline, allowing smugglers to make arbitrage profits by buying gasoline in these countries and then selling it elsewhere. Indonesia reportedly estimated that, in 2005, it lost US$862 million by subsidising fuel that was then smuggled out of the country. Malaysia estimated that it was losing US$175 million.[12]

Visitor arrival numbers can be fraught with problems. Thailand typically claims astounding figures of 10 million arrivals in a year. But many of these are Malaysians who repeatedly slip across the border to the southern Thai city of Hat Yai for a Saturday night of cheap beer and prostitutes. Singaporeans who come across the Causeway on a Sunday afternoon in search of cheap durians, seafood, and so on bolster Malaysia's figures, which oscillate between 8 and 13 million.

Population and demographic figures can similarly be highly distorted. Illegal migration is one reason for this and in Asia it's a huge problem. It is commonly said, for example, that there are as many as 1.0 million Indonesians who illegally reside in Malaysia. In Myanmar, thousands and probably many more Chinese citizens have come in from Yunnan province illegally. Many buy the identity papers of dead Burmese and so not only is the population distorted but so too are figures on its ethnic composition. Even legal migration can produce distortions. Singapore has a population of 4.4 million. But there are not 4.4 million Singaporeans. Around 800,000 or almost 20% of Singapore's population comprises resident foreigners.

Another great statistical ruse in Asia occurs in relation to initial public offering (IPO) subscriptions. Nowhere more than in Asia are stock offerings routinely oversubscribed by ridiculous multiples. Often this is achieved by having government pension funds take up huge numbers of shares, with few left over for other institutional investors and members of the public. But the main way in which IPOs become oversubscribed is because rarely in Asia is more than 25% of a company's stock freely floated on a stock exchange. Take the case of the Indonesian Government's Bank Mandiri, Indonesia's biggest bank and hitherto state-owned. It is difficult to think of a bank with a greater history of mismanagement. It was formed in the wake of the Asian economic crisis by merging Indonesia's many corrupt and largely insolvent state banks into one entity. But frankly, piling pieces of junk into a heap doesn't change the fundamental characteristics of the heap's components, although it does make for a more tidy landscape.

And so what happened to Bank Mandiri's IPO in mid-2003? It was more than three times oversubscribed.[13] Frenzied excitement over a worthy company? Well, no. The reality was that the IPO was for just 10%

of the bank's total stock. The other 90% was to be retained by the government. Institutional investors that track the Jakarta Stock Exchange were compelled to acquire the stock, as inevitably Bank Mandiri would be included in the exchange's composite index. With such a slim offering, how could it not be oversubscribed?

Lumpy investments are another source of distortion. FDI approvals in Indonesia surged in the first quarter of 2003. It seemed a fantastic result; a signal that investor confidence was returning to Indonesia perhaps? Well, not quite. In that quarter, a 41.9% tranche of state-owned telephone company Indosat was sold to Singapore Technologies Telemedia, a Singapore government-linked company. The agreed sum was S$1.1 billion. Subtracting this from the investment approval figures showed not that FDI in Indonesia had surged in the quarter, but rather that investment approvals had actually fallen by a massive 45%.[14]

Fibs from the Middle Kingdom

But when it comes to questionable statistics, it is China that leads the way. China is one of the world's great exporters. It exports cheap, manufactured goods in ever-increasing numbers. The other thing it exports in vast quantities is lies.

The IMF said in its *World Economic Outlook* of December 1998 that "the quality of Chinese statistics remains a major difficulty for both policy-makers and outside analysts, both in the national accounts and in other areas". That's a diplomatic way of saying that the IMF thinks that China's statistics are rubbish.

China has a long history of lying about statistics. Minor officials all over China tell little lies about production in their area and in aggregate these combine to become big lies. *Guan chu shuzi, shuzi chu guan* ("officials produce numbers, numbers produce officials") is the saying in China that nicely encapsulates the situation.[15] Report the types of statistics that those who are more senior want to hear and you will be promoted.

Thomas Rawski, an economics professor at the University of Pittsburgh, wrote a paper in 2001 titled "What's Happening to China's GDP Statistics?"[16] He pointed out that Chinese Government estimates showed that between 1997 and 2000, real GDP grew by 24.7%. So far, so good. But during those same three years, energy consumption was recorded as having dropped by 12.8%. And that implied a reduction in energy consumption per unit of production of a whopping 30% in three years. That, said Rawski with polite understatement, "seems implausible".

He then looked at the data specifically for 1997–98. Yet again he found more inconsistencies. "Could farm output increase in all but one province despite floods that rank among China's top ten natural disasters of the twentieth century?" he asked. "Could industrial production rise 10.75% even though only 14 of 94 major products achieved double-digit growth and 53 suffered declining physical output? Could spending jump 13.9% even though steel consumption and cement output rose by less than 5%?" Rawski then looked at consumption figures for the years 1998–2001 inclusive. With one exception, national figures for retail sales grew more rapidly than per capita expenditure figures shown in household figures. The discrepancy was too large to be accounted for by population growth during the period. Plainly, the official growth figures that Professor Rawski was looking at were rubbish. Rawski demonstrated unequivocally what many had long suspected: that statistics in China are press-ganged into the country's propaganda efforts.

It's likely that the government also adjusts high numbers down and low numbers up to smooth data out and avoid the appearance of booms and busts. The practice leads to more deception: the Chinese economy is less stable than the government lets on. It might also do this in lieu of seasonally adjusting figures which it doesn't do. This means that trends can really only be determined by looking at year-on-year data rather than month by month or quarter by quarter.

China's National Bureau of Statistics (NBS) ceased basing national economic growth figures on provincial data in 1998. It considered them too unreliable. Since then, the NBS has sought to create a statistical collection network that bypasses local and provincial governments. It sounds like a positive development. But resources remain a problem and interference from lower level officials is difficult to avoid. The NBS also has a transparency problem of its own. Since 1998, it has not explained how it derives the figures that serve as the official estimates of China's growth. Professor Rawski says that pressure to affirm official growth targets overwhelms local and provincial statistics agencies and it seems likely that the NBS also is unable to resist the pressure.

At the end of 2005, China announced that it had understated its gross domestic product by an extraordinary $250 billion. But on what basis? And how then should all other macroeconomic figures be treated? With caution? With suspicion? Or should they just be dismissed? Each year China announces huge foreign direct investment results, usually very close to the end of the year for which the figures relate. That alone ought to raise suspicion. The figures receive widespread international media coverage. But why? They never stack up, they never correspond to other countries' estimates of investment outflows and they do not tally with figures estimated by international economic agencies. China claimed US$5.42 billion in FDI from the US for 2002 for example, but the US put the figure at $924 million. The Organization for Economic Cooperation and Development (OECD) for its part has said that FDI to China between 1995 and 2000 was $39.3 billion. China claims to have received double that.[17]

Can the private sector be relied upon to do any better? Maybe not. Even international investment banks eager to get their share of China's trade have an incentive to affirm official forecasts rather than question or contradict them.

And the result? Billions of dollars have poured into China's economy on the basis of the spectacular growth forecasts and the just as stunning growth results. But where are the returns? Few foreign investors have earned what they had expected to earn. The surging middle class with its swelling disposable income exists but not in the numbers that many had thought. Typically, foreign investors conclude that maybe China is just "too hard", they haven't got the right product mix or their messages to consumers haven't worked. But it could also be that although China's economy is doing well, it's not doing *that* well; they have been duped and poured billions into China that they shouldn't have.

The nationwide preference for dressing things up better than they actually are naturally infects China's corporate sector. China's Ministry of Finance reviewed the books of 192 listed companies in China in 2002 and found that 103 or 54% of them had misreported their profits by 10% or more.[18] But then such corporate misreporting is hardly unique to China or Asia. Huge stock options give Western executives an incentive to lie about all sorts of things to get their stock prices up.

The SARS epidemic of 2003 provided another example of China's economy with the truth. For a long time, China's government refused to admit that it had a problem. Then it did, but the problem was not serious. Then it decided that the problem might be a little more serious. But by then people in Hong Kong, Canada, Taiwan, Singapore, and elsewhere were infected and dying – to a large degree because China hadn't told the truth. If it had, then neighboring countries and regions might have been better prepared for the epidemic.

China routinely confuses information with propaganda. It has one of the most comprehensive systems of rules and regulations in the world aimed at suppressing truth. Many statistics and other data are declared state secrets and those that reveal them face jail. A case in point is Dr Wan Yanhai, a former official in China's health ministry who was detained in 2002. Wan was fired from the ministry after he clashed with other officials about how best to warn people of the consequences of high-risk behavior when it comes to HIV transmission.[19]

In August 2002 he was detained by China's State Security Bureau for posting an internal government document on two online chat groups. The document showed that Chinese health authorities were well aware of a serious HIV problem in Henan province in the mid-1990s and yet continued with unsafe blood collection practices between 1994 and 1997. Ridiculously, Wan's actions amounted to "revealing state secrets" under Chinese law.

His detention met with an international outcry and so, after a month, Wan was unexpectedly released without charge. But not because he had not broken the law but because the authorities had decided to be "lenient" on this occasion.

Mainland journalist Wu Shishen was not so fortunate. He was jailed for life in 1993 for sending a document to a Hong Kong colleague that was declared a state secret. And what was the great secret? An advance copy of a speech that then President Jiang Zemin was to give to the 14th Communist Party Congress. Wu remains in jail.

Shi Tao, a local journalist, was jailed in 2005 for 10 years for posting on a New York-based, Chinese-language website details of a communication from Communist Party officials to media outlets around China. The information involved routine instructions on how officials were to ensure social stability during the fifteenth anniversary of the 4 June 1989 democracy movement.[20]

Other journalists, foreign and local, and their research assistants are kept under watch and face threats. Even Ching Cheong, the chief China correspondent for Singapore's *Straits Times*, was arrested in 2005 on charges of spying.

The absurdity of China's rules on the release of information were highlighted in September 2005 when the body charged with restricting information, the National Administration of State Secrets, announced that disaster-related death tolls would no longer be treated as a state secret. Henceforth, China's media would be able to report on the numbers killed in purely natural disasters such as earthquakes, floods and hurricanes. The rationale was that such reporting would help in disaster prevention and relief efforts.[21] That such information was ever deemed a state secret in the first place demonstrates the chronic insecurity of China's government.

Information is gold in business. In much of Asia, information from official sources is fool's gold – it looks like the real thing but isn't. Becoming an Asian Insider means discerning the difference between the two, or at least learning to take many government-supplied statistics with a pinch of salt.

Chapter 9

THAKSIN BERLUSCONI AND SILVIO SHINAWATRA

When the first edition of this book was published, a prominent bookstore chain in Thailand first took copies from the publisher to sell. Not long after, they asked if they could return those copies. They felt I had been too critical of the Thai Prime Minister Thaksin Shinawatra and they didn't want the political risk of being seen to stock it on their shelves. Was their move a reflection on my writing? Or on Thaksin? Or perhaps the climate that Thaksin and his colleagues have allowed to evolve in Thailand whereby people self-censor, thereby saving the government the need to do it. Probably the latter. The messages are often mixed. That keeps people guessing and often means that they err on the side of caution. In 2005, a book was brought out in Thaksin's name in which he lists the 109 books that he feels all Thais should read. Curiously, an earlier book of mine, *Asian Eclipse: Exposing the Dark Side of Business in Asia* was among the 109 listed. Like I said, the messages are mixed.

Still, Thaksin's rule must be seen in the context of Thailand's other governments in recent decades, many of which were either overtly corrupt, dominated by the military, or both. Thaksin is a civilian leader and the electorate largely is approving of his administration. It must also be said that whatever blemishes it has – and there are many – governance at the provincial level is almost invariably far worse. It is notoriously corrupt, prone to patronage and cronyism and frequently at the mercy of feudal-like "godfathers". In February 2005, Thaksin's Thai Rak Thai Party was returned to office with an even greater majority (377 seats in the 500-seat Parliament). His main electoral support comes from Thailand's rural areas. Bangkok voters tend to be hostile to his government and the English-language press there, which has a strong local intellectual and professional readership, is particularly vehement in its anti-Thaksin sentiment.

The Rise to Power

Prime Minister Thaksin's career echoes that of another rich prime minister: Italy's Silvio Berlusconi. The billionaire Italian businessman had everything that money could buy. Except perhaps the prime ministership of Italy. And so in 1994 he formed and bankrolled his own political party, Forza Italia, with himself as its head. He did this just in time for his country's elections and in three months he had what he wanted: he was Prime Minister of Italy. Getting favorable media coverage wasn't difficult. He owned a near monopoly of commercial television stations across Italy, his empire being held under his Fininvest Group. Berlusconi's coalition government lasted just nine months. But he was back a second time in 2000.

But it was not plain sailing. Berlusconi was charged in 1999 with bribing a judge. The case, like many cases in Italy, dragged on for several years and then, without it being resolved, the Italian Parliament approved a law in June 2003 to grant immunity from criminal trials to whoever held the position of prime minister. (That law was overturned by Italy's Constitutional Court in January 2004.) Berlusconi has also been accused of many other abuses of power, including attempts to constrain the media from providing negative coverage of his government to using his position to benefit business colleagues.[1] Such are the dangers of rich men in politics. Do they know at what point they are to stop making money?

On the other side of the world in Thailand, Thaksin Shinawatra's career followed a remarkably similar path. His family had been involved in the local silk business. Various family members had dabbled in politics too, including his father who had served as the local MP. But Thaksin turned his family's significant means into something far more substantial. He became a telecommunications and media billionaire who enjoyed near-monopoly market power. Then he bankrolled his own political party, Thai Rak Thai, and this became the vehicle that catapulted him to Thailand's prime ministership. In January 2001, Thaksin led his two-year-old Thai Rak Thai Party to the first ever majority control of the Thai Parliament. He was aged 51.

So, who is Thaksin Shinawatra? He is from the northern Thai city of Chiang Mai. Like many senior Thai politicians, he is of largely ethnic Chinese ancestry (former Prime Minister Chuan Leekpai, for example, is half Hokkien Chinese and Banharn Silpa-archa is fully ethnically Chinese). He is a former high-ranking police officer who had his start in business with movie distribution before moving onto computer leasing and then telecommunications. The bulk of his fortune derives from government concessions that gave him a virtual monopoly in mobile and satellite telecommunications. Today, what was his flagship, Shin Corp is one of Thailand's largest companies and encompasses satellites, mobile telephone networks, television, paging and internet services.

Thaksin and his family maintained a controlling interest in Shin Corp. until January 2006 when they and the Damapong family, with whom they are related by marriage, sold their entire stake for US$1.87 billion to Singapore's Temasek Holdings.

Thaksin's business interests did not suffer nearly as much as most other large Thai companies during the 1997–98 economic crisis. Shin Corp had stuck to telecommunications, its core area of competency. Privately, Thaksin concedes that his personal diversion into politics probably saved the company. Had he remained focused on business, he too probably would have succumbed to temptation like most other senior Thai business figures and diversified into banking and property.

The political "diversion" included serving as foreign minister (1994–95) under Chuan Leekpai's earlier prime ministership and as deputy prime minister (1995–96) under Prime Minister Banharn Silpa-archa. Neither stint was particularly noteworthy.

And then in January 2001 he became prime minister. Thaksin drew his cabinet ministers from some of Thailand's biggest conglomerates. His commerce minister came from the family that owns the Jasmine telecommunications group. The transport minister was from the family that owns the Thai Summit automotive group. His deputy interior minister came from the family that owns the BEC broadcasting group. And his deputy commerce minister (and later, his commerce minister) was from the family that owns the CP agribusiness group. Cabinet meetings took on the hue of meetings of the Thai Chamber of Commerce under Thaksin.

Conflicts of Interest: Who, Moi?

To get around constitutional rules that prohibit the prime minister and cabinet ministers from holding more than 5% of any listed company while in office, the ownership of Shin Corp has ricocheted around Thaksin's family and people connected with Thaksin since he entered politics. In 1997, Boonchu Rienpradab and Duangta Wongpakdi, Thaksin's two maids, became two of Thailand's wealthiest people after Thaksin transferred shares to them. A driver and a bodyguard also became big shareholders. These transfers later were the subject of fraud charges – Thailand's National Counter Corruption Commission indicted Thaksin. He denied having done anything wrong, and in any event the disputed assets amount to just 3% of his total assets. He could have been banned from politics for five years if the indictment had been upheld. It wasn't and Thaksin was able to continue as prime minister.[2]

Then in September 2000, Panthongtae Oak Shinawatra, Thaksin's only son, reached adulthood and suddenly he emerged with 25% of Shin Corp. Overnight, the 20-year-old became Thailand's richest man. Thaksin's wife Khunying Potjamarn also had millions of Shin shares, as did her brother Bannapot Damapong. Other Thaksin relatives did too, such as his younger sister Yinglak. Bannapot Damapong was made chairman of Shin Corp. The entire arrangement made a farce of the constitutional limits to curb conflicts of interest.

Shares in other companies were transferred to Panthongtae. In 2001, he emerged as one of the biggest single shareholders in Thai Military Bank, the country's sixth largest bank. This produced yet another conflict of interest in 2003, when the bank had to be bailed out by the government for the second time in three years.

In September 2001, Panthongtae sold half his stake in Shin Corp to his sister Pinthongtha. The 367 million shares were sold for one baht each. The then market price was almost eleven baht. And so now the major owners of Shin Corp were Bannapot Damapong (13.77%), Pinthongtha (12.50%), Panthongtae (12.49%), an investment holding company called Ample Rich Investments (7.8%) and Singapore Telecom (5.8%).[3]

In September 2002, Panthongtae, a third-year political science student, was caught in the exam room at his Ramkhamhaeng University with two smuggled pieces of paper that contained answers to the political analysis examination that he was taking. One can imagine the spreading horror at the university when news of the discovery got around, that the apparently cheating student was the prime minister's son. The chairman of the university panel charged with considering the matter helpfully offered that "Bringing paper into an exam room is a violation of exam rules. But it isn't always proof of an intention to cheat." Panthongtae claimed that he had taken the papers into the exam room by "accident".[4]

By 2006, Panthongtae, now graduated and still only 25, was a celebrity photographer and Thailand's richest man. Apart from his massive stake in Shin Corp, he also controlled How Come Entertainment which, in April 2005, was awarded a 10-year concession to manage advertising space in Bangkok's new subway system.

Like Thaksin, Berlusconi claims he plays no decision-making role in his many business interests. Instead, his two daughters and a son sit on the board of Fininvest, his holding company. One or more of his children sit on each of its main subsidiaries, including Mediaset, Italy's largest television company. The youngest daughter and board member, Barbara Berlusconi, was aged 19 around the time of her appointment and was a philosophy student at the University of Milan.

Many other Thaksin family members are in business. For example, Thaksin's younger sister Monthatip Kovitcharoenkul runs the listed M Link Asia Corporation, a mobile distributor and retailer. It has won several contracts to supply the Thai Civil Service with handsets. M Link Asia is jointly owned by the family of Monthatip's husband and the family of her sister Yaowapa Wongsawat. Thaksin's sister Yaowapa Wongsawat is the Thai Rak Thai Party MP for Chiang Mai and also heads the Party's Wang Bua Ban faction. She's also a prominent business-woman in Chiang Mai and owns a bus company among other assets. Her daughter Chayapa Wongsawat emerged in 2004 as the owner of a 7% stake in prominent Thai media company Traffic Corner Holding (TCH). Its subsidiary Traffic Corner Publishing (TCP) publishes a large range of magazines, including *Bangkok Today, Maya Channel, A Day, A Day Weekly, Hamburger, Take a Seat, MTV Track, Knock Knock* and *Rai Wan Tan Hun*.[5]

At least until the sale of Shin Corp, it's difficult to think of another political leader in the world who has been as potentially compromised as Thaksin. Other than Berlusconi that is. But not all conflicts of interest are so obvious. Some are more subtle. In January 2003, the Education Ministry stopped publication of the final 100,000 copies of a booklet printed for schoolchildren to mark Children's Day after complaints that it excessively promoted the use of mobile telephones among children. The booklet contained an article, ostensibly written by the daughter of the ministry's spokesman who happened to be a Thai Rak Thai MP, in which a child outlines all the reasons why she would like to own a mobile telephone. The story's character also specified which model she wanted, the prices and the promotion packages available.[6] Around 620,000 copies of the booklet had already been printed. What was the Thaksin family's Shin Corp enjoyed a near monopoly on mobile telephone operations in Thailand at the time.

Just two months later and the prime minister's name was being mentioned in conjunction with something much murkier. A body was found near Chiang Rai with three bullet wounds in its forehead, ear and neck.[7] Numerous bodies are found each day around Thailand. But this one was different. It belonged to Kornthep Viriya, the man who had supplied information on a deal in which Shin Satellite, a company owned by Thaksin's family, was alleged to have evaded taxes on imported satellite equipment. Kornthep, a former Shin employee, had apparently lived in fear since giving his evidence and had moved to what was considered a "safe" house in the Chiang Rai district for his protection. But the house was searched repeatedly by police and Kornthep had apparently feared that he would be "silenced". He had changed his name twice and used 10 different telephone numbers.

Right away, Thaksin was forced on the defensive. "I will repeat clearly and simply that members of my government and I are in no way involved in the murder of Kornthep", Thaksin told Parliament.[8] No evidence was produced that linked Thaksin to the killing. Nonetheless, it's not often that the prime minister of any country is forced to deny his involvement in a murder.

Reining in the Media

Thailand has one of the freest media in Asia. The coverage of high-level corruption is excellent, as is the subjection of senior political and military figures to scrutiny. The *Bangkok Post* simply is one of Asia's best English-language newspapers. So too is *The Nation*. This does not mean that journalists in Thailand are not free of intimidation and harassment. Nor does it mean that Thaksin has not brought legislative and other changes that have had the effect of muting criticism of him, his government and his family. In this, Thaksin once again is comparable to Italy's Berlusconi who stands similarly accused.

Thaksin's government has been accused of changing executives, news editors, reporters and program hosts at electronic media outlets under the control of the government's Mass Communication Authority of Thailand; shutting down programs that were critical of the government and the prime minister; allowing Thaksin family-owned companies to oversee the placing of government advertising so that sympathetic media outlets could be rewarded with advertising expenditure; using state-run media outlets to push the Thai Rak Thai Party's line and suppress news of the opposition; and intervening in the selection of national Broadcasting Commission members. In addition, the Thaksin family's Shin Corporation bought a 76% stake in Thailand's fifth television network iTV.[9] The first tranche of iTV shares were bought just six months prior to Thaksin becoming prime minister. Shin Corp subsequently upped its stake in the "independent" television company.

Promoting Friends and Relatives

The Military

Two of the fastest rising stars in Thailand's military during Thaksin's prime ministership have been his two cousins, the brothers Chaisit and Uthai Shinawatra.

In August 2001, Chaisit was promoted to deputy chief of the Supreme Command's Military Development Unit and Uthai became chief of the Defense Ministry's Office of Policy and Planning and then deputy permanent secretary of the Defense Department. At least 20 former class 10 classmates of Thaksin from pre-cadet school also were promoted, including 8 at the air force, each of whom was promoted from group captain to air vice marshal.[10] Such elevations have become standard each October when the annual round of military promotions is held.

In 2002, Chaisit, now a general, but still a supreme command specialist (an inactive post) was made an assistant army chief to the collective gasps of just about everybody in the Thai civil and military elite. Later that year, he was put in charge of defense logistics, arms procurement and construction. For good measure, Uthai was put in charge of defense arms procurement, budgeting and intelligence work.[11]

Thaksin promoted Chaisit to army chief in October 2003 and then to supreme commander of the armed forces in 2004, a post that was largely inactive, because Chaisit was a year away from the mandatory retirement age of 60.[12] But the move did give Chaisit a seat on the board of the Thai Military Bank and control of the military-owned Channel 5 television network. Chaisit retired from the position in September 2005, but not before pushing through his own candidate to replace him.

Chalerm Chuemchuensuk was unexpectedly promoted from a specialist position to air force deputy commander in 2002. Chalerm's wife is one of Thaksin's wife's closest friends.[13]

In March 2003, Thaksin was instrumental in having Major General Picharnmet Muangmanee promoted to commander of the Third Army in the north. Picharnmet is a class 16 graduate of the army cadet school, the same as General Chaisit. He is also a close associate of Payab Shinawatra, Thaksin's younger brother.

Thaksin also had Lt-Gen Songkitti Chakkabat promoted to commander of the Fourth Army in the south. Songkitti is a former class 10 classmate of Thaksin's at the Armed Forces Academies Preparatory School. He'd also been the commander of the UN peacekeeping forces in East Timor. (Thaksin had him removed as commander of the Fourth Army in the south six months later, after criticism of Songkitti's performance. Connections are not always enough.) Another class 10 classmate of Thaksin's was appointed as the new commander of the 1st Cavalry Division.[14]

The October 2003 army reshuffle that saw Chaisit promoted to army chief also saw a stunning array of former class 10 classmates of Thaksin's promoted to senior military positions. The chief of the office of the permanent secretary, deputy chief of the First Army, the commander of the 1st Infantry Division (the army's main force in Bangkok), the commander of the 1st Development Division, the head of the Phetchaburi Army Circle, the head of the army's Directorate of Civil Affairs, the commander of the 2nd Cavalry Division and the deputy director of joint operations of the Supreme Command were now all former Thaksin classmates.[15]

Thailand has a long history of military coups. It's unlikely that the military will ever move against Thaksin now. Instead, the military has been converted from a rival power source to another instrument of state that Thaksin can call upon to do his bidding. And help to entrench his power.

The Judiciary, the Civil Service and the Police

But it's not only Thailand's military that is being converted to an adjunct of the Court of Thaksin. In March 2002, Pol Lt Gen Priewphan Damapong, the elder brother of Thaksin's wife, was appointed at Thaksin's behest as a deputy national police chief, even though he was the most junior of all the candidates.[16] In early 2005, Damapong was assigned to oversee crime suppression in the northern and northeastern provinces, the areas considered Thai Rak Thai strongholds.

In 2003, Thaksin oversaw the promotion of his former classmates Pol Lt Gen Wongkot Maneerin to the post of Police Central Investigation Bureau commissioner and Pol Lt Gen Chalor Chuwing to police regional commissioner.[17]

In 2003, several new judges were appointed to the Constitutional Court. Each was claimed to have a "special" relationship with Prime Minister Thaksin.[18] The new court president happened to be one of eight judges who cleared Thaksin of charges of concealing assets in a case brought against the Prime Minister in 2001. The judge's role in that case made him,

along with several other judges, the subject of an impeachment investigation by the National Counter Corruption Commission. Another new judge
to the Constitutional Court was the prime mover in mobilizing police
support during the hidden assets case. He also happened to be one of
Thaksin's teachers when Thaksin was a cadet at the police academy.
Another newly appointed judge was director general of the Customs
Department when a questionable ruling was delivered in a tax case that
related to Shin Satellite Company, then owned by Thaksin's family.

Around the same time, trouble brewed at the Justice Ministry. The
minister, Purachai Piumsombun, did not get on with the ministry's
Permanent Secretary Somchai Wongsawat. That was bad news for the
minister because his permanent secretary happened to be a brother-in-law
of Thaksin. The differences became very public. Thaksin publicly took
sides in favor of his brother-in-law and the justice minister was soon
replaced.[19] Once more, the state proved servile to the family. Unusually,
Wongsawat had his term at the justice ministry extended twice and then,
in January 2006, it was announced that he would be appointed to head up
the labor ministry.

Just prior to Thaksin becoming prime minister in 2001, Thailand was
leading the way on human rights in Southeast Asia. The armed forces had
retreated from politics, the media had few concerns about government
censorship and political pressure, a new constitution had been put in place,
and a series of independent bodies had been established to check the
power of the executive. One of these bodies was the National Human
Rights Commission. It has no powers other than investigation and
publishing reports. Its first report was issued in August 2004. It painted a
dismal picture of retreat on human rights over the Thaksin years, which
had worsened over the past three years, it said. Police torture was cited, as
were the thousands of killings associated with Thaksin's 2003 "war" on
drugs. It argued:

> Thailand is worryingly regressing towards a culture of authoritarianism, instead of
> progressing to a culture of human rights. Freedom of expression and the right to
> monitor the government have been virtually treated as undermining stability and
> prosperity and economic and social development.[20]

On being reelected in March 2005, Thaksin appeared to respond: "I
will uphold human rights in this country", he said. To date, he has not
done that.

Thaksin holds a position in Thai politics enjoyed by no other past prime
minister. His party controls a majority of seats in the Thai Parliament

outright. Thaksin has power like no other previous elected Thai leader. And what has he done with this mandate? Instead of professionalizing government and strengthening the rule of law in Thailand, he is converting the process of politics to that of a traditional Asian family firm. He is remaking government in Thailand into something that's akin to the image of Shin Corp. He often refers to himself as CEO of Thailand. He is the owner/manager who brooks no dissent. He is both referee and player. He is Silvio Berlusconi with an Asian flavor. Both though understand the importance of business and the economy to improving the welfare of their citizens and that at least puts them a long way ahead of many of their predecessors.

Chapter 10

THE END OF INDONESIA

Who would want to be president of Indonesia? It is a job obtained by making bright promises. But Indonesia's problems are manifest and intractable and so any incumbent, no matter how earnest and qualified, inevitably must leave office disappointed. This is the fate of Susilo Bambang Yudhoyono who was elected Indonesia's president in 2004. A good man but with a near hopeless task.

Indonesia comprises some 242 million people split among 300 different ethnic groups, with 365 distinct languages or dialects spread across more than 13,000 islands. That might be a selling point to tourists but it is not a recipe for political stability. It's not a country that you would ever design by choice. In fact, it's highly questionable whether a country this diverse can ever be expected to function with any degree of efficiency and deliver reasonable security and livelihoods for its people. And if it can't, is it reasonable to expect it to stay together? It's a consideration that all investors and potential investors in Indonesia need to keep in mind.

Talk of a sizable and increasingly affluent middle class and even GDP per capita statistics mask the reality of a population that remains largely rural and far from affluent. Seventy-five million Indonesians do not have access to electricity.[1] Ridiculously, half that number reside on Java, Indonesia's small, densely populated main island, for which electrification ought to have been completed decades ago.

Indonesians are heavy smokers but few realize that many if not most cigarettes in Indonesia are not sold packet by packet but stick by stick. Even though cigarettes are priced and taxed low in Indonesia compared with most other countries, Indonesia's smokers by and large are too poor to afford a whole packet at a time. What point then are new World Health Organization requirements that packets carry health warnings when many Indonesians simply don't see the packets?

Managers in multinationals who implement worldwide minimum health and safety standards in their factories report that they sometimes have difficulty in getting their workers in their Indonesian factories to wear the steel-capped boots with which they are issued. Instead, they prefer to operate dangerous plant and equipment without them, and wear flips-flops. Why? Because they simply aren't used to wearing any shoes, let alone those that are steel-capped.

Overestimating Indonesia and assuming too much is a common problem when approaching the country. Jakarta has a few glitzy streets but the veneer is very thin indeed.

I'd just given a speech in Jakarta at a conference held at the Aryaduta Hotel. The organizer was a think tank attached to a German political party. It was a curious but well-funded affair in which Wan Azizah Wan Ismail, wife of then jailed Malaysian politician Anwar Ibrahim, was among the other speakers. (I'd only just written a guest column for the *Far Eastern Economic Review* in which I'd questioned her husband's credentials as a reformer.) Chee Soon Juan, an opposition figure from Singapore, attacked me during the Q&A part of my session because I'd dared to say something nice about the Singapore Government. Upstairs on the hotel's in-room viewing system, televangelists from the southern US belted on about the devil; the hotel being owned by the Christian fundamentalist Indonesian Chinese Riady family in this, the world's biggest Islamic country. And at lunch a Malaysian MP buttonholed me to tell me in some detail about the corruption of his cabinet colleagues. A prominent Indonesian political activist also sat at my table. And so the discussion turned to Indonesia.

"Indonesia is ungovernable," he said. "It is too big. It's impossible to govern. Impossible!"

"So you think that Indonesia should be broken up?" I asked.

"Oh no! It should not be broken up. No, that cannot happen. But it is ungovernable."

A Chronic Underperformer

Indonesia is resource-rich and yet its people are poor. The country is not some desert blighted by endemic famine but one of immense fertility, with massive sea and mineral resources. And yet GDP per capita (PPP basis) languishes at around US$3,700.

Brazil offers an analogy. With a population of 186 million, it is close to Indonesia's 242 million, it too was a European colony and it too has resources. But at US$8,500, its GDP per capita is more than double Indonesia's, even though Indonesia produces more than twice as much oil and about twenty times more natural gas. If Indonesia is impossible to govern, there is a logical next step for Indonesia. But it seems that no-one wants to take it. At least no-one in Jakarta.

Indonesia's territorial definition comes not from any rationale based on shared culture or language but on the basis of a greedy and murderous land grab by Dutch colonizers. They sought to pull in as many islands as possible into a conglomeration that became known as the Dutch East Indies. The Dutch were after the spices and other commodities that could be harvested from the islands. They were interested in building a corporation, not a country. And so there is no great logic to Indonesia's borders and precious little history. The Dutch had grabbed what they could and by and large that comprised what others had left and somehow out of this a country called Indonesia was born.

Frankly, Indonesia should never have happened. But it did. And now everyone has to live with the consequences. Politicians in Jakarta are left with a country that they admit they can't govern and Indonesia's regions must exist with a central government that many don't want.

Indonesia hasn't worked because it cannot work. Indonesia is too big and too diverse. Orwellian slogans such as "unity in diversity" are just that. And with 300 sometimes warring ethnic groups, at best Indonesia is not a nation state but a state of nations; it is a false construct.

Empires as Dinosaurs

Javanese culture is like a tapeworm ... It is "aesthetic" and silent; it is polite (no commotion); it is insinuating. It weakens without turmoil and it is ultimately deadly. Javanese culture cannot be yanked out or cut out. It will require strong and repeated doses of medicine to free it out.

So says retired Catholic priest and social activist Romo Mangun, as quoted by Theodore Friend in his book *Indonesian Destinies*.[2] It is a view that is outrageously politically incorrect. And it is accurate. Javanese culture is rent seeking, stultifying and energy sapping. And yet politically, numerically and culturally, Java, where more than half the country's population lives, dominates Indonesia. (About 59% of Indonesians live on Java: 45% are ethnic Javanese and 14% are ethnic Sundanese who live in west Java.) Java is sometimes portrayed as imperialistic, a colonizer, even, of the rest of Indonesia.

Indonesians are obsessed by the control that ethnic Chinese Indonesians have over the economy, as if other Indonesians are not themselves from trading minorities. They are. It's just that Javanese political and military leaders have conspired to keep them in check so that they do not pose a threat to Javanese political dominance. In this way, the Minangkabau of west Sumatra, the Acehnese of north Sumatra and the Bugis of south Sulawesi have been prevented from realizing their full commercial potential, despite trading traditions that go back centuries. The Bugis particularly have a history of international sea trade, with their wooden sailing ships being integral to trade not just between Indonesia's many islands but throughout Southeast Asia and occasionally beyond. Where are the Bugis today among the Indonesian commercial elite? Largely, they are impoverished and maginalized; they are victims of Javanese imperialism.

The world continues to pay the price for such empires. The problems of Europe are the results of the old Austrian Empire and even the Roman Empire. The problems of Chechnya derive from the old Soviet Empire. The problems of the Balkans and the Middle East are due in part to the Ottoman Empire. The First World War was due partly to the disintegration of the Austrian Empire. The problems that empires cause reverberate for centuries.

Empires are the dinosaurs of statecraft. Their time has come and gone. Even the US, the richest country the world has ever seen, has not sought to expand its borders when at the peak of its power and wealth. Of course the US wants to be influential. What country doesn't? But it has not sought to acquire and incorporate new territories.

Governments should enhance the wealth and wellbeing of their people. But too often the Indonesian state, mismanaged and riddled with corruption, destroys these things. Partly, the state is in the hands of the military. Former President Abdurrahman Wahid sought to water down the influence of the military but it remains powerful. Ultimately, the prime function of Indonesia's military is not to protect its citizens, but to protect the Indonesian state, often at the expense of its citizens. Why? Because of the artificiality of its construct. And so its job is not so much to keep potential invaders at bay, but simply to hold the country together, a job that is more akin to that of a jail warder than a policeman, keeping people in rather than keeping them out. Its job is to keep the high-energy cultures of Indonesia's outer islands caged by the introversion and dull moderation of Java.

Thinking the Unthinkable

What if Indonesia does disintegrate? Will the sum of the parts be greater than the whole? We live in the age of microstates. Big countries often are poor countries. Small countries tend to be disproportionately rich. For example, consider Iceland and Singapore. And then think of India and Indonesia. The economies of scale of public administration seem to diminish quickly, particularly when administering across cultures. Countries have an optimal level of diversity beyond which public administration grows increasingly ineffectual.

Malaysia, that other Malay country in Southeast Asia, shows what Indonesia could be: a series of ten or twelve Malaysias across the Indonesian archipelago. Malaysia's GDP per capita is more than US$10,000 (PPP basis) – about three times that for Indonesia. And yet Sumatra and the Malaysian peninsular are barely a stone's throw apart, and Sarawak and Kalimantan actually share a border. Malaysia shows the value of sound public administration for promoting national wealth. It also suggests something about the optimal size and complexity of a country.

None of Indonesia's near neighbors supports its break-up. The governments of Singapore and Australia particularly are terrified by the prospect. "Regional security" is the foremost concern. An Indonesia that is tearing itself apart could produce a big outflow of refugees and in any event both countries have significant investments in Indonesia. Singapore, for example, was Indonesia's biggest direct foreign investor in 2002. But in an age of terrorism, more borders and border checks enhance security. Perhaps the Bali bombings that occurred in 2002 might not have happened if Bali had control of its own borders and the perpetrators could not so easily have slipped in from Java.

On top of that, one national government is administratively less troublesome to deal with than are ten in its place. Independence for East Timor meant that many countries had to open embassies there. Convincing diplomatic staff to serve in Jakarta is difficult enough without having to get them to agree to be posted to places like Dili. But is it fair to hold 242 million people hostage for the convenience of the neighbors? Is it fair that these 300 cultures should remain colonies of just one? Increasingly, this is a question that will be asked inside Indonesia and outside.

> With independence being the right of every nation, colonialism must be eliminated from the face of the earth as it is contrary to the dictates of human nature and justice.

Admirable sentiments of course. It is the opening line of the Preamble to the Constitution of the Republic of Indonesia. The paradox is that Indonesia was formed by shrugging off colonialism but now stands accused of being a colonizer itself.

On all sorts of measures, particularly economic ones, Indonesia has failed. It is questionable whether it can do much else. The tendency worldwide has been for empires to dissolve, often in a violent manner, as the central government fights to maintain control. Indonesia might well not break up. But what is certain is that it will always be subject to secessionist tendencies in at least some of its provinces and that will continue to create instability and use up scarce central government funds. Possibly, Jakarta itself might become more prone to terrorist attacks as secessionists seek to be heard. Police confirmed that they questioned Aceh rebels about a bomb explosion at Jakarta's international airport in mid-2003. It seems likely that more of the same can be expected. And again, that is a risk that foreign investors in Indonesia, be they American, Singaporean, European, Malaysian or Australian, need to consider.

In terms of leadership, Indonesia has not thrown up quality options. The founding Indonesian President Sukarno's idea of connecting with voters was to race them or at least their wives and daughters off to bed and if his government needed more money, it simply printed more of it.

Soeharto turned the country into the biggest kleptocracy the world has seen. Despite the rhetoric of progress during his time, there was little economic diversification during the decades in which he ruled. Farmers learning how to grow more rice largely due to the application of fertilizer accounts for much of the economic growth during the 1970s and 80s. Then came Habibie, who had all the mannerisms of someone who was mad and had the industrialization policies to match. Next was Wahid, largely blind and well meaning but a chaotic and random manager who was ultimately impeached and removed. Megawati, whose main claim to fame is that she is someone's daughter, replaced him. She was not known for initiating policy ideas and her two favorite topics of conversation were often described as being what she ate for dinner and Indonesia's weather, neither of which vary much. Rarely have so many people been led so poorly.

Then in 2004 came Susilo Bambang Yudhoyono. But one man can only do so much. And with a hopeless legal system, an appalling bureaucracy and rampant corruption, that won't be very much at all. He has had his symbolic corruption convictions, such as that for the former governor of Aceh province who was given a 10-year sentence for ordering a Russian-made helicopter in 2002 at a vastly inflated price, the proceeds of which mostly ended up in his private bank account. He suspended another governor, that of Banten province, in October 2005 on suspicion of graft.[3]

And the former president and chief executive of Bank Mandiri, the listed but largely state-owned bank, also went on trial that month on suspicion of improperly giving loans to wealthy businessmen, presumably in return for inappropriate inducements.[4]

But there is a risk that such instances serve only to placate an electorate that wants to see something done about corruption, rather than being genuinely culture changing.[5] It remains the case that literally everything in Indonesia is tainted by corruption. In September 2004, the World Bank even saw fit to ask Indonesia to repay a US$10 million loan intended to buy school textbooks after it was found that the money had been stolen by corrupt publishing companies.[6] Going from 2004 to 2005, Transparency International's Corruption Perception Index ranking for Indonesia actually worsened, from being ranked at 133 in 2004 to 137 in 2005.[7] That may have been due partly to more countries being considered in 2005. But importantly, there appears to have been no improvement in perceptions of Indonesia as a country that is particularly corrupt.

Yudhoyono set up an anti-corruption court in 2004 as part of his efforts to stamp out high-level corruption. By January 2005 only three of the nine positions on it had been filled.[8] There was a shortage of judges willing to serve on it. No doubt some were shy of hearing cases that involved powerful people. Others perhaps didn't feel that it would be a good place to make money. After all, judges in an anti-corruption court would be expected, above all others, to be free of corruption.

Ironically, the Ministry of Religious Affairs is one of Indonesia's most corrupt institutions. A recent former Minister for Religious Affairs went on trial in January 2006 for corruption in connection with US$70 million that went missing and which had been collected from pilgrims intending to make the Haj to Mecca.[9] He received a five-year jail sentence the following month.

The acquisition in early 2005 for US$5.2 billion of HM Sampoerna, Indonesia's third largest cigarette maker, by Philip Morris of the US, was portrayed as a vote of confidence in Indonesia. It did after all mark the largest foreign takeover of an Indonesian firm ever. But it was forgotten that the acquisition also represented a selling out: the cigarette company's founding family, a local ethnic Chinese family, essentially was selling out of Indonesia. Already many of its key members had physically relocated to Singapore. So how much of a vote of confidence was the transaction really? After all, investing in cigarettes is not particularly risky. No matter what political and economic strife Indonesia will face in the future, the majority of its male citizens at least will continue to smoke.

Meanwhile, Indonesian commercial courts persist in making the most bizarre decisions, due to gaps in the written legal codes, inadequate training of court officials, lack of the use of precedent to guide judges, and bribery. In 2003, for example, a Jakarta court decided that the loan documents, in respect of a US$180 million loan made by a syndicate of foreign creditors to the company that built the Jakarta Stock Exchange building, were incorrectly specified so the loan did not need to be repaid.[10]

In 2004, the Indonesian arm of the UK's Prudential, a massive multinational insurer, was declared bankrupt by a commercial court in Jakarta over a dispute with a former sales consultant, who had complained that the insurer had not paid bonuses and travel allowances to his satisfaction.[11] A district court declared a US$184 million bond issue, underwritten by a number of US banks on behalf of a local petrochemical company that had defaulted on the bonds, to be invalid because some of the terms were against Indonesian law. The court then determined that the company did not need to repay any of the money.[12] The impact of such decisions on foreign investment in Indonesia has been predictable. Apart from the Sampoerna sale, and even then that represented a transfer of physical assets rather than the creation of new ones, it has collapsed.

The Law and Other Amusements

One of Indonesia's many problems is inequality before the law. There is one set of rules for the poor and middle class and almost no laws for the rich and well connected. It means that ordinary people tend to be incessantly hassled by various levels of government for petty bribes and gratuities as they go about their daily lives. At the other end of the scale, Indonesia's rich can avoid almost any problem with a well-placed phone call.

The Jakarta rich and well connected need not even bother with immigration queues when they return home. They can pay for a special express service which allows them to more or less walk through immigration proceedings, barely stopping. When the wealthy and well connected are accused of crimes, often they can head off prosecution with a few well-placed bribes or phone calls, or if they must go to trial and are found guilty, the sentences tend to be light.

An important case cropped up in 2005. Many Indonesians watched it to see if and how the legal system for criminal law cases might have improved under the administration of President Yudhoyono. It involved a Jakarta businessman, Adiguna Sutowo, who owns major stakes in Jakarta's Hard Rock Café, Bali's Hard Rock Hotel, its Four Seasons Hotel and several magazines. He was accused of shooting a waiter in the head at the Jakarta Hilton's Fluid Nightclub in the early hours of New Year's Day.[13]

After a hard night's drinking, cocaine and crystal methamphetamine use, Adiguna, who was in his forties, gave the waiter a credit card to settle his tab. The card was declined and when the waiter, a 25-year-old law student, returned with the news, he was shot dead. The pistol used belonged to Adiguna and the waiter's blood was later found on Adiguna's clothing. Witnesses to the killing were too fearful to testify against Adiguna but several were prepared to say that they saw him holding the gun seconds after the shot was fired.

After the shooting, Adiguna wiped his fingerprints off the weapon, forced it into the hand of a man nearby – presumably so that he would take the rap for the murder – and then fled the nightclub. In any event, Adiguna was arrested. And the case went to trial. It had attracted far too much local media comment for it not to. Prosecutors demanded life in prison, the maximum punishment for murder. Adiguna was also charged with illegal possession of a firearm for which the maximum sentence is death by firing squad.

Adiguna comes from a rich family. His brother Ponco Sutowo owns the Jakarta Hilton where the murder took place, and four other Hilton Hotels in Bali and Surabaya. But the Hiltons are in a curious state. Ponco's company stopped paying Hilton International marketing fees in 1999 and so the international chain withdrew its services from the hotels. A settlement was negotiated but Hilton International had little chance of redress, given Indonesia's poor legal system and the power of the Sutowo family. Each of the hotels retains the Hilton name but has little else to do with the international chain.

The brothers' sister, Endang Utari Mokodompit, is also in business. She ran the family's Jakarta-based Bank Pacific into the ground in 1995 by having it guarantee commercial paper issued by a finance company that she owned, the proceeds of which she used to speculate in Singapore property and buy other assets such as the listed Singapore operations of Australia's Goodman Fielder. By the time her bank was taken over by the central bank, it had net capital of just US$50 million and more than US$800 million in bad debts and guarantees.[14]

A local business magazine published an investigative issue on Endang and her bank. Apart from financial wrongdoings, the magazine also hinted at marital infidelities. Before the magazine could be distributed, a buyer blockaded the printers with trucks and refused to leave until the entire print run of 30,000 copies had been acquired. The magazine had exhausted its licensed print run under Indonesia's then restrictive printing laws and so essentially the story was killed.[15]

But from where did the siblings get their wealth in the first place? Their late father Ibnu Sutowo was a retired general who was close to then President Soeharto. He was made head of the state-owned oil company Pertamina in the late 1960s. Also around this time, the massive site on which the Jakarta Hilton now sits was "lent" to Ibnu by the Indonesian Government which technically still owns the land, a claim that the family denies.

Ibnu's mismanagement and corruption at Pertamina was so extraordinary that rather than attain record profits when oil prices were at historic levels after the oil shocks of the early 1970s, Pertamina nearly collapsed with US$10 billion in debts.[16] He and his fellow executives pocketed millions in kickbacks and millions more in contracts were given to private Sutowo family companies. Millions meant for Pertamina ended up in Ibnu's private accounts and he leased oil tankers on behalf of Pertamina even though it had a fleet of its own so that he could take millions in commissions. Pertamina's accounts were such a mess that the government had the humiliating task of writing to 200 banks around the world to ask if and how much Pertamina owed them.

Ibnu was forced out in 1976 and spent a period under house arrest. At no stage, though, was he required to repay what he had taken, although no doubt he shared the proceeds around to ensure that bygones would be bygones. He was left to build up his business empire of hundreds of companies from the comfort of his fortified mansion and Rolls-Royce with gold fittings.

But by 2005, when Adiguna went to trial, Ibnu was dead. And so in June of that year, he was sentenced by the Central Jakarta District Court, not to life but to seven years. A "mockery" of justice is how lawyers for the victim's family described it. But it was a conviction, nonetheless. Still, jail is not often that onerous for Indonesia's rich. Conditions usually can be "negotiated".

One of the more celebrated cases of a rich businessman going to jail in Indonesia was that of Eddie Tansil, who was convicted in 1994 for bribing state bank officials to obtain US$430 million in unsecured loans – loans on which he later defaulted. Several months into his jail term, Tansil was sighted in Bali playing a round of golf. It turned out that he routinely bribed jail warders to let him out for days at a time so that he could run his many businesses and occasionally get away for the weekend. But then one May day in 1996, Eddie simply didn't come back. The warders took days to raise the alarm – they assumed he'd been delayed, presumably on a pressing business matter. That was the last that anyone ever heard of him.

As has been mentioned in Chapter 5, back in 1997, a retiring Indonesian Supreme Court judge claimed that half of Indonesia's judges were corrupt. The figure was hotly disputed by the then chairman of the Indonesian Barristers Association. He claimed that a more realistic figure was 90%.[17] Has much changed? In Adiguna's case, the judges argued that a life sentence was too severe because there were "mitigating" circumstances. No doubt there were.

Part III
SINGAPORE AND MALAYSIA

Singapore and Malaysia are among my two favorite places in the world. But how they have squabbled. Like Siamese twins, joined via a causeway, they cannot live with each other and they can't live without each other. The squabbling is all the more frustrating because both countries have such strong and obvious virtues that too often each refuses to acknowledge of the other. The departure in 2003 of Dr Mahathir Mohamad from the prime ministership of Malaysia has allowed ties to be less prickly but old vestiges of suspicion remain.

Singapore might be small but it matters. It is the regional purveyor of professional services. In the words of one former Indonesian minister, Singapore "feeds off the inefficiency of its neighbors". But Malaysia is up and coming. Increasingly, its economy is a threat to that of Singapore's. So this section includes chapters that look at these two countries.

Among them are chapters that consider why Singapore is so different, what now for the Singapore economy, the diversity and decency of Malaysia, and the role of gossip and rumors in Malaysia. Also included is a chapter on Malaysia's Syed Mokhtar Albukhary. His ascendancy has profound implications for both Malaysia and Singapore. And there's also a chapter on one little known aspect of Singapore: its commercial sex industry. It is a thriving, government-regulated industry, which puts the lie to Singapore's image internationally as strait-laced and conservative. Singapore is, above everything, pragmatic and this chapter demonstrates that.

WHY SINGAPORE *IS* DIFFERENT: THE *BABAS* OF SINGAPORE

The success of Singapore rests on its rule of law. But why should Singapore have succeeded so well in this regard when other countries in the region have not? The backgrounds of Singapore's political elite suggest a clue.

There is a dichotomy in Singapore that continues to this day. Historically, Singapore's Chinese were divided between the *baba* and the *sinkeh*. The *sinkeh* comprised the majority of the island's population. They were the Chinese who came from China, or whose parents were born there. They spoke Chinese, lived like Chinese and considered themselves overseas Chinese. In Indonesia such Chinese were called the *totok*.

The *babas,* on the other hand, were Chinese more in name than practice. (The womenfolk were called *nonyas* and collectively they were also called the *peranakan*.) They were acculturated with both the local Malays and the British, whom they especially admired. Many *baba* families had intermarried with Malays or even with Christian Batak or Hindu Balinese women from Indonesia, for whom Islamic restrictions on marrying non-Muslims did not apply. The *babas* developed their own ceremonies, their own cuisine and even their own language, known as *Baba Malay* – a version of Malay with a sprinkling of Hokkien. They used chilli in their cooking like the Malays and pork like the Chinese. Brides would give grooms fabulous gilded silver belt buckles as part of their wedding ceremonies. The buckles were large and ovoid in the Malay style but with repoussé Chinese flowers and Chinese gods. The accoutrements of their culture are unique to the point that, between 1995 and 1997, the London-based auction house Christie's held auctions in Singapore at which the special porcelain, jewellery and gold and silver utensils commissioned by the *babas* were sold.

Of course the *sinkeh* picked up some local habits but the *babas* had been around longer and had picked up more. The Chinese, after all, are adaptable wherever they are. It's what makes them such successful migrants. I've eaten at Chinese restaurants in Rome and Venice that are decorated with dragons and red lanterns but with Italian espresso machines and menus that include pizza and the Thai dish *laab gai,* made not with mint but with pinenuts from Pisa. Would such compromises be possible in a French restaurant? And there is no shortage of Chinese restaurants in Kuala Lumpur and even London that are halal.

The *sinkeh* looked to China for guidance. The *babas* looked to London. Their admiration for the British was such that they became known as the "King's Chinese". They had their enclaves in Singapore – *baba* pockets in a *sinkeh* sea. One such pocket was what is now called Peranakan Place off Orchard Road. Many of the old *baba* homes are now bars and restaurants. It was behind here on Emerald Hill that Dr Lee Choo Neo, the first Straits Chinese woman to graduate from the Singapore Medical School in 1919, lived. She was the daughter of businessman Lee Hoon Leong. And he was the grandfather of Lee Kuan Yew.[1]

The *sinkeh* were the traders, the coolies and the shop house owners. The *babas* became the lawyers, the civil servants and the politicians. For them it was Oxford and Cambridge or the local English-language schools run in the tradition of England's public schools. For the *sinkeh*, if they received an overseas education at all, it was Nanking or some other university in China. And so although the *sinkeh* dominated Singapore's population, it was the *babas* who dominated public decision-making. In effect, a *baba* minority captured *sinkeh* Singapore. And that minority had attitudes that were more those of Victorian England than they were Chinese. Singapore's then Prime Minister Goh Chok Tong hinted at this in his 2003 National Day address when he explained why his administration had decided to loosen some restrictions: "What I had done was to signal a shift in our mindset to being more relaxed and open-minded, and less strait-laced *and Victorian*."[2] Goh does not come from a *baba* background. His predecessor does. As does his successor.

It was the *babas* who were the framers of Singapore's rules and institutions. Many of Singapore's most prominent Chinese have *baba* backgrounds. Lee Kuan Yew, who incidentally became prime minister of Singapore when aged just 35, is the most obvious example. He claims a Hakka heritage, although his upbringing was that of a *baba*. At home, he spoke English with his parents and *Baba Malay* to his grandparents.

"Mandarin was totally alien to me, and unconnected with my life". Lee has said of his childhood.[3] But then that was true of other Chinese dialects too.

Lee's paternal great-grandfather was a Hakka born in China. He married a local Hakka girl. His paternal grandfather was locally born. Lee describes him as an "Anglophile". He married a Semarang-born Chinese.

His maternal grandfather was a Hokkien from Malacca. His maternal grandmother was a Pontianak-born Chinese who spoke Hakka and Malay. They were a wealthy Straits family. Their daughter – Lee's mother – was married in 1922 at the age of 15. Lee says in his autobiography that part of her dowry included a little slave girl whose duty it was to help bathe and dress her.[4] And when Lee himself married, he chose a local *nonya* woman, Kwa Geok Choo, whose father was a Java-born Chinese and mother was a Straits-born Chinese, "like my own mother", says Lee.[5]

Lee's mother, Lee Chin Koon, was a highly respected authority on *nonya/baba* cuisine. She wrote a book on the subject, *Mrs Lee's Cookbook,* first published in 1974.[6] It was edited by her Hawaiian-born daughter-in-law Pamelia Lee, who married Lee Kuan Yew's brother Lee Suan Yew. The preface was written by Wee Kim Wee, another *baba*, and in fact, her cousin. Wee, who passed away in May 2005, served as the high commissioner to Malaysia (1973–80) and between 1985 and 1993 served as president of Singapore. Wee's wife was a *nonya* and the two showed significant interest in *baba* history and culture.

Those who doubt Lee Kuan Yew's *baba* origins (and some do) should consider the opening lines of his mother's cookbook:

> We Straits-born Chinese are known as the *Peranakan* – the ladies are called *nonyas* while the men are called *babas.* We are the descendants of the early Chinese in the Straits Settlements of Penang, Malacca and Singapore ... Malay influence, because of mingling and intermarriage, has produced a unique *Peranakan* culture and set of customs distinct from those of the Chinese community who came from China.[7]

Learning to be Chinese

For Lee, Chineseness was something of an acquired skill and later a political necessity. He was not brought up as a Chinese with a focus on China, but as a *baba* who looked to England. His language, food and culture were not that of a Chinese. And he followed the conventional career path of a *baba*. Not for him shopkeeping or trading. He went to London to study law. And so Lee Kuan Yew of Singapore became Harry Lee of Fitzwilliam

College, Cambridge. His father had given him and two of his brothers English as well as Chinese names.

Did Lee run Singapore as a piece of Asia mired in Chinese ways? No. He ran it in a manner to which a British colonial administrator would have aspired. He ran it as a *baba*.

Goh Keng Swee, that other great framer of Singapore's institutions, who rose to become finance minister and deputy prime minister, was the epitome of the *baba* elite. Goh was born in 1918 in Malacca, the epicentre of *baba* culture, into a local *baba* family. His parents were English-oriented Chinese Methodists. His cousin, also a Malacca *baba*, was Tan Siew Sin, who became Malaysia's first finance minister.

Goh attended the Anglo-Chinese School and Raffles College in Singapore – standard schooling for a *baba* son. He then joined the colonial Civil Service in Singapore. After the war he decided to study in London and so it was to the London School of Economics (LSE) that he went. Goh returned to Singapore, then returned to the LSE to complete a PhD, after which he returned to Singapore to resume a life in public service. He was instrumental in setting up many of Singapore's most well-known government bodies: the Economic Development Board, the Development Bank of Singapore, the Housing and Development Board (HDB) and the Jurong Industrial Estate. It was all about development – but development that proceeded along structured and paternalistic lines.

It was also Goh's Victorian attitudes on savings and frugal government spending that has given Singapore the huge external reserves that it has today. And it was at Goh's instigation that the Singapore Symphony Orchestra was established. No noisy, clanging Chinese opera for the *babas*. Their musical tastes were far more restrained.

I had the opportunity to meet with Goh at his office at the Singapore Totaliser Board in 1994. As he entered the room with an outstretched hand, my immediate impression was that he looked more Malay than Chinese. He was charming and welcoming, his voice was deep and his accent English upper class. He wore a pinstripe suit. As a fifth and sixth generation Australian with little interest in and knowledge of England at the time, could it be that I was more of the region than him?

We talked about Singapore's then plans to invest heavily in China. Goh was not a fan. "A lot of Singaporeans will lose their shirts in China", he'd said. China was messy, its legal system too poor and the going would be tough. Singaporeans were not used to operating in such an environment, Goh had said. Singaporeans might have been descended from China but the ways and means of China were no longer theirs. The *babas* had seen to that.

Another influential *baba* was Lim Kim San. He was born to a wealthy local family and as a fourth generation Straits-born Chinese did not speak Chinese at home but Malay. In 1960, he became chairman of the HDB where he made a remarkable contribution in a short time. He was appointed minister for national development in 1963. Later, he headed many other ministries in successive Peoples Action Party (PAP) governments. He was appointed executive chairman of Singapore Press Holdings in 1988 and then became chairman of Singapore's Presidential Board of Advisors.

Long-term PAP chairman Toh Chin Chye is another of the old guard with a *baba* background. His first language was not Hokkien, Teochiu or Hakka, but English. With Goh, Lee and Sinnathamby Rajaratnam, Toh formed the inner core that ran Singapore from 1959 until about the mid-1970s when his influence waned.[8] And so this is the coterie that designed and ran Singapore – three *babas* and a Jaffna Tamil.

Tony Tan, who retired as deputy prime minister and defense minister in late 2005, is a prominent second generation politician with a *baba* background. He was appointed deputy chairman and executive director of the Government of Singapore Investment Corporation (GIC) on his retirement. He also accepted a seat on the board of government-linked Singapore Press Holdings, which publishes Singapore's most prominent newspapers, and was later made non-executive chairman. And he was made chairman of Singapore's National Research Foundation. The GIC is instrumental to the Singapore state. Its chairman is Lee Kuan Yew. And so the GIC is another Singapore institution firmly in the grip of prudent *baba* management. Singapore's current prime minister is Lee Hsien Loong, Lee Kuan Yew's son. (Hsien Loong also serves as the GIC's deputy chairman.) With both a *baba* mother and father, Hsien Loong's *baba* pedigree is actually stronger than his father's.

Victorian Values

Of course the influence of the *babas* has been no bad thing. It is to the *baba* elite and their values that Singapore owes its prosperity and stability. Their insistence on sound public administration, education and the rule of law had made Singapore what it is. They took over from the British and continued in their tradition.

But that has also given Singaporeans trouble when it comes to investing successfully in the region. Used to doing business in a structured environment, many have had trouble investing in markets where legal structures are poor. The Singapore-Suzhou Township, an industrial park that the

Singapore Government invested in heavily in China, proved a flop, for example. So Singaporeans have tended to invest in the mature markets of the West – markets that operate in a manner like their own. "There is always the insider-outsider problem in Asia", complained Dr Teh Kok Peng, president of the Singapore Government's GIC Special Investments. "The US is more open. We are not at a disadvantage there."[9] Singaporeans, it seems, might be Asian but being an Asian Insider is more than simply looking the part.

Largely, it was the *babas* who were responsible for the concept of Asian values that we used to hear so much about prior to the 1997–98 Asian economic crisis. The proponents of Asian values liked to emphasize the sense of family and community. But just how Asian are these values when it comes to the early *sinkeh* population in Singapore – with its opium dens, brothels and gambling houses? The *sinkeh* settled into parts of Singapore according to dialect. There was not so much a sense of community but communalism. Families were torn apart by gambling and other vices. Many Chinese of earlier generations were polygamous – they took second and sometimes many subsequent wives.

Sago Lane in Chinatown is still remembered by older Singaporeans as the street of the "death houses" where many old and sick spent their last days. Funeral parlors and shops that sold the paraphernalia associated with death operated from here. Chinatown residents called it Sey Yan Kai or the "Street of the Dead". Death houses were abolished only in 1961. They did not fit in with the values of the *babas*. Families were supposed to look after their own sick and elderly, not leave them somewhere else to die.

Also, Asian values or at least their contemporary manifestations were about strong, if not autocratic, leadership. But submitting to authority was not a strong point of the *sinkeh*, who largely came from China's unruly southern provinces. The *babas,* on the other hand, admired authority, after all, that was what the British stood for. In fact, those values that have come to be labeled as "Asian" – strong, patriarchal leadership, frugality, community and family – are the values of Victorian England, the period in which Singapore's *baba* community had its genesis and which was so admired by them. It was in Victorian England that moral order was linked to economic development and where the natural goodwill of men was deemed an unreliable guarantor of order and so was supplanted by a structure of deterrents and incentives to constrain and cajole.[10] These were the very sentiments that lay behind the efficacy of strong leadership in the Asian values debate.

And so "Asian" values were not particularly indigenous to Asia, which in any event was mired in banditry, polygamy, concubinage, and narcotics usage, if China is taken as an example. A *baba* elite whose values drew not so much on Asian but the British values of the late nineteenth century propagated them. The debate over Asian values really was a debate about the efficacy of old English values supplanted from another century – the same values that underpin the apparently "decadent" but nonetheless successful West. And so this is the true Singapore story: a little piece of Victorian England off the Malay peninsular. Not so much a red dot in a green sea but a banana palm in a forest of durians.

Chapter 12

REINVENTING SINGAPORE?

My fellow Singaporeans,
Compared to the bright sunshine of the early 1990s, the recent years look much darker ... I know that you are worried that we have lost our way.

(then Prime Minister Goh Chok Tong's opening lines
for his National Day address, 2003)

Since Goh uttered these lines, the Singapore economy has picked up. But they underscore its essential fragility. The problem with being at the peak of success is that every way you look, it's all downhill. That is Singapore's problem. Another problem is that it is heavily dependent on the rest of the world for its living and so its economy is like a cork buffeted by the vast sea in which it floats. As one analyst whose presentation I sat through in late 2005 said, Singapore's economy, when mapped on a graph for the last 20 years, is beginning to adopt the boom-and-bust profile that we've come to expect of a South American economy.

And yet Singapore is a beacon for sound corporate governance in the region. Indeed, there is a view among some outside Asia that corruption is part of the Asian way; that Asians are somehow culturally predisposed to corruption. But there is an obvious flaw in the argument: Singapore. The Lion City is something of an embarrassment to the argument because it shows that it is possible to be both Asian and not corrupt.

Singapore has done extremely well. But embedded in this success are problems for the future. Singapore will continue to enjoy high living standards. But it cannot keep growing as fast as it has. Its economy is services-oriented. It fills the niches that others in the region cannot and so it is said that it feeds off the inefficiencies of its neighbors. But the competition is closing in.

I saw something in Singapore in 2003 that I hadn't thought that I'd need to see. I was about to give a speech at a marketing and advertising congress at the Suntec Convention Center, when across from the hall in which I was due to speak I noticed a seminar room in which corporate training seminars were being held. And the topic of the seminars? "Management training on handling staff retrenchments". So things have come to this, I thought.

Unemployment in Singapore reached a 17-year high in 2003. (This when unemployment had reached a 30-year low in the UK and a 14-year low in Australia that year, for example.) The hysteria over the SARS virus had taken its toll, but economic growth in any event was not going to be spectacular. In fact, Singapore's economy for the year was forecast to be the slowest growing in Asia. Why? The unpalatable truth for Singapore is that it is losing its comparative advantage. The most important competitor is Malaysia.

But Singapore and its government perform well when backed into a corner. A politically difficult decision had to be made toward the end of 2004, as to whether Singapore should allow a casino to operate to attract the growing numbers of wealthy mainland Chinese tourists. The government took everyone by surprise and announced that it would license two casinos. It has also provided big incentives to attract biotechnology investment. The government itself planned to spend S$12 billion (US$7.1 billion) on research between 2005 and 2010 and has built a US$300 million biotechnology research park. Perhaps such spending will pay dividends. But profiting from having a biotechnology industry and merely having one are two very different things. The challenge for Singapore will be to keep producing rabbits out of the hat.

Enter Malaysia

Singaporeans tend to be fairly dismissive of Malaysia, unnecessarily so. Its inefficiencies are derided, as is its general "messiness". But that messiness permits a certain amount of creative thinking. There is a plurality of ideas and dynamism in Malaysia that is beginning to see its entrepreneurs kick some real goals. Malaysian politics tends to be chaotic and unscripted. The government comprises many parties and not just one. And positions within the ruling United Malays National Organization (UMNO) party and the two other leading Barisan Nasional component parties, the Malaysian Chinese Association (MCA) and the Malaysian Indian Congress (MIC), are contested fiercely. That is not necessarily the case within the Peoples Action Party (PAP) in Singapore, for which people often have to be asked to stand.

A sound rule of law and putting in place excellent infrastructure are the two things that allowed Singapore to boom. But these are two things that

Malaysia has been working on. It does it with more chaos and less focus than Singapore but Malaysia is now heading in the right direction. And every Malaysian step forward is a step back for Singapore in the race for relative comparative advantage. The business that the Singapore Port Authority has lost to Johor's Tanjong Pelapas port is one obvious example of this. There are others.

Malaysia was hit hard by the region's 1997–98 economic crisis. But it recovered quickly and efficiently. Incompetence got Malaysia into the crisis but its recovery was managed with surprising competence. The work of Malaysia's economic restructuring agencies Danaharta, Danamodal and the Corporate Debt Restructuring Committee (CDRC) rightly received praise far and wide. The professionalism and efficiency of these bodies ensured that they will serve not just as models for the region in future but for all countries when they run into severe financial difficulties.

Malaysia now has a better securities law, fewer and bigger banks and stockbroking firms and better bankruptcy provisions. The work of the Kuala Lumpur Stock Exchange (KLSE) in educating directors and enforcing codes for better governance has been exemplary. The fines that it can impose on aberrant companies are too low, but the KLSE has shown that it is prepared to reprimand and fine companies without fear or favor.

Singapore remains ahead of Malaysia on all these counts. But Malaysia is closing the gap. Singapore now faces the problems that all mature economies face: how to stay ahead when its competitors can play catch-up?

Regional HQs

Singapore has always prided itself on attracting the regional headquarters of multinationals. But Kuala Lumpur is becoming more competitive in this regard. Boeing, Lafarge and Patria have chosen Kuala Lumpur over Singapore in recent years for the location of their regional headquarters. GE has moved its corporate, oil, gas and medical systems Southeast Asian headquarters to Kuala Lumpur. BMW cars, BHP Steel and Philips Luminaires also shifted their Asian headquarters from Singapore to Kuala Lumpur. And in 2003, Standard Chartered of the UK, one of the world's biggest banks, chose Malaysia as the location for one of its two global service centers, which now employs more than 1,000 staff.

These companies might represent a drop in the ocean, especially given that some 3,600 international companies have their regional operations and HQ-related functions in Singapore, but then this figure shows how much Singapore has to lose.

Philips cited Malaysia's "lower costs", "excellent infrastructure" and "highly trained workforce" as the reasons for its decision to leave Singapore for Kuala Lumpur.[1] Singapore has these last two factors but it's on the first that Kuala Lumpur wins. Increasingly, Malaysia represents better value for money. It is becoming more attractive as a place to live for expatriates. Its shopping facilities are just as good as Singapore's, the restaurants are comparable but cheaper and education facilities are improving all the time, to the point where Malaysia now attracts fee-paying students from Thailand and Indonesia, for example.

But Kuala Lumpur isn't the only destination for multinationals that are opting to exit Singapore. In 2003, Honeywell decided to shift its regional headquarters from Singapore to Shanghai. Honeywell's president in China said:

> In addition to opening up new growth opportunities, this move will enable us to draw from a larger pool of talent for recruitment, and help our suppliers and partners support our growth initiatives.[2]

It's not that Singapore is no longer as good as it once was. It's more that other places no longer are as bad as they once were.

Bread and Circuses

So what choices does Singapore face? One is to drop its standards and pursue any opportunity. Elsewhere I have called this the Boat Quay option.[3] By that I mean that Singapore's famous Boat Quay restaurant strip used to have a certain elegance. But as business has dropped off, gradually that elegance has been lost, as ugly bars emiting loud and competing music, with girls who hang out front to push cheap beer, spring up along the Quay. The quality of the food on offer has declined as the vigor of the touts has increased. Boat Quay now offers shades of Pattaya or Patpong.

A recent walk down Boat Quay one evening took me past a statue urinating into a trough decorated by fairy lights. This tacky ensemble had been dragged out onto the sidewalk to lure passersby into the adjacent seafood restaurant.

A manifestation of the Boat Quay option was then Prime Minister Goh's announcement in 2003 that the government would permit table-top dancing in Singapore. Bungee jumping would be allowed too.

In 2005 it was announced that the Crazy Horse cabaret from Paris would be opening a local version in Singapore, at Clark Quay, along from Boat

Quay. Nudity would be allowed, at least of a kind. Singapore's Media Development Authority reportedly provided guidelines stipulating that the nudity could not be full frontal, no acts would be permitted that suggested or depicted homosexual themes, and there should be no physical interaction between performers and members of the audience.[4] Unlike the Paris version, the Singapore version will offer patrons a restaurant service while they watch the show and there will be lingerie and perfume merchandising.

And then of course there are the two casinos, permission for which was granted in early 2005, although the local media was encouraged to refer to them as "integrated resorts", which it dutifully did, thereafter referring to them as IRs, as if gambling was not to be at the very heart of their *raison d'être*.

But the reality is that such moves smack of desperation; a form of government by gimmick. They do not represent changes in "mindset". They happen only because the government says that they can, explicitly and on a case-by-case basis. When local political activists said they wanted more freedom, they didn't mean they wanted to go reverse bungee jumping.

Pulau Kiasu

Everyone knows that good problem-solving within a company comes from discussion, debate, canvassing all options and then letting the best idea win. Good problem-solving does not come from the founder or CEO simply dropping solutions onto the company from on high. And so it is with countries. Public debate fosters ideas and the messy process of the contest for ideas ensures that the better ones come up. To a large degree, Singapore is still being run like a Chinese family-owned and managed firm, whereby the patriarch issues edicts and the managers follow. It works when the family patriarch is unusually clever. But such unusual cleverness and benevolence often comes down to good fortune as much as anything else. The more assured way of getting good decisions is to have a market-place for ideas from which they can originate and be tested.

And yet no other government in the world with citizens with a comparable per capita income persists with the sorts of media controls as does Singapore's. No other government in the developed world is as paranoid about the media, information control and control in general as is this one. But to what end? At this point it is important to state that media freedom is not simply a political issue. Just as importantly, it is a business and economic matter. A strong and questioning media doesn't just act as a check on government but on companies. The threat of exposure is a valuable one. Economies that lack this are poorer for it.

Singapore accepts that free trade in goods and services is essential to having a successful economy. But that's only half the equation if a country that's rich wants to stay that way. The other half is that there must be a free market for ideas. People must feel free to offer their opinions and ideas. Markets need marketplaces and what is the most obvious marketplace for ideas, the place where they can be exchanged? It is the media.

The result of the Singaporean mismatch – a free market for goods and services and a near monopoly in the market for ideas – is that Singapore and its economy do not benefit from the vibrancy and dynamism of a free ideas and information marketplace as do other mature economies. The market for ideas which, after all, is the market for progress has become stifled. For too long, civil servants have been allowed to be the main source of ideas, the Civil Service to be the font of development and progress. And for too long, the media has been relegated to the role of simply reporting rather than scrutinizing. And it is this last role that is so important in a country where the political opposition is embryonic.

But there does seem to be a growing ability to accept criticism and endure self-analysis. Some changes, though, are false starts. The most obvious is the proposal to allow a Speaker's Corner in Singapore's Hong Lim Square. Demands for free speech were taken literally. And so now, contingent on the successful application of a police permit, any Singaporean (but no foreigner) is able to go and stand in that (usually deserted) square and make a speech. It's an idea from nineteenth-century London. It belongs in the nineteenth century and is ridiculous now. Of course, London has its Speaker's Corner in Hyde Park but it is a tourist attraction. It is a venue for cranks. No-one pretends it is a venue for serious public discourse and in no way does it play any role whatsoever in public debate in mainstream British society today. In Singapore there was a contemporary problem but it received a *baba* solution.

But there are signs that the media is freeing up in Singapore. A process of developing a culture of competition among competing ideas is under way. I began to write an occasional column for Singapore's *Today* newspaper in 2003. In June of that year I wrote in a piece on Hong Kong's planned anti-subversion and sedition laws under Article 23 of the territory's Basic Law, that:[5]

Historically, sedition has been used to suppress political dissent. Many former British colonies still have it on their statute books. But it's either falling into disuse or being repealed in most modern countries. But Hong Kong is going the other way. It intends to introduce it. That will bring it into line with Singapore. And mainland China. Countries like Cuba, North Korea and Iran have similar laws.

That's right. On this matter I put Singapore in the same league as mainland China, Cuba, North Korea and Iran and it was published, by a Singapore newspaper and one that is ultimately owned by the Singapore Government.

Things are changing in Singapore. Increasingly, newspapers publish a range of views that would not have been published a few years ago. One golden rule is whatever you say, make sure that it is correct. Get it factually wrong, particularly if it is in relation to a politically contentious matter, and you can expect to face heavy criticism and possibly legal action.

Ravi Veloo wrote a piece headlined "For the sake of Singapore the PAP should split" for the same newspaper a few months before mine had appeared.[6] The headline itself would have made many outsiders lift at least one eyebrow. But what followed shows that the gap between the reality of Singapore and its image abroad increasingly has grown apart.

In relation to the PAP's unbroken rule of 44 years, Veloo said that it had done well, despite the fact that "it faces none of the usual checks and balances, such as free and responsible media". Nonetheless, he then went on with a blistering attack on the PAP as it is today:

> So strong is the conservative culture within the main ranks of the party that even the brightest, most exciting people it recruits soon echo hackneyed old lines … Just look at the Economic Review Committee. Given the mandate to think the unthinkable, it came up with a thumping endorsement of the status quo instead, with just minor tinkerings here and there.

Veloo went on to criticize the top-down approach to public decision-making in Singapore:

> How did we come to this? Well, for one thing, when you crush alternative opinions steadily with a sledgehammer in the name of pragmatism and social unity, you encourage people not to have any strong opinions … So no wonder that Senior Minister Lee Kuan Yew could face hordes of our better educated, better traveled, better fed at a university gathering recently and lament that it was hard to find world class leaders among the 40,000 or so babies born each year [in Singapore]. The clue to the problem was right before him — not one of our students had the self-respect to stand up and correct him. The young are more dull and less rebellious than their parents — another Singapore first!

The solution, Veloo suggested, is clear:

> The PAP needs a real threat to its own dominance to make the difference. It needs to split down the middle. Strategically, it would be the best legacy the founder of the party, SM Lee, could leave the country.

So there you have it. The PAP is conservative, turns new recruits into hacks with hackneyed old lines, crushes dissent with a sledgehammer, has led to young Singaporeans having insufficient self-respect and being dull, and should be split in two. And all that published in a Singapore Government-linked newspaper. Clearly, change is afoot. But does this journey have a predetermined destination? Journeys in Singapore usually do. But this one might be different.

Humpty Dumpty Sat on a Wall

But it's not quite a Prague Spring. In October 2003 I wrote another column for *Today*. Again, I took advantage of what appeared to be Singapore's new *glasnost*. The newspaper gave it the headline "Is Singapore being paranoid?"[7] To provide a flavor, here are several paragraphs from that piece:

> Why does the Government still feel the need to license newspapers and other media outlets? Why do editors feel the need to self-censor? Granted, the list of "sensitive" topics appears to have grown shorter. So, why maintain the old fashioned, out-moded trappings of a Third World dictatorship? What does Singapore have to hide?

> For too long, civil servants have been allowed to be the main source of ideas. To their credit, their professionalism has got Singapore to where it is. But now, such control threatens Singapore's prosperity.

> I accept that the media has become more open in recent years. *Today*, for example, publishes challenging opinion pieces increasingly of a nature that would have been unthinkable several years ago. But five minutes of sunshine does not make a sunny day.

> The Government should abolish the system of annual licensing and editors should have greater independence. Instead, what reforms have been made in the direction of liberalism? Bungee jumping and bar-top dancing.

> I was walking along Boat Quay recently and saw four ladies standing on a bar in a pub, each writhing to music in a sexually-suggestive manner. This is not reform. This is not liberalism. This is sleaze. And sleaze should not be equated with freedom. The most important aspect of freedom, which is aligned to the freedom of the media, is the freedom to be wrong. And it's that freedom that Singapore needs to cultivate.

Many outsiders were stunned. They were amazed that a Singapore newspaper would publish such remarks. One said to me that I'd never be allowed into Singapore again. Another inquired, half in jest, where he should send the wreath. An expatriate reader in Singapore wrote to the editor to say that he was "simply floored" when he read the piece and he offered his congratulations to all concerned.

Many Singaporean readers wrote to express their agreement with the sentiments that I'd expressed. In all, about 20 letters were received and only one was not supportive. Such a reader response to a serious opinion piece is almost unheard of in Singapore. But there was one other letter. *Today* was obliged to publish it. It was from the press secretary to the minister for information, communications and the arts. She was not happy. Of course I had it all wrong, she said (as did presumably the Singaporeans who had written in support of what I'd said). She finished by saying that, as a foreigner, I was entitled to my views but I had "no right to campaign for them [in Singapore] or to change our system to something else that he prefers".[8] This last remark attracted more letters in my support from ordinary Singaporeans. One reader said that it contradicted all that the Singapore Government had said about the country's need to attract foreign talent.

The letter was followed up by a speech a few weeks later. Dr Lee Boon Yang, the minister for information, communications and the arts, said in an address to a Singapore press club luncheon attended by around 100 journalists and other people involved in the media that by "attacking" the government's media policy and urging the adoption of the Western model, I had "clearly crossed the line and engaged in our domestic politics". He also described how the government had issued more media licenses since 2000 and defended the government's role in censorship. When asked in the Q&A session what the government would do if another article like mine appeared in Singapore, Lee said: "If any newspaper, whether it is *Today* or some other newspaper, persists in publishing such articles, we will certainly take it up." Ironically, the topic of Lee's speech was "Towards a Global Media City".[9]

That same day, the *Today* newspaper ran another of my columns but, unusually, did so on page one. The following day, its front page was devoted to Lee's speech. And so I was in the odd position of having written what turned out to be the newspaper's lead story on one day and then being in it on the next. But the fact remains that *Today* had published my offending column and it is a government-controlled newspaper. Presumably, the editors at *Today* would not have published if they thought that it was outside the government's boundaries and if they were unsympathetic toward it. Indeed, if Dr Lee's boundaries are so clear, why did a Singapore newspaper publish my column in the first place – a newspaper that is ultimately owned by a government holding company headed by the wife of the deputy prime minister? The boundaries are not clear and that seemingly is their point. They encourage the erring on the side of caution.

I did email the minister's office to say that everyone would be helped if what constitutes "politics" was defined by the Singapore Government and then codified. It did not occur to me that I had written about domestic politics but rather about Singapore's institutional arrangements. But on that point I received no reply. The government's position is evocative of Lewis Carroll's *Through the Looking Glass*. "When I use a word, it means just what I choose it to mean – nothing more nor less", said Humpty Dumpty to Alice. The Singapore Government's position also runs counter to the Universal Declaration of Human Rights. Article 19 of that Declaration states in its entirety:

> Everyone has the right to freedom of opinion and expression; this right includes freedom to hold opinions without interference and to seek, receive and impart information and ideas through any media and regardless of frontiers.

The global media city seems a long way off.

Dr Lee's singling me out with the claim that I had "crossed the line" was reported across the region in newspapers in Singapore, Malaysia, Hong Kong, the Philippines, Brunei and Taiwan and on several wire services. It was also reported in the *International Herald Tribune* ("Singapore calls article on politics out of line"). But arguably most damagingly for Singapore, it was the subject of an editorial in the *Wall Street Journal* in the US and in that newspaper's European and Asian editions ("How does an authoritarian government get its journalists to toe the line without having to micromanage them?" it began).[10] Dr Lee's reaction also earned a rebuke from the international organization of journalists, the Reporters Sans Frontières (Reporters without Borders), which was described in its 2004 annual report as "acrimonious". How all this promotes Singapore as a global media city isn't obvious. Of course it doesn't. It does the opposite.

Dr Lee's remarks even managed to propel me (and him) onto the well-known satirical website TalkingCock.com. The piece – a spoof of an interview with the minister – sat alongside another that called for a "national day of civil disobedience" in relation to the Singapore Government's ban on oral sex unless such sex leads to full intercourse. There's probably no need here to go into what form the suggested civil disobedience should take. Singapore's Court of Appeal had upheld the oral sex ban in 1997. The court referred in part in its decision to an Indian case that dates back to 1817 in which a man was charged with having intercourse with a buffalo's nostril. The Singapore Government's preference for control and the self-defeating contortions and absurdities to which that leads was highlighted once more.

In any event, the Singapore Government is not above intervening in the domestic political processes of foreign countries itself. It retains a range of lobbyists and law firms to push its case in the US, for example. One firm it retains is Washington-based APCO Worldwide Inc. The firm describes itself as "a global communication consultancy specializing in building relationships with an organization's key stakeholders". In short, the company works as a political lobbyist. According to US Department of Justice records, Singapore's embassy in the US paid APCO US$50,441.53 in the six months to 30 September 2000 alone for "strategic advice and counsel ... concerning trade and foreign policy issues. [It] also contacted Singapore Government officials, *and* members of Congress concerning the interests of positive US/Singapore relations."[11] APCO is still in the pay of the Singapore Government. So, it seems to be a case of "do as I say, not as I do".

Finally, it needs to be asked why Singapore needs the position of information minister in the first place. It is not a position that rich, successful and modern countries have. For example, the US, Britain and Australia do not see the need for an information minister. But Iran, Zimbabwe and Burma do. And, famously, Iraq used to have one. The trouble is, rarely is the position of information minister about giving out information but about controlling it. It's a coveted post for governments that like to control. It was no accident that in November 2003 when Sri Lanka's President Chandrika Kumaratunga suspended Parliament and seized power from the elected prime minister unilaterally, she also took control of the Ministries of Defense, Interior *and* Information in addition to remaining president.

Once more, it needs to be remembered that media freedom is not simply a political or social issue. It is a business issue. Having a free media, a media that doesn't only report but also scrutinizes and questions, is consistent with having a strong economy. A free media is consistent with good government and nation building. A shackled media is certainly not consistent with the aspiration to be a global media city. And importantly, calls for a free media should never be dismissed as meddling in politics. How the media is regulated is as much a business issue as it is about politics.

Evolution not Revolution

But Singapore *is* changing, even if it's often a case of two steps forward and then one back. These combative opinion pieces were published in

Singapore, after all. Singaporeans are learning to criticize. Not for its own sake but because it is constructive: it helps the government and leads to better policy outcomes. The challenge for the Singapore Government is not to see such criticism as a loss of face. The odd PAP MP has begun to be more vocal in criticism. Tan Soo Khoon, a former speaker of the House for 13 years and an MP for 25 years, began to subject Singapore to a degree of self-analysis that it has rarely heard. In a speech to Parliament on 4 April 2002, Tan let fly with a series of criticisms. The government had called an election in 2001. It was called before the government's current term had expired but the government said that it wanted to go to the people to renew its mandate in the face of all the problems the world was facing and in the face of Singapore's own difficulties.

Tan said in a speech to the Parliament:

So it did somewhat baffle me that while we went out to seek a new mandate from the people very quickly, it took almost five months for Parliament to be convened for the representatives of the people to meet and discuss the issues that are so crucial to Singaporeans and our future.

The former speaker went on to express a number of other dissatisfactions at how the government and most particularly government ministers conduct themselves:

It is indeed a rare occasion in this House where a minister accepts changes to be made to his Bill, except as one minister puts it: "I guess I can live with the changes if they are just commas and full-stops." ... Much buzz is now given to the lifting of the Whip. [The Whip is the process whereby all government MPs are required to vote with the government regardless of their personal views on a matter.] MPs of the ruling party may ask for permission to vote freely on a case-by-case basis, except for some crucial areas. And the Whip will be lifted for all matters of conscience and selected issues. So what's new? I still have to get permission to disagree. Matter of conscience? It's a term that has never been clearly defined. And as if to show how generous we have been in lifting the Whip, we always take a kind of skewed praise in parading, as an example, our lifting of the Whip during the debate on the Abortion Bill. But that was 33 years ago!

Tan's criticism grew more specific the following month. Speaking in the government's budget debate, he referred to the "seven wonders of Singapore". It has become something of a modern classic in Singapore and had those few Singaporeans who bother to watch local politics smirking in the coffee shops, for Tan's seven wonders were all new government offices.

His list included the offices of the Ministry of Education, the new Supreme Court building and the Foreign Affairs Ministry, which Tan observed sits on "choice district 10 land". He said that he could remember when government offices had "the Spartan look". But not any more. "I think there must be a competition among them ... to see which can look better than the Four Seasons Hotel." The nation of immigrants had become decidedly comfortable.

Tan also complained that too much public money was spent by government departments to produce glossy flyers, colorful charts and fancy name changes. For example, the Standards, Productivity and Innovation Board had become Spring Singapore and the Trade Development Board had been renamed International Enterprise Singapore. Who would now know what Spring Singapore actually did? Tan joked that it "sounds like the name of a nightclub". For all the money spent on renaming the boards and then telling people about it, "at the end of it all, you're still doing the same things but nobody is any wiser what you actually do or how to look for you".[12]

Such criticisms represent steps forward in Singapore's striving for political maturity. But then another step back occurred in 2005 when Singaporean film maker Martyn See was threatened with prosecution over his 26-minute documentary *Singapore Rebel*, based on the opposition politician Chee Soon Juan. The government ordered the film to be withdrawn from Singapore's annual international film festival on the grounds that it breached the Films Act, which prohibits "party political films", defined as those films that contain "either partisan or biased references to or comments on any political matter". Such a definition is, as any rational human being will know, an utter absurdity, particularly in a country with pretensions of modernity. See was placed under police investigation with a view to prosecution under the Act, for which the penalty is a jail term of up to two years or a fine of up to S$100,000 (approximately US$59,000). See's video camera and tapes of the documentary and other related material were seized.[13] For his part, he denied making the film in support of any political belief but rather was curious about why Chee bothers to do what he does when, as an opposition politician, the odds are so stacked against him in Singapore. No doubt many would like to know.

Also in 2005, Dr Vivian Balakrishna, a cabinet minister, toured a housing estate in August that had been affected by the construction of the Buangkok Mass Rapid Transit (MRT) train station. Protestors had made several large cut-out white elephants, which they attached to a fence near to the site as their means of quiet protest against the inconvenience caused by the construction. It was not a big deal and was done with reasonable humor. But it turned out to be an illegal act: a permit from the police should have been obtained first. Some joyless individual made a complaint to the police and after much to-ing and fro-ing, the police decided not to charge the "culprit" but to give the individual a "stern warning". This was deemed progress because the "culprit" had not been charged. But even a "stern warning" for putting up cut-out elephants? Oh please.

Of course it's not true to say that Singapore is a one-party state. Voters are given the choice to vote for parties other than the PAP, but by and large they prefer the PAP. It is a preference that is genuine. But a government that espouses free trade because competition helps manufacturers to be more efficient cannot deny that political parties also need effective competition. In a sense, the PAP has become a victim of its own success. Singapore now does seem starved of sources for new ideas and creativity when it comes to public decision-making. There might not be a dictatorship politically, but to a degree there is a dictatorship of ideas, if for no other reason than because alternatives are not offered up. As the joke goes, "we in Singapore are very lucky because we don't need to think. The government does it for us." Ordinary Singaporeans have by and large opted out of the marketplace for ideas. They have done so for good reason.

Some quip that Singapore is not so much a one-party state as a one-family state. It is true that relatives of former Prime Minister Lee Kuan Yew now hold key positions of power in Singapore. His sons Lee Hsien Loong and Lee Hsien Yang serve as prime minister and head of Singapore Telecom respectively. Lee Hsien Loong's wife, Ho Ching, is the head of Temasek Holdings, the government's principal holding company. Sister-in-law Pamelia Lee has served as a senior director at the Singapore Tourist Promotion Board. Kwa Soon Bee, the brother of Lee's wife Kwa Geok Choo, is a former permanent secretary of health and a member of the Singapore Tourist Promotion Board. Even Wee Kim Wee, former president of Singapore, was a cousin of Lee's late mother. It's said that when Lee resigned as prime minister, he did not so much step down as step aside. And then there is Lee himself. Since 1990 he has served as the senior minister and then minister mentor in the prime minister's office. He also serves as chairman of the all-important Government of Singapore Investment Corporation (GIC).

Malaysia's former Finance Minister Daim Zainuddin, someone for whom Lee has expressed considerable respect, said to me that, although Lee is no longer Singapore's prime minister, it was his view that no-one should "doubt" that Lee still "runs the place".

The problem, however, is not that the Lee family has deliberately moved its members in place to exclude others. The members who have won prominent positions have done so on merit. The Lees genuinely are an exceptional and talented family. It's also the case that Singapore is small, with a lot of demand for talent but an insufficient supply of it. Ho Ching's appointment as executive director of Temasek was a classic case. Then Prime Minister Goh Chok Tong acknowledged the apparent conflict of interest inherent in the appointment but said that it was the result of Singapore's small talent pool relative to the demand for talent. "It is awkward, we know that", said Goh, exhibiting his typical flair for sounding reasonable. "There is some conflict, but you know, we work for the larger good."[14]

Goh made it very clear in his 2003 National Day address that Lee Hsien Loong would succeed him as prime minister and that Lee was his choice. But he also astonished Singaporeans by breathing new life into an old rumor:

> You may have also heard this old story about [Lee Hsien] Loong. Back in 1990, Loong had a quarrel with Richard Hu [the then finance minister]. Dhanabalan [the then minister for national development] sided with Richard. Loong lost his temper, reached across the table, and gave Dhanabalan a tight slap! The whole Cabinet was thrown into commotion. I then forced Loong to apologise. I must be suffering from amnesia. I just cannot remember this incident!

Raising the matter was an extraordinary thing for Goh to do. Particularly in what is considered to be the prime minister's most important speech of the year. And notice how he did not say that the incident did not happen but rather that he could not remember it. Singapore was abuzz with the story and theories as to why Goh had brought it up. Someone even developed an email attachment that was quick to do the rounds, showing action figure toys including a BG GI Joe doll with one arm in a slapping position ("comes with special slapping action to bring critics to their knees"). At its feet was a doll on its knees, on which Dhanabalan's face had been transposed. (BG stands for "brigadier general", Lee's last post in the army, and not for "baby god" as some quip.) As Hsien Loong's appointment as prime minister grew closer, the local media were advised to stop referring to him as "BG". Presumably the powers to be were keen to craft a less militaristic image for the new prime minister.)

But ultimately, the real problem with fostering a culture of debate and the free flow of ideas is that Singaporeans (and foreign writers) don't yet know where the boundaries are. And if the boundaries are unclear, the best way to avoid crossing them is to remain as cautious as possible. In mid-2003, a government subcommittee charged with examining ways to make Singaporeans more creative in their thinking said that the idea that "out-ofbounds markers" exist in Singapore was having a "dampening" effect on people expressing their views. The committee recommended that various forums be set up in which various strata of the community could voice their opinions. Young Singaporeans could air their views in a national youth forum, for example.[15]

Would that work? Of course not. The media is the means by which ordinary people voice their concerns in other modern countries. And that's how it needs to be in Singapore. There has been greater public debate in Singapore's media of late. But people still tread with caution.

I say things in Western newspapers in ways I feel I could not in Singapore's media. But then I might be wrong. I don't know. No-one knows. And yet my Singaporean friends regard me as outrageously outspoken. But when I did write an outspoken piece that I genuinely did believe to be permissible, as did the newspaper's editors, we all later found out that it wasn't.

The political culture in Singapore encourages self-censorship and that constrains the flow of ideas. But ideas are a middle-class consumption good. Revolution is not. And Singapore, thanks to the success of its government, is overwhelmingly middle class, the first such middle-class country in Southeast Asia. So what is the danger? Why the phobia of criticism? Ideas and creativity are good for business and good for the economy. How dangerous to Singapore can freethinking be? The place is an outstanding success. Its story is an excellent one. It is a story that can stand up to scrutiny. And it can do so without the clutter of outmoded media licensing laws and other restrictions that suggest otherwise.

Chapter 13

SINGAPORE INC. OR SINGAPORE SINK?

British shoppers who go to the chilled section of their local Sainsbury's or Tesco supermarkets and choose a Covent Garden fresh soup are doing more than simply buying a pre-prepared meal. The same goes for Irish shoppers who buy Cresset soups. They are becoming customers of the Singapore Government because the soups are made by two companies that are ultimately controlled by one of its commercial arms.[1] While governments in the world are getting out of business, Singapore's is not only staying put but expanding the scope of its commercial activities. It is expanding its domestic role and investing heavily overseas. Hence the soup.

In Singapore, the government, or its arms, owns or controls enterprises that operate in almost every conceivable sector. From television to selling computers to mobile telephones to inflight catering – the government, or its entities, is involved in it all. Of course, the private–public partnership that is Singapore Inc. has got Singapore to where it is today, one of the wealthiest small nations on earth. But that does not mean that such a mix is optimal for all time.

Overseas, the Singapore Government's investments are even more diverse. Arms of the Singapore Government empty household dustbins across Brisbane, sell weapons in the US and operate serviced apartments from London to Jakarta.

The means by which the Singapore Government has direct ownership in the commercial sector are via two massive holding companies: Temasek Holdings and the Government of Singapore Investment Corporation (GIC). Until recently the former has had largely a domestic focus. The latter always has been focused on overseas investment. Both are notoriously secretive. Neither publicly disclose their consolidated accounts, their total assets or total liabilities.

Temasek Holdings

Singapore is a free trade port by and large. But free trade need not mean free of government ownership. The government owns even the port through which most of that trade occurs. Writing in the *Asia Times*,[2] Gary LaMoshi said:

> Rather than the sharp elbowed unabashed capitalism of Wall Street, Singapore's economic philosophy more closely mirrors that of another tropical island with a signature rum cocktail: Cuba.

This is true in so far as government ownership is concerned. There's very little that Singaporeans can do to avoid being a customer of a Temasek-linked company. The companies permeate practically every sphere of economic activity and often dominate it.

Singapore Inc. means Temasek Holdings, for it is Temasek that is the ultimate holding company for the government's interests in every government-linked company. Singapore's Ministry of Finance is Temasek's only shareholder. It was from the ministry that Temasek was spun off in 1974.

Temasek owns major stakes in many of Singapore's most important companies including Chartered Semiconductor, Singapore Telecom, Singapore Airlines, Singapore Press Holdings, MediaCorp, DBS Bank, Capitaland, Ascott Group, Singapore Petroleum Company, SMRT Corp, PSA Corp, SembCorp Industries, Keppel Corporation, MobileOne, Singapore Technologies, Singapore Food Industries, and Singapore Power. Each of these has many subsidiaries. There was one surprising sale, however. It occurred in mid-2005 when Temasek sold the Raffles Hotel brand which included the iconic, historic Raffles Hotel itself in Singapore, demonstrating that the Singapore Government is able to put return before nationalistic tendencies.

In all, Temasek ultimately controls some 40 listed companies in Singapore, with an estimated market worth of around S$60 billion.[3] About a quarter of the market capitalization of the local stock exchange is accounted for by the companies controlled by the government. (Government-linked companies (GLCs) account for almost half of the 20 largest listed companies that make up the local Straits Times Index.) And there are several major unlisted companies too that it controls. The contribution to

Singapore's GDP of all the companies in which the Singapore Government has a stake, plus the public sector itself, has been put as high as 60%.[4]

Very often, there is not one Temasek company in a market but several. It means that Temasek sometimes owns both sides of the fence and probably the fence too. This leads to some extraordinary and awkward situations in corporate Singapore: companies competing against one another even though they share the same ultimate shareholder; companies seeking to outbid each other for third companies even though they are related parties, and so on. And then there is the matter of the Singapore Government being both umpire and a player. Essentially, the Singapore economy is a seething mass of conflicts of interest.

An example of the contortions that Singapore Inc. sometimes finds itself in occurred in November 2002, when the *Business Times* and *Today* newspapers were required to publish apologies to DBS Bank on account of statements in an article on the sale of DBS's stake in NatSteel.[5] DBS claimed that the articles implied that the chairman and directors of DBS had failed to appropriately discharge their fiduciary duties in relation to the sale and that Temasek had influenced DBS to make the sale. At the end of each newspaper's apology were the words: "We have agreed to pay DBS damages and costs incurred by them in connection with this matter." The extraordinary thing is that the *Business Times*' parent company Singapore Press Holdings, *Today*'s parent company at the time MediaCorp, DBS and NatSteel all share the same ultimate major shareholder: the Singapore Government. On top of that, the chairman of Temasek and the chairman of DBS were one and the same man: S. Dhanabalan.

Irrespective of the merits of DBS's claims to damages, many Singaporeans who are long used to such things were confounded by the circularity of it all. I was in Singapore at the time and the apologies came up in several conversations. The increasingly incestuous nature of corporate and government Singapore seems to worry many Singaporeans. A big part of the worry is that no-one seems to know what the solution is. A government committee set up to look at Singapore's economic direction came back with recommendations for little apparent change. Earlier there was a review of Temasek's charter. It too recommended against sweeping change. *The Economist* magazine claimed that the new charter used "ambiguous jargon" and that "all possibilities are covered".[6]

And then there was the revelation in mid-2003 that Ang Kong Hua, the then chairman of Singapore Telecom (Singtel), had not only bought shares in rival telephone services provider MobileOne but at the time of the purchase he held more MobileOne shares than he did Singtel shares. He also appeared on MobileOne's register of significant shareholders as its

19th biggest shareholder.[7] There was no suggestion of any wrongdoing on the part of Ang but it did strike some as unusual that the chairman of Singapore Telecom had in fact emerged as a significant shareholder in the company's rival. But then how separate are the companies anyway? MobileOne is controlled by a consortium that includes the GLCs Singapore Press Holdings and Keppel Corp. So while MobileOne is a rival to Singtel, they're still both ultimately controlled by Temasek Holdings.

And yet what is the role of the private sector in Singapore? Clearly it is engulfed. And it is small. Small and medium-sized enterprises generate three-quarters of GDP in Taiwan and Hong Kong. But in Singapore they generate about one-fifth.

But have the GLCs performed well, given all that they control? The answer is mixed. Analysts have pointed to poor returns from most major listed GLCs compared with the market in general.[8] Routinely the GLCs win awards for having the best annual reports but annual reports are just one marker for sound corporate governance. "While GLCs figure prominently in Annual Report Awards, I have not seen conclusive evidence that their performance as companies, or the price of their shares, with some notable exceptions, is decidedly superior. Indeed, I have come across reports that argue otherwise", said J.Y. Pillay, chairman of Singapore's stock exchange in a speech at Singapore's 29th Annual Report Awards dinner in January 2003. Annual reports are important, said Pillay, "but one event in the governance calendar does not constitute the sum and substance of corporate governance".[9]

GLCs Offshore

GLCs have expanded not only to the point of crowding out the private sector in Singapore. Increasingly, when it comes to Singapore's investments overseas, it is the commercial arms of the government that do the investing.

World Wide Web

Here are just some of the interests that GLCs have accumulated around the world in recent years:

■ Singapore Airlines has a 49% stake in Virgin Atlantic Airlines.

- The Civil Aviation Authority of Singapore has a 50% stake in the UK's Alterra Partners which has a key role in running Luton Airport as well as international airports in Chile and Costa Rica.
- Singapore's Port Authority has a 49% stake in China's Guangzhou Container Terminal Co. Ltd, 80% of the giant Belgium port operator Hesse Noord Natie NV, which operates container terminals in Antwerp and Zeebrugge, and operates port terminals in Italy, Portugal, Yemen, Brunei, China, India and Belgium.
- A consortium 85% controlled by Temasek has a 51% stake in Indonesia's Bank Danamon.
- DBS Bank owns 71% of Hong Kong's Dao Heng Bank Group and 60% of the Philippines' bank, the Bank of Southeast Asia.
- Singapore Technologies Telemedia has a 42% stake in Indonesia's international telephone carrier PT Indosat. And in October 2003 it finally won approval to acquire a majority stake in bankrupt US telecoms group Global Crossing.[10]
- SingTel owns Australia's second biggest telephone company Optus, and has stakes in 20 other countries, including a significant stake in Belgium's telecommunications company Belgacom, 36% of Indonesia's bigger mobile phone operator Telkomsel, a US$500 million stake in India's Bharti Group and 30% of Digital, Thailand's third-largest mobile phone operator. SingTel's outside operations now account for 70% of its total revenue.
- Singapore Power owns the electricity transmission network for the entire Australian state of Victoria which takes in Melbourne, Australia's second largest city, plus additional parts of the gas distribution network in that state, 50.1% stakes in each of LG Energy and LG Power of South Korea and cogeneration interests in China, Indonesia, South Korea, the Philippines and Taiwan.
- Singapore Food Industries owns 70% of UK-based chilled food maker S. Daniels plc.
- SNP Corporation, a GLC involved in printing, has a 56% stake in Hong Kong-listed printing company Leefung-Asco Printers Holdings.
- SITA Environmental Solutions, an associate company of SembCorp Industries, won Australia's single largest rubbish collection contract in 2002, when it was awarded a A$151 million contract to provide waste and recyclables collection in the Australian city of Brisbane.
- Capitaland also controls Australand Holdings, one of the biggest property developers in Australia, which, in turn, controls the listed property developer Walker Corporation.

- The Ascott Group, Asia's biggest serviced apartment operator, owns the French-based Citadines hotel chain, acquired over 2003 and 2004.
- Temasek has a 19% stake in Australian international budget airline Jetstar Asia and a 3% stake in Qantas.
- Temasek has a 73% stake in Pakistan's NDLC-IFIC Bank, has 10% of the Bank of China in mainland China, and is a member of the consortium that controls Indonesia's Bank Danamon.

Temasek and the GLCs have made some good investments abroad. But often they are accused of paying too much when they buy abroad, so much so that it has become conventional wisdom. A piece in *Asiamoney* magazine in September 2005 said:

> Chinese officials love Temasek. It is the perfect passive partner ... It also tends to overpay – witness its purchase of a 4.6% stake in China Minsheng Bank earlier this year at 3.4 times book [value], the highest level paid for a share in a Chinese bank.[11]

Foreign Uneasiness

Investments like these bring their own unique problems. Host governments can become suspicious of what the Singaporean entities are up to. Singtel, then 76% owned by the Singapore Government, bought a majority stake in Australia's second major telecommunications company Cable & Wireless Optus in 2001. The sale amounted to a quasi-nationalization of Optus, except that the source of control was somebody else's government. The acquisition included the purchase of a yet-to-be-launched satellite, with military communications facilities, which was a joint venture between Optus and the Australian Department of Defense. And so the acquisition first had to be cleared with the Pentagon as well as the Australian defense establishment.

That came after Malaysia's then Prime Minister Mahathir Mohamad rejected a bid by Singtel to buy 20% of Malaysian telecommunications company Time dotCom, a subsidiary of a local conglomerate, the Renong Group. The Singtel deal would have meant a big cash injection for the heavily indebted Time dotCom and valuable skills transfer for the company. But Mahathir opposed the deal because he considered Time dotCom to be a strategic company and he did not want it to fall under the control of an arm of a foreign government. (Singtel had also lost out in a bid for Cable & Wireless Hong Kong Telecom partly due to similar concerns.)

When asked at a news conference about his objections, Mahathir, with his usual panache for a good one liner, remarked that people worry about Singtel, "maybe because they sing and tell". And that will always be the problem with investments abroad by the commercial arms of the Singapore Government: are such investments always motivated by commercial considerations alone or might there also be some political or strategic motivation as well? To what degree are they stand-alone entities or do they gather information to be passed back to the Singapore Government? This is the legitimate concern of many.

An added consideration in respect of Singtel's investments overseas is that the company has been headed by Lee Hsien Yang, a son of Singapore's former prime minister and now Minister Mentor Lee Kuan Yew, thus further strengthening Singtel's ties to the Singapore Government. Lee Hsien Yang also served as a member of the Singapore Government's Defense Science and Technology Agency.

Other GLCs have faced problems abroad on account of their pedigree. Singapore Technologies submitted a bid for a 50% stake in Hong Kong-based ASAT Ltd, which had been put up for sale by its parent, integrated circuit manufacturer QPL International Holdings, a company that's listed in Hong Kong. Singapore Technologies' bid of around US$200 million was 16% higher than one submitted by Chase Asia Equity Partners but QPL opted to go with Chase anyway. QPL feared that Singapore Technologies as a partner would be slow at decision-making and introduce bureaucratic meddling, QPL's chairman Tong Lok Li reportedly said.[12]

And in 2003, a GLC once again came up against foreign resistance on account of its government ties. Singapore Technologies Telemedia had offered US$250 million for a 61.5% stake in the bankrupt US company Global Crossing but officials from the FBI, CIA and Pentagon all objected on security grounds. It was only after then Prime Minister Goh Chok Tong made representations on the matter to President George Bush that Bush said that he would not block the acquisition.[13]

But the GLCs can offer one major plus. Singapore is known around the world for being largely free of corruption and the same can be said of its GLCs. Hence, as foreign investors, they are clean and cashed-up. Too few multinationals can genuinely be ascribed both these attributes.

The GIC

The government established the Government of Singapore Investment Corporation Pte Ltd (GIC), its principal investment vehicle, in 1981. The

Currency Act requires all Singapore currency on issue to be fully backed by foreign assets and so the GIC manages Singapore's foreign reserves (and not, as is commonly assumed, the retirement monies contributed by Singaporeans to the Central Provident Fund.)

The GIC's precise holdings are a secret – it makes neither its accounts nor the extent of its holdings public – but it does admit to owning a portfolio worth more than US$100 billion, although that is a figure that has been in use for many years. Either the total amount now is far greater or the GIC has been investing poorly. Until recently, the GIC did not even disclose who sat on its board. In any event, it means that Singapore's currency is backed many times over by foreign assets, because by the start of 2006, the US dollar value of all the Singapore currency in circulation was about US$8.7 billion (the M2 money supply was about US$133.3 billion.)

About a quarter of its investments are thought to be in the UK and Europe. It is also believed to be one of the largest shareholders in Citigroup Inc in the US and has almost US$2 billion invested in Taiwanese equities. It has offices in London, New York, San Francisco, Beijing and Tokyo to manage its existing investments and search out new ones.

The GIC itself invests in equities, fixed income and money market instruments. But it also has two principal subsidiaries: GIC Special Investments Pte Ltd and GIC Real Estate Pte Ltd. The corporation as a whole is overseen by a board of 12 directors, almost all of whom are drawn from the cabinet or are senior officers of Temasek Holding companies. Lee Kuan Yew serves as chairman and his son, Prime Minister Lee Hsien Loong, is deputy chairman.

GIC Special Investments was set up in 1982 as the private equity investment arm of the GIC. It manages a portfolio of investments in venture capital and private equity funds worldwide. And it has direct investments in private companies.

What sorts of companies does the GIC invest directly in? The answer seems to be any company anywhere in which it thinks it can invest cheaply. In Thailand, the GIC has stakes in many listed companies. Bangkok Bank, the Nation Publishing Group, Thai Union Frozen Products, Thai Danu Bank, National Finance, Nation Multimedia, Quality House and Land & Houses are among them. In China it has stakes in companies such as Beijing Capital Land, sanitary-ware manufacturer Eagle Brand, Nanfu Battery Factory and Li Ning Sports Goods, a sportswear retailer. In Malaysia there are stakes in Proton, Telekom Malaysia, Malaysian Plantations (which controls Alliance Bank), Shell Refining, the Sunway Group, New Straits Times Press, Star Publications, Tanjong,

Resorts World, Berjaya Sports Toto and Public Bank. In India there are stakes in HDFC Bank and ICICI Bank. In Australia, there is a stake in niche telecommunications company EasyCall International. In Indonesia, there is a stake in the Adaro coal mine, Indonesia's largest, and PT Astra International, that country's largest vehicle assembler. In October 2003, it and two partners acquired the private hospital arm of Australian company Mayne Group for US$570 million. And so on. The list is suggestive rather than exhaustive. It's worth repeating that the GIC does not make its holdings public. Typically, holdings such as these only come to light when local stock exchange rules require the GIC to make a public announcement.

What it all means is that the Singapore dollar is backed not only by gold but by private hospitals in Australia, hotels around the world, stocks in Asia and elsewhere, and part of Citibank. And for a while it was even backed by Kentucky Fried Chicken outlets in Malaysia.

The GIC is the principal investor in the AIG Asian Infrastructure Funds, the largest privately held infrastructure funds in Asia. They include the US$1.2 billion AIG Asian Infrastructure Fund I and the US$2 billion AIG Asian Infrastructure Fund II.

It is a major investor in the China International Capital Corporation (CICC), China's first joint venture investment bank. Other investors are the China Construction Bank, Morgan Stanley, China National Investment and Guarantee and Hong Kong-based Mingly Group. The CICC has been involved in various landmark deals such as the floats of China Telecom and PetroChina.

GIC Special Investments also co-manages Singapore's US$1 billion Technopreneurship Investment Fund (TIF), which was established to nurture a venture capital industry in Singapore itself.

The GIC claims to have been one of the earliest institutional investors in venture capital funds in Silicon Valley and to have invested in some of the best-known venture capital names in the US, such as Sequoia Capital, Matrix Partners, Summit Ventures and TA Associates. More obscure funds too are an investment target, such as Israel's Giza GE Venture Fund III, established by Giza Venture capital, a pioneer in venture capital funds in that country. There are stakes too in New Margin Ventures and CDH China Fund, both based in China.

Sometimes, GIC Special Investments operates in concert with the funds in which it also has a stake. For example, it bought a 40% stake in Indian cement producer Gujarat Ambuja Cements in 2000, along with AIG Asian Infrastructure Fund II and the AIG Asian Opportunity Fund.

GIC Real Estate takes care of property investment. It owns dozens of office towers, hotels and apartment blocks around the world, including the AT&T Corporate Center in Chicago; the Grand Millennium Plaza in Hong Kong; the AMEX Centre, the International Broadcast Center, the tower at 175 Liverpool Street, the Shangri-La Hotel and Westin Sydney Hotel, all in Sydney; the Park Hyatt Hotel in Melbourne; the Hotel Intercontinental in Prague; the Shiodome City Center in Tokyo; The Exchange building in Beijing and the Tianjin Exchange; the 41-storey Menara Standard Chartered in Kuala Lumpur; and the Seoul Finance Center in downtown Seoul. There's also a 25% stake in Fininvest, one of Manila's largest property developers.

But these are just some of the flagship holdings. It buys big and it buys often. In 2001, for example, it committed US$75 million to a San Francisco partnership that will own and operate 59 industrial buildings around the US; it paid around US$170 million for seven Tokyo residential apartment blocks; US$170 million for a 20-storey Tokyo office tower; and with a Thai partner shelled out almost US$19 million for Wave Place, a 21-storey office building in downtown Bangkok. And in Australia, Sydney's historic Queen Victoria Building shopping arcade and the equally historic Strand retail arcade are among its assets.

In 2005, it committed US$600 million to a Japanese property fund, which, with another fund, would give it majority stakes in almost 60 buildings in major cities such as Tokyo, Osaka, Kobe and Nagoya.[14]

At 620 square kilometers – or just 9% of the size of Tasmania or 0.25% the size of the UK – Singapore's physical size no longer meets its national aspirations. It's as if Singapore has become a nation in search of a country that is commensurate with how it sees itself in the world, now that it has burgeoning capabilities and wealth. Historically, governments have expanded their borders by military conquest. But that's not an option for Singapore. Instead, it is its government corporations that are marching overseas. They are pushing Singapore's economic space way beyond its geographic space to create a type of virtual economy. And given the massive government ownership and influence in that economy, it's as if a virtual government is evolving to match. And that is a trend that not everyone is happy with.

Chapter 14

SINGAPORE'S THRIVING SEX INDUSTRY

Hollywood director Peter Bogdanovich filmed the movie *Saint Jack* in Singapore in 1979. Based on a book by Paul Theroux by the same name, the movie features easygoing expatriate American Jack Flowers, who becomes a pimp in 1970s Singapore furnishing prostitutes to foreigners. He opens a successful brothel, but pressure from local mobsters soon puts him out of business. Along the way he becomes involved in a blackmail scheme with an American mobster.

Bogdanovich filmed part of the movie at Singapore's Mitre Hotel. The film has largely been forgotten. But the hotel survives. It is one of the most curious sights in Singapore today. Few know of its existence, even long-time Singapore residents. It's reached by a leafy lane off Killiney Road some way behind Somerset MRT Station on Orchard Road. A rough hand-painted sign that says simply "Mitre Hotel" provides testament to its existence. It is a large old Straits mansion with louvered windows and high ceilings on a big piece of land. What's odd is that the "hotel" is largely broken down and in a terrible state of disrepair. A pile of broken office chairs is heaped under the carriageway.

Just inside, the owner sells beer from a small bar. Customers can bring wine if they like but they must pay a corkage fee. The rooms are in an unbelievable state of disrepair. They are let to very low budget travelers and prostitutes, for as little as S$25 a night. The place is a shambles. And yet the land must be worth tens of millions of dollars being in the heart of Singapore, not far from Orchard Road and otherwise surrounded by expensive condominium blocks.

The owner, an elderly Hainanese Chinese man, who has lived at the hotel for most of his life, is known to the few customers only as "Uncle". At 12am he drags an iron grate across the front entrance (presumably because of licensing laws) and patrons can retire to the carriageway where they can pull up a broken chair. Uncle then falls asleep in a chair inside the gate, but a mop is kept handy just outside that patrons can use to poke him awake so that he might supply another drink, which he passes through the grate before retiring once more to his chair. The hotel attracts few visitors and possibly more rats, though to be fair I saw only two when I visited.

Cheap beer, broken chairs and rats – what is this doing in the heart of Singapore? Rumor has it that the Mitre Hotel has not been redeveloped because of a family dispute and so one of the few, valuable remaining pieces of land in central Singapore remains undeveloped. That such a place can exist in modern Singapore when so much other valuable real estate has fallen victim to compulsory acquisition laws has given rise to talk of political connections. But what the Mitre Hotel demonstrates more than anything is that there's more to Singapore than most realize. There always has been.

Liberal Singapore

"Liberal" and "Singapore" in the same heading? If ever there was an oxymoron, that is it. Well, no. Singapore has long been more liberal than most give it credit for. The rhetoric has been strait-laced but the reality has been quite different. Nor has it been the case that Singapore has turned a blind eye to issues of sexual diversity and commercial sex, for example. Rather, it has been quietly pragmatic, regarding the issues very much as private. Generally, the Singapore Government doesn't mind what people do in private but it still maintains the right to regulate the public arena. So movies like *Eyes Wide Shut* and *Lolita* have been banned, as have magazines such as *Playboy*. But these headline acts help to create an image – one that is at odds with reality. Pornography, for example, is not hard to find in Singapore. It's sold openly, particularly in Singapore's red-light districts. Sex toys, videos and magazines are sold most evenings from lean-to stalls along Desker Road in Singapore's Little India district. Indeed, Desker Road is the only place in Asia that I've seen child pornography available for sale. This in a red-light district that's licensed by the government. To be fair, it was not copious and I saw it on only one occasion.

Of course, child pornography is something that the Singapore Government would never condone but, in practice, the government is and always has been more liberal than it lets on. Sex changes were first legally permitted in the 1970s. But a few years ago, a marriage involving a sex-changed person was declared null and void by a court because marriage laws refer to the sex at birth. And so, the law was changed to allow gender-reassigned Singaporeans to marry based on their new sex. It was a reasonable and pragmatic solution. It marked out the Singapore Government as more progressive than some of its Western counterparts, at least on this issue.

In the last two to three years, sex shops have opened in Singapore that sell all manner of plastic devices. It's unlikely that the government welcomes their arrival but pragmatism demands that it looks the other way. The internet revolution, whereby such products can be ordered easily over the internet and delivered by post, means that there is little benefit in prohibiting the opening of fixed shops that sell these items. Shops that sell politically sensitive books are more likely to attract official attention. After all, a vibrator is hardly going to bring down the government.

Homosexual acts are against the law (the laws date from the colonial era) but unless those acts occur in a public place, the police do not prosecute. Gay men who self-identify as such are excused from the military aspects of national service. Minimal attempts might be made at counseling but by and large they are given desk work and otherwise left alone. Per capita, Singapore probably now has as many or even more saunas for gay men as does London. According to a *Time* magazine survey of Singapore published in mid-2003, there were seven saunas "catering exclusively to gay clients".[1] (Spartacus was one early such establishment which occupied a prominent place near Boat Quay. "Enter through the rear", famously read a note attached to its front door.)

And there are several obviously gay bars and clubs. The government's unwritten rule seems to be don't make a fuss and neither will we. "We are born this way and they are born that way, but they are like you and me", then Prime Minister Goh was quoted as saying in the *Time* survey.

And in July 2005, the Central Provident Fund, Singapore's government-run national retirement scheme, changed its rules to allow non-related single people to dip into their retirement savings to jointly buy private property. This allowed unmarried couples to buy a residential property. But it also allowed same sex couples to do the same. This was not an unintended consequence of the rule change on the part of the government.

But where the Singapore Government has been at its most liberal is prostitution. Singapore's marketing job has been so efficient and so slick that its carefully concocted image as strait-laced to the point of being boring has actually been taken seriously worldwide. Many foreigners simply refuse to believe that Singapore even has a sex industry, let alone one that is thriving and government-approved.

Some History

Singapore's economy has always been dominated by the trade in services and one of the services that has always been on offer has been prostitution. It's something that is acknowledged. Singapore's government-run Chinese Heritage Museum in Chinatown has a re-creation of a prostitute's room in a brothel. It contains a bed with some rumpled bedding, a dressing table and an artfully hazy projected image of a young lady sitting before a mirror and preparing for work.

Being an island of trade and immigrants, Singapore was largely an island of men in the nineteenth century. Many of the Chinese who came from China were married but they left their wives in China. Not surprisingly, Singapore became home to a thriving sex industry. It's said that four out of five women arriving at Boat Quay from China by the late nineteenth century were soon employed in the settlement's brothels.

Many prostitutes came from Japan. Indeed, Japan was a supplier of prostitutes across Southeast Asia. And they weren't there just to service visiting or expatriate Japanese, but the locals too. It's a thought that might horrify many Japanese today. Southeast Asia after all was a source of "comfort women" for the Imperial Japanese Army during the Second World War, a reverse of the situation a few decades earlier.

Georgetown on Penang has Lebuh Cintra (Cintra Street) that is still known locally as Jeep Pun Kay, or "Street of the Japanese", for that is what it was, a street full of brothels of Japanese prostitutes. And in Singapore, Banda Street in Chinatown and the neighboring Spring Street were referred to by locals as Japan Street or Phan Tsai Mei (the Lane of Foreign Prostitutes) because of the many Japanese prostitutes who operated there.

The Contagious Disease Ordinance was passed in 1870. It required brothels to be registered and prostitutes to be examined medically for diseases. In 1887, the Ordinance was repealed, and the registration of brothels was stopped in 1894. The result was an even greater proliferation of brothels. Record increases in the arrivals of migrant laborers saw the demand for prostitution escalate. The demand was met by the specific importation of women who were prepared to work in the sex industry. The trade was banned in 1927 and brothels were made illegal in 1930.

The three-storey building in Chinatown at the corner of Smith Street and Trengganu Street was a famous brothel called Hui Fang Lou. Prostitutes could call down to passers-by to attract their attention from the large balconies and terraces overhead. The building is still patronized by visitors to Singapore. It is now home to the China Town Classic souvenir shop.

Malay Street close to Singapore's Arab district was another early center for brothels. Today, the actual street has been completely enclosed and glassed over and turned into a shopping mall as part of the Bugis Junction development. The redevelopment was undertaken in the early 1990s, spearheaded by a group of Indonesian investors.

Opium went hand in hand with the sex industry. By 1823 in Singapore there were 423 government-run shops from where opium could be purchased over the counter. The shops were distinguished by their dark red doors and were open to the public from 6am to 10pm. Opium could be purchased in the brothels until 2am. In this respect at least, things have changed. But Singapore's commercial sex industry remains.

The Government's Administration of the Sex Industry

It's just on 6pm on a Tuesday evening. I'm sitting at the Coffee Bean & Tea Leaf outside Borders bookshop on the corner of Singapore's Orchard and Patterson Roads. The afternoon sun is blazing but will soon ebb. Two Thai prostitutes have taken up a position on one of the concrete pavement seats nearby. There's little action as far as they're concerned so they spend their time watching the big outdoor television screen that's attached to the side of the shopping center across the road. An American music video plays over and over, interspersed with advertisements for mobile telephones. Prostitutes often solicit for business along Orchard Road in the evenings. But they are operating illegally. And many male visitors to Singapore will have had the experience of being accosted by an *ah quah* – a Hokkien term that has been adopted locally and in Malaysia to denote a transvestite – along the same road when it has emptied out and the shopping malls have closed.

Stamford Raffles established Singapore as a free port, a place of commerce. So he was not greatly troubled that sex would be one of the commodities bought and sold in his new settlement. His main concern was who would profit. "The unfortunate prostitute should be treated with compassion, but every obstacle should be thrown in the way of her service being a source of profit to anyone but herself."[2] The position is not unlike that of the current Singapore Government.

Prostitution is permitted. But pimping, soliciting and streetwalking are not. Pimping can attract stiff penalties including lengthy jail terms. But prostitutes who are registered are quite able to work in licensed brothels that operate openly in Singapore's several designated red-light areas (DRAs).

Prostitutes are required to register and carry a "yellow card" supplied by the government. It is the same size and in the same style as a national identity card and carries the holder's photograph and thumb print. Card holders are obliged to submit to a health check every two weeks.

How many prostitutes are there in Singapore? No-one knows for sure. One estimate is that there are around 6,000.[3] Singapore has as many as six DRAs in which as many as 400 licensed brothels operate. The principal DRAs are located in Geylang, Flanders Square, Keong Saik Street and Desker Road. Additionally, escort services and private call girls are permitted. Most brothels cater to locals. Women from mainland China, Malaysia (especially Sarawak and Sabah), Thailand, Laos and the Philippines make up the core of the workforce in this sector.

During the SARS crisis of 2003, brothels in Singapore had notices posted to all their front entrances to say that prospective clients who had been in China, Hong Kong and Vietnam in the previous two weeks were prohibited from entering the premises. Clearly, the notices were at the behest of the government but of course the Singapore Government does not want to be seen to be openly endorsing the sex trade, so there were no government coats of arms or any other insignia on the warning posters, but each brothel displayed exactly the same poster.

To further emphasize the government-monitored nature of the sector, DRAs are lined with posters that advise that condoms should be worn, the advice appearing in English, Chinese, Malay and Tamil.

The government's relaxed attitude to brothels means that the industry is not underground and so has not been targeted by organized crime syndicates in the way that it has in other countries. Most brothels seem to have individual owners. The fractured nature of the sector appears right for a major operator to move in and set up a branded chain of brothels across the island. Perhaps the chain might then list on Singapore's stock exchange in the way that a Melbourne-based brothel listed on the Australian Stock Exchange in 2003 (although a year later, the Australian company opted out of the brothel business and into tabletop dancing.) But then that would go against the nature of the implicit contract between those who operate on the margins of society in Singapore and the Singapore Government, this being "keep your head down and don't attract attention and, in return, we won't make an issue of it".

An odd convention is followed among Singapore's many brothels. Rarely do they have a name displayed on the outside. There are no shop hoardings and other signage. Instead, they typically display an oversized street number on an otherwise empty façade. Buildings like this – no name, just a big number – almost certainly are brothels. Those few with touts outside tend to cater to tourists, but most do not.

Geylang

The Geylang area has the biggest concentration of brothels in Singapore. It is nowhere near the main tourist precincts. By and large, it does not cater to tourists and especially not Western ones. David Brazil in his book *No Money, No Honey!* estimates that around 250 brothels operate in Geylang. The busiest evenings for Geylang's brothels are said to be Mondays and Tuesdays rather than weekends. That way errant husbands can say they were detained at business meetings.

Geylang is home to many budget hotels, many of which have opened recently. Many rent rooms by the hour. Briefly – for a period of three months in 1998 – the Hotel Licensing Board instructed hotels not to engage in this practice, but the instruction was suspended, probably on account of the Asian economic crisis. There's even a chain of these hotels, Hotel 81, that is low-budget and amenable to short-term occupancies.

Keong Saik Street

The Chinatown brothel area is bordered by Keong Saik Road, Teck Lim Road and Jiak Chuan Road. It is Singapore's oldest, still-operating, approved red-light area. Traditionally, it served the poorer segment of Singapore society and this holds true today. As in Geylang, the brothels identify themselves from other commercial establishments, not with names but simply by having huge street numbers displayed on their façades. Large red lanterns hang from the eaves of many of the brothels and large statues of the God of Prosperity T'sai Shen sit just inside many of the entrances. (For the record, there is a goddess of prostitutes in the Chinese pantheon, P'an Chin Lien.) But the brothels are now under pressure from the area's transformation into a spot for trendy bars and boutique hotels. Ten or fewer brothels still operate in this area. The government is tending not to renew licenses for them to operate here if there is a change of ownership, so in a few years this DRA will no longer be functioning.

Around the corner from Keong Saik Road on New Road in the restored and now brightly painted Chinese shop houses is the "Numbers" massage service that offers "all-male massage" according to a notice near its door bell. Further along is Rairu, one of the seven saunas that cater to gay men, alluded to in the *Time* survey.

Spend the Night with the Soehartos in Singapore

The Royal Peacock Hotel was one of the first new boutique hotels to open in the area. It comprises about 10 old shop houses that have been converted into the hotel. Several operated as brothels in the past. The hotel now is owned by Bambang Trihatmodjo, son of Indonesia's former President Soeharto. Bambang's son Jason Trihatmodjo takes care of the hotel on behalf of his father, according to hotel staff.

The Soeharto family, via a Singapore-based company called Viewpoint Investments, owns the hotel. That company developed plans in 2003 to open a new hotel in late 2004 on Erskine Road, also in Singapore's Chinatown area. Its US$17 million St Gracelil Hotel will be a five-star, 110-room hotel and have a Tuscan look. The company also said that it planned to form a hotel management group and then look for hotel management contracts in Indonesia, Australia, Japan and China.[4]

Bambang meanwhile has been busying himself since the fall of his father by being a very active member of the International Practical Shooting Confederation. He attended the confederation's general assembly in South Africa in September 2002, according to the minutes of the meeting and voted on various resolutions. He has also attended quite a few international shoots.

Desker Road

My first introduction to Singapore's large and thriving commercial sex sector occurred along the back alley between Desker and Rowell Roads, near to Singapore's Little India district. "I'll show you a side of Singapore that you haven't seen before", said a friend who worked at one of the big London-based art auction houses that had recently opened up in Singapore. She certainly did. I was stunned. It wasn't the activities that were carried out in the dirty cement floor shacks along the alley that stunned me, but that the alley was there at all. The alley, which runs nearly all the way from Serangoon Road to Jalan Besar, contains not just a handful of brothels but dozens. Mostly, Indian women, probably from Tamil Nadu, work in them. They gather in the evenings in the brothels' porches where they sit on cane chairs, preening and posing and awaiting custom. Sunday evenings is perhaps the best time to visit. It's the evening that the Bangladeshi guest workers have off and they assemble in the alley in their hundreds. Few of the Bangladeshis actually seem to enter the brothels. Instead, they crowd around each porch, gawking and gesticulating at the women in an atmosphere of rising excitement. For their part, the women either completely ignore the men or entertain them with an (apparently) erotic display of combing their long black hair, an event which causes the crowd of onlookers to swell significantly and chatter even more excitedly. Every so often, one of the men would enter a porch, urged on by two or three of his mates, only to return within minutes, presumably having decided that the requisite S$30 would be better spent by his wife back in Bangladesh.

Desker Road was named after the owner of the largest slaughterhouse in the area in the early twentieth century. The area was the site for cattle yards and meat markets. There's an analogy here that I could draw on but I'll resist.

Flanders Square is another DRA that's a short distance from Desker Road. But instead of Indian women, its workers are almost exclusively Chinese.

Other Areas

It's not a DRA but you wouldn't know it. The Orchard Towers complex, right on Orchard Road, Singapore's premier shopping district, has earned the moniker of the "four floors of whores" and seems to have become almost as famous around the world as Singapore's Jurong Bird Sanctuary. It contains several discotheques that cater mostly to a Filipino crowd. Sunday afternoons and the place is swinging. It's the Filipino maids' day off. By 4pm the San Miguel flows freely for the men, Coca-Cola for the women and the dance floors bustle.

The KTV bar downstairs at Orchard Towers is well known for mainland Chinese prostitutes. Once every few months the police raid it. They typically bring along several buses that they park behind the complex and fill with apprehended prostitutes – many are illegal visa overstayers from China, the Philippines and Thailand.

The Golden Mile Shopping Center on Beach Road is another area that has become a center for illicit prostitution. The conventional shops and restaurants there cater to local Thais and so too do the prostitutes. They are Thai themselves and mostly service locally employed Thai construction workers.

Keepsakes for Memories

What do Singaporeans think of their sex industry? The reality is that they are the industry's main client base. It could not survive on tourism alone. An online charity auction was held in April 2003 for some 3,400 old black and white street signs. Which street signs were among those that attracted the greatest interest? Mohamed Sultan Road, the road famous for its night-clubs, attracted the highest bid at S$1,338. The eighth highest was the sign for Keong Saik Road, with a final bid of S$589.

There was more interest in the sign for this relatively obscure street of brothels than there was for a world-famous name like Boat Quay. It sold for S$550. The sign for Desker Road was also among the top prices, coming in at S$471. Bidders were after a souvenir with a difference for their living rooms. Or maybe their bedrooms. That signs for street names associated with red-light districts finished among the top dozen or so lots out of a total number of 3,400 says something about Singaporeans. Probably that they're not much different from anyone else.

Kuala Lumpur's Chow Kit

Of course every city has its red-light precincts, although not all are designated by the government as they are in Singapore. Kuala Lumpur has several, the most famous of which is Chow Kit. It is akin today to what Singapore once had in the form of Bugis Street.

Lorong Haji Taib, a narrow street in the Chow Kit area, is famous in Kuala Lumpur for one thing: transvestites. Dozens of aging transvestites, mostly Malay but also some Indian and Chinese, take up positions on either side of Lorong Haji Taib as night falls. The street is so famous among locals that most nights it is jammed with traffic as dozens of middle-class local families drive through it for an evening's family entertainment of wildlife spotting, as if on safari in a drive-through zoo.

Lorong Haji Taib wraps around a small night market. Most of the stall-holders are Malay and most of the stalls sell cheap clothing. But the oddest aspect of Lorong Haji Taib is not so much its transvestites but the dozens of individual Malaysian men who come to the street, not to walk through it and steal quick glances but take up a position of their own from where they stare at the transvestites, not for just a few minutes but possibly all evening. They don't approach them, they don't discuss the transvestites with each other, poke fun at them or in fact respond in any obvious way. They just stand there, impassively, and stare.

In mid-2002, Kuala Lumpur's mayor Mohmad Shaid Mohd Taufek talked publicly about the plight of Chow Kit's transvestites:

> These people are the most misunderstood and mistreated members of our society and people must sympathize with them. Sometimes they resort to negative activities because the society looks down on them so much that they have no opportunity or confidence, which is not the case as they are people with talent, intelligence and skill.

He said that he was considering plans for a vocational training center for them.[5] Attitudes to the sex industry in Asia sometimes are surprisingly enlightened. Some Western governments could do well to learn from them.

Chapter 15

DIVERSITY AND DECENCY IN MALAYSIA

One evening in London, I was enjoying dinner at the Gay Hussar, a famous Hungarian restaurant in Soho. (It's been open for more than 40 years. In that time the only thing that has changed about it is the meaning of the word gay.) My choices were pressed boar's head with fresh horse-radish sauce, followed by duck with red cabbage and apple, Hungarian potatoes, red pepper salad and smoked baked beans. The food is heavy, hearty and traditional. Surely a family-owned restaurant I thought. Possibly, the owners' relatives from Hungary staff the kitchens. I did some research and discovered that I could not have been more wrong. The Gay Hussar is owned by the Corus & Regal Hotels Group, which is controlled by a company called London Vista Hotel Ltd, a part of Malayan United Industries (MUI) owned by Malaysia's Khoo Kay Peng. So the Gay Hussar in London's Soho – London's most famous Hungarian restaurant – is owned by a Malaysian. It turned out that other restaurants in London shared the same ownership: Simply Nico, Nico Central, Elena's L'Etoile and Thierry's.

I was both disappointed and fascinated. Disappointed because my romantic notions of a former Hungarian peasant family making good in the cutthroat London restaurant trade had been dashed. And fascinated because I've long been interested in Khoo Kay Peng. Khoo is a deeply committed, fundamentalist Christian, one of several prominent Southeast Asian Chinese who have used their Christian beliefs to further their business interests by setting up international joint ventures and the like with fellow fundamentalists. For example, when Indonesia's Lippo Group, founded by Mochtar Riady, another fundamentalist Christian Southeast

Asian Chinese entrepreneur, sold its Hong Kong-based travel company Morning Star Holdings in 1994 it did so to Khoo's MUI Group. Khoo and Riady later formed a joint venture in 1995 with International Family Entertainment Inc., a company controlled by American evangelist Pat Robertson (who founded the Christian Coalition) to operate China Entertainment Television Broadcast, a family-oriented cable television service, out of Hong Kong. Khoo, in turn, acquired two "family" hotels in North Carolina, previously owned by Jim Bakker, another former tele-evangelist, whose fundamentalist Christian business empire collapsed after he was convicted of fraud. And after Khoo acquired control of the UK-based clothing and homewear retailer Laura Ashley, he appointed Pat Roberston to its board.

It's an interesting side-story. But the bigger story of which Khoo is a part is the overseas expansion of Malaysia's entrepreneurs. Malaysia is a country that is beginning to punch above its weight, to borrow a boxing analogy. Former Malaysian Prime Minister Mahathir helped with this. His frequent attacks on the West helped to keep Malaysia's profile higher internationally than it otherwise deserved to be. But so too have Malaysia's entrepreneurs with their investments abroad. Khoo's Corus & Regal Hotels has 80 hotels across Britain. But it's Hong Leong of Malaysia, a group controlled by Quek Leng Chan, that controls Thistle Hotels, the biggest hotel chain in London, with 24 hotels in that city and 56 overall in the UK. Malaysians have been South Africa's biggest foreign investors in recent years. Even Snappy Tom, the number one brand of canned cat food in Australia, ultimately is owned by Malaysian investors. In southwest England, the entire water and sewerage network is owned by a Malaysian company.

Ethnic Complexities

Malaysia is a nation of migrants, or at least those descended from migrants. The Chinese and the Indians obviously have a migrant background. But so too do many Malays. Many are the descendants of migrants from west Sumatra, Java, Sulawesi, Aceh or even the Middle East. Many of the royal houses of Malaysia – there are nine – are themselves of Indonesian ancestry.

Malaysia's population comprises Malay and other indigenous groups (58%), ethnic Chinese (24%), Indians (8%) and other groups (10%). But these categories can be broken down into other subgroups.

Of course the Chinese can be split into dialect and subdialect groupings, although the dividing lines between these are weakening with cross-dialect marriages and so on. In Kuala Lumpur, the lingua franca of the Chinese community has become Cantonese, whatever dialect background the local Chinese have. Other dialect groups are more important in other towns and cities, for example the Chinese of Penang are overwhelmingly Hokkien. In Sabah, the Hakka are more dominant. In Johore Bahru, it's the Teochiu and Hokkien. The Chinese in the so-called "New Villages" that were formed in response to the Communist threat in the 1950s typically are Hakka. In Sibu and Sitiawan, it's the Fuzhou, and so on.

The Indian category is dominated by ethnic Tamils. Around 90% originate from southern India. They were brought to Malaya during the time of the British as indentured laborers, usually to work in the rubber plantations. The remaining 10% are Jaffna Tamils (Tamils from Sri Lanka). They were more wealthy, educated and mobile. Typically they settled in Malaysia for business or to work in public administration. Ananda Krishnan, one of Malaysia's wealthiest entrepreneurs, is ethnically a Jaffna Tamil. And so, today, about 80% of Malaysia's Indians are Hindu, 8% are Christian, 7% are Muslims (called *mamak* in local parlance; they dominate the Indian food stall sector) and around 3% are Sikhs (most Malaysian sports stores are run by Sikhs; whereas in Bangkok many operate tailor shops). There is a significant ethnic Thai population, particularly in the northern state of Kedah.

And then there are the Malays. There is much regionalism among the Malays, of which most outsiders remain unaware, even on peninsular Malaysia. The Malays of Penang tend to be mixed with other Islamic trading groups, such as Arabs, Turks, Javanese and Acehnese, and so many Penang Malays have Arab-like features.

Other Malays in Penang have intermarried with Muslim Indians and are known as the Penang *mamaks*. Unlike *mamaks* elsewhere in Malaysia, the Penang *mamaks* are more Malay than Indian. Dr Mahathir himself, although not from Penang but from nearby Kedah, is of mixed Malay-Indian ancestry. Prominent Penang-born Malays with a Penang *mamak* background included Azizan Zainal Abidin, the late chairman of state-owned oil company Petronas, and Ali Abul Hassan, a former governor of Malaysia's central bank.[1]

The Malays of Negri Sembilan state are largely of Minangkabau descent. The Minangkabau came from west Sumatra several hundred years ago. Malaysian Minangkabaus retain a unique dialect, many words of which are not intelligible to other Malays. They are matrilineal, meaning that property in families passes from eldest daughter to eldest daughter and not from eldest son to eldest son. Many Malays in Negri Sembilan still follow this custom. A friend of mine, a Malay with a Minangkabau background, was told by his mother that he will not inherit the family's not inconsiderable wealth but that it will all go to his sister. But to compensate him, his mother gave him a small rubber plantation, although under Minangkabau tradition she was under no obligation to do so. And so Malay women in Negri Sembilan are often wealthy and strong-willed; local Malay men tend to be passive and estranged from household decision-making. Minangkabau food, culture and art is also distinctive.

And then there are the Kelantan Malays. Many Kelantanese have migrated to Kuala Lumpur for economic reasons. Kelantanese are particularly clannish. They have their own dialect, which differs substantially to standard Malay. They tend to employ one another and trade with one another. They also have distinctive names that are readily recognized by other Malays as Kelantanese. There are distinctive Kelantanese pockets in Kuala Lumpur. Many operate food stalls in the capital that sell unique Kelantanese-style food. Other Malays see them as particularly distinctive and insular, not just in their home state but when they live as pocket communities in Kuala Lumpur and Malaysia's other larger towns. Nik Aziz, the Islamic Party's Menteri Besar (chief minister) of Kelantan, slips into Kelantanese when addressing political rallies in Kelantan to stress his local pedigree. Wan Azmi Wan Hamzah, head of the Land & General Group, is a prominent Kelantan-born Malay entrepreneur.

But even among other Malays, there are regional Malay accents (*loghat*). There is a northern accent, for example, but even this is split into identifiable Penang, Kedah and Perlis accents.

Slowly, very slowly, Malays, Chinese and Indians are blending in Malaysia. But the blending is a top-down phenomenon. Intermarriage is more common among the business and educational elite, but at the lower end of Malaysian society the races still live very much apart.

Malay and Chinese customs are blending at the margins. There is a whole separate class of blended Malaysians: the Straits Chinese or *babas* who took on many Malay characteristics but essentially were still Chinese. But *baba* culture in Malaysia is now marginalized and dying out. Typically, the Malays borrowed less culturally from the immigrant Chinese than the immigrants borrowed from the Malays. But with education and wealth has come more borrowing. In some places in Malaysia, Malays celebrate Hari Raya at the end of the Muslim fasting month of Ramadan by letting off green fireworks (a blending of the Chinese predilection for fireworks with green, the universal color of Islam). Also, some Malays have taken to giving one another green *ang pow* at Hari Raya. (Traditionally, Chinese give *ang pow* at Chinese New Year, red envelopes that contain cash.)

Generally, Malaysia is a society that is calm, well ordered and always eager to adopt the accoutrements of modernization and progression visible elsewhere. Speed humps adorn the roads of many Kuala Lumpur suburbs (and not just the better ones), for example, and the public toilets for the overhead commuter train service in Kuala Lumpur feature baby changing facilities in the men's toilets as well as the women's. Small instances of thoughtfulness such as these are the physical indicators of a civil society.

Tending the Grass Roots

Malaysia, particularly during the time of Prime Minister Mahathir's rule, typically was portrayed in the Western media as bordering on a dictatorship. It is a view that was wrong. The Malaysian Government typically enjoys an overwhelming majority in Parliament, something that by and large renders the Malaysian Parliament an irrelevancy in Malaysian politics. The real forum for debate and politicking is within the United Malay National Organization (UMNO).

Also there is a huge imbalance between metropolitan (Kuala Lumpur) and rural electorates, with the latter being significantly bigger in terms of registered voters than the former. Such malapportionment is explicitly allowed for in the Malaysian Constitution (Part I of Schedule Thirteen). It means that the electorate in Kuala Lumpur is largely estranged from the political process.

For example, at the time of the 1999 general elections, Malaysia's biggest federal electorate (Ampang Jaya in Kuala Lumpur) had 98,527 registered voters, which was more than six times the voters of the smallest electorate (Hulu Rajang, a rural seat) with 16,018 voters. Such discrimination is justified in terms of voters who live in cities having access to a far greater and better range of services than do rural voters. But it also ensures that the Malay vote will count for much more than the Chinese vote, as most Chinese are urbanized.

The mainstream Malaysian media also heavily favors the government and often only gives the opposition any degree of prominence when it is involved in infighting or is being attacked by the government, the government's attack being what is reported. This too helps to keep the government in power.

Nonetheless, the government is sensitive to the whims of the electorate. The Malaysian Constitution can be changed with a vote supported by two-thirds of the Malaysian Parliament and so winning by a simple majority is never enough for the ruling coalition. A real victory is to have a two-thirds majority and so to ensure it gets that, come election time, voters are listened to very carefully.

The prime minister too is not nearly as dictatorial as is often assumed. Heading up a coalition of many parties means that his role is considerably constrained. His choice for his ministry is similarly constrained by state considerations, racial balance and the need to ensure that the head, at least, of most constituent parties has a cabinet position. All this substantially reduces the prime minister's flexibility. So in cabinet, Prime Minister Mahathir, for example, was not the aggressive dominator that many might assume. Rather than walk into the room, announce his position and then expect everyone to fall into line, I was told by several of his cabinet ministers that Mahathir tended to stay quiet, listen to the various positions, weigh them up, assess which points of view had majority support around the table and which key players held what view, and only then would he announce his view. "Mahathir [was] too smart to announce his view and expect others to follow", one told me.

The degree to which Malaysia's politicians do attempt to communicate with and listen to voters was brought home to me on one occasion, around mid-2000, when I was able to travel with Daim Zainuddin to his Merbok electorate in Kedah state. Daim had made it a practice to visit Merbok at least once a month in the wake of the November 1999 national elections in which UMNO had lost significant ground, particularly to the opposition PAS.

We flew in Daim's private jet to Alor Setar where we were met by local UMNO officials. From there we spent the entire day traveling the electorate in a cavalcade, occasionally with a police escort. It was an exhausting business. And I was just following the minister around. He, on the other hand, made four speeches in four locations, attended three lunches, had several meetings with party officials, called in at the house of one, called in at his sister's house, opened a new motor vehicle repair shop owned by a local Malay cooperative, gave several media interviews, stopped to pray at a local mosque, and visited two rubber estates to meet with Tamil Indian rubber tappers. We also narrowly missed a collision with a buffalo that had wandered onto the road. And that was all in one day. Typically, the lunches were served at long tables and in the traditional style. No cutlery was provided, all ate dishes such as rice and fried padi fish with their right hands, including Daim.

Aboard the jet on the way back to Kuala Lumpur, he gossiped with an UMNO Kedah official who accompanied us for the return flight, read through various begging letters that had been directly handed to him by constituents during the day and then went on to read several ministry briefing papers. Later that night, Daim hosted a large prayer gathering of the local Malay business elite at his Kuala Lumpur house.

Malaysia's is not a government that verges on the totalitarian. Accordingly, outside commentators need to update themselves on the true situation in Malaysia. I had once worked in Australia as the senior adviser to a shadow minister and been through one federal election and several by-elections and, if anything, the direct contact that Malaysian politicians appear to have with voters is more intense and regular than is the practice in Australia and perhaps in most other Western democracies. Nonetheless, there are important institutional rigidities to ensure that the Malaysian Government will not easily be voted from office, although, again, that need not mean that the government is therefore insulated from the concerns of ordinary citizens. These rigidities have allowed the Malaysian Government to wield enormous social and economic influence in a way that governments with a more precarious hold on power would never dare to do.

The other important consideration in Malaysian politics is the military. The military is important because it is not important. At all times since independence, even during times of crisis (for example the 1969 communal riots), Malaysia's armed forces have remained entirely professional and under the direction of the elected government. It is a rarity among Asian countries.

Capitalism the Malaysian Way

The Malaysian Government is pro-business. But it is not pro-market. It has intervened heavily in the market to ensure a better distribution of wealth and business opportunities, not between rich and poor but between Malays and Chinese. Many have criticized such explicit race-based policies but it cannot be denied that they have been instrumental in ensuring that race-related violence is no longer a feature of Malaysian society, when it is a routine occurrence in Indonesia, where most race-related violence simply goes unreported.

Part of the modus operandi of the Malaysian Government has been to award contracts without a tender or with a closed or limited tender. Partly this is because if open tenders were held, invariably the cheapest bidders would be companies owned by local Chinese or foreign companies – precisely the situation that the Malaysian Government is keen to avoid. Sometimes the contracts have gone to well-connected entrepreneurs. But the truth is that in Malaysia so many government contracts are awarded to so many people that invariably some of those awarded will be to those with good connections. So it might be that it's not a select few being treated differently but, rather, the well-connected being treated no differently to anyone else. Daim Zainuddin once said to me that during his time as finance minister, the one item of business that used up the most time was supervising the awarding of government contracts. The time went into making sure that their distribution was widespread and balanced, particularly with due regard to regional and political considerations.

Not that this sort of thing isn't replete with inefficiencies and unfairness. Occasionally balance is lost and the result is a scandal, as was the case in 2005 in relation to the allocation of approved permits (APs), the permits Malaysians need to import foreign-made cars. Thousands are handed out and it turned out that too many had been handed out to too few who happened to be too well-connected. There were calls for the resignation of Rafidah Aziz, the responsible minister, but in reality Rafidah is one of Malaysia's most competent ministers. It is true that the allocation of APs had become a shambles, but it's also true that Rafidah was operating in a wider context of broad patronage that allows the ruling coalition to stay in power.

As for big contracts, Malaysia is hardly alone in awarding them without open tenders. The US Government did just that in the aftermath of the 2003 Iraq War, when it selected the US giant Bechtel for a US$680 million Iraqi reconstruction contract via a closed, restricted tender. Why Bechtel was chosen above other companies was not clear. But what is clear is that George Schultz, Republican Party stalwart and secretary of state under President Reagan, was a board member at Bechtel, a senior counselor and its former president.[2]

The controversial policy devised by Daim, and fully backed by Mahathir, of picking Malay entrepreneurs for rapid advancement led to enormous waste and inefficiency. It also led to few obvious successes. But what it did do was break the nexus between super-wealth and race. Arguably, the waste and the failures have been worth it for this alone.

Although Daim and Mahathir created Malay entrepreneurs who operated at the upper echelons of Malaysian business, it did not mean that they orchestrated their every moves thereafter. The biggest of the created Malay entrepreneurs was Halim Saad who headed Renong Group. Halim owed almost everything to Daim but that did not mean that Halim on occasions did not embark on strategies or take routes that either surprised Daim or of which Daim had no prior knowledge. An approach made by expatriate Malaysian investor Khoo Teck Puat in 1996 to acquire a stake in Renong is a case in point.

According to Daim, Khoo offered to swap all, or almost all, of his stake in Standard Chartered Bank with Halim for a large chunk of Renong.

(Khoo's stake in the UK bank of almost 15% was valued at around US$1.6 billion at the time.) The deal seemed an astonishingly good one to Daim. Halim would be getting a large tranche in a blue-chip bank of world standing in return for giving up part of his stake in Renong, much of which was yet to prove profitable. The deal would not have handed control of Renong to Khoo but would have left him as one of its largest single share-holders. Daim says he even flew to Singapore to personally examine and approve the deal. But Halim later rejected the deal, much to Daim's surprise. "I couldn't believe it", Daim said to me while Halim was still in control at Renong. "Sometimes, I don't know who he gets his advice from."

Both Mahathir and Daim justified the government's intervention in the economy by portraying the government as a quasi-shareholder in Malaysia's business sector. "The government after all is an indirect shareholder of all your companies", Daim told the Malaysian Institute of Directors' Round-table Conference back in October 1986. "If you make more money, govern-ment revenues will increase."[3] It was a sentiment repeated again, 14 years later by Mahathir, when he wrote in his book *The Malaysian Currency Crisis* that: "The government wants to see business profitable because it has a 28% stake in the profits made through corporate tax."[4]

Inevitably, preferential treatment raises the ire of those who are not preferred. But the necessity of such treatment in a racially fractured society such as Malaysia's should be beyond dispute. The debate should focus on the degree of preferment. Below is an anonymous email that was distributed in Malaysia in April 2003. It may be factually incorrect but the degree to which it was circulated among Malaysian Chinese and Indians was remarkable:

Most of us are aware of the unofficial quota system employed by Petronas [the national state-owned oil company] in awarding contracts, jobs and tenders. (For those who don't know – a ridiculous 90% for *bumis* [Malays] and 10% to be shared by all other races!!!) However, it has come to our knowledge that from now on 100% of dealings with Petronas must be by a *bumi* company (unless there are no *bumi* companies in specialized fields). All non-*bumi* contractors have been politely told not to waste their time. Petronas fuel stations will from now on only be given to *bumis*, and for the existing non-*bumi* run petrol stations, their contracts will be nullified and given to *bumis*. This from our national petroleum company.

Many non-*bumis* in the Klang Valley are now boycotting all Petronas stations and all Petronas products, and suggest the rest of you do the same as a silent protest. Please forward this mail to as many non-*bumis* as possible.

It is a measure of the success of Malaysia's race-based policies that sentiments such as these only lead to angry (but nonetheless polite) emails rather than rioting. Even Malaysia's Chinese have come to realize the value in the government's Malay preferment policies. But again, the debate is not over whether such policies should operate at all, but rather their degree.

Corruption and Professionalism

Malaysia is an odd mixture of low-grade corruption and civility. A friend of mine was observed talking on his mobile telephone while he was driving his car. The fine for driving and using a mobile telephone is M$1,000. After much negotiating, in which my friend protested his poverty and that in any event he was running low on cash, he managed to negotiate "tea money" of just M$30 with the policeman. Only then did he realize that he did not have the right amount; he had only M$50 notes. He gave the policeman one of these. The policeman, without any discussion, then opened his wallet and gave him M$20 change. The deal, after all, had been struck. The exchange was civil but corrupt nonetheless.

Another example of the propensity for Malaysia's traffic police to accept bribes becomes particularly prevalent in the lead-up to Ramadan, the Islamic fasting month, when extra money is needed for each evening's fast-breaking activities and the celebrations at the end of the month. At several points around central Kuala Lumpur, roads turn into bus-only lanes. The police erect barriers along the lanes so that once motorists turn into them they cannot get out. They then set up a position and stop each motorist for illegally using the bus lane. At night, the queues of motorists trapped and awaiting their turn to negotiate with the police can reach a dozen or more. The process is reminiscent of how dolphins herd schools of fish into estuaries where they can dine on them at leisure.

But other things work as they should. Some streets in Kuala Lumpur now have parking meters. They function, motorists pay what they need to and those that don't often receive a parking ticket on their windscreens. It's all as unexceptional as it should be.

There is also greater equality in the application of the law in Malaysia than in, say, Indonesia, Thailand or the Philippines. Ministers pay speeding fines if they accrue them. Ministers' convoys also stop at toll booths on toll roads to pay the toll. Even when the prime minister's car is travelling on official business, it always stops at toll booths to pay the toll. This does not surprise Malaysians but this will surprise many outsiders. And many in Indonesia wouldn't understand at all.

Higher level corruption exists in Malaysia, but once more it is something that is perceived to be more of a problem by Western commentators than it probably is. Malaysia is the envy of Southeast Asia. It's seen as relatively rich, its government is seen as relatively competent and clean of corruption and its infrastructure is viewed as first rate. As the daughter of one of the Philippines' wealthiest families said when I mentioned to her that the view expressed in the Western media often is that the administration of Dr Mahathir was corrupt: "Corrupt?" she said. "Malaysia is not corrupt. That's why it's rich. I'm from the Philippines. I can tell you about corruption."

Malaysia's Civil Service is one of the most professional in the region. It is also relatively less corrupt than most others in the developing world. Partly, this is due to the number of women employed at senior levels in the Malaysian Civil Service. And frankly, women the world over tend to be less corrupt in official positions than men.

The Australian Government's Department of Foreign Affairs and Trade said in its 1999 report, *Asia's Financial Markets: Capitalizing on Reform*, for example, that "Bank Negara is considered one of the best regulators in Asia, renowned for its strict interpretation of rules and transparency".[5] It was strong praise by one government's agency of another.

The oil and gas sector always attracts corruption on account of the government approvals needed to operate in the sector the world over and the easy, unearned economic income that oil and gas generate. But even here, Malaysia looks relatively good. Its state-owned oil company Petronas is one of the most widely respected companies in Asia. Routinely it is rated as one of Asia's best-run companies. And it has the profits to prove it. It announced a net profit for 2002 of US$4 billion and revenues of US$21.4 billion.

Indonesia's Pertamina, on the other hand, is famously riddled with corruption. Arguably, it would do more for the Indonesian economy if it simply closed down. One external audit calculated that it lost around US$5 billion in two years alone during the mid-1990s due to corruption and poor management. Its 2002 net profits were US$697 million off revenues of US$23.7 billion, meaning that it had higher revenues than Malaysia's Petronas but made almost six times less in profits.[6]

In any event, Prime Minister Abdullah Badawi, on coming to office in late 2003, quietly and perhaps cautiously went about sending some important signals that he would not be prepared to tolerate some of the more overt abuses. The land and cooperative minister was charged with cheating and corruption in early 2004.[7] No doubt that got his cabinet colleagues talking. In June 2005, the federal territories minister was suspended from UMNO for six years for vote-buying.[8] And in August 2005, a former UMNO member of the Perak State Assembly was fined M$35,000 (US$9,500) and given a four-year jail sentence for bribery.[9] Importantly, both the latter two were seen as important supporters within the party of Abdullah.

Also, the media has become more open. Under Abdullah it is now more likely to report the views of the opposition. This is an encouraging development. Anecdotally, most Malaysians only seemed to bother to buy a daily newspaper to check out the job advertisements section. They relied on the gossip networks for their news. There has been more openness elsewhere too. A debate on the Internal Security Act attended by more than 1,000 people was held in a public hall in mid-2004 between a government minister and an opposition figure. And as ever, government ministers and even the prime minister can be "door-stopped" by journalists and asked impromptu questions as they enter and leave public events. No such thing is ever permitted in Singapore.

Meeting Mahathir

Toward the end of 2005, Dr Mahathir remarked to someone who knows me that he'd like to meet me. He'd read some of what I'd written in the past and was keen to discuss it. It so happened that I was due to be in Singapore and Malaysia to speak at several conferences, so I was able to meet with the former prime minister. We met at his private residence at Country Heights, a gated estate outside Kuala Lumpur.

I'd been warned that Mahathir would take a while to warm up. He might be fiery, abrupt and difficult. Certainly, none of that would be out of step with his public image.

His hospitality was evident before I'd even entered the house. I was sitting on the porch removing my shoes to go inside as is necessary in many parts of Asia. When I got up, there was Mahathir standing on the doorstep waiting for me. We shook hands and we went inside. He directed me to a living room with little more than a large, comfy lounge suite and a large television on which a sports program was playing. He switched the television off and we sat down together and started to talk.

He could not have been more open and engaging. He was mild mannered, charming even, and proved a great talker. It was another side of this complex and thoughtful figure of history.

He was now 80 but had the looks and stamina of a 60-year-old. And he's tough. It was Ramadan and he was fasting, meaning no food or drink during sunlight hours. And yet he'd been horse riding that morning and by four in the afternoon showed no signs of fading.

The house is not particularly large; certainly it's no mansion. Probably Mahathir is one of Asia's poorest ex-leaders, which says a great deal about the man and how he ruled Malaysia. Only one household staff member was visible. And a solitary police box stands outside the gate. It did not appear to be manned.

Only the day before I'd been asked at a conference to confirm that Mahathir really still pulls the strings in the way that Lee Kuan Yew continues to in Singapore. But this is not the case. It helps to demonstrate the degree to which Malaysia is a functioning parliamentary democracy compared with some of its neighbors. When Mahathir left office, he left power, something that Singapore's leaders have so far felt unable to do.

He told me that he had only seen Prime Minister Abdullah Badawi twice since the latter came to office in late 2003. The first occasion was prior to the 2004 elections. Abdullah came to see Mahathir to enquire if any of Mahathir's children wanted to stand. If so, then a seat would be found for them. But Mahathir said no. He is the politician in the family; it was not his intention to found a political dynasty.

On the second occasion, Abdullah wanted to brief the former prime minister on government policy. Mahathir told me that he simply listened and stayed quiet.

We talked about Anwar Ibrahim, the former deputy prime minister who fell out with Mahathir and was subsequently jailed on abuse of power and sodomy charges. I asked Mahathir if he felt it was appropriate for sodomy to be an offence in a country with modern pretensions like Malaysia. Malaysia is a conservative society but Mahathir's main concern, which has largely gone unreported, was that, if in fact the allegations about Anwar were true, then he was unfit to be prime minister – not particularly because of the moral issue but because Anwar would have been open to blackmail threats from all directions. So for Mahathir, Anwar's alleged behavior might have led to private moral concerns but the much larger concern related to security.

Anwar, who has since been cleared of the sodomy charges by Malaysia's federal court (although not of the allegations), had repeatedly asked to see him since being let of jail, Mahathir said. But Mahathir felt that any such meeting would be seen by the Malay community as a rapprochement, an impression that he did not want to give.

I asked Mahathir why he was always so aggressive toward the West and if he felt that such aggression was counterproductive because it may damage how he will be remembered, particularly outside Malaysia. He explained that the Malays had peacefully traded with the Arabs and the Chinese for 1,000 years and that the latter had come to the Malay peninsular in trading vessels. But when the Europeans arrived, they did so in warships. They did not want to trade but to take control. He feels that vestiges of this attitude survive today.

Has he made mistakes? Of course he had, Mahathir replied, but not knowingly. Mistakes are only clear after the event. And his biggest regret? That he was unable to do more to change Malays' attitudes, to make them more entrepreneurial and less reliant on handouts and special favors.

Still, Malaysia is prosperous and peaceful. The race-based preferment policies that Mahathir introduced did sever the link once and for all between great wealth and Chineseness, thus giving Malays their own heroes in the business community. There has been a lot of waste and inefficiency along the way. But it has been a small price to pay for the social cohesion that Malaysia now enjoys. Chauvinistic communalism has been replaced by multiculturalism and, today, the three main races in Malaysia – the Malays, the Chinese and the Indians – have one thing in common: they all think of themselves first and foremost as Malaysians. And for that Dr Mahathir should feel justly proud.

Malaysia has a lot going for it. But not everyone knows that. How that has come about is discussed in the next chapter.

Chapter 16

RUMORS AND GOSSIP IN MALAYSIA

Many readers who live in Malaysia or who are frequent visitors realize that Malaysia represents hidden value. Living standards are high, there is stability and peace and the infrastructure is excellent. Even Malaysia's mega-projects, most of which are of dubious economic value, prove something more than Malaysia's engineering capability: when Malaysia says it is going to build something, it actually does it. If this were India, Indonesia, Thailand or the Philippines, the project would be grounded by corruption, political squabbling and mismanagement. Malaysia is not perfect but it is much closer to that state than most countries in Asia. The problem is that outside Asia few people know this. Why then is the value hidden?

The answer lies in the fact that for all its achievements, the Malaysian Government has not performed as well on the public relations side, particularly for the international, and especially the Western audience. Former Prime Minister Mahathir went out of his way to offend the West and so its media responded in kind, by portraying him as a dictator and Malaysia as politically and economically backward.

Too often, government decisions and the processes behind them are not fully explained. Too little effort is given in Malaysia to cultivating the media, be they foreign or local journalists. The media is seen as a foe, when it should be seen as a friend and the means by which the government's policies can be communicated and justified. Ministerial explanations are often too defensive or simply lack sophistication. Journalists are the link between government and the electorate, they are the middlemen of democracies and they need to be treated as such.

Conspiracies Galore

The Malaysian Government's paying too little regard to the PR side allows two things to happen. It allows some foreign journalists to assume the worst motives and see conspiracies where often there are none. And it allows the Kuala Lumpur gossip mill to work overtime. One classic example was the rumor in the midst of the 1997–98 economic crisis that the businessman son of then Prime Minister Mahathir had committed suicide. He hadn't; he'd simply been seen visiting a hospital of which he was a part owner.[1]

Perhaps the most obvious example of the outcome of the value of Malaysia being hidden was a speech that the then US Vice President Al Gore made in Kuala Lumpur in 1998. It was calculated to do as much damage to Mahathir as possible. At the height of small but noisy street demonstrations after the sacking of Deputy Prime Minister Anwar Ibrahim, Gore said:

> Among nations suffering economic crisis, we continue to hear calls for democracy in many languages, "People Power," "*Doi Moi*," "*Reformasi*" ... We hear them today – right here, right now – among the brave people of Malaysia.

Mahathir was in the audience, as was President Joseph Estrada of the Philippines and President Alberto Fujimori of Peru. It was a calculated attempt to humiliate Mahathir to his face. After delivering the speech, Gore left the room.

Malaysians were stunned. Malaysian Trade Minister Rafidah Aziz said:

> It's the most disgusting speech I have ever heard in my life. I hope I never live to hear another one from anyone like that.[2]

Rafidah was right. Al Gore's speech was disgusting. And it was ignorant. It made me wonder what sort of briefing the US embassy in Kuala Lumpur had been giving Washington. In a similar vein was an Australian Broadcasting Corporation news report that year that showed a video montage of Indonesia's former President Soeharto, Burma's Than Shwe and Mahathir, with a voice-over saying that 1998 had been a "bad" year for Asia's dictators.

The fact that the realities of Malaysia are not clear to the rest of the world is a great pity because the Malaysian story really is a good one. Malaysia succeeds in so many ways. The Western media's attacks on Mahathir were well earned but not well deserved.

Malaysia's media outlets are partisan and tend not to probe issues, particularly on matters of local politics. It's not the done thing and in any event all the major newspapers and private television stations are owned by interests that are allied to the ruling coalition government. Also, rarely are government decisions explained to the satisfaction of the general population. So what is the inevitable consequence? Rumor and gossip. In fact, Kuala Lumpur must be home to some of the most sophisticated and fabulous gossip of all the Asian capitals. The more cynical, preposterous and damning it is, the better. Indeed, gossip that is mundane tends not to be believed, whereas outlandish gossip is. And the more outlandish it is, the more quickly it circulates, and the quicker it goes around, the more likely it will get back to the gossipmongers (which is practically anyone and everyone in Kuala Lumpur) but this time from fresh sources which of course only confirms its "truthfulness".

A Classic Case

A friend of mine who lives in Kuala Lumpur told me with absolute certainty that, at the height of the 1997–98 economic crisis, the then Finance Minister Daim Zainuddin had boarded a flight out of Malaysia with six bags of cash. He had bought two first class seats, one for himself and one for the bags of cash. How did she know this? A friend had "told her". One evening several days later, I had the chance to chat with Daim. It was a relaxed and free-ranging conversation so I thought I might relay this story to him to gauge his reaction, but I didn't have to. Before I could, he told me his own version.

The Times of London, he said, had reported that he had left Malaysia aboard his own jet with the six bags of cash. "Can you believe that! *The Times* said that! *The Times* actually said that!" He was more incredulous than hurt. Clearly, the story was ridiculous. "Why didn't you just do a telegraphic transfer like everyone else?" I jokingly asked Daim. He simply shook his head with an air of resignation.

Daim has been the target of as much innuendo as any politician in Malaysia. An essay entitled "Who is the real Daim?", which appeared on the oppositionist *Reformasi* website, "Justice for Anwar", in 1998, ridiculously suggested that Daim's wealth was once as high as M$65 billion (US$17.1 billion), although it was now significantly lower. It went on to say that Daim had demanded big "fees" when negotiating contracts with two Japanese banks. Additionally, it alleged that during the economic crisis, Mahathir had asked Daim for help in propping up the ringgit and

Daim had lost "$1 billion" trying to do just that. The *Reformasi* website became home to many absurd and extreme claims, and this was one of them. Ultimately, such claims were self-defeating. Over time, the website lost much credibility among many ordinary Malaysians.

When I read to Daim some of the essay's more extravagant claims and asked him to comment, his reaction was genuine laughter, albeit tinged with some disappointment that the site had claimed that his wealth was now down to a third of what it claimed it once was. "I can't be a very good businessman if I'm down to just a third", he quipped. He had met the chairman of only one of the two Japanese banks mentioned, and the chairman had later sent him a collection of press clippings and certainly "no money", he laughed. After examining the document, Daim recognized it as having started out as one of the many poison-pen letters (*surat terbang* or *surat layang*) that circulate in Malaysian politics, although it had since been added to and embellished. *Surat terbang* are unique to Malaysia, not so much for their existence as their volume. Hundreds of these often lengthy, well-researched anonymous letters fly around, particularly in the lead-up to UMNO assemblies. Typically they are heavily libellous but often extremely well written.

Rumors and speculation play a big role in politics in Malaysia, perhaps more so than in many other countries. Why are Malaysians so often prepared to believe the worst? Perhaps the reason is partly cultural. But it might also be because there is insufficient public disclosure. The absence of full information leaves room for untruths. Policy formulation in Malaysia, and the rationale behind it, is another area that is constantly the target of rumor and supposition. The government might well have pure policy motives for this or that change, but almost invariably the change is seen as part of some conspiracy or a rebalancing of interests between ministers and their backers in the business sector. Rarely is it accepted at face value.

A case in point is an article that appeared in the *Asian Wall Street Journal* on 26 May 2000. The article ("Change in state-corporate relations could exacerbate Malaysia troubles") described how the Ministry of Finance had just issued a directive that restricted chief executives and presidents of government agencies to holding only one management position at the parent body. They were to relinquish their positions as directors or executives of subsidiaries and associate companies of their parent bodies, as well as directorships in private companies not linked to the government agencies they serve.

The article portrayed the move in terms of what the journalist saw as the "growing rift" between Mahathir and Daim – a rift that both had denied existed. The Finance Ministry directive allegedly was a sign that Daim was trying to "reassert his influence" in government after supposedly having seen it diminish during the previous six months, suggested the article. But this was all conjecture. The fact that the directive was prudent, likely to enhance corporate governance and improve account-ability and that Daim had pushed for a similar move in the 1980s was not mentioned in the article. A rationale so mundane as this is almost never part of government reasoning in Malaysia, or so it seems, if the pundits are to believed.

Why should this be so? Perhaps ministers, and the Malaysian Govern-ment more generally, do not adequately explain their policies and inten-tions. They might have good intentions, but in the absence of full information there is a tendency on the part of those in the wider community to assume the worst – hence the propagation of rumors and speculation. I put this to Daim. His explanation is that government in Malaysia is difficult out of necessity. The quotas for states, parties and ethnic groups mean that senior members of the government have little flexibility in selecting the composition of the cabinet. This means that many ministers are chosen not so much for their policy and communi-cations skills as for other factors. Accordingly, many are insufficiently articulate when it comes to explaining government policies or govern-ment's reasons for doing things. When questioned by reporters, "they might perhaps seem shallow in their answers", offered Daim. Also, Daim feels that once many politicians reach a certain level on the political ladder, they become more concerned with politics and less with policy. They feel that they no longer need to be well briefed on government policy – certainly not as well briefed as they should be. It's not that Daim believes that his ministerial colleagues are lazy, but rather that the system encourages them to be too preoccupied with playing politics. And who pays the price for this? It is the Malaysian Government. Motives are questioned and achievements are underreported in the foreign media. And so the strengths of Malaysia are obscured. Change is coming under new Prime Minister Abdullah Badawi, but it proceeds by necessity at a cautious pace. Malay culture is more disposed to evolution than revolu-tion. It all means that the country represents good value for business and tourists. So be quick.

Chapter 17

MEET SYED MOKHTAR ALBUKHARY

Syed Mokhtar Albukhary never gives interviews. Or at least almost never. "This is something of a record, Michael", he said, as we were introduced. "This is the first time that I've agreed to be seen by anyone for many years. Maybe only once have I given an interview. I think about ten years ago." But it wasn't to be a formal interview. It was to be a "chat". A few months later he met with a journalist from the *Far Eastern Economic Review*. Syed Mokhtar appeared to be opening up. "Why don't you meet with more journalists so that you can explain who you are and what you're doing", I'd asked. I want to get my businesses in order first, he'd replied. Syed Mokhtar controls companies with annual revenues of at least M$17 billion (US$4.68 billion) and employs 75,000 people.[1] It was time, he seemed to have decided, to start giving an account of himself.

I had first met his right-hand man Mohamed Sidek Shaik Osman. We met for dinner at the Mandarin Oriental Hotel in Kuala Lumpur. Sidek is well-spoken and unassuming. He is quintessentially Malay. Shipping and ports are his interests. He'd studied this area in Stockholm and had then come back to Malaysia to work in the Civil Service before joining Syed Mokhtar. Now he is the CEO of Syed Mokhtar's Port of Tanjung Pelepas. Not only did Sidek turn out to be well spoken, he was also well read and able to discuss almost any writer that I cared to name. Right away I could see that some of my assumptions about Syed Mokhtar were wrong. Unlike many other Malay businesspeople who'd been given privileges on account of their good political connections, Syed Mokhtar must be serious. Why else would he be entrusting a lot of his newly created business empire to someone so obviously capable and professional?

(Another of Syed Mokhtar's executives is Megat Najmuddin Khas, the president of the Malaysian Institute of Corporate Governance. He is the chairman of Syed Mokhtar's Tradewinds hotel group. "He doesn't try to micro-manage things", Megat has been quoted as saying. "He surrounds himself with professional managers who know they must look after the interests of all shareholders.")[2]

We left the Mandarin Oriental at about 10.30pm and together we drove off to meet Syed Mokhtar. Sidek half-apologized for the black Mercedes-Benz in which we were traveling. "Actually, this is not our style", he said. "I said to Syed Mokhtar that we should have at least one good car if we are going off to meet senior foreign government officials and so on. Reluctantly he agreed. He's happier with a Proton." Syed Mokhtar's frugality is one of the few things known about him. He does indeed have a locally made Proton as his main car, albeit a top-of-the-range Proton Perdana. His corporate headquarters famously are in an unassuming three-storey building in a shabby part of Kuala Lumpur.

Other Malay entrepreneurs who have been given a state-sponsored kick-start had responded not by building up their companies into first-rate competitors able to compete on the world stage but by buying themselves a corporate jet. Halim Saad, when CEO of Renong Group, had kept his parked alongside that of his mentor, the then Finance Minister Daim Zainuddin, at the private jet hanger at Subang in Kuala Lumpur. I once sat next to Halim at a dinner. Despite my telling him that I was not from New Zealand, he insisted on telling a sheep joke. This time it was going to be different it seemed.

Sidek and I were driven out of central Kuala Lumpur and along Jalan Ipoh. Our destination was to be a Muslim Indian coffee shop where Syed Mokhtar likes to work each night. He has a private room. It's spotlessly clean and air-conditioned. Its windows are blacked out. He arrives at 10pm or later, and likes to meet people there to discuss business over *teh tarik*. Or he just sits there alone, working through his papers.

It turns out that this is his regular routine; largely he is nocturnal. He commences work at about 10 or 11pm, having spent the evening with his wife and children, and then works through the night, going home at 6am to pray, after which he goes to bed, sleeping throughout the morning and perhaps into the early afternoon. It's a routine that suits him but not all his staff. Appointments can sometimes be at 2 or 3am. This is tough on his subordinates who don't keep the same hours as he. Sidek tells me how recently he was working at 4am with Syed Mokhtar on some important matters. But he's philosophical about it. It seems the negatives are more than compensated for by the positives when it comes to working for Syed Mokhtar.

Sidek and I waited a while. Syed Mokhtar then arrived. He is tall, middle-aged and thin. He has a youthful, restless energy. His dress is sober and neat but it's perfunctory; no tie graces his neck. Apparently one hardly ever does. He is polite, humble and softly spoken. His large brown eyes give him the appearance of a bush baby. The frothy *teh tarik* arrives in metallic cups and Syed Mokhtar begins to talk.

So who is Syed Mokhtar Albukhary? It's a question a lot of people are asking. Not that many years ago, few had heard of him. But now he is one of the brightest stars in Malaysian business. He grew up in Malaysia's Kedah, the home state of former Prime Minister Mahathir Mohamad (with whom he enjoys close relations) and former Finance Minister Daim Zainuddin (with whom he does not). His family were traders, with a mixed heritage.

His immediate ancestral roots are in what is now northern Pakistan, but prior to that the family originated from the Hadramawt coastal region of southern Yemen, a heritage shared with many successful Southeast Asian Muslim trading families (see Chapter 20).

An Overnight Success (in 30 Years)

He started with trucks. The year 2003 marked his 30th year in business. It was the 30th anniversary of his first truck license. "That truck is still in use and making money for us", he told me. Then he moved into cattle trading, then rice trading, then textiles and clothing making in Penang. He is also now one of the biggest exporters of rubberwood furniture in Malaysia. The interest in textiles continues with his control of listed Malaysian clothing manufacturer Amtek Holdings. Its core business is the manufacture and distribution of shoes and denim jeans under the Lee Cooper brand name.

Syed Mokhtar had a lot of early partnerships with local Chinese. But his is not a story about opportunistic nominee relationships. He, like them, is a trader. He loves to trade. It is a topic on which he becomes animated, his large hands waving to make points and his eyes widening even more. "I am a trader", he'd told me. "Sidek has to stop me!" He looked at Sidek and Sidek smiled, looked down at the table and shook his head in bemused exasperation. Syed Mokhtar must be a good manager. He does not call all the shots.

His interest in trade and early involvement in the rice trade explains his purchase in early 2003 of a 15% stake in Padiberas Nasional, Malaysia's sole rice importer. The stake cost him more than US$26 million.[3] He now controls that company. There's also a stake in listed Ocean Capital which owns 16 low-end retail outlets around Malaysia. Trade, once again, is the attracting feature.

Syed Mokhtar rode the stock market boom in the 1990s and with astute buying and selling was able to build up a local stock portfolio worth several billion ringgit, but much of it was lost in the 1997–98 regional economic crisis. Banks called in loans as his collateral diminished and he suffered accordingly.

But in recent years Syed Mokhtar has gone from being a commodities trader to a giant in infrastructure development. Infrastructure means government approvals and that means connections. Syed Mokhtar's friendship with Mahathir when he was prime minister is what elevated him to the Malaysian corporate stratosphere. But it wasn't always like that. For a long time, Syed Mokhtar was frozen out of the Malay business elite – those who were routinely awarded contracts and government privatization deals. Generally, those who did receive major contracts were the protégés of Daim Zainuddin, the two-time finance minister. Almost invariably, "Daim's Boys", as the group became known, had been trained as accountants and then were hand-picked by Daim for promotion. They were entirely creatures of Daim's patronage. Syed Mokhtar, however, was his own creation.

He went to see Mahathir to state his case as someone deserving of the sort of opportunities that until then had passed him by. Mahathir was frosty at first but then warmed to him. Syed Mokhtar, Mahathir decided, was someone who could get things done. Syed Mokhtar went on to buy billions of dollars in assets from the Malaysian Government, particularly as the Mahathir era was drawing to a close.

In 2000, Syed Mokhtar bought from an arm of the Malaysian Government a controlling interest in Malaysian Mining Corporation (MMC). The acquisition was via a restricted bid. Syed Mokhtar has said that he paid approximately M$3 per share, beating two other bidders who'd offered M$1.80 and M$2.20 respectively.[4] MMC has many key assets, including control of the independent power producer Malakoff and a 40% stake in Gas Malaysia.

MMC has since served as the listed holding company of Syed Mokhtar's other interests. These include controlling stakes in the Malaysian Port of Tanjung Pelepas, electrical appliances maker Malaysia Electric Corporation and Pernas International. This last owned a string of interests that included what was the Kuala Lumpur Hilton, the Hotel Istana in Kuala Lumpur, the Pelangi Beach Resort in Langkawi and seven other Malaysian hotels. All these assets were acquired in the brief period of 2000–03.

Pernas was renamed Tradewinds Corp. It was not a company that Syed Mokhtar wanted to buy: he was asked to. It was a mess and riddled with fraud. The government was keen for someone to quietly take it off its hands and sort it out. After Syed Mokhtar's auditors had been through its books, they presented him with evidence of a great deal of corporate wrongdoing. They thought that he should contact the authorities, with a view to those responsible being charged. As much as M$500 million (US$130 million) was missing but Syed Mokhtar elected to look to the future. Let bygones be bygones was his view. "I don't want to go on a witch-hunt", he said, or words to that effect. "Don't even give me the details." Pernas had been a *bumiputera* or Malay trust company managed on behalf of the Malays. Charges would have meant a public scandal and no doubt it was better for everyone concerned not to lose face. Mahathir no doubt wanted Syed Mokhtar to fix the problem and to do so without a damaging fuss.

He had the massive renovation work on the old Kuala Lumpur Hilton completed at a cost of around M$150 million (US$40 million.) It now operates as the Crowne Plaza Kuala Lumpur. On the second occasion that I met Syed Mokhtar, I complimented him on how professional the renovation work was (I've been in a few five-star hotels in Southeast Asia where the owners turned the interior design over to their wives, with disastrous consequences – the Gran Melia in Jakarta is an example). He was pleased but then admitted that he hadn't seen it himself. This is partly because he's happier in a small-scale Indian coffee shop. And partly no doubt because the sight of so much having been spent probably would distress him. And yet he knows that for an international hotel, money must be spent, so better that it's left to the professionals. Later when I met Syed Mokhtar again, he said that he still hadn't eaten at the Crowne Plaza but had attended friends' weddings there. To this day he has not seen inside a room.

In June 2002, a subsidiary of MMC acquired a controlling stake in the prominent Malaysian construction group IJM. The ethnic Chinese owners had done well with the company but it was felt that IJM could do a lot better in winning government construction contracts with a well-connected Islamic businessman as a strategic shareholder. Syed Mokhtar did not initiate the contact, he told me. IJM's owners were looking for a buyer and approached him.

In October 2003, MMC and a partner clinched a US$290 million contract to help build and operate a monorail on the island of Penang.[5] MMC and another partner also were given a US$658 million contract for stormwater and road tunnel management in Kuala Lumpur, and a US$3.9 billion project to build and electrify the North–South Railway, which could be as long as 800 kilometers, stretching the length of the Malaysian peninsular.[6] (This last project, however, was suspended by Mahathir's successor – Abdullah Badawi.)

Syed Mokhtar is fast developing Johor state into what might one day be Southeast Asia's alternative transport hub to Singapore. He is influential in the state and with the state government. He befriended Muhyiddin Yassin, a young politician in the late 1970s who later became Johor's chief minister. This paved the way for land deals and state government projects.

He acquired the state's two container ports, the Senai Airport concession and permission to build a 2,100 MW power plant. He was also awarded the right to jointly build a M$7 billion road network in the state. And in late 2002, MMC announced that it would design and build a light rail system in Johor.

Sidek told me that Syed Mokhtar's main intention with Senai is to turn it into an air cargo hub. "While Singapore's Changi is handling premium passengers on premium airlines, we can handle, for example, air-freighted fruit and vegetables coming in from Indonesia for Singapore's supermarkets", Sidek had said. Germany's Hochtief Airport is advising Syed Mokhtar on the airport's development.

Syed Mokhtar added that his longer term vision was to have Senai Airport used as a base for low-cost airlines. It is his intention to turn Senai into a Stanstead Airport, with Singapore's Changi Airport functioning more like Heathrow, out of which premium service airlines function. By 2005, Sidek had been moved from active involvement in the Port of Tanjung Pelepas to developing Senai. China Eastern Airways staged its inaugural flights between Kunming in China and Senai late that year and Singapore Airlines was using it for pilot training, with the airport earning several thousand dollars each time a training flight landed and took off from its strip. Formerly, Singapore Airlines had been using strips in Australia for this purpose.

But it is the Port of Tanjung Pelepas (PTP) that is Syed Mokhtar's biggest success. Construction got under way in 1996. By 2002, the port was ranked at number 21 among the world's busiest ports. The port has caused Singapore and its Port of Singapore Authority (PSA) a lot of concern. Singapore is one of the world's busiest ports. About 250 shipping lines with over 100,000 ships connect it to about 600 ports around the world. The PSA is big and very profitable – it earns around US$500 million a year. But the Port of Tanjung Pelepas is just four nautical miles away. The PSA did negotiate with PTP about the possible acquisition of a stake but, in return for buying a 30–40% interest, the PSA wanted PTP to slow down its growth in capacity, so that it would be less of a competitor to the PSA's own port. The offer was rejected.

Initially, Syed Mokhtar's executives couldn't even get a meeting with the head of the PSA but then in 2000, PTP attracted Maersk Sealand – the world's largest shipping company – away from Singapore. Syed Mokhtar sold the Danish shipper a 30% stake in PTP to boot. And in 2002, Evergreen Marine, the second largest shipping line calling in at Singapore, also migrated to PTP. It would channel more than one million containers through PTP instead of Singapore.

In 2003, Johor Port, the other of Syed Mokhtar's ports, attracted UK-based Gearbulk (co-owned by Norwegian interests and Mitsui OSK Lines of Japan) away from Singapore. Gearbulk said it would channel its entire volume of 600,000 tonnes of bulk cargo annually through the Johor port instead of Singapore.[7] Suddenly, everyone in Singapore was available for meetings, from the head of the Singapore Government's principal holding company, Temasek Holdings, down. Many meetings were held between Temasek, the PSA and Syed Mokhtar's people to investigate ways in which the two ports might cooperate.[8]

Syed Mokhtar's companies also were involved with building a customs, immigration and quarantine complex at Senai Airport and three dedicated highways to link the airport and the two ports. And in mid-2002, he signed an agreement with Ballast Ham Dredging, the world's biggest dredging company, to set up a land reclamation and dredging company in Malaysia.[9] It will be useful to further develop the ports in Johor and elsewhere in Malaysia.

By 2004, many wondered if Syed Mokhtar would survive the change of political leader. His friend and supporter Dr Mahathir was no longer prime minister. Instead, Abdullah Badawi was now leader, a man with whom he had little connection. But by year's end, Syed Mokhtar was back on the acquisition trail and with a major purchase too: a controlling stake in DRB-Hicom, a car distributor, that also came with interests in finance, insurance, hotels, real estate and defense technologies. He acquired the stake after an intense four-month battle against other possible buyers. He ended up paying M$3.60 per share. The trading price around M$2.10.

But where was all the money coming from? The answer is diverse and complex. Personal income, bank loans, bond issues, dividend streams from listed and private companies and retained earnings are all sources. "Instead of buying a personal jet or a yacht, he uses his earnings to invest in his companies", one associate was quoted as saying.[10] Some funds come from selling privately owned assets to listed companies that he controls, a maneuver not without its critics. But Syed Mokhtar has plenty of cashed-up partners as well. Many are foreign.

The Arab Connection

Syed Mokhtar is one of a new breed of international Islamic businessmen who use their connections from across the Islamic world to mobilize capital and look for opportunities. Western, or at least non-Islamic, businesspeople are invited into the network, but generally only if what they have cannot be sourced readily from within the international Islamic community.

In 2003, Syed Mokhtar and Mohamed Ali Alabbar, a Dubai-based businessman, announced plans for a joint venture company to be called the Gulf International Investment Group (GIIG). The company would attract the "huge pool" of funds, initially M$1 billion (US$263 million) that had been built up in the Middle East following the pull-out of Middle Eastern investors from the US in the wake of the 2001 attack on New York's World Trade Center.[11]

Alabbar, a citizen of the United Arab Emirates, serves as the director general of Dubai's Department of Economic Development. He is close to Dubai's Crown Prince Sheikh Mohammad Al Maktoum and the rest of the ruling royal family and has acted as a troubleshooter for the family's investments since about 1980. In the late 1980s, he came to Singapore to restructure Al Khaleej Investments, the family's Singapore-based holding company. Among its assets in Singapore is Wisma Atria shopping mall on Orchard Road.

Alabbar is the chairman of listed Singapore fashion retailer Royal Clicks, which operates Zara, Reebok, Nautica, Lacoste, Rockport, Royal Sporting House and Mango stores in Singapore and owns 26% of Australia's Westco Jeans, which has more than 140 stores across Australia.[12] Several Royal Clicks outlets are located in Wisma Atria. (So too at one stage was a clothing shop called Fiasco. It was owned by the Mimar Industrial Group, one of the groups owned by the estranged family of Osama bin Laden.)

Alabbar is also deputy chairman of the Dubai Aluminium Company (one of the biggest smelters in the world) and chairman of EMAAR Properties, the UAE's biggest property company.

As if to underscore the close relations between the two men, on a subsequent meeting I had with Syed Mokhtar at his foundation's Islamic Museum in Kuala Lumpur, he received a call on his mobile telephone from Mohamed Ali Alabbar. The tone of the conversation was very jovial. The two obviously enjoy dealing with one another.

One of the projects in which Alabbar and Syed Mokhtar wanted to invest in is a US$2 billion aluminium smelter to be built in Sarawak state, if plans are realized. The main partner in this is to be the Dubai Aluminium Company.

Why had Alabbar and his fellow Middle Eastern investors chosen Malaysia for their attentions? "My Arab colleagues have a lot of respect for the way Malaysia manages it affairs ... And it is also a matter of trust and an ability to see eye to eye with your business partner."[13]

The Sarawak smelter will rely on cheap power from the massive Bakun dam project. I asked Syed Mokhtar about the environmental consequences. Previous plans for the dam drew a lot of criticism for the damage that the dam would do. "We need a dam and we need power, but there's no need to destroy everything", he told me. "We're now looking at the best ways to save the orang-utans and so on."

Visitors to Kuala Lumpur's International Airport will have noticed a Harrods outlet among the duty-free concessions. Syed Mokhtar was instrumental in bringing Harrods to Malaysia which is part of his Amtrek Holdings. The London-based Egyptian businessman Mohamed Al Fayed owns Harrods. It's the Islamic network at work again.

And again, Syed Mokhtar imports luxury Patchi chocolates from Lebanon – there's a Patchi outlet in his Crowne Plaza Hotel and two others elsewhere in Kuala Lumpur. Patchi was set up in Lebanon in 1974 by Nizar Choucair.

Capitalism with an Islamic Face

In October 2002, Syed Mokhtar bought the Singapore-based, 30-store, bookstore chain MPH Books, which has outlets in Malaysia, Singapore and Indonesia. The price was S$46 million. The vendor was a company controlled by Singapore businessman Simon Cheong.

MPH sits very oddly with Syed Mokhtar's infrastructure interests. It looked like reckless diversification. Syed Mokhtar bought it at the government's urging and it seems to be part of the "national service" obligation that he concedes he must undertake in return for having been granted valuable concessions and contracts. (His acquisition of the loss-making Malaysia Electric Corporation also falls into this category. It was a near basket case that the government was keen to get off its hands.)

The government could see that most of MPH's bookstores are located in Malaysia and so felt that it was really a Malaysian company but was in Singaporean hands. I asked Syed Mokhtar about the reasons for buying MPH. Right away he conceded that it did sit oddly with his other interests and that it did look like a reckless diversification. But he said that he saw MPH as fitting in more with his charity arm. He wanted MPH to open up more bookstores around Malaysia, to take English-language books closer to the Malay communities outside Kuala Lumpur. "English is important", he told me. "I want to see more Malay children able to read and write English." Shortly after the acquisition, MPH's management asked Syed Mokhtar if the chain should continue to sell Christian books (it stocked a considerable range, particularly at its flagship Mid-Valley Megamall store in Kuala Lumpar, where there is a large section devoted to Christian literature). Syed Mokhtar's response was "Why not?" But he did suggest that they might also like to increase their range of Islamic books too.

Syed Mokhtar mentioned his interest in Islamic banking. (Islamic banks do not offer or charge interest. Instead borrowers and lenders enter into profit-sharing arrangements.) From the way his eyes bulged, it was clear this was becoming a passion. "Would you like to own a bank?" I asked. "Yes", was his emphatic reply. I mentioned several banks and asked if he'd like to buy those. But then he added that he was interested in buying into an Indonesian Islamic bank perhaps and it could open branches in Malaysia. The local Islamic bank Bank Muamalat was mentioned. And then not long after we met, the Malaysian Government announced that it would open the door to foreign Islamic banks, by issuing licenses to operate locally to such banks and introduce other measures to help Malaysia become a regional hub for Islamic finance.[14] Soon after, Syed Mokhtar emerged with a 70% stake in the bank.[15]

Syed Mokhtar sees his business interests as having two arms: a commercial arm and a charity arm. He wants to move more executives between the two. It is Syed Mokhtar's Islamic community work that was especially attractive to Dr Mahathir. He contributes to mosque construction and Islamic schools. Syed Mokhtar is the biggest single donor to charity in Malaysia, reportedly having given M$127 million (US$34 million) to his personal foundation in the past two years.[16] (Ananda Krishnan probably donates more but a significant proportion of his donations are not of his own volition but a requirement on account of his having gaming concessions.)

The Albukhary Foundation, Syed Mokhtar's private charitable foundation, has built a large mosque and Islamic school complex in Alor Setar in Kedah state. Millions have been spent and a great deal more remains to be spent. The centerpiece is a large and impressive mosque with twin minarets, but the complex will include a hospital, an orphanage, a budget hotel, a college and educational facilities for pensioners. The orphanage can accommodate 120 children. I asked Syed Mokhtar if his charitable facilities were available to non-Muslims. Yes, he said, they were. The hospital, for example, would be available for anyone to use.

Syed Mokhtar hopes that by 2007 the college will have 3,000 students from both Malaysia and countries where Muslims are in a minority (such as the Philippines, Thailand and certain African countries). Ten percent of places will be earmarked for capable non-Muslim students from poor backgrounds.

In mid-2005, he paid US$1.1 million for a church in central Capetown, South Africa, which will be converted to a mosque. The vendor was Jewish. The fact that he, a Muslim, had bought a church from a Jew amused him, and accords with his view of the world where all are equal in business and business brings people together. Why did he buy it? A brother is involved in an international charitable organization and had drawn to his attention that the Muslims in Capetown had inadequate praying facilities.

The Albukhary Foundation also underwrote the cost of building Kuala Lumpur's Islamic Arts Center, a lavish, four-storey museum filled with Islamic antiques and art from around the world, and the cost of keeping it open, which runs to almost US$100,000 a month. Its displays could not be more professional. The Sultan of Brunei keeps a similar museum of Islamic arts in Brunei's capital Bandar Seri Begawan. The Sultan's collection is bigger and has many more rare and beautiful objects but they are crammed into cases, seemingly haphazardly and with poor labeling. The Sultan's collection is more about acquisition than scholarship. This is not the case with the carefully curated collection at Syed Mokhtar's Islamic Arts Center. Syed Mokhtar said the museum was not his idea. "The government asked me to do it", he said. His brother Syed Mohamad takes care of the day-to-day running of the museum and has accumulated around 4,000 artworks. Syed Mohamad has turned the museum into an important repository of Islamic art for Malaysia and also for the world. A recent acquisition is the earliest known hand-written Koran to have been made in China, acquired for around US$150,000 from a New York dealer.

No-one can challenge Syed Mokhtar's Islamic credentials. His charity work is there for all to see. He is a great supporter of Islamic banking and actively promotes cross-border ties between Muslims. But he is adamant that women should not have to wear the *tudung*, the Islamic headscarf. Indeed, there is no explicit reference in the Koran that women should. Other parts of the body are mentioned for coverage, such as the breasts, but there is no explicit mention of hair.

What Next?

I asked Syed Mokhtar if other family members are involved in his group of companies or if they will be. "No", he said. "This is not family. This is me." He said that only one family member, Syed Mohamad, was involved in any of his interests but then only at the museum.

Will Syed Mokhtar survive? The longevity of Malaysian Malay entrepreneurs has been fickle. But then that's because they have not delivered ultimately. He should survive if he steers clear of political partisanship and does well with the assets with which he has been entrusted. He does not appear to be making the same mistake that many big ethnic Chinese businesspeople make – try to manage everything all the time. Instead he tends to set key performance targets and strategies for the group and then leaves day-to-day operation in the hands of competent CEOs.

In late 2005, he told me that he did not plan to make any further significant acquisitions. Even he seemed to agree that he was stretched as far as was prudent. But not everyone agreed. When I asked Mahathir around the same time if he felt that Syed Mokhtar had grown too big, Mahathir replied simply that there were so many opportunities in Malaysia for someone like Syed Mokhtar. In some respects, Syed Mokhtar might be fortunate that Mahathir no longer is prime minister.

In any event, he said he had developed a program to "institutionalize" his corporate and charity holdings so that by 2010, the lot would be professionally managed and he could walk away, if he so chose. By 2010, he wants the business side to be running well and profitably and it could then donate a significant part of its earnings to Syed Mokhtar's various charities, which also would be running on a fully professional basis.

Does he want his children to inherit his empire and take over the running of the group, I asked? Not necessarily, was his reply. If they are capable, then maybe. Although judging from the expression on his face, that appears not to be his intention. Would he fold all of his businesses into a charitable foundation along the lines of the Tata family in India, I asked? (The Tata Group is largely owned by several Parsi charitable trusts.) Syed Mokhtar replied that he really hadn't thought about it but, yes, that is a possibility.

In another way, Syed Mokhtar is different: he proved that he was capable and shrewd before he was given government contracts. There are few big Malay or Muslim entrepreneurs in Malaysia who can genuinely say this. As he said to me in a veiled reference to "Daim's Boys": "I'm not an accountant." Has he benefited from his connections? Of course he has, as he is the first to admit, but the connections took years to arrive. First, he had to prove himself as a businessman. But he rests easy. "All my money is halal money, Michael", he said to me, late one night over roti chanai at his favorite coffee shop. He also told me that the first edition of this book had served an unusual purpose. One evening he went home and found his wife upset. She had been surfing the internet and had read various claims that he had unfairly benefited from his government connections and had taken government money. He has benefited from his connections, but it's probably true that the government has taken money *from* him, considering some of the appalling state-owned companies that he has been asked to buy and bail out. He showed his wife a copy of *The Asian Insider* and asked her to read the chapter on him so that she could see a more even viewpoint. "So you see, Michael, you saved me. If it wasn't for you, I would have been sleeping in the garage that night," he joked.

But the big question remains. Why does he do it? What has driven him to accumulate so many companies? The enjoyment factor is obviously a big part. His enthusiasm for business is boyish and infectious. But there's a more serious side. In late 2005 he told me

> I have 75,000 employees. I need to look after them, to make sure that they have enough retirement money and so on. But also there's the foundation, the charity work. This is what's important to me. Making sure that all of that is looked after. That is what drives me.

Part IV

ISLAM, BUSINESS AND ASIA

Most of the world's Muslims do not live in the Middle East or even near it. They live in Asia. Over the centuries, Arab and Indian Muslim traders linked East Asia to Europe, trading in textiles, timber and spices. And so today, these old links are emerging again – investment is flowing along these old Islamic trade routes between the Middle East and East Asia.

Islamic consumers are becoming more powerful in Asia too, a potentially discrete spending bloc that business must be aware of and sensitive to.

What follows are several chapters that look at Islam, not as it's practiced in the Middle East but as it exists in East Asia, the role of Asians of Arab descent in business and politics, where the East Asian version of Islam fits among the many schools of Islam, and more on the growing business links between Malaysia and the Middle East.

Chapter 18

ALLAHU AKBAR!
ISLAM IN ASIA

One evening on a recent visit to Kuala Lumpur I was in that city's Mid-Valley Megamall. I was about to see a film with a friend. Before it was due to start, I visited the public conveniences in the mall. As I stood there at the urinals, I became aware of a presence behind me and not too far away. I looked and saw a Malay girl, dressed in a *tudung* (Islamic headscarf). She held a mop. She was waiting for me to finish so that she could continue mopping the floor.

I thought about that. It occurred to me that often in men's toilets in Malaysia, I have found myself in the company of female cleaning staff dressed in Islamic attire. Until then I'd thought nothing of it, it is such a commonplace occurrence in Malaysia. But then I wondered what would happen if I was in a public toilet in Saudi Arabia alone with a woman who was not my wife. I suppose we'd both be whipped. Or maybe stoned. Or maybe I'd have an amputation to look forward to, although of what I'm not sure.

Islam as it's practiced in most of Southeast Asia is moderate. It trusts people. It treats adults like adults and does not attribute impure motives as the default response. It's more about community and taking care of one another than about imposing a checklist of rules and regulations.

Ordinarily, Islam is a religion of tolerance. The vast majority of Muslims in Indonesia and Malaysia do peacefully coexist with other religious groups. The manner in which multicultural and multiethnic issues are managed in Malaysia, a Muslim country, is world-class. Around 58% of the population is ethnically indigenous or Malay and Muslim, 24% are ethnically Chinese, 8% are ethnic Indians and the remainder belong to other smaller groups. And yet Malaysia is not on the brink of civil war. There are few tensions between Muslims and non-Muslims. Nor is Malaysia a place in which women are oppressed.

So how unfortunate it is that the world's perception of Islam has been tainted and even captured by political extremists in the Middle East. All too easily it's forgotten that Arab Muslims and Sephadi Jews existed in relative peace as neighbors for centuries; that Christians and Arabs also coexisted peacefully in the Middle East. And is it not the case that 24 of the 25 Islamic prophets are also Christian figures? That the Jesus of the Christians is the Isa of the Muslims? "Ojalá" say the Spanish or "I hope that ...". It stems directly from the Arabic "inshallah" which means "God willing".

Most fundamentalist Muslims are not interested in history and precedent. They prefer to return to the "simple" truths of the Koran. But as Middle East scholar Robert Irwin has said:

> The Koran, however, is not simple, and in many centres in Britain, Pakistan and elsewhere the standard of training in the basic tenets of Islam, including the meaning and context of the Koran, is staggeringly poor. Naïve literal readings are soldered onto modern preoccupations with the menaces of Zionism, globalization and feminism, and this third-rate religious education is one of the things that fuels fundamentalist violence.[1]

One thing on which the Koran is very clear is that Muslims are not to proselytize. Islam is, or it ought to be, a tolerant religion in terms of those of other faiths. "For you, your religion; for me, my religion" intones the Koran.

The Muslims of the Middle East have been politicized by tribalism and the Palestine–Israel issue. And so arguably, to get a truer picture of Islam, one that is less tainted by politics, it is to Asia that we should look. This is all the more so, given that the vast majority of the world's Muslims live nowhere near the Middle East; most Muslims are not Arabs. They are Asian. Most Muslims live east of Karachi, although you wouldn't know it, judging from the headline-grabbing antics of the Muslims of the Middle East.

The world's Muslim population is more than 1 billion. And that number is growing, both in absolute terms and as a proportion of the world's total population. Around 30% live in the Indian subcontinent. Another 20% live in sub-Saharan Africa, 17% are in Southeast Asia, 10% live in the former Soviet Union and China and 18% are in the Arab world. (Incidentally, around 1.5 million Muslims reside in the UK and around 5 million live in the US. Muhammad entered the list of the 20 most popular names for newborn boys in the UK for the first time in 2004.)

The countries with the five largest Islamic populations are all in Asia. They are Indonesia (with about 213 million Muslims), Pakistan (158 million), India (145 million), Bangladesh (120 million) and then there's China. (The richest man in India, Azim Premji, the owner of Wipro, is an Indian Muslim.) No-one is quite sure how many Muslims there are in China but the ratio is usually put at 1–2%. If the true figure is 2% or 260 million, that would mean that China has the world's largest Muslim population.

The great bulk of Indonesia's 242 million plus population are Muslims. So too are about 60% or 14.4 million of Malaysia's 24 million population, most of Brunei's 372,000 population, around 4.6% or 3 million of Thailand's population (concentrated in the southern provinces), 15% or 660,000 of Singapore's population, 5% or 4.4 million of the Philippines' population (also concentrated in the south) and 4% or 1.7 million of Burma's population.

Islam might have started in the Middle East but no longer can it properly be considered a Middle Eastern religion. In fact, the principles of Islam and those of traditional Malay culture are very similar, so that the two are reinforcing. Jonathan Raban wrote in an essay published in Britain's *Guardian* newspaper:

> Muslims put an overwhelming stress on the idea of the individual as a social being. The self exists as the sum of its interactions with others. [Lawrence] Rosen puts it like this: "The configuration of one's bonds of obligation define who the person is ... the self is not an artifact of interior construction but an unavoidably public act." Broadly speaking, who you are is: who you know, who depends on you, and to whom you owe allegiance – a visible web of relationships that can be mapped out and enumerated.[2]

Substitute "Malays" for "Muslims" in this quotation and it still has applicability.

Women and Southeast Asian Islam

Women in largely Muslim Malaysia and Indonesia increasingly wear headscarves. Obviously, they cannot be anything but repressed. Or at least that is the general perception in the West. The fact that women play a role that is both full and prominent in Malaysia and Indonesia is little appreciated. But the position of women in these two countries is in some respects more advanced than in some Western countries. Just how much more was suggested by a Malaysian minister when I asked him if he thought that he should introduce affirmative action policies to favor women in his ministry. He couldn't see the point. Why? Already many of the senior officials in his ministry were women. In fact, it is very common to see women in senior management positions in both the Civil Service and the private sectors of both Malaysia and Indonesia.

Malaysia recently amended its Constitution to prohibit discrimination on the grounds of sex. Many laws still need to reflect this change but the symbolism is important. The Malaysian Government also has recently enacted laws in relation to domestic violence and the distribution of property to further benefit the position of women in society.

In the professional and managerial category in Malaysia's federal public sector, almost 43% of officers are women. Given that women do take time out to have babies and raise young children when men don't, such a high figure is extraordinary. Several women have also served as secretary-generals of ministries. And in higher education, the number of female students at higher learning institutions is more than 50% of total enrolment.

A woman was appointed as the head of Bank Negara, Malaysia's central bank in May 2000. Little fuss was made in Malaysia when the appointment of Zeti Akhtar Aziz was announced. And yet no woman has ever been appointed to head the central banks of, say, the US, the UK or Australia. One can imagine the media attention when one is.

Rafidah Aziz, another prominent Malaysian woman, has been the country's long-serving trade minister. Not for her the traditional "nurturing" ministerial portfolio of social affairs, health or education that women traditionally are given in the West, but a hard-edged economics portfolio.

Over in Indonesia – the world's largest Islamic country – women have served as ministers in the various cabinets for years and in 2001 Megawati Sukarnoputri became the country's first female president. Raden Ajeng Kartini, the Javanese woman who wrote about her plight as a noble woman in nineteenth-century Java, is remembered with an annual national public holiday, called Kartini Day. Kartini wanted emancipation and it is that for which she is celebrated.

A woman was made CEO of car assembler Astra International in 1998. Astra is one of Indonesia's largest listed companies. It was no sinecure. Rini Soewandi's first task was to fire 25,000 people. Ultimately, she was fired herself but that had nothing to do with her sex. The government-controlled restructuring agency IBRA demanded it after she blocked the sale of a controlling stake in Astra to US interests. Soewandi was later appointed as Indonesia's industry minister.

Labor force participation rates for women are still relatively low in Indonesia and Malaysia. In Malaysia, about 50% of prime age women participate in the paid workforce – compared with the OECD average that's in excess of 60%. Former Malaysian Finance Minister Daim Zainuddin mentioned to me that he views the low female participation rate as wasteful, particularly as he now considers that some of the best Malay entrepreneurs in the country are women because they are more prepared than their male counterparts to "get their hands dirty". In the past he has also called for more flexible terms of employment to attract more women into paid employment. This from a man who prays every day, has made the pilgrimage to Mecca on several occasions and has a small mosque in the grounds of his Kuala Lumpur house.

Islamic Banking

Islamic banking is a growth area in Asian finance. Usury is haram or forbidden under Islamic law. Islamic banking finds ways to bring lenders and borrowers together on a commercial basis without interest being explicitly charged. Malaysia and the Gulf state of Bahrain are the two leaders in Islamic banking. Bahrain is the larger, with almost 30 Islamic banks and several multilateral organizations based there, including the Accounting and Auditing Organization for Islamic Financial Institutions, which sets standards for Islamic accounting and transparency, and the International Islamic Financial Market, which seeks to bring about common standards for Islamic finance.

The Islamic Financial Services Board, however, is based in Kuala Lumpur. It seeks to coordinate regulatory and supervisory bodies worldwide to develop one set of guidelines for prudential practices in Islamic banking.

Global financial institutions such as HSBC, Citigroup and BNP Paribas have set up either Islamic divisions or separate banks that operate on Islamic principles. And within Asia, Malaysia's central bank, for example, has relaxed restrictions on allowing foreign Islamic banks to operate in Malaysia, and Singapore's Monetary Authority has allowed its banks to offer Islamic financial products. Ironically, Malaysian banks have found substantial demand for Islamic-based loans from the local Chinese community, largely because the loans offer more attractive terms for borrowers.

Ramadan

Muslims do not fast for the entire month of Ramadan but only during daylight hours, when they should not eat, drink or smoke. Some, who are particularly strict, even choose not to swallow their own saliva and instead spit it out.

Ramadan has a lot of significance for Southeast Asian Muslims, even if they are not regular mosque-goers. Many who are not still choose to fast. The fasting involves not eating, drinking, smoking or having sexual relations during daylight hours. Ill people, menstruating women and travelers are exempted from fasting for that period of the fasting month that they are affected, but time lost should be made up for later. The insane are excused altogether. The abstinence is to teach self-discipline and develop empathy with the poor.

It is a time of the year that requires considerable forbearance on the part of employers, as many staff are irritable, productivity is low and for the first few days at least it is not uncommon to see staff practically collapsed on their desks by mid to late afternoon. Headaches cannot be relieved by aspirin because that would mean eating.

There are several important business elements to Ramadan. The first is that, counterintuitively, food consumption rises dramatically in Malaysia, Indonesia and Brunei during the fasting month.

Beef imports rise substantially – much of it comes from Australia – and cold storage companies usually carry excess capacity throughout the year so they can cope with the huge rise in demand for cold storage space during Ramadan.

How is this so? Each night during the month, many Muslims break the fast together after sundown and do so in a festive atmosphere that involves consuming a great deal of food. People take it in turns to hold an open house at which large trays of pre-prepared food are offered to friends and relatives.

Also, many hotel buffets tend to double their prices during Ramadan. Demand is high. A practical consideration is that people breaking their fast tend to eat far greater quantities of food at the one sitting compared with usual. Ironically, the Holy Ramadan fasting month is actually more a food festival.

Extra permits are allocated in Kuala Lumpur for the fasting month for stallholders to sell food that they have prepared. This both helps meet the demand for extra food and allows the sellers to make extra cash for the post-Ramadan spending. Often types of food appear on the streets that simply aren't available at other times of the year. Night markets spring up for the month in places where normally there aren't any. And in Kuala Lumpur near to the Indian quarter, a spectacular, massive street market appears each evening. It comprises dozens of food stalls each selling regional Malay foods. It's one of the best places to obtain certain Kelantan or Kedah-style Malay dishes that otherwise are difficult to find in Kuala Lumpur.

With all the extra eating during the fasting month, food companies are quick to advertise their wares. Fast-food companies sponsor advertisements in newspapers that advise readers at what time in the evening they could break their fast according to their location. The time depends on when the sun sets (*Maghreb*) and that varies at each location and a little each subsequent day.

One of the more pernicious aspects of Ramadan in Indonesia is that requests for bribes made by government officials rise dramatically and the incidence and frequency of demands for bribes is explicitly linked to the need to get extra money to buy presents and food for the post-Ramadan celebrations. Expatriates find themselves an easy target during the month and are stopped more than usual by traffic policemen who allege minor traffic infringements (real or imaginary) so that they can then ask for a bribe. The closer the end of the fasting month, the more desperate (and intimidating) can become the demands for cash. Also Indonesian Chinese who operate shops often are visited by representatives from the local military and police commands and reminded that the post-Ramadan festivities are approaching and that their "generosity" would be appreciated.

Ramadan has been falling in the European winter in recent years. And so wealthier Southeast Asian Muslims have been known to fly to Europe for the fasting month. For much of winter, the sun rises in London at about 7.15am and sets at about 4.15pm. Anywhere near the equator, such as Singapore, Indonesia and Malaysia, and the sun rises at about 5.40am and sets at about 7pm. The practical outcome of this is that Southeast Asia's Muslims must fast for more than four hours longer each day than Muslims in London. A Muslim friend in London confirmed this to me. Ramadan "is a breeze" he said, but only while it falls in the northern hemisphere winter months.

Many senior business and political figures break their fast by holding an open house each evening. This means that influential people who might be inaccessible all year suddenly are easily accessed. It's quite possible, for example, to drop in on cabinet ministers at their private residences (providing they are Muslim) when at other times of the year it would be unthinkable to do so. So while Ramadan might mean a loss of productivity in Asia for the month, it also presents a month of excellent networking opportunities.

The Rise of Extremism

Extremist terrorist groups have been operating in Southeast Asia for some considerable time. The Pattani Liberation Front is one of the oldest. It's an insurgent group of Thai Muslims who seek the independence of the largely Malay-populated southern provinces of Thailand. It is believed to have links to Malaysian Malays who live along the Malaysian-Thai border. There's also the Moro Islamic Liberation Front which operates in the southern Philippines.

But the newer groups are more pernicious for they are linked to international terror networks and Osama bin Laden, someone who claims to be a Muslim but clearly isn't. So Jemaah Islamiyah, which has links to Osama's al Qaeda and operates across Southeast Asia, has become the new face of terror in Southeast Asia. It has brought in money from the Middle East and its members are professionally trained.

Some Southeast Asian governments are more flexible than others when it comes to whom they chose to consort with. In May 2002, Indonesia's then Vice President Hamzah Haz paid a personal call on Ja'far Umar Thalib, the head of the Indonesian terrorist organization Laskar Jihad, when Umar was arrested and held in jail in 2002. The pair chatted for one and a half hours. Haz called those who disapproved of his visit to Umar as "unIslamic".

Haz followed that up with a visit to the radical cleric Abu Bakar Ba'asyir, who Singapore, Malaysian and Philippines authorities believed was connected to Jemaah Islamiyah and who was later arrested. Haz, who headed Indonesia's main Islamic party, claimed at the time that there were no terrorists in Indonesia.[3] And then in October 2002, several massive bombs exploded in Kuta on Bali, killing 202 people. There were more attacks in Jakarta, including a large bomb that exploded outside the Australian embassy in September 2004 and another in August 2002 at the JW Marriott Hotel – which mostly killed local Silver Bird taxi drivers who queued near to the hotel's lobby awaiting customers. In 2005, there were more bomb attacks on Bali. Several tourists were killed but most of the victims were locals, including Muslims.

Two Malaysians residing in Indonesia were believed to be the masterminds behind the attacks. One, Azahari Husin, an engineering graduate from Australia's Adelaide University, was killed by Indonesian police when they raided an explosives-filled house in central Java in November 2005. Fellow students from his Adelaide University days remember Azahari Husin as fun-loving and friendly and driving an Audi sports car. He liked Australia and Australians but somehow over the intervening period he changed, to the extent that his 1992 Kuta bombing claimed almost 100 Australians among those killed; the bars chosen seemingly for their popularity with young Australian holidaymakers.

Married with children, Azahari had also gone on to to complete a doctorate in the UK, with a thesis entitled "The construction of regression-

based mass appraisal models: a methodological discussion and an application to housing submarkets in Malaysia".[4] What turns someone like this
who has had, and taken, so many opportunities into a mass murderer
remains a mystery.

At the 1999 election, Malaysia's opposition Islamic PAS party (Parti
Islam se-Malaysia) won control of the state governments of Kelantan
and Terengganu. Previously, it controlled only Kelantan. Its leader also
became, for the first time, the official opposition leader in the federal
Parliament, a position held in recent years by the leader of the Chinese-
based Democratic Action Party. The two PAS state governments would
be more extreme if it were not for them being overridden by the federal
government. Abdul Hadi Awang, who became the PAS chief minister of
Terengganu, for example, twice sought to introduce bills into Parliament
that would allow for the execution of Muslims who converted to another
religion. PAS, in both Kelantan and Terengganu, indicated its desire to
introduce the harsh *hadud* punishments (hand amputations for thieves
and so forth) but the federal government again has blocked this. Then in
the national elections of 2004, PAS lost enormous ground as Malays
flocked back to support the ruling UMNO party, with its new leader
Abdullah Badawi. PAS won just 15.2% of the national vote and lost 20
of its 27 parliamentary seats. Abdul Hadi Awang, who served as federal
opposition leader after the original PAS leader had died, even lost his
federal seat. At the state level, PAS lost control of the Terengganu state
government and only narrowly retained power in Kelantan.

Under PAS, both Kelantan and Terengganu treated Friday as the start
of the weekend and Sunday as the first day of the working week. Anecdotally, local Chinese in these states said that they were little troubled by the
Islamic preferences of the state governments. PAS is more interested in
regulating the lifestyles of Muslims than it is in imposing its values on
non-Muslims. Both states had also introduced laws that were particularly
constraining on local Muslim women, laws that are more intrinsic to the
Middle East than they are to Southeast Asian Islam. Nik Aziz, the PAS
chief minister of Kelantan, reportedly went so far as to describe women as
the main cause of "social ills and moral decadence".[5]

In 2001, the Malaysian Government detained Nik Adli, the 34-year-old
son of Nik Aziz, under the Internal Security Act. Allegedly, he was a
leader of the Kumpulan Militan Mujahideen (KMM), a local chapter of the
extremist group, the Militant Holy Warriors. The group was accused of
plotting to overthrow Mahathir's government, planning assassinations and
sending fighters to Indonesia's ethnically riven Maluku Islands. To cap it
all, Nik Aziz confirmed that his son had indeed been to Afghanistan on

several occasions where group members were alleged to have received training. He also confirmed that his son had actually fought alongside the Mujahideen in the civil war in Afghanistan.[6]

For a time, Thailand's Prime Minister Thaksin Shinawatra appointed a Muslim to be his interior minister. The appointment of Wan Muhamad Nor Matha, a Thai Muslim from the country's southern Yala province, coincided with the government getting tough on the more salacious side of Thai society. Raids were conducted on brothels and nightclubs, there was the so-called "war" on drugs described in Chapter 7 and women were told not to wear tight-fitting or skimpy tank tops during Thailand's water festival season. I was actually a witness to one drug-related raid on a bar in Bangkok in 2003. Close to closing time, about a dozen uniformed police arrived and prevented the patrons from leaving. All Thai nationals were presented with a paper cup and told to form two lines, one for the men for the men's toilet and one for the women for the women's toilet. They were required to provide a urine sample, which a policemen who was seated at a temporary table that had been placed on the dance floor then tested by dropping in blotting paper via his latex gloved hands. It was one of many such raids that were conducted in Bangkok at this time.

Wan Muhamad Nor Matha was Thailand's first Muslim interior minister and one of the few Muslims to have served in the Thai cabinet. Thaksin believed that his inclusion would help his Thai Rak Thai Party in the south to attract Muslim votes. The party had won just one seat in the southern provinces which traditionally have been a Democrat Party stronghold. But Thai Muslims are not necessarily a cohesive group. In February 2003, for example, Maha Marom Muri Kora, the deputy chairman of the southern Yala province's Islamic Committee, and a close aid to the interior minister, was shot and seriously wounded in a car park.[7] And then in January 2004, serious trouble flared up in the south. Islamic rebels set fire to 17 schools, three police posts and raided a military camp, killing four soldiers and making off with as many as 360 M-16s and other weapons. The defense minister declared martial law in the three southern provinces of Pattani, Narathiwat and Yala, each of which has a majority Muslim population.

Since then the trouble has barely abated. A few days later two bombs exploded in Pattani, one at a police box in a park and another in a shopping mall. Then in April 2004, organized uprisings were staged across the three provinces, which erupted in bloody street battles in which more than 100 militants and 5 police officers and soldiers were killed.

In October that year, the security forces arrested 1,300 protestors outside a police station in Narathiwat province. Many or most were packed onto police trucks for six hours in the heat and were packed so densely that 78 suffocated to death. Another 6 people were shot and killed. The deaths were condemned worldwide and did little to build trust between the central government and the local people.

The illegal Pattani Liberation Organization, practically dormant for years, has been revived. Its aim is to see an independent Islamic state comprising Yala, Pattani and Narathiwat provinces. There is some logic to its aim. The three southern provinces did once form the Islamic Sultanate of Pattani. In the early twentieth century, the British planned to remove Pattani from Thai sovereignty and hand it to the colonial administration in Malaya, as they did with what became the Malaysian states of Kedah, Kelantan, Terengganu and Perlis. A similar plan was hatched during the Second World War as a punishment for Thailand for its pro-Japan wartime posture but it was not carried out.[8]

Certainly, the southern Thai Muslims culturally are closely allied with the Malays of northern Malaysia. The food, dialects and artwork of the two are similar. And today, it is common to find southern Thai Muslims working in Kuala Lumpur, probably illegally, in Malay food courts and hawker centers. They have greater acceptance among the Malays than the many Indonesian workers similarly employed.

Interestingly, the problems, whilst having an Islamic dynamic, do appear to be unrelated to Islamic extremist groups that operate elsewhere in Southeast Asia, such as Jemaah Islamiyah. Anecdotal suggestions are that the Thai Muslims have spurned approaches by outside Muslim extremist groups for assistance and even any sort of significant linkage.

Islamic Consumer Boycotts in Asia

The Iraq War of 2003 was the first occasion on which significant Muslim consumer boycotts of US products and brand names were initiated in Southeast Asia. There was some targeting of obvious US brand names in Asia by protesters. McDonald's fast-food restaurants in Indonesia were the scenes of anti-war and anti-US protests. Members of Indonesia's small Islamic Youth Movement approached the main McDonald's in central Jakarta to look for Americans to force into signing promises that they would leave Indonesia. The protesters were arrested before entering the restaurant. The group then announced that Americans had two days to leave Indonesia or be forced out. The irony was that the McDonald's franchise holder for Indonesia is a local Muslim, Bambang Rachmadi, a son-in-law of former Indonesian Vice President Soedharmono.

Muslims in Thailand's five most southern provinces called for a boycott of US brands of goods and services. A list was drawn up of 100 US and British brands and products and distributed in the form of leaflets at an anti-war rally of more than 20,000 local Muslims in the southern seaside town of Songkla. Among the companies and brands on the list were Coca-Cola, Procter & Gamble (Olay, Vicks, Pringles), Colgate-Palmolive (Fab, Colgate, Palmolive), Unilever (Rexona, Pond's, Omo) and Johnson & Johnson (Johnson talcum powders, Carefree). Fast-food chains listed to be boycotted included KFC, McDonald's, Pizza Hut, Starbucks and Burger King.

Nestlé was also on the list, despite it being Swiss-based. Nestlé executives in Bangkok responded by sending teams to the south to explain to consumers that Nestlé was not in fact American.

The rally was staged at a local sports stadium with the cooperation of the provincial government. Hat Thip Co Ltd, the Thai distributor of Coca-Cola, was asked to remove its booth from the stadium for safety reasons.

I was in Songkla at the time and apart from the rally, there was little obvious protest activity visible in the streets of Songkla or nearby Hat Yai. Not so in nearby Malaysia, where the government had endorsed the local anti-war movement, so blue and white banners declaring "Malaysians for Peace" hung all over Kuala Lumpur, including in the lobbies of some major hotels.

Zam Zam Cola, the Islamic-owned competitor to Coca-Cola that is produced in Iran, has made an appearance in Malaysia. It's aimed at Muslim consumers and its appeal is simply that it is not Coke. It had become popular in some parts of the Middle East, its consumption being tantamount to a political statement. After six months of going on sale in Malaysia in 2003, its local distributor, a company called Al-Fajr (M) Sdn Bhd, reported that it had sold almost 500,000 bottles in Malaysia. The company was considering setting up a local bottling plant. Mostly, Zam Zam was sold through Indian Muslim (*mamak*) food stalls.[9] Mecca Cola, a Zam Zam imitator, was a sponsor of the expo that accompanied the Organization of the Islamic Conference meeting held in Kuala Lumpur in October 2003.

Another risk to companies, particularly food companies, is the spreading of malicious rumors that halal food is in fact not halal. This is not infrequent, in Indonesia particularly, but also in Malaysia. Such rumors may be spread by competitors or those with a grudge against the targeted companies. They spread now at astonishing speed via mobile phone text messages and chain emails that can lead to almost instantaneous consumer boycotts. Such instances can be particularly costly to companies, because of the speed with which they can eventuate, the decentralized nature of the passing on of the misinformation and the difficulty in locating the source of such rumors. Gardenia Bakeries, a major manufacturer and distributor of bread and bread-like products, faced such a campaign in mid-2004. Messages were spread across Malaysia via SMS texts and poison-pen letters that Gardenia products contained non-halal products. The company had to respond with prominent and costly media advertisements, in which it explained that it had been manufacturing bread and similar products in Malaysia for almost 20 years, that the rumors of non-halal ingredients were "blatant and malicious lies designed to injure and undermine Gardenia" and that it had allowed its factories to be inspected by representatives from the Muslim Consumers Association of Malaysia.[10]

Rising Islamic consciousness in Southeast Asia not only has a political dimension but also a business one. It is a trend for the future, something of which business planners and investors need to take account.

Chapter 19

WHERE DO ASIA'S MUSLIMS FIT IN?

Islam is an important East Asian religion, so it is essential for those who wish to become Asian Insiders to be aware of at least its basic precepts. It's also important to know where in the Islamic world Asia's Muslims fit.

The level of ignorance about Islam is enormous and surprising, given that it has been with us for around 1,300 years. But the ignorance is not only confined to the West. The level of ignorance about Islam among non-Muslims in Singapore, Malaysia and Indonesia, for example, is as deep as it is self-defeating. The lack of a central religious authority in Islam contributes to this problem. With no clear leader and thus no obvious point of reference, non-Muslims find it difficult to distinguish between what is extreme and what is mainstream.

How does one become a Muslim? One merely needs to say (and presumably believe) that "There is no god but God, and Muhammad is the Messenger of God." Being a *good* Muslim is more onerous. One must adhere to the five "Pillars" of Islam: the Oneness of Allah, the importance of prayer, payment of *zakah* (tithes), the fast of Ramadan and the pilgrimage to Mecca (Makkah).

Despite all the noise that would appear to suggest the contrary, Islam, Christianity and Judaism have similar origins. The principal figure of each is descended from Abraham – Muhammad from Abraham's eldest son Ishmael and Moses and Jesus from Isaac. Muslims hold that Abraham founded the city of Mecca. Jesus and Moses are revered by Muslims, even by extremists and fundamentalists.

Some Muslims believe that Judas was crucified in Jesus' place. Others believe it was Simon of Cyrene. Nonetheless, Jesus was raised to Heaven.

The Koran also allows for the Second Coming of Jesus. And as mentioned, it teaches adherents to respect the rights of followers of other faiths. "There is no compulsion in religion" (surah 2. 256) says the Koran. Islam would prefer non-Muslims to convert but it does not compel them. Instead, they must be led to the faith by God. And so it is not a proselytizing religion, unlike Christianity. The life and property of all citizens and residents in an Islamic state is to be considered sacred, whether a person is a Muslim or not. Orthodox Christian minorities in Syria and Coptic Christians in Egypt experience little overt state-sponsored discrimination, for example. (Boutros Boutros-Ghali, the former secretary general of the United Nations, is an Egyptian Coptic Christian.) This means that Islam is far more tolerant of competing religions than Christianity. Clearly, though, a lot is done in the name of Islam that is not especially Islamic. But that is true of most religions. The problem for Islam is that it has become entwined in Middle East political issues, thus distorting the outsider's view of what Islam is and what it is not. The Prophet Muhammad had 11 wives in his lifetime. His tenth wife Safiyya was Jewish. In the face of teasing by two of his other wives, he told her that she should be proud of her origins. After all, they are the same as those of Muslims.[1]

That Islam, Christianity and Judaism are three trees from the same root stock is apparent from the main figures. The Jesus of the Christians is the Isa of the Muslims. Nuh, Yusuf, Yunus, Yahya, Ayub, Musa and Sulaiman are among the prophets of the Koran. Noah, Joseph, Jonah, John the Baptist, Job, Moses and Solomon are the names they're given in the Bible. The Koran has Isa (Jesus) born of a virgin.

> [I have come to you] to attest the Law which was before me [the Law of Musa/Moses] and to make lawful to you part of what was forbidden to you; I have come to you with a sign from your Lord. So fear Allah and obey me. It is Allah who is my Lord and your Lord; then worship Him.

says Isa (surah 3. 50–1). Christians believe that Jesus was the end of the line. Muslims believe that there was one more: Muhammad. The Jews are still waiting. However, Muhammad has only ever been regarded as a prophet. Jesus has a position far more exalted than that among Christians.

Oddly, the Muslim world has become synonymous with economic backwardness and a suspicion of technical innovation. But this is a comparatively new phenomenon. Arguably, the greatest contribution from the Islamic world is the number zero. It simply hadn't existed in the Western world. One does not, after all, go the market and buy zero eggs or cabbages. As the author Peter Bernstein writes in *Against the Gods*:

Zero revolutionized the old number system [of Roman numerals] in two ways. First it meant that people could use only ten digits, from zero to nine, to perform every conceivable calculation and to write any conceivable number. Second it meant that a sequence of numbers like 1,10,100 would indicate that the next number in the sequence would be 1000.[2]

This wasn't possible or obvious with a number sequence that went something like I, X, C and so on, as was the case with Roman numerals. Slowly, the new numbering system was adopted in Europe between 1000AD and the 1500s. The new numbering system with zero as its centerpiece brought with it the possibility of doing algebra. And with that came the possibility of quantifying risk, according to Bernstein, which gave birth to the insurance industry. The possibility of insuring against risk reduced the cost of international trade (one could insure cargo, for example, against loss at sea) and therefore promoted it. Mass international trade suddenly became possible and the world changed forever. No zero would have meant no mass trade. We have the Arabs to thank for globalization, or at least their ancestors. But what would they make of their descendants?

The prowess of the Islamic world reached a zenith between the sixteenth and seventeenth centuries. The Ottoman Empire conquered much of Eastern Europe and was on the verge of conquering Austria in 1529. The Ottoman army had laid siege to Vienna. Its attempt to mine the city at night was stopped only when the city's early rising bakers heard the noise and alerted the city's army. Vienna was saved and the bakers created a pastry in the shape of an Islamic crescent to mark their efforts. Marie Antoinette, an Austrian princess who married the future king of France, took the pastry with her to Paris, where it survives today in the form of the famous French croissant (*croissant* being French for "crescent"). Few in France today are aware of the Islamic associations of what is one of their country's most famous breads.

Factions

The vast majority of Muslims in Southeast Asia are Sunni Muslims. But the majority of the Hadramis (a small Arab group who are discussed in the next chapter) who came to Southeast Asia are Zaydis, a Shiite subgroup. Where these two groups fit in the Islamic world is described below.

Islam is viewed by most non-Muslims as a monolith. The reality is that Islam probably is more fractured and factionalized than Christianity. The oldest and largest Islamic grouping are the Sunni Muslims who account for about 90% of all Muslims. But the Sunnis are divided between various schools. In addition, independent sects such as the Wahhabis (dominant in Saudi Arabia), the Mutazilites, the Qadiyanis and the Kharjis (dominant in Oman) are also under the Sunni umbrella.

Differing interpretations of the Koran are one reason for the factionalism. So it seems that the Koran, with its "simple" truths, is not so simple after all. The Wahhabis, for example, insist that the penalty for adultery is stoning, but the Koran prescribes no such thing. Instead, it recommends flogging. Nowhere in the Koran is it ordained that women must cover their faces. It does insist that their breasts be covered, though.[3] Osama bin Laden, his entire extended family and his close followers are Wahhabi. It is this sect that has sought to expand and proselytize within the worldwide *ummah*, or Islamic community. And so Wahhabism is being transplanted to Muslim communities across Southeast Asia via radical clerics subsidized with oil money from Saudi Arabia.[4]

Yet Muslims insist that the Koran is inimitable; it is absolute and invariable. Strictly, this means that the Koran cannot be translated as such, for its Arabic form is the only and perfect form. Thus English and French "translations" are only versions of its meaning.[5] This is why even across Southeast Asia, strict Muslims insist on learning Arabic so that they can read the Koran in its unadulterated, "pure" form. To settle for a translation means compromising and accepting the translator's judgment as to the meaning of words and the imprecisions of converting words from one language to another.

But the biggest split came when the Shiites split from the Sunnis over a dispute as to the proper successor to the Prophet Muhammad. The Shiite position is that there can only be one true teacher in the world at any one time – one true Imam. The Sunnis believe that there can be many teachers, each offering various doctrinal opinions.

The Shiites themselves split. There are the Nusayris. The Asad ruling family in Syria subscribes to the doctrine, although only about 11% of other Syrians do. Then there are the Zaydis (most prominent in Yemen) and the Ismailis. The latter disagreed with the rest as to the identity of the Seventh Imam, hence they're also known as the Seveners. But the Ismailis also soon split apart into two factions: the Qarmatis (now largely extinct) and the Fatimids.

The Fatimids then split into at least three subgroups – the Mustalis (those who settled in India are known as the Bohras today), the Druze (Lebanon is their stronghold) and the Nizaris, who were known as the Assassins in the Middle Ages. The latter group is divided into the Qasim-Shahis and the Muhammad-Shahis. To further complicate matters, the term "Nizari" has become synonymous with "Ismaili", although, strictly, the Nizaris are a subset of the Ismailis.

The Qasim-Shahis branch of the Nizaris is the biggest group of Ismailis in the world today. There are maybe 20 million of them. The Aga Khan is their leader. He lives outside Paris and is probably one of the wealthiest men in the world. There is even an Ismaili flag which is used when the Aga Khan visits friendly countries. Earlier Aga Khans were based in Iran, then India. Nizari-Ismailis are exhorted to save and pay a monthly tithe from their savings. The tithes are paid to the Aga Khan and, although the tithes historically have been used for charitable works in the Nizari-Ismaili community, the sums collected were regarded as the personal property of the Aga Khan.

The various Aga Khans' private fortunes have made them independent of the tithes of their followers so that the tithes can be distributed as charity. The Aga Khan and his charitable foundations claim to give around US$100 million away each year to development projects in the least developed countries. The Institute of Ismaili Studies serves as the Aga Khan's London headquarters. It is opposite the main entrance of the Victoria and Albert Museum and has an interior that is both lavish and well maintained.

Many of the Nizaris in the world are Muslims from India and Pakistan. They are known as the Khojas. Many Khojas left India for East Africa in the nineteenth century. Tens of thousands were expelled from East Africa in the 1970s. They didn't head back to India. Instead they made their way to the West, mostly to the UK, Canada and the US.

There are thousands of Nizaris in London and across the rest of the UK. Many run off-licenses. There is at least one in the House of Lords. Lord Amirali Alibhai Bhatia is an Ismaili Muslim originally from Tanzania. The Jumabhoy family in Singapore who founded the Ascott serviced apartment chain (but then lost it through family infighting) are descended from Ismaili Khojas.

Most Muslims in Asia are indigenous. However, those who were involved in international trade early on were from the Middle East. They are the subject of the next chapter.

Chapter 20

SOUTHEAST ASIA'S ARABS

Arab traders have long operated in Southeast Asia. They traded in spices, timber and textiles. So an important trading minority in Southeast Asia that goes largely unrecognized comprises the local descendants of Arabs. But this minority is more specific than simply coming under the rubric of "Arab". Most of the prominent Indonesians, Malaysians and Singaporeans of Arab descent have their origins in southern Yemen in the Hadramawt coastal region. They are the Hadramis.

As many as four million Indonesians are of Hadrami descent. Today there are almost 10,000 Hadramis in Singapore. The Alkaff, Alsagoff and Aljunied families who settled in Singapore in the nineteenth century and managed to tie up most of the land in what is now Singapore's central business district and a lot more too were Hadramis.

Several prominent Southeast Asian politicians are also Hadramis. Among them are Ali Alatas who served as Indonesia's foreign minister under President Soeharto, Alwi Shihab who was foreign minister under President Abdurrahman Wahid and Syed Hamid Albar who was appointed Malaysia's foreign minister in early 1999.[1] His father was a founding member of UMNO. Zeti Akhtar Aziz, who was appointed the governor of Malaysia's central bank, Bank Negara, in 2000, is half-Hadrami. Her mother was an Alsagoff.

Quraish Shihab, Alwi Shihab's older brother, served as the Soeharto family chaplain and was appointed by Soeharto as religious affairs minister in March 1998 in the dying months of his presidency.

Another Hadrami is Mari Alkitiri, prime minister of East Timor. East Timor is a predominantly Catholic country. Alkitiri's brother is the leader of Dili's Islamic community and Alkitiri himself is a practicing Muslim.

There's another prominent Hadrami family that has attained worldwide fame on account of the activities of one of its members: the bin Laden family. Osama bin Laden's father was a Hadrami who emigrated to Saudi Arabia from Yemen in the 1920s.

Unwittingly, Yemen has played a significant role in international terrorism. Fifteen of the 19 hijackers responsible for the September 11, 2001 terrorist attacks on the US are believed to have been from Saudi Arabia, while six were from Saudi Arabia's Assir province, which borders Yemen. Assir was under the control of Yemen until its incorporation into Saudi Arabia, and Yemen only relinquished its claim on the province in 1934. Several of the tribes in the province still refuse to accept their incorporation into Saudi Arabia.

Even Osama bin Laden's driver, Salim Ahmed Hamdan, who was captured by US forces in Afghanistan, is a Yemeni.[2]

In November 2002, CIA operatives fired at a car travelling in northern Yemen, killing all six occupants. All were believed to be operatives in bin Laden's al Qaeda network. One was Qaed Salim Sinan al-Harethi, al Qaeda's chief operative in Yemen and a suspect in the October 2000 bombing of the destroyer USS *Cole* that killed 17 American sailors.

And then there are the Islamic extremists in Indonesia who have caused that country and the region so much grief. There is Abu Bakar Ba'asyir, the head of Jemaah Islamiyah which was founded by another Hadrami, the late Abdullah Sangkar, Ja'far Umar Thalib, the head of Laskar Jihad, and Habib Husein Habsy, the head of the Indonesian Muslim Brotherhood. These men are not drawn from the general Muslim population. Each one is a Hadrami and so descended not from Indonesia but from southern Yemen.[3] And each one has made it his business to rally Indonesians not so much in support of Indonesia but in support of his own version of Islam.

Once again, the importance of family and clan networks is demonstrated. International terrorism is like international trade – it works best when it can be organized among people who trust one another deeply and yet who are spatially dispersed and so can operate across borders. It's why the international diamond trade is now largely in the hands of the Jains of India, the international rice trade remains largely in the hands of Teochiu Chinese and the international heroin and opium trade, for that matter. So international terrorism, as per al Qaeda now, is not in the hands of Muslims, Arabs or even Yemenis – but renegade Hadramis. Others have come on board but the central nervous system is Hadrami, from the top and stretching to Southeast Asia.

Some History

Arabs have had a close connection with India for over a thousand years. Persian trading communities were established in India by the eighth century. And from the thirteenth century, Muslim rulers ruled in India for the next 600 years. The Mughal Empire that ruled in India from 1526 to 1761 used Persian as its official language.

Arabs and Southeast Asia have connections that go back hundreds of years. Arab traders had settled in the Indonesian archipelago by the seventh century. It was through them that Islam arrived at the archipelago.

Sir Stamford Raffles wanted to build a settlement based on trade. So when he founded Singapore in 1819, he earmarked a considerable part of the new settlement as the Arab district. Slowly, they trickled in. But not directly from the Middle East. Mostly, they came from the Indonesian archipelago where they had settled first to trade in spice. First to arrive were Syed Mohammed bin Harun Aljunied and his nephew. Hadramis, they came from what had been their base, Palembang in Sumatra.

Syed Abdul Rahman Alsagoff was another early arrival. He came with his son Syed Ahmad to Singapore in 1824 from Indonesia. He was active in the spice trade between Malacca, Singapore, Java and other Indonesian islands. They established Alsagoff and Company in Singapore in 1848 to trade in spice, sago, rubber and cocoa. A subsidiary company owned the Perseverance Estate in what is now Geylang, Singapore. It was a lemon grass plantation. They also set up the Straits Cycle and Motor Company. And they owned many ships as befitting their huge export-import business.

Syed Ahmad married into the Sultan of Gowa's family. (Gowa was a small sultanate in southern Sulawesi (the Celebes) in what is now Indonesia.) Their eldest son Syed Muhamad inherited all the family's businesses in 1875. He acquired land in Johor on which he established rubber, sago, pepper and cocoa plantations.

The best-known *keramat* or Islamic holy place in Singapore is the tomb at Tanjong Pagar of Habib Noh bin Mohammed al-Hahshi who died in 1866. Habib Noh supposedly had supernatural powers. Syed Muhamad paid for the construction of a shrine over the grave and today the site is still maintained by members of the Alsagoff family.[4]

One of the largest mansions still standing in Singapore is the Alkaff Mansion at Telok Blangah Green. Until recently, it served as a restaurant and function center. The Alkaff family arrived in Singapore in 1852 from Indonesia and traded in coffee and sugar. In Singapore they branched into property development. Originally the family was from South Yemen. Syed Abdul Rahman Alkaff was the head of the family. He owned the Hotel de

L'Europe, which was the Raffles Hotel's main rival in its day. Later the family sold it, possibly because they were no longer comfortable owning premises from which alcohol was served.[5] Ironically, the Raffles Hotel was built on land owned by Syed Muhamad Alsagoff. Raffles was built by the Sarkies brothers: Martin, Tigran, Aviet and Arshak. They were Armenians from Julfa in Turkey.[6] At least one surviving member of the family still resides in Singapore. Impoverished and a maverick, other than for a maid, she lives alone with around 3,000 porcelain Chinese figurines, her uncles having suicided after losing the family fortune. (Famously they also built the E&O Hotel in Penang and the Strand Hotel in Rangoon.) But, essentially, nearly all Singapore's rich Hadrami families bought land. Lots of it.

The Alsagoffs, the Aljunieds and the Alkaffs controlled the Mecca pilgrimage traffic and much of the inter-archipelago sailing ship trade by the turn of the twentieth century. They were all active in endowing mosques, schools and hospitals. It was in the inter-war years that the Arab community in Singapore reached the zenith of its wealth. The community also controlled Singapore's Malay-language press in the 1930s. The Alsagoff family founded *Warta Melayu* in 1930. It also founded Arabic language and culture schools, where Arabic children could learn Arabic and how to pray. The Alsagoff Arab School still functions in Singapore.[7]

Much of the Arabs' land holdings were transferred into *wakafs*, charitable trusts. And, ultimately, via these *wakafs,* Arab families owned almost all the land that is in Singapore's central business district today.

The commercial power of Singapore's Arab community was curtailed by the Rent Control Act 1947. The Arab community had put most of its eggs in the property basket and so the effect of the Act fell disproportionately on them. Then came the Land Acquisition Act which saw a lot of the land held by the *wakafs* compulsorily acquired by the government in the 1970s and 80s, with little compensation. Some land still remains in these old trusts. A large part of the land along Purvis Street remains in the Talib family trust, established by Salim Talib, a Hadrami businessman, in the nineteenth century.[8]

Also, Singapore's Hadramis had long maintained close connections to Yemen and male members typically were sent back to acquaint themselves with their roots and polish their Arabic. But all that changed in the late 1960s as the regime in South Yemen grew more Marxist.[9]

About 90 *wakafs* remain in existence in Singapore. The government-linked Islamic Religious Council of Singapore administers 53 of them. Syed Haroon Aljunied, another Hadrami, serves as its secretary.

Much of the property owned by the *wakafs* today comprises three- or four-storey shop houses. Many are dilapidated or ready for development, their upkeep having been hampered by decades of rent controls that were lifted only in 2001.

Alkaff, Alsagoff and Aljunied are common family names among Singapore's Islamic community today. Faisal Alsagoff is the president of Horizon Education and Technologies, a company listed on the Singapore Stock Exchange, for example. Such surnames suggest a Hadrami ancestry.

Syed Mokhtar Albukhary is perhaps the most prominent Malaysian businessman with Middle Eastern roots. As mentioned in Chapter 17, he considers himself partly of Hadrami descent, although his immediate forebears came to Malaysia from northern Pakistan.

Other Middle Easterners

Several prominent Indonesian businesspeople have Arab roots. The Bakrie family which heads up the Bakrie Group is one. They champion *pribumi* (indigenous) concerns and they are seen as *pribumi* by virtue of their adherence to Islam, but essentially the Bakries are a migrant Arab trading family. So too are Fadel Mohammad and his family. He controls the Bukaka and Gema Groups.

Thailand has long attracted Middle Eastern traders, but not Hadramis so much as Persians. It is believed that a Persian trading community was established in Siam as early as the sixteenth century. There are Persian loan words in the Thai language today that reflect these old trading ties. The Thai word for rose is pronounced as *dork kulaap*. *Golaab* is the Persian word for rose water, for example. The Thai word for grape is pronounced *angun*. In Persian it's *anguur*.[10] The Persian traders won favor with the then king of Siam and so several became high officials at the court. Descendants of some of these early traders still enjoy close proximity to the court, some three hundred years later. They have surnames such as Bunnag, Siphen and Singhaseni, which betray their Persian origins. Such ethnic links to the Middle East and West Asia are there to be utilized. One country has been very active in pursuing such links to serve its commercial interests. That country is Malaysia.

Chapter 21

PAX ISLAMICA: MALAYSIA AND THE MIDDLE EAST

All countries want a sphere of influence. Malaysia has chosen not to be particularly influential in Southeast Asia. Instead, its horizons are wider, much wider. A hint as to where its ambitions lie was suggested by a three-day visit to Malaysia by the then President Mohammed Khatami of Iran in July 2002. He arrived with a 91-member delegation that included five ministers and deputy ministers. Malaysia pulled out all the stops. Why? Because Iran and Malaysia are close trading partners? No, they're not. Because they're big investors in each other's economy? No, not that either. There's another reason that is evident from all the fuss that was made.

On one of the three days, I was near the Mandarin Oriental Hotel next to the Petronas Twin Towers as Khatami was leaving the hotel. He was on his way to call on then Prime Minister Mahathir at his office. The scene was extraordinary. A police helicopter buzzed low overhead and flew between and around the Twin Towers. Dozens of police on motorcycles were everywhere. And traffic all around the area was stopped. Khatami appeared at the front of the hotel and climbed into his car. It and an enormous cavalcade of black limousines and security vehicles, some with bizarre dish-like antennae on their rears, then snaked their way out onto the streets of Kuala Lumpur. The cavalcade was accompanied by the biggest formation of motorcycle police outriders that I've seen. The helicopter followed overhead. It was better than James Bond. And it would have been impressive too, if it was all necessary. Around the same time, the US was briefing the Western media that it no longer considered Khatami to be sufficiently powerful in his own country to be worth dealing with. The news hadn't reached Malaysia. But then the real point of such an extravagant display was that Khatami was a visiting leader from the Muslim world. And in Malaysia that counts for a lot.

Cultivating Islamic Governments

In global terms, Malaysia is a small country on the periphery of the world economy. It's a problem faced by other small countries that want to have more influence on the world stage than suggested by their populations or economies. Countries like Australia and Norway are also in this category. What can such countries do? They can attempt to develop their own sphere of influence in which to be a significant player. Accordingly, Malaysia has sought to be influential in the Islamic world.

So Malaysia has sought to develop close bilateral ties with other Islamic countries. Visiting heads of government of Islamic countries are given huge welcomes. And Malaysia has sought a prominent role in multilateral forums such as the 57-member Organization of the Islamic Conference (OIC) and the Non-Aligned Movement (NAM). Malaysia hosted a NAM meeting in 2002 and for that it spent large sums on beautifying Kuala Lumpur. And it hosted an OIC meeting in late 2003. Once again, no expense was spared. Scarcely a lamp-post in Kuala Lumpur was left without a yellow banner that heralded the meeting that was held in the futuristic convention center at the government's new administrative center, Putrajaya, outside Kuala Lumpur. And in mid-2005, Malaysia hosted the thirtieth annual meeting of the Islamic Development Bank, the financial arm of the OIC.

Malaysia is a founder member of the OIC. Its headquarters are in Jeddah but it was actually established at the Conference of Islamic Nations held in Kuala Lumpur in 1969. Malaysia's first Prime Minister Tunku Abdul Rahman was its first secretary-general. The idea behind the OIC was that it should be modeled on the British Commonwealth or the United Nations and would foster closer ties among Islamic countries.

While it is true that the OIC's members are among the world's poorest countries and Muslims account for perhaps 15% of the world's population, Malaysia argues that OIC members control approximately 60% of the world's natural resources. They also point to 10 of OPEC's 11 members also being OIC members.[1] Other not insignificant oil producers such as Malaysia and Brunei are OIC members but do not belong to OPEC. Malaysia has also sought to become a world leader in Islamic banking (on this see Chapter 18.)

Malaysia has also sought to develop a leadership role in exploring the intellectual aspects of international Islamic cooperation. It hosts many conferences and meetings on this theme. Syed Mokhtar Albukhary's Islamic Arts Center hosted the Fourth International Islamic Political Economy Conference in November 2000, for example. "Asia–Europe Muslim Partnership" was the theme of the conference. The Albukhary Foundation was a sponsor, as was the Da'wa Foundation of Scotland. (Da'wa means to preach or undertake missionary work in Arabic.)

Abdalhamid Evans from the Da'wa Foundation was on the organizing committee. Shaykh Abdalqadir as-Sufi al-Murabit, who is the director of the European Islamic Center that's also based in Scotland, was co-patron. The European Islamic Center was sponsored by former Finance Minister Daim Zainuddin. He bought a Scottish castle to serve as its premises. Acts like this serve to highlight the theme of international Islamic cooperation that the Malaysian Government is keen to promote.

The Palestinian issue is a unifying issue for most of the world's Islamic countries, including Malaysia. Malaysia does not recognize Israel. That means that Israeli citizens are unable to enter Malaysia unless they do so using some other country's passport. Nor can Malaysians visit Israel using a Malaysian passport. Each Malaysian passport states very clearly that it is not to be used for travel to Israel. I asked Daim Zainuddin when Malaysia would recognize Israel. "When they [the Israelis] treat the Palestinians better", was his reply. "And how will you judge that?" I asked. "The Palestinians will tell us when", he said.

Arab Tourists

The real value of Malaysia's attempts to cultivate the international Islamic community became apparent after the attack on New York's World Trade Center in September 2001. Middle Eastern tourists found that their visa applications for travel to the US or Europe were held up or refused altogether. Many turned to Malaysia.

The number of visitors to Malaysia from Arab countries more than doubled in 2002 from a year earlier, to 115,000. By 2005, the figure had doubled again to around 200,000.

Accordingly, Malaysia has encouraged Middle Eastern airlines to put on more flights to Malaysia. It has engaged public relations companies in the Middle East to help promote Malaysia as a safe, clean and well-priced tourist destination for Muslims. And Malaysia's tourism agencies have undertaken roadshows across the Middle East. At the 2004 three-day

Arabian Travel Market held in Dubai, there were no less than 70 exhibitors from Malaysia, including 39 hotels and 20 tour operators.[2]

The Arab holiday season is from June to August and during that time, Malaysian Airlines scheduled 70 extra flights between Middle Eastern cities and Kuala Lumpur in 2005. In 2005, for the first time, Malaysia's Tourism Ministry also extended the closing time for Kuala Lumpur shopping malls to midnight from 9pm for seven weeks from mid-July to better cater to visiting Middle Eastern tourists. This is more in keeping with Middle Eastern shopping hours but also, Middle Eastern tourists tend not to adjust their body clocks when holidaying in Southeast Asia and instead prefer to keep Middle Eastern time. So they get up late in the day and then go to bed late.

Another initiative in 2005 was to have as many as 500 Arabic-speaking students from Malaysia's International Islamic University act as part-time tour guides stationed at the international airport, in hotels and at tourist attractions during the Arab holiday season.

Malaysian Government research has shown that tourists from the Middle East spend more per capita while in Malaysia than tourists from any other region and stay almost twice as long, so its initiatives are well grounded in commercial self-interest. Tourism is Malaysia's second largest foreign exchange earner after exports of manufactured goods.

Malaysia offers several attractions for Muslim tourists. It's good value for money. Saudi women can appear fully robed and veiled in the streets and not face harassment or even puzzled looks. (An unfortunate aspect of this is that they are mistaken by some Western tourists as local Muslim women, when in fact almost no Malaysian women dress in this style. Most locals regard it as extreme and unnecessary.)

Halal food is available everywhere. And so too are mosques. Malaysians know the right etiquette for dealing with Muslims. For example, men know not to offer their hand in greeting to Arab Muslim women. And male housekeeping staff in the hotels know not to enter a room in which a female Arab guest is alone. Many Malaysians have direct familiarity with the Middle East too, having traveled there to undertake the haj and the *Umrah* (minor haj).

Middle Eastern tourists are drawing Malaysia culturally closer to the rest of the Islamic world. Kuala Lumpur has long had Mughal-style elements to its architecture. Its colonial-era railway station and the law courts are the most obvious examples. But to cater to the ever-growing numbers of Middle Eastern visitors, Kuala Lumpur's cafés and restaurants are undergoing Arab makeovers.

The peak season for Arab tourists is the four months around the middle of the year. Saudi Arabians, Jordanians and Kuwaitis, probably in that order, are Malaysia's main Middle Eastern visitors. Major hotels in Kuala Lumpur now employ Arab-speaking staff. Their restaurants also stage Middle Eastern food promotions and buffets.

Coffee shops and restaurants in Kuala Lumpur offer complimentary *sishas* (hookahs or hubble-bubbles) during this time too. Otherwise, many Arabs bring their own. And so, increasingly, groups of Arab men are seen in the open air cafés of Kuala Lumpur smoking *sishas*.

Kebab stands and Lebanese restaurants have appeared in the main tourist districts, such as Tabush opposite Bintang Walk and another outlet at Ampang. Kuala Lumpur's chefs and food writers have had to embark on a steep learning curve with this quick invasion of new food. A feature in the *Star* newspaper in mid-2002 that sought to introduce readers to Middle Eastern food told readers that hummus is a mix of egg white, mayonnaise and Arabic spices.[3] It's anything but. It's a mixture of ground chickpeas, sesame seed paste (tahini), garlic and lemon juice.

Pan-Islamic Investment and Trade

Linkages between Malay entrepreneurs and Muslim businesspeople from the Middle East and elsewhere are growing but are largely unnoticed outside Asia and the Middle East. The role of Syed Mokhtar Albukhary in linking up with cashed-up Middle Eastern businessmen to invest in Malaysia was highlighted in Chapter 17.

The Malaysian Government under Prime Minister Mahathir pushed for the adoption of the gold dinar as the means of international payments for trade between Islamic states. The Malaysians proposed that each dinar would have the value of one ounce of gold. It sponsored conferences in Kuala Lumpur on the matter and underwrote research into the dinar's use. The idea was to reduce Islamic states' reliance on the US dollar in international trade. However, such a move is likely to be little more than symbolic. The US dollar is so well entrenched and the trading complementarities between Islamic countries too few for the dinar ever to be of much significance.

Still, the suggestion does have some historical underpinnings. The dinar was far more important in world trade in the sixteenth century than it is now and Islamic sultanates beyond those in the Middle East, including that in Aceh in Sumatra, adopted a local version also known as a dinar. Similarly, the sultanate in what is the Malaysian state of Kedah today coined local silver rials. Both the Achenese dinar and the Kedahnese rial were stamped with Arabic inscriptions.

Malaysia's efforts to woo other Islamic countries is beginning to pay off. Deals announced recently would not have happened if it were not for the efforts of the Malaysian Government in cultivating such links.

Malaysian car manufacturer Proton has established a completely knocked down assembly operation in Iran. Proton hopes to sell 25,000 Protons each year in Iran in the medium term.[4] Trade Minister Rafidah Aziz announced in January 2003 that Proton had won a tender to ship 5,000 Proton cars to Iraq by the following August. Proton had won an earlier contract in 2000 and shipped 1,500 Protons to Iraq. Proton had beaten Nissan, Toyota and Peugeot to win the new contract. But timing is everything and within a few months Iraq and its government was being obliterated by the US and the UK and presumably was no longer in a position to honor anything, including its contract with Proton.

A subsidiary of related Hicom Holdings won a waste management and cleaning contract in 2002 for the municipalities of the Kingdom of Bahrain.[5] Malaysian company UEM won a US$238 million contract in 2003 to build an expressway in Qatar. The company had earlier won a US$91 million contract to build a college of technology in the oil state.[6] Malaysia's national oil company Petronas also has utilized international Islamic links to further its interests. It now has operations in Algeria, Egypt, Iran, Sudan and Turkmenistan.

Dian Kreatif, a Malacca-based composite dome manufacturer, even won a contract in late 2004 to supply 40 domes for the Grand Mosque in Abu Dhabi.[7]

And in late 2005, a Malaysian–Saudi consortium won a US$2.5 billion power and water desalination construction project in Saudi Arabia. The Malaysian parties included Khazanah Nasional, Malakoff Power and Tenaga Nasional. Malaysia's Islamic links and credentials undoubtedly helped in furthering the bid. But true to Malaysia's multiracial character, the minister who flew to Riyadh to seal the contract was Energy, Water and Communications Minister Lim Keng Yaik.[8]

Investment is going the other way too. In mid-2003, a Bahrain-based private equity fund IDB Infrastructure Fund announced that it intended to spend up to US$200 million on infrastructure projects in Malaysia. The fund is sponsored by the Islamic Development Bank, the government of Brunei, Dar al-Maal Al-Islami Trust, the Saudi Pension Fund, Bahrain and a Malaysian consortium led by Lembaga Tabung Haji.[9]

And there are the massive investment commitments that Dubai investors have made in Malaysia in conjunction with Syed Mokhtar

Albukhary. Links are being formed. Deals are being done. The Arab–Malaysian link is another little-known dynamic that is shaping Asia today. Other countries like Singapore talk about furthering their investment and trade interests along ethnic Chinese lines. Malaysia does that too but is leading the way on using international Islamic networks to further its interests.

Part V

JAPAN, CHINA, INDIA AND KOREA: ASIA'S MONOLITH ECONOMIES

Why can't Japan get its economy back on track? If it has one good quarter of growth, invariably this is followed by many more of flat growth. And what of the only two countries in the world with billion-plus populations: China and India? One is the focus of the investment world, while the other, save for a few key growth sectors, lags far behind. And then there is South Korea, a country that has risen, phoenix-like, from the Asian economic crisis to be stronger and richer.

Chapters in the following section look at Japan and Korea, the rule of law in China, China as a consumer market rather than simply a low-cost place for manufacturing and exports thereafter, what democracy has done for India and what totalitarianism has done for China, India's economy, and its IT and IT-enabled sectors. There are also two chapters that allow for a comparison of Mumbai (Bombay) with Shanghai. Both are the financial capitals of their respective countries but that's where the similarities end.

There is also a chapter on the Dalai Lama. Tibet is a perennial international political problem for China. China is in one corner and the Dalai Lama is in the other. China is always heavily scrutinized but the Dalai Lama rarely is, so here is a chapter that does that. This might seem out of place in a book aimed at business. But that's the key to being an Asian Insider: no stone should be left unturned.

Chapter 22

LAND OF THE SETTING SUN: THE INEVITABLE DEATH OF JAPAN

When will Japan's economy revive? When will it grow like it once did? When will Japan's legislators finally make the right decisions to get things moving again? The answers are that it won't and they can't.

It doesn't matter what the Japanese Government tries to do, Japan's economy refuses to ignite in any sustainable way. Massive spending on infrastructure, government buy-ups on the stock market and forcing interest rates to zero by flooding the economy with cash have all been tried and have failed. Interest rates have been low for so long in Japan to encourage investment and consumer spending but instead many Japanese simply withdrew their money from banks and now hold it as cash because bank and building society fees and charges more than wipe out any interest earnings. And in January 2003, official interest rates even dipped below zero. Japan's central bank had released yet more liquidity into the banking system but there were few takers at any price. ABN Amro's Tokyo operations, for example, actually lent around US$150 million to two other foreign banks at a negative rate. It still made a profit on the deal because it was able to borrow US dollars at an even lower rate. The average overnight call rate at the time was 0.001%.[1]

Growth could come from exports but thanks in part to the "hollowing out" of the Japanese economy in the 1980s, whereby a lot of Japanese manufacturing was shifted offshore to lower cost countries, there are now many more countries that produce what Japan produces and can compete with it on world markets. In any event, the relative size of Japan's export sector has never been as important to the Japanese economy as commonly assumed. The American economist Richard Katz has pointed out that as a share of GDP, Japan's exports in 1999, at 10.4%, were no higher than in the 1950s. Nothing is so sacred to the Japanese as protecting its rice growers from foreign competition. Japan still persists with a quota system to import less than 10% of all rice consumed. Imports beyond this face an incredible 500% tariff.[2]

Japan's economy has become more open to outside investment. Foreigners have been allowed to take large and often controlling stakes even in Japanese icons like Mazda Motor Corp. It is now owned by Ford Motor Co. of the US. Mitsubishi Motors is now 22% owned by German-US auto giant DaimlerChrysler, who acquired a one-third stake in Mitsubishi Motors in 2000, although this was pared down until the remaining 12.4% stake was sold in November 2005 to Goldman Sachs, which then became the largest shareholder in Mitsubishi. Nissan Motor Co. is 44% owned by France's Renault SA. The supermarket chain Seiyu Ltd is 37.7% owned by Wal-Mart of the US. Chugai Pharmaceutical is 50.1% owned by Roche Holding AG of Switzerland. This infusion of capital and know-how has helped these companies but it has made little discernible impact on the Japanese economy overall other than to slow its slide.

Nothing seems to work. But there should be no mystery as to why. Nor should there be any mystery as to why Japan's economy will never recover. Japan's problem is not asset deflation, for that is merely a symptom. Economies, after all, are nothing more than the summation of people doing things to and for one another. And if the number of people who comprise the economy contracts, then so too will the economy. Exports might help, but then contracting populations are not conducive to ensuring competitively priced labor so that a country's products can compete on world markets.

Endangered Species?

And so this is the story of Japan today. Its population has or will soon peak. Most forecasters believe that Japan's population will have peaked by 2007 at around 127.6 million.[3] It's all downhill after that. Japan's population will fall by 20% over the next 30 years, by 30% over 50 years and by 50% within 100 years. Not only that, but by 2050, 800,000 more Japanese will die each year than are born and the country will have more than a million people aged 100 years or more.[4] Consultancy Asian Demographics has calculated that the absolute number of Japanese women of child-bearing age has been, and is projected to continue, declining. In 1982, there were 30.4 million women aged between 15 and 49 years. By 2002, this number had declined to 28.8 million and by 2022 it will fall to 23.8 million.[5]

The Japanese Government discovered in 2004 that the fertility rates of Japanese women were falling even faster than had been believed, having dropped from 1.32 babies per woman in 2002 to 1.29 in 2004. It had only just enacted a new pension scheme which assumed a fertility rate of 1.39.[6]

Other sources are similarly pessimistic. Japan's Institute of Population and Social Security Research forecasts that the population will fall to somewhere between 92 million and 108 million by 2050. The UN forecasts that it will fall to 105 million.[7]

Extrapolating from current trends, it's even possible that there will be relatively few Japanese left after several hundred years, and that eventually the Japanese might be spoken of in the same way that we speak of Bombay's Parsi community today: prosperous but heading towards extinction. That might seem a preposterous proposition but do the sums yourself.

Japan now has around 21.5 million people aged 65 or more – that's more than 17% of its 120-million strong population. And the number of Japanese aged 65 or more is currently growing by about a million a year. There are also more people in Japan aged over 65 than under 15 – the only mature economy in the world where this is so. Not only that but about a third of all households have one or more members older than 65. There's nothing new about Japan's aging population. It has simply become more acute. In 1950, there were 12.06 Japanese of working age (15–64) per person aged 65 or older. By 2000, there were just 3.99. By 2050, there will be just 1.71.

How things have changed! The CEO of one of Australia's business councils described to me how he was visited by a business delegation from Japan. The Japanese visitors noted the health of the Australian economy, its resilience in the face of economic downturns among its major trading partners and its flexibility.

"What are the secrets of your success? What should we be doing in Japan that we are not?"

My friend and his colleagues were flabbergasted. They were astounded that a delegation from the world's second biggest economy had been reduced to having to look to Australia for answers.

"We told them that Japan needs to reform its banking system, that it should further open up its domestic markets to outside competition, things like that. They listened, but you could tell that it was not what they wanted to hear."

It's true that these sorts of measure will help the Japanese economy. But will they be enough? Almost certainly not. Demographics are at the heart of the problem. Japan simply doesn't have enough young people forming families and new households, with all the spending that goes with it, to keep the economy growing.

Instead, it has a lot of older people who are retired or are facing retirement, who have spent their lives acquiring all the goods they need and are now more concerned with looking after their savings. And those savings amount to a very large pool – the average savings balance of elderly Japanese households is a whopping ¥25.3 million, which is more than 50% higher than that for all households. Loosening these purse strings would go a long way to reviving economic growth. But how to do that? Should each retiree be required to have two hip replacements instead of one, or add on new bedrooms to their houses? Of course not. The elderly cannot be a source of economic growth and no government stimulus package will ever make them that.

Not only is the higher spending base of Japan's population quickly shrinking as a proportion of the total but so too is the number of wage and salary earning taxpayers. This is happening so fast that the next generation of Japanese will face a net increase in lifetime taxes of 170% on that faced by the current generation, assuming that the number of old people who will then be in Japan are to have the same government benefits that Japan's elderly currently enjoy.

Most of the rest of the world is used to the idea of buying property, particularly residential housing, with the reasonable expectation of making a capital gain. Speculating in residential property has become a profitable hobby for many Australians, Britons and Americans. But in Japan, it is almost a certainty that any house or flat bought today will be worth less in future.

Will the Japanese property market ever pick up? How can it? In 50 years time, there will be 25 million fewer Japanese than there are now. For each of the 12 years to 2003, land prices in Japan fell for both commercial and residential areas. The falls are not slight. Residential land prices in the year to January 2003 declined by an average of 5.8%. Commercial prices fell by an average of 8%.[8] Prices for commercial land across Japan are now roughly equivalent to the levels they were in the late 1970s, before the asset bubble of the 1980s.

The parlous state of the property market is exacerbating the poor financial position of Japan's banks. Many of their customers who borrow to make property purchases soon find themselves with negative equity. Japan's banking system lurches from one crisis to another. The government had to bail out Resona Bank, the country's fifth biggest bank, in 2003. The cost: around US$17 billion. Analysts agreed that it was only a matter of time before the biggest, second, third and fourth biggest banks also would need further bailing out.[9]

What is the solution to all this? The answer is not another round of tax cuts, spending more on highways or another loosening of monetary policy. The *only* answer is to boost immigration. But by how much? United Nations' demographers have calculated that just to stabilize Japan's population, it will need to have 17 million new immigrants by 2050. Those 17 million would represent 18% of Japan's then population.

But Japanese society is one of the most homogeneous in the world. An astounding 99.4% of Japan's population are ethnic Japanese (including the indigenous Ainu people). The other 0.6% are almost entirely ethnic Koreans and some ethnic Chinese. Only the Koreans are accepted to any great degree and then only grudgingly. Son Masayoshi, the founder and CEO of Softbank, is perhaps the most prominent Japanese businessman of ethnic Korean ancestry. But it's instructive that Softbank is part of the new economy. This has allowed him to leapfrog old prejudices to be as prominent as he is today. If he had to work his way up through an existing Japanese company instead of founding his own, age-old racial prejudices would probably have halted his career at around middle management level. (One manifestation of this insularity is that English-language skills among Japanese remain at very low levels, possibly on a par with North Korea, according to some estimates.)

Immigration keeps labor costs low for menial jobs (this is one of the reasons why England is booming right now – relatively few lower paid jobs, particularly those in the services sector, are now done by the English). It brings new ideas and methods into an economy. It helps to promote international trade because a lot of trade is done via ethnic and family networks. But most of all, it helps to rejuvenate an aging population stock. Japan benefits from none of this. The US accepts around a million migrants a year. This is the sum total that Japan has accepted in the last 25 years. Those who have been accepted have largely been marginalized. And so Japan's economy, like its population, is slowly dying.

I Shop Therefore I Am

But is all this a disaster for Japan? Maybe, but it's not necessarily a disaster for the Japanese. Unemployment has risen to 4–5%. But then that was the rate in the US throughout the boom years of the 1990s. Japan's economy is stagnant but on a very high plateau.

One of the great sights of Asia is not in Asia. It's in France. The Louis Vuitton boutique in Galeries Lafayette, the famous department store in Paris, is a fantastic place to observe what's happening in Japan. The queue for the upmarket handbags and backpacks, which sell for thousands of dollars each, is made up almost entirely of young visiting Japanese and it is to be found there, on the ground floor of the store on Boulevard Haussmann, all day, every day. Two security men are on hand the whole time lest things get out of control. But what is especially interesting is that the queue has shown no signs of abating. Even with Japan's economy in the doldrums. Similar fervor can be seen in London's Soho in the West End, where several alternative clothing stores that are barely known to locals are deluged with young Japanese, forming a niche world known only to itself. Clearly, these are not people who are frightened to spend money.

Why? Because Japan still is among the richest countries on earth. Its workers don't work the long hours typically assumed and they tend to take holidays more often than believed (which is why Japanese tourists are so ubiquitous from Alice Springs to Trafalgar Square). They pay less tax than their counterparts in Europe, the US and Australia and their homes are filled with more gadgets. Younger Japanese are spending – as the queue at Galeries Lafayette shows. But how does this fit in with a Japan that is apparently in terminal decline? The answer is that while Japan's economy in total is either stationary or contracting much of the time, per capita incomes will rise. This is because Japan's population will shrink faster than its economy. Not only that, but with asset price deflation, homes and other big purchases in Japan are becoming more affordable. So not only are per capita incomes rising but so too are living standards. Already this effect is becoming apparent. Japan's per capita GDP on a PPP basis (the measure that attempts to capture living standards) has risen significantly in recent years, outstripping real per capita GDP growth. But in aggregate, Japan will continue to take fewer exports from the US and elsewhere. So it seems that everyone needs Japan's economy to grow. Everyone that is but the Japanese.

All the cheap credit, tax cuts and government spending that are designed to reflate Japan are doomed to fail. Like pumping an octogenarian full of vitamins, such measures prolong life and make it more comfortable but they do not make it younger. Japan has had its heyday. The smile of youth has moved on.

Chapter 23

LAW, ORDER AND CHINA

Hong Kong businessman Harry Lam sat in the Lok Yu Tea House in central Hong Kong finishing his breakfast one Saturday in late November 2002. His table was at the rear of the downstairs part of the Lok Yu. At a table near to the door, another man was also finishing his breakfast. He paid for it, got up, walked calmly over to Harry Lam's table, pulled out a handgun and shot the millionaire businessman in the head. A single bullet was fired and Lam was dead. The gunman then walked out of the restaurant, as calmly as when he'd paid for his breakfast.

The Lok Yu Tea House is a Hong Kong institution. The fact that such a brazen murder could occur in the heart of the local traditional Chinese establishment was deeply shocking to many in Hong Kong. It's the favorite haunt of the city's big traditional Chinese businessmen and it is famous for its dim sum. It's the sort of place where locals deep in discussion about prices and deals tap the tablecloth with their index fingers, without glancing up to acknowledge the waiter as he pours more tea, rather than say "thank you", which would interrupt conversation. It's a small cultural nuance that I've noticed only in Hong Kong.

The Lok Yu Tea House is also the only place in which I have experienced overt, in-your-face racial discrimination. Not being Chinese, I was told that I could not sit downstairs and instead was directed upstairs where I was shown to a table that was actually behind a screen. Apparently this is the standard treatment for a *gweillo*.

There was a similar no-nonsense killing in London six months later. You Yi He, a mainland-born Chinese, was enjoying a drink with friends in the BRB Bar in the Chinatown district in London's Soho in June 2003.

The bar is located at the top of the T-junction between Gerrard and Macclesfield Streets. The feng shui could not be worse. A Chinese man walked into the bar, raised a handgun to You's head, fired twice and walked out. You was dead within three hours.

The killings of Harry Lam and You Yi He occurred on opposite sides of the world but were remarkable for the professionalism with which they were carried out. The other similarity is that no-one saw anything; patrons and waiters were "unable" to give descriptions of either gunman.

Lam had business interests in mainland China over which there were some legal wrangles. You, on the other hand, was unemployed but possibly connected to people smuggling from the mainland into the UK. The easy assumption is that Chinese triads killed both Lam and You. But did they? Traditionally, the triads kill or preferably maim using knives and machetes. You's killing was in fact the first murder in London's Chinatown to be committed with a gun. The killings appeared to point to some other force at work.

China's People's Liberation Army (PLA) numbered some 4.75 million in 1981. By the mid-1990s, it was down to around 3 million. Some of those shed were picked up by the expanding People's Armed Police Force. But others were made unemployed. Some of them appear to have been absorbed by the "Snakehead" gangs that originate, not in Hong Kong and China's Guangdong province, the traditional homes of China's triads, but with renegade ex-PLA cadres in China's Fujian province. The new groups, trained in weaponry thanks to their PLA links, have muscled in on the old-style triads. The new gangs are far more violent. No longer is kidnapping merely about detention. Now it also involves torture. Throughout the 1990s, Snakehead gangs staged several spectacular bank robberies in Hong Kong. They used infantry tactics, with light machine guns set up in the street to provide covering fire, while the banks were stormed by gang members wielding AK47s and throwing stun grenades.[1] Essentially, the banks were attacked as if they were enemy positions, presenting some-thing altogether quite new for Hong Kong's police to deal with.

Organized crime is a problem everywhere. But it thrives most where the rule of law is weak and law enforcement officials are easily paid off. And that is a good description of China.

The Rule of Law

A sound system of law needs to be funded. Law enforcement officials and the judiciary need to be well paid. But in China, the tax take is too low.

China does not collect enough taxes to pay for an efficient and professional system of public administration and what taxes are collected often end up subsidizing inefficient state-owned companies rather than the machinery of law enforcement.

Back in 1997, tax revenues in China were just 6% of GDP and that was when the economy was much smaller than it is now. By 2003, the tax take had grown to almost 12% of GDP.[2] And in 2004, the tax take reached a new record, US$311.4 billion, excluding taxes earned from customs duties and agricultural taxes.[3]

Better compliance measures were introduced. Some are ingenious. For example, the government required that restaurants, cafés, bars and taxis issue receipts on specially printed paper that had scratch-off lottery games on its reverse. And so now patrons request receipts because they want to play the scratch-off games that can reward them with free meals and the like. Once a receipt is issued, the revenue enters the establishment's accounts and it becomes visible for tax purposes. Despite improvements, China's tax collection still lags behind more developed countries. In the US, for example, tax revenue amounts to around 19% of GDP.

Law enforcement is one thing. But actually having well-drafted laws is another. China has made significant progress in recent years in drafting laws, particularly for business, albeit from a remarkably low base. Under the planned economy that was set up from 1949, the state controlled almost all property and business in China. Citizens had almost no legal protection for their personal possessions. Even their bank savings did not have legal protection, although a law to provide protection for personal savings was proposed in late 2002.

Having said that, it remains the case that many of the laws promulgated by China's National People's Congress are contradictory, poorly drafted, vaguely worded and might not even be known to members of the legal profession or fully understood by the officials responsible for enforcing them. The opportunities for discretion on the part of officials, who are invariably poorly paid, are many and the consequences obvious. Bribery renders the rule of law patchy and inconsistently applied in many parts of China.

A big challenge for China is to implement and enforce adequate bankruptcy laws. But that will be only half the battle. Bankruptcy courts will need to contend with vague property rights and the confusion as to who owns what. How can a state-owned enterprise be forced into bankruptcy when the extent of its assets is unclear? It might be insolvent. But then it might not.

The law in China is not applied equally when it is applied. The more than

60 million party members, the judiciary and the police all feel themselves to be above the law. Law enforcement officials view themselves as an arm of the state that aims to control rather than as servants of the people there to assist. The police offer little direct assistance to ordinary citizens. I did hear though of a case when an expatriate worker in Tianjin had his laptop computer stolen. The police located it and returned it to him within three days. The expatriate was as astonished as he was grateful. It turned out that the thief had also stolen two other laptops. Unbeknownst to him, they belonged to two senior Chinese PLA officers and held sensitive material. He hadn't merely stolen two laptops, he'd stolen state secrets, which explained the police's uncharacteristic competence in retrieving the stolen items.

I asked a Chinese friend who had arrived in London from China what surprised him most about London. It was his first time outside China. I expected him to mention the food or the weather. He thought for a minute and then said "the police". "Why?" I asked. "Because they are very, very polite. They go out of their way to be polite. That is so surprising", he said.

Another surprise for him was the way in which Britain's prime minister was grilled in Parliament and even by journalists. Seeing that, he said, "shocked" him. He felt "embarrassed" at the sight of the most senior politician in the country having to justify his policies on television. Simply, he had not seen anything like it. He could see the sense of it but somehow it just didn't seem right. But then centuries of conditioning cannot be overturned in a few days.

Typically, leaders in the West are seen as "servants" of the people. On the other hand, China's leaders care mostly about one thing: their power and how to preserve it. A well-developed, well-enforced legal system is essential for the sustained economic and social wellbeing of any country. But in China, the rule *of* law is substituted with rule *by* law. A legal system in which everyone receives equal treatment before the law means that no longer are the rulers all-powerful. Instead, they must share power with the law and, ultimately, be subject to it.

"In his 13 years in power, the outgoing president and party chief, Jiang Zemin, gave low priority to strengthening the legal system", commented prominent China watcher Jasper Becker after Jiang stepped down in 2003.

He preferred to beef up the secret police. He cut the ambitious targets set in the 1980s to train 2 million lawyers and judges by 2000. Only 100,000 were trained. The legal system functions so badly and enforcement of court decisions is so unpredictable that commercial and also civil disputes, such as divorce, become intractable or a matter of whom you know and how much you can bribe them.[4]

China desperately needs a better legal system. But China's interests and the interests of its leaders are miles apart. It can be expected that improvements in this area will come only grudgingly.

China's entry to the WTO came after 15 years of haggling and negotiating. Part of China's commitment was that it would upgrade its laws. Its trade pledges ran to 900 pages of text. More than a thousand new laws needed to be passed and 570 existing laws needed to be amended.[5] But to be frank, an appropriate response might be, so what? There's a chasm of difference between a law as it is written and a law as it is enforced in a country like China. A rule-based system such as the WTO works very well in rule-based societies that are transparent and open, but is largely irrelevant to a country like China. China had relatively little to lose from WTO membership since many of the laws that it agreed to pass are not being enforced anyway. But it had much to gain.

Corruption

When has public administration in China ever been anything other than highly corrupt? Even many of the thousands of eunuchs who ran Beijing's Forbidden City on behalf of the emperors amassed huge fortunes for themselves, despite being paid a pittance. The opportunities for material advancement that service in the Forbidden City provided meant that many young men and boys lined up for the medical procedure that would be their passport to the palace.

The eunuch clinic where they were required to sit in a special chair with a hole in the seat for the operation is near to the Forbidden City. As many as half the candidates died shortly after the operation. Mutilation was thought to be grounds for exclusion from the next life, so the eunuchs carried their severed testicles with them in pouches or jars wherever they went so that they might appear whole to the spirits responsible for accompanying them to the next life should the moment of death strike.

Today, there are some extraordinary mansions and villas in the semi-rural area just north of Beijing close to the Miyun reservoir, as there are in many parts of China. One in particular was so large that I imagined it might be a five-star hotel and convention center. "No", I was told bluntly by a guide. "That's the house of an official." Corruption in China can be somewhat brazen.

It remains rife in China despite the government's ongoing anti-corruption campaign and the existence of the death penalty for the worst "economic crimes". One of China's best known bankers Liu Jinbao was convicted of corruption in 2005, for example. He had been the chief executive of the Bank of China's Hong Kong subsidiary and also a vice chairman of the entire bank. He was convicted of taking US$173,000 in bribes and embezzling another US$2.7 million with several colleagues. He was sentenced to death with a two-year suspension, although he is unlikely to face a firing squad as suspended death sentences normally are converted to life in prison in China.[6]

Nonetheless, presumably the probability of getting caught is low, otherwise capital punishment would be more of a deterrent. Hu Angang, a professor at China's Tsinghua University School of Public Policy and Management, has estimated that 15–20% of the funds for any project in China are illegally diverted to private hands via fraud and bribery.[7] Seemingly, everyone is at it. One Chinese told me:

> I know of one official and he's really quite low ranking and even he has sent his son to school in Switzerland and bought his son a house to live in while he was there. Can you imagine how much money there is to be made even at these very low levels?

Officials send their children abroad to establish a foreign foothold. Ostensibly, they go abroad for schooling but while there they arrange offshore banking facilities, property transactions and so on. When a company needs to bribe an official to get approvals or whatever in China, the money need never enter China. It can be paid by the company's offshore arm into the official's children's offshore bank accounts. That way, the bribery is practically untraceable. Once the officials feel that they have profited enough, they can then emigrate to the ready-made foothold established by their children.

Typically, those who get caught are those who have fallen out politically. And so charges of corruption often are masks for some other misdeed, probably some sort of misdeed that actually doesn't violate criminal codes. In 2001, for example, 175,000 members of the Communist Party were punished for corruption.[8] It seems a lot but given that the party has more than 60 million members and the only question is whether many or most of them behave corruptly, then this figure might appear surprisingly low. It is said among the Chinese themselves that if the anti-corruption campaign doesn't succeed, China will die. If it does, then it will be the party that dies.

Misallocation of scarce capital is rife. Chinese Government auditors admitted that a staggering US$15.1 billion of state funds was either misused or embezzled across the country in 1999. It's probably an underestimate. The previous year, it was revealed that cumulative losses from fraud and mismanagement in state grain purchases alone were US$25.8 billion for the previous six years.[9] The sums that are embezzled, pilfered or just wasted are astronomic in China.

Corruption in China can sometimes work in favor of foreign investors. Foreign retailers have expanded very quickly across China, much to the chagrin of local domestic retailer associations. By 2006, the French hypermarket operator Carrefour had turned itself into China's second largest chain of such stores and Wal-Mart of the US had around 60 stores, for example. Foreign retailers have proven themselves to be better at retailing, inventory management, store design and marketing than the locals. But they also are the preferred customers of many of China's domestic suppliers. They pay promptly and tend not to demand kickbacks.[10]

Intellectual Property

Harry Potter, or Ha-li Bo-te as he's known in China, is immensely popular on the mainland. Cheap, authorized local editions of J.K. Rowlings' novels sell in their millions. When *Harry Potter and the Half Blood Prince* was released worldwide in July 2005, how long did it take for China's copyright infringers to translate this mammoth work into Chinese, print it, bind it and distribute it on China's streets? Less than two weeks after the English-language version of the book was published.[11]

One of the legal system's greatest failings is in the area of intellectual property protection. China did update its trademark, copyright and patent laws to comply with WTO requirements but again enforcement is quite another matter. It has been estimated that 15–20% of all products in China are counterfeit.[12] Fast moving consumer goods manufacturer Procter & Gamble found that around a third of its shampoos sold in supermarkets outside Beijing and Shanghai were counterfeit. Similarly, Henkel, the German household products manufacturer, commissioned market research firm A.C. Nielsen to survey its sales in the late 1990s. A.C. Nielsen showed Henkel that it was doing rather better than it had expected. It was selling 130% more product than was leaving its factories.[13] The excess was made up of counterfeit goods. And the cigarette company British American Tobacco claims that its biggest competitor in China is not Philip Morris or China Tobacco but counterfeiters – illicit producers that fabricate its brands and packaging to sell cheap cigarettes at premium prices and outside the tax system. Similarly, two-thirds of the pirated goods that were seized at US ports in 2004 came not from its neighbor Mexico or indeed from Central and South America but from China.

Product faking and switching occur everywhere and with everything. On one occasion I ordered a Corona beer at a bar in Beijing's Bar Street. The bottle arrived in the usual way, opened and with a lime quarter stuffed in its neck. But the beer was not Corona. The bottle had been refilled with some cheap, local alternative. (To be fair, bar rip-offs occur everywhere. A few weeks earlier, I'd watched a barman in a tapas bar in San Sebastian in northern Spain top up a pint of beer with tap water.)

China's decentralized nature does not help with intellectual property rights enforcement. Consultants in Beijing speak of helping multinationals to organize raids with the central government. The central government's police arrive at factories where counterfeit goods are known to be produced, only to have the local mayor turn up with local police to stop the raid. "If you close this factory, I'll have 200 unemployed workers to look after. What am I supposed to do?" is the typical response from such mayors. The same attitudes are mirrored in the courts. The Beijing-based Property Rights Tribunal of the Chinese Supreme People's Court is relatively sophisticated and has a genuine desire to act on intellectual property rights infringements. But lower courts are still very much under the control of local governments and so are sensitive to local political concerns.

When China actually does operate within its own laws, the world reacts with surprise and excitement reminiscent of the overcompensatory praise given to a small child who's learning to walk. "Isn't she clever!" A case in point was the victory of Lego, the Danish manufacturer of children's building blocks, in a copyright infringement case in the Beijing's High People's Court in January 2003. Lego had filed a suit in 1999 against a local Chinese company that, it claimed, was infringing on its intellectual property by copying 53 characteristics of Lego toys. The Chinese court agreed on 33 of those characteristics. It demanded that the local company stop production of the look-alikes, turn over the offending molds to the court, publish an apology to Lego in the *Beijing Daily* and pay Lego unspecified damages. "It is the first time that the Chinese legal system has delivered a judgment that confirms copyright protection of industrial design/applied art", said Lego triumphantly.[14] But it had taken more than three years to come and then it wasn't clear whether the court's decision would actually be enforced. But Lego was delighted and the court's decision made it into the international press.

Since the Lego case, judges have tended to favor plaintiffs more when they can show clear cases of intellectual property infringement, and obtaining effective enforcement has now become the more serious problem.

Another way to fight back is to take legal action against Chinese companies when they venture offshore. BASF, the world's largest chemicals producer, did that in late 2005. Lawyers acting on its behalf and two other agrochemical companies served 37 injunctions for intellectual property infringements on 19 separate companies – all of them from mainland China – at Glasgow's three-day BCPC International Congress and Exhibition, Europe's largest agrochemical trade fair. Two of the Chinese companies were even ejected from the fair as a consequence of the legal action.[15]

The Courts and Convictions

Nearly all developed, wealthy countries have a notion of the need for a separation of powers – that various arms of the state are independent of one another and so can act as checks on each other's power. Such institutional arrangements are essential to the functioning of a modern, successful state. But in China there is simply the Communist Party and everything else is subservient to it and dependent on it. There is no separation of powers. No part of the state is independent of any other. And that includes the judiciary.

Judges are nominated by local and provincial party committees and approved by local people's congresses. The congresses provide the salaries, housing and other benefits for judges, many of whom have little or no legal training but instead are ex-military personnel. They are expected to discuss sensitive cases with members of their local Communist Party political-legal committees before making rulings.[16] There is not even a pretence that judges are in any way independent.

A manager in a Malaysian company described to me how his company had taken a Chinese bank to court in Dalian over a dishonored letter of credit. When it came to the lunch break, the lawyers for the government-owned Chinese bank and the bank officials had a sumptuous lunch with the judges, the bank officials and the judges had all been appointed by the same government officials after all. No prizes for guessing which way the case went. Such examples are the rule rather than the exception.

In addition, many judges are corrupt. Joe Studwell in his book *The China Dream* writes of the experience in China of US fund manager ASIMCO.[17] It ran two automotive private equity funds and seemed to be targeted for every scam going. An employee of a joint venture in Zhuhai, Guangdong conspired with the staff of a local state bank to defraud the venture via a fake letter of credit. ASIMCO took the matter to court. The judge asked if ASIMCO might help him get an American green card. ASIMCO refused and the judge ruled against it. ASMICO took the case to China's anti-corruption bureau. The bureau said that it was willing to investigate but it would first require a car and some working capital. Ironically, the employee fled to the US in the meantime where he was safe from extradition because of US concerns over China's human rights records.

Procedures for commercial cases in China are a mess but arguably its criminal courts are worse. They do not exist to uncover the facts of the cases that appear before them. Their prime function is to mete out punishment. Most criminal cases in China are undefended and the situation is deteriorating. In 1995, 22% of criminal cases were defended. By 2002, the rate was just 15%.[18] Defense work is hardly attractive. In a totalitarian regime such as China's, the perception is that the state only brings a case against a defendant who is guilty, so therefore there can be only one logical conclusion to a case. And indeed that's what happens. In 2004, 770,947 criminal defendants appeared before China's courts and of those 768,634 or 99.7% were found guilty as charged.[19]

Responding to perceptions that China's courts are unfair, the Chinese government has made some changes. From May 2005, two jurors and a judge, rather than simply one judge, now decide both civil and criminal cases, or at least that is the intention. The jurors are not chosen anew for each trial, however, but serve a five-year term.

Nonetheless, other problems abound. Not only is defense work financially unrewarding, sometimes it's seen as almost subversive. Defense lawyers run the risk of jail themselves. Lawyers can be charged with perjury and falsification of evidence if they are too vigorous in overturning the prosecution's evidence. Courts cannot or do not compel witnesses called by defendants to attend hearings and if the police are summoned, perhaps to be cross-examined on the evidence they have collected, typically they refuse to attend the hearing. Arrest in China is tantamount to guilt. Trials are a mere formality.

China's Advances on Paper

Corporate governance is a huge problem in China, as it always is in economies with weak legal systems. Probably China is as backward on this as any other country in the world. But even as state-owned companies modernize and list, they still indulge in behavior that is at odds with even the most basic principles of sound governance. There is a tendency among most of them not to use funds raised from an IPO to strengthen their core business but to expand in utterly unrelated activities. China Travel International Investment is one such company. It is China's biggest travel operator. And for some reason it also has a joint venture in the form of Shaanxi Weihe Power Plant. Haier, the well-known white goods producer, is yet to

list and so no audited accounts are made public. But despite a core competency in producing washing machines and refrigerators, its management is
keen for it to get into finance. Already it has an insurance joint venture,
Haier New York Life Insurance, with offices on the 36th floor of the
opulent Jin Mao Tower in Shanghai's Pudong area. One study found that
around 120 Chinese state-owned companies had sought permission for
their IPO plans, raised cash from the IPO and then, contrary to what had
been agreed, immediately changed their intentions on how to spend the
cash. Many had used it to buy assets from their parent companies, contrary
to undertakings in their IPO prospectuses.[20]

In any event, of the 1,200 mainland Chinese companies that are listed,
almost all have less than a third of their shares freely listed. In this way,
minority shareholders are not so much part-owners in these companies but
milch cows from whom funds can be gathered by the majority shareholder.
With few enforced safeguards for minority shareholders, listing does little
to enhance corporate governance. Majority shareholders readily ride
roughshod over the interests of other shareholders.

Still, measures designed to improve corporate governance have been
introduced. For example, in August 2001, China unveiled new rules that
require listed companies to hire at least two independent directors within a
year and for boards to comprise a third of independent directors within
two years. A study undertaken by the Shanghai Stock Exchange in 2000
had found that of the 3,000 directors surveyed, only eight could be considered independent.[21]

In February 2002, it was announced that stocks in companies listed on
the Shenzhen and Shanghai Stock Exchanges with two consecutive years
of losses would be suspended for six months. If they returned to profitability in that six-month period, then trading in their shares could recom-
mence. A third year of losses would result in delisting.[22]

Like the case of Liu Jinbao mentioned above, there have also been many
high-profile arrests, jailings and even some executions of officials and
state-owned enterprise managers who have been involved in corruption and
fraud. Yang Rong, the former chairman of Brilliance China Automotive,
China's largest manufacturer of mini-vans, for example, was arrested for
"economic crimes" in late 2002.[23] Zhu Xiaohua, the former head of China's
state-run Everbright Group which controls China's sixth largest commercial
bank, is another. He was jailed for 15 years in October 2002 for taking
bribes in cash and stock worth US$500,000.[24] But again, the application of
the law is selective. Being corrupt is not enough to be arrested. One must
also be vulnerable and out of favor. But isn't that the same everywhere,
some readers in Asia might be tempted to ask? The answer is no.

CHINA AS A CONSUMER MARKET

China is routinely portrayed as the workshop of the world. It isn't. It still accounts for only about 6% of world international trade. But increasingly companies all over the world have shifted manufacturing operations to China, not just US and European manufacturers but Japanese and Korean too. But China also represents a vast potential consumer market, with its 1.3 billion population. So what are Chinese consumers like? The word "potential" needs to be emphasized. For, largely, that's what it is and that's what it will remain for many years to come for most would-be sellers into the Chinese market. China has a lot of people but mostly they cannot afford to buy much. And even if they can, their tastes and needs need to be accounted for.

It's that last factor that's often forgotten. I grew up in Australia and at one point, the anti-competitive, monopolistic wool board, which bought up wool from Australian wool growers and then attempted to manipulate the world wool price, got it so wrong that an enormous wool stockpile was created. "If only every Chinese would buy a pair of socks" was a refrain often heard at the time. But at the time, probably 70% or more of China's working-age population was involved in agricultural production, many in rice cultivation. And for those millions who grew rice, standing around barefooted in water and mud all day, what use would a pair of woollen socks have been?

Similarly, foreign breweries have flooded into China, hoping to sell beer to the Chinese, as if China didn't already produce beer. Beer drinkers the world over tend to be loyal to "their" brands, loyalties which are usually attached to a region. Why would Chinese beer drinkers be any different?

Foreign soft drink companies have not done as well as could be expected in China, although Pepsi, for example, did manage to sell a billion dollars worth of soft drink in China in 2004, but that was after years of struggle. One reason is that China is largely a tea-drinking society. But there's another reason: most Chinese continue to believe that cold drinks are unhealthy and will induce a hot–cold imbalance in the body. This is a belief that's prevalent among traditional Chinese in overseas Chinese communities of Southeast Asia too. The average Chinese in China consumes just eight soft drink servings a year.[1] There might be room for growth but it's not simply a matter of spending power.

In any event, how affluent are Chinese consumers? The answer is not very, but more than before. Generally, incomes are rising. But many have been made poorer not richer by the country's economic advancement. Millions have lost their jobs through the collapse of many state-owned enterprises and not just their jobs but all the healthcare, housing and education benefits that went with such jobs.

Officially, around 30 million people in China are unemployed. But as is usual anywhere with such figures, the underemployed are not fully accounted for. When they are, perhaps 96 million people are unemployed and underemployed.

What about those with real disposable incomes? How is the size of China's middle class best determined? A conventional measure is to count all those who earn more than US$5,000, this being the level at which discretionary purchases can start to be made. Probably, there are around 250 million people in China who earn US$5,000 or more. But that is not most people's idea of middle class. Perhaps US$25,000 or more is a figure closer to what many people would consider a middle class, in which case there are around 40 million such people in China. Add to them their immediate families and the figures grows to around 100 million. That's significant but it's not huge when compared with the world's mature economies. Income per capita in the US on a non-PPP adjusted basis is around US$25,000 for every man, woman and child, employed or not, and there are almost 300 million people living in the US. China, on the other hand, has just 40 million people who earn this or more.[2]

Alistair Nicholas, managing director of AC Capital Strategic Public Relations, a consultancy based in Beijing which helps foreign companies come to grips with the realities of the Chinese market, says:

The market for high-end consumer goods, while growing, is still small by comparison to the total size of the population. These high-end consumers are concentrated in the more developed coastal cities of China and much more so in the

three key cities of Beijing, Shanghai and Guangzhou. Also, the rural–urban divide
must be considered. It is particularly pronounced when it comes to income: rural
household incomes are about a third of urban households.

Of course, some people in China have become very rich. Large upmarket housing estates, with houses that sell for hundreds of thousands of
dollars, are being constructed outside Beijing and elsewhere. But these
estates will house thousands not millions and certainly not tens of
millions. They are showy and tend to distort outsiders' perceptions about
how rich China really is.

Still, China is a booming market for smaller, discretionary consumer
goods. Or at least it should be. China is well known as the world's biggest
manufacturer and exporter of branded sports shoes such as Nike and Adidas,
but what about China as a market for such shoes? Adidas already had 1,300
stores in China by 2005. By the 2008 Beijing Olympics, it intends to have
no less than 4,000. The numbers sound good. But sales are yet to match:
Adidas' sales in China by 2005 were over US$130 million, or just
US$100,000 per outlet, and Nike's sales in 2003 were US$300 million.[3]

Another pointer to China's potential as a huge consumer market is its
current national savings rate. At around half of national income, it is the
highest in the world. A lot of the saving done by households is precau-
tionary in nature. There's little by way of state-sponsored welfare or
healthcare for most people and so households save to meet unforeseen
contingencies. As China's provision for these sorts of things grows and the
insurance sector broadens its coverage, ordinary people will feel the need
to save less, thus releasing more cash for spending.

Then Economic Minister Zhu Rhongji exhorted the Chinese to spend
more back in 2000 but to no avail. Five years later and the same exhorta-
tions were still being made. The US Government believes that if Chinese
households saved less, then the US trade deficit would be reduced. US
Treasury Secretary John Snow, on a trip to China in October 2005, urged
the Chinese to buy "more stuff". Snow said: "We see the growth of
consumerism … as going directly to what is most on our mind, which is
the global imbalance."[4] So far, ordinary Chinese have been reluctant to
save less, even as incomes have risen. But that will change as China grows
richer – it always does.

Reaching Consumers

Survey findings suggest that the Chinese don't like to shop nearly as much as, say, Americans do. It's not a cultural thing but has more to do with the practicalities. Shopping in China can be difficult and unpleasant. Good retail infrastructure is only just being built. Many places are still without supermarkets, much less modern shopping malls that present shopping as entertainment. Even with modern supermarkets and malls, the consistent availability of goods remains a problem. Says Alistair Nicholas:

> Distribution continues to be a nightmare for companies as there are few truly national supermarket chains and most goods are still bought through very small corner shops (*xiao maibu*). Scarcity of goods is very common. Quite often, when shopping for one item or another, consumers are told *meiyoule* (we've run out) followed by *mingtian* (try again tomorrow).

The biggest revolution for consumers with some spending power in China has been not the internet or even the shopping mall but the supermarket. Why? Because in the centrally planned era, consumers would have to queue at a counter to ask an invariably indifferent assistant for permission to look at products kept behind the counter. Now, customers can walk down aisles of products and look at products for themselves. They can touch the items, compare them and properly consider them before they buy. Further, the range is greater. Supermarkets have empowered ordinary Chinese consumers. They also are helping to educate them.

Direct selling was an early way to circumvent China's lack of decent retail infrastructure: the retailer went to the consumers rather than the other way around. It took off in China in a big way. Amway, Mary Kay and Avon all did well but then the rules were changed (or reinterpreted) and such selling was suddenly banned in 1998.

But appetites had been whetted for good reliable products and a choice of products. So when foreign retailers worked out how to navigate China's regulator obstacles in the sector, their businesses took off. French hypermarket chain Carrefour quickly grew into China's second largest chain of stores by ignoring central government's requirement that it approve retail joint ventures.[5] Instead, it signed deals with local governments, rightly assuming that once stores were open and hundreds of locals were employed, central government would not shut them down. It didn't. Carrefour has revolutionized wholesaling in China, achieved wide name recognition, and good consumer and supplier acceptance, all *without* central government approval.

Other foreign retailers with a significant presence in China today are IKEA (Sweden), Makro (Holland), Metro (Germany), and from Hong Kong: U2, Giordano and Watsons. And as has been mentioned, by 2006 Wal-Mart had around 60 stores in China.

Plenty of Western food and beverage franchises have opened too, including Starbucks, Pizza Hut, McDonald's and KFC, which had 1,300 outlets in 280 cities by 2005. Starbucks has become one of China's most recognized foreign brands in the cities. There's even a Starbucks in the heart of Beijing's Forbidden City.

The first Starbucks opened in Shanghai in May 2000. In Shanghai, 50 stores were planned in partnership with Uni-President Enterprises.[6] Renmin Square was the site for big protests in 1989 that echoed those in Tiananmen Square in Beijing. Today, the square is lavishly landscaped and there's a Starbucks in one corner. Another Starbucks is at an equally strategic spot in the city, on the Pudong waterfront, where it's visible from almost anywhere along the Bund on the opposite side of the Huangpu River.

In southern China, more Starbucks stores were planned, this time in conjunction with its 50:50 partner, Maxim's, a Hong Kong cake shop company that's 50% owned by Dairy Farm International. By 2005, 111 Starbucks stores had opened across mainland China (including 44 in Beijing and 43 in Shanghai), plus another 34 in Hong Kong and one in Macau.

The Golden Resources Shopping Mall in the western part of Beijing opened in 2004. With a total area of 680,000 square meters, it is the world's largest shopping mall. To put it in context, it has three times the lettable space of Minnesota's Mall of America, the largest shopping mall in the US.

You would think that was enough. But by 2006, China also had the world's third, fourth and fifth largest shopping malls: Beijing's Beijing Mall (440,000 square meters in total area), Donnguan's South China Mall (430,000 square meters) and Guangzhou's Grandview Mall (420,000 square meters).

But even that's not enough. Two shopping malls under construction in 2006, one in Wenzhou and the other in Qingdao, will far eclipse anything the world has seen to date. Both will have around 930,000 square meters when they are completed. That's equivalent to four Mall of Americas all under one roof. And there will be two of them.

By 2010, at least 7 of the world's 10 biggest shopping malls will be in China.[7] Overall, more than 400 large shopping malls were built in China between 2000 and 2006. Many more are planned.

Foreign investors are finding ways to become involved in mall development too. Simon Property Group, one of the largest property developers in the US, announced a partnership in mid-2005 with Morgen Stanley of the US and the state-owned Shenzhen International Trust and Investment to develop as many as 12 malls around China.[8] All the malls will have a Wal-Mart store as the anchor tenant. Some will also have cinemas run by Warner Theaters, a unit of TimeWarner. In this way foreign and, in this case American, chains can arrive in China, courtesy of deals already done back home and so in the company of partners with whom they are familiar.

It remains to be seen how many malls will actually prove profitable. Many might well be filled with people but are they filled with shoppers? This is the problem in many developing countries. Often the public promenade spaces are full but the shops themselves are largely empty and many visitors are happy to satisfy themselves with just a two-dollar coffee at Starbucks, a small but affordable glimpse at Western-style consumerism.

Credit Cards

China's backward payments system is a major impediment to China becoming a significant shopping destination. Credit card usage is still very low. Around 30% of retail transactions occur on credit cards in developed countries, but in China the figure is less than 3%. And personal cheques are not used at all. ATM cards and machines have become common, but typically they are used to obtain cash which is then used to pay retailers. There are 350,000–400,000 merchants equipped to accept credit cards but mostly these are local currency credit or debit cards issued through the local system China UnionPay. Visa is the largest foreign card accepted, but by 2005, Visa was accepted by about 105,000 merchants, compared with an estimated 20 million merchants in China in total.[9]

The situation will evolve more quickly after 2007. Local currency-denominated transactions are off limits to foreign institutions until 2007, after which China will adopt WTO rules for its financial markets. Foreign credit card companies can then be expected to make a push for greater credit card usage and acceptability.

Advertising

A boom in advertising has come with the growth in shopping and shopping facilities, which will no doubt reach a crescendo as the 2008 Beijing Olympics approach. The advertising spend on Chinese television alone was US$24 billion in 2004, with annual growth rates of 20–30%. The number of television stations in China has expanded rapidly too, from a few dozen to almost 300 by 2005. The number of households with a television set has also grown: most Chinese homes now have one. And by 2005, around 110 million homes also had cable television access.[10]

Newspapers and magazines are another route for advertisers, as is outdoor advertising such as billboards. In 2004, a total of 2.58 trillion copies of national and provincial newspapers were produced and 2.69 billion copies of magazines were printed.[11]

Outdoor advertising opportunities are growing exponentially as toll roads and other highways are built, meaning more places to place billboards. The construction of thousands of high-rise office towers around China affords another opportunity in the form of naming rights on prominent buildings.

Internet Retailing

Is the internet a good way to sell to consumers in China? There's a lot of interest in the internet in China on the part of investors. There's no doubt that it is an important way to reach young, educated Chinese, but why it should become a significant vehicle for retailing in China any time soon isn't clear.

Around 80% of China's internet users use Baidu.com as their primary search engine.[12] It listed on the Nasdaq in August 2005 and its shares soared. But even with 700 staff, its revenues in 2004 were just US$13 million.[13] Presumably this will grow with online advertising.

And then there is online retailing. Profits are a long way off but investors are positioning themselves. Amazon.com acquired Joyo.com, the largest online bookseller in China for US$75 million. But how many books are actually sold online in China? Furthermore, books in China have very low retail prices, far lower than in the West, and that's for non-pirated versions. Pirated versions of popular books and expensive textbooks and technical guides abound and sell for even less. The mainland Chinese rights for a previous book of mine were sold for just US$1,000 – that's $1,000 for a country of 1.3 billion people. The publisher was of the view that it's better to get $1,000 than to get nothing at all. They expected that the book would appear in China whether permission was granted or not. Furthermore, the cover price of even legitimate copies would need to be so low that royalties even on tens of thousands of copies would be almost negligible.

EBay finalized its acquisition of the Chinese auction site EachNet.com for US$180 million in 2003. And then in August 2005, Yahoo! bought a 40% stake in Chinese portal Alibaba.com for US$1 billion and agreed to hand control of its Yahoo China operations to Alibaba's management. These were worth an additional US$700 million for the purposes of the deal.[14] Alibaba.com principally operates a business-to-business portal but also owns Taobao.com, a Chinese auction site that rivals eBay locally. But Alibaba had less than US$50 million revenue in 2004. Still, as in the West, the attraction of an auction site is that the auctioneer never has to actually handle the goods that are bought and sold and at no point carries the risk of owning them.

Branding

When it comes to attracting consumers, for a relatively poor country, one would expect price to be paramount. But counterintuitively, branding is at least as important and probably more important to Chinese consumers than price. This doesn't mean that luxury goods necessarily do well in China. It is more that when shoppers buy goods in a supermarket, quality and brand recognition matter as a proxy for quality. Prices need to be competitive but not necessarily the cheapest. Harold Chee provides an example of the power of brands over price in his *Myths about Doing Business in China*: Kodak and Fuji films both charge "about 50% more than their local competitor, but less than they do in developed countries. Between them they have 90% of the Chinese market."[15] The message is: don't be cheap so much as give value for money.

A survey by Kurt Salmon Associates of middle-class consumers in China found that characteristics such as brand, impact on health and customer care were all regarded above price when it came to the decision to buy. Among those surveyed, 78% said they buy toiletry products based on brand and that if their preferred brand was unavailable, they would be unlikely to switch.[16]

The survey also found that consumers' preference for foreign or local brands differs according to the type of product they are buying. When it comes to home improvement products and electronics, the consumers surveyed showed a strong preference for foreign over local brands. When it comes to food and personal care products, they prefer local brands. And in the case of clothing and footwear, no strong preference is shown. Accordingly, KSA advises that home improvement products and electronics entrants should retain their foreign identity in their marketing. But food and personal care product entrants should try to appear more Chinese; to appear more localized.

Consumer Boycotts

The Chinese are increasingly nationalist too and sentiment can turn extremely quickly. Foreign sellers into China are more prone to consumer boycotts and scaremongering than in many other markets. Among the global brands to be targeted for boycotts and consumer scares in 2005 alone were Haagen-Dazs, Procter & Gamble's Pantene Pro-V shampoo and SK-II anti-aging cream, Colgate-Palmolive's Colgate toothpaste, Lipton instant tea, and KFC.[17] Japanese products face even more risks.

Anti-Japanese protests in April 2005, staged in response to Japan's perceived lack of remorse for its wartime hostilities in China, were accompanied by attacks on the Japanese embassy in Beijing and Japanese shops and restaurants.

The China Chain Store and Franchise Association even urged members to take products made by Japan's Asahai Breweries and MSG manufacturer Ajinomoto off their shelves. "Any Chinese customers with patriotic spirit and morality will understand and support us", said the association in a statement.[18]

But Japanese companies need to be cautious at all times about how they present themselves and react to provocation. The previous year an advertisement created for Nippon Paint was pulled before it was used due to local sensitivities. It showed a Chinese dragon unable to keep its grip on a pillar coated with Nippon paint, suggesting the smoothness of the paint. The use of a dragon was meant as a display of cultural awareness. Instead, when news of the campaign surfaced, it became clear that customers would be offended by such an obviously Chinese symbol being defeated by an overtly Japanese product.[19] On other occasions, when Japanese products have been found to have breached safety standards, the official and public condemnation tends to be more severe and longer lasting compared with for other foreign products.

Ice-cream producer and retailer Haagen-Dazs found itself in the middle of a consumer scare in early 2005, after a Shenzhen newspaper reported that the hygiene certification of a local manufacturing facility had expired. A news piece on the lapse was accompanied by various exaggerations about hygiene problems at the facility. These were quickly spread on the internet and before long Haagen-Dazs outlets across China were experiencing a dramatic slump in sales. The company believed the story was planted by a manager who had been fired. The newspaper offered to kill the story if Haagen-Dazs promised advertising money but the company refused. It subsequently paid for its refusal.

Newspapers are an important source of scares partly because the range of subjects that local journalists can safely cover is so restricted. Writing sensationalist stories about foreign brands does not raise the ire of the government and it helps to sell newspapers.

The most efficient way to counter bad news pieces is to pay journalists not to write negative, misinforming stories, which of course is what many journalists want. Until China has better enforced libel laws and greater journalistic standards, there may little choice other than to do this.

Such shakedowns and scares in relation to global brands have become so common that the American Chamber of Commerce in Beijing hosted a seminar in mid-August 2005 entitled "Foreign Firms under Fire". Foreign brand manufacturers have been advised to monitor internet bulletin boards, a prime source of transmitting scares, and aggressively counter misinformation. The internet and mobile phone texting mean that localized scares can quickly become national ones.

Aging Consumers

From a retailing perspective, the important characteristic of China's population other than its sheer size is that it's aging. The UN estimates are that in 2025, China will have 326 million people aged 50 or more. Fewer than 278 million will be below the age of 20 and 598 million will be aged 20–49.[20] Indeed, China's age/population profile is similar to a developed country. Median population age in China is 32.26 years. In India it's 24.7 (the figure for the US is 36.27 years). More than 10% or around 140 million Chinese are classified as elderly. By 2030, that number will be 300 million.[21] This is a consequence of the one-child policy introduced in 1979.

The aging will be more pronounced in the cities than in rural areas because people in the cities tend to live longer and the one-child policy was enforced with more vigor in the cities than in rural areas.

This aging is already having a direct impact on the consumer market. There's strong demand for tonics and vitamins, for example, as people attempt to stave off the effects of aging.

Foreign life insurance and pension companies have come to realize that China's size, the current lack of adequate pension and insurance provisions and, most importantly, China's unusual demographic profile makes China a huge potential market for them.

By 2006, 76 insurance companies operated in China – 38 of them domestic insurers and the other 38 foreign investment insurers. The majority specialize in life and property insurance. Insurance premiums reached Y432 billion (US$53.5 billion) in 2004, making China the largest insurance market in Asia after Japan and South Korea.[22]

But there's a long way to go. By the end of 2004, 163.42 million people, or less than 25% of the working population, participated in a basic pension program. And 123.86 million people were covered by basic health insurance programs, or less than 10% of the population.[23]

Healthcare

China's aging population and the appalling state of its healthcare system mean that healthcare has huge potential in China for investors. Deregulation will lead to plenty of opportunities.

The scale of the sector is confounding. By the end of 2004, there were 277,000 healthcare institutions in China, including 62,000 general hospitals and healthcare stations, and 3,000 maternal and childbirth healthcare institutions. There are more than 3 million hospital beds in China.[24] Quantity, though, is no substitute for quality. China's healthcare standards are so poor that it poses a huge potential political problem for the government. By 2005, even the state-controlled press was openly criticizing the sector and officials' management of it.

The current problems have had a long gestation. At no stage in its 5,000 year history was surgery a significant part of Chinese traditional medicine and healthcare. The body was seen as an inviolable whole. Acupuncture was about as invasive as healthcare generally got. Meanwhile, in Europe, doctors were experimenting with cadavers and eventually on live people to develop surgery, a whole new discipline of medicine.

Apart from Confucian restrictions on human vivisection, one theory as to why surgery did not take off in China is that circumcision was not practiced, on account of Chinese males having small foreskins. And without this starting point, surgery had little to build on. Eunuchs who were employed by the emperors as their palace servants, bureaucrats and advisers – up to 70,000 at a time – present a counterargument, however.

The practice of castrating men had occurred in China for at least 3,000 years. By the time of the Manchu emperors, castration had become a profession and specialist castrators earned a living beside the imperial palace. Keith Laidler, in his *The Last Empress,* writes how the genitals were washed in pepper water to partially anaesthetize them, the stomach and upper thighs were tightly bandaged to reduce blood flow and once the candidate was settled on a heated couch, the castrator would then slice through with a knife, severing both penis and scrotum.[25] A plug was then inserted in the urethra and the lesion bandaged. The patient was not allowed to drink for three days, after which the urethra was unplugged. If the patient could then pass urine, the operation was a success. If not and the urethra had healed shut, the patient would die within days. The severed genitalia were never discarded but kept by each eunuch in a jar so that on his death he could be buried whole.

Access to the palace often meant influence and great wealth. Many eunuchs became rich through bribe taking and were able to afford their own mansions and country houses. Consequently, and contrary to expectations, the demand to become a eunuch was actually very high.

Surgery in China has moved on. But there is still a preference for traditional healing. One reason might be the state of China's conventional healthcare system. The absence of market forces has left it moribund and crowded. There remains an almost total absence of conventional primary care: there are few independent doctors, or even neighborhood clinics, so people attend hospitals for almost every healthcare need.

Hospital funding is complex and confused. The central, provincial and local governments fund hospitals, and in the past, medical care was provided either at no or very little charge. Patients are now being asked to pay for some of their care and that is helping to promote rapid growth in the healthcare insurance market. This market is worth around US$5 billion and growing at 15–20% per annum.

But it's also leading to overservicing as cash-strapped hospitals and doctors attempt to raise funds whenever they can. One study has found that around half of all babies delivered in China's hospitals are delivered by Caesarean section, with the figure as high as 70% in some hospitals.[26] Drug sales too have risen dramatically. Some hospitals earn up to half their operating revenues by selling drugs to patients.

Hospitals vary widely in competence and quality. Beijing, for example, has several specialist hospitals that are well equipped, but in many rural areas, hospitals have almost no modern equipment to speak of.

There are long waiting lists for many procedures and this has encouraged significant bribery, whereby better off patients are able to queue jump and have the doctor of their choice by giving unofficial payments to nurses, doctors and administrators, all of whom tend to be paid poorly.

By 2005, the Ministry of Health had recognized that China's healthcare system needed substantial reform. Accordingly, the sector is being opened up in varying degrees to competition and foreign investment.

State-owned hospitals increasingly are being permitted to contract out some or all of their management. The municipal government of Suzhou, for example, issued tenders in 2004 for the management of most of its public hospitals, while retaining ownership. Others are being permitted to partially privatize by accepting private capital. And in some regions such as Zhejiang-Jiangsu, foreigners have been allowed to invest directly in new hospitals.

China Hospitals Inc. is one company that has sought to capitalize on the growing liberalization of China's healthcare sector. By 2005, it operated two hospitals in China through Beijing-based associates. It filed for an IPO with the US Securities and Exchange Commission in mid-2005, with aspirations to become the largest hospital chain in China by acquiring as many as 29 hospitals.

The market for medical equipment in China is also growing rapidly and is worth around US$13 billion annually. The China International Medical Equipment Fair, held twice a year in Harbin, is Asia's largest international medical equipment show and only opened to foreign exhibitors two years ago. The May 2005 exhibition attracted 900 exhibitors from around the world. It has become an important means by which foreign medical equipment suppliers find agents and distributors in China.

So, in short, China as a consumer market is diversified, regionalized, not rich but growing more comfortable, brand conscious (but that's more in terms of what brand of soap is preferred not whether Rolex is preferred to Longines) and it's aging. There's more to it than it simply being big. The opportunities will come from the detail rather than the mere magnitude.

Chapter 25

SHANGHAI: CHINA'S FINANCIAL CAPITAL

Shanghai worries the world. And Hong Kong is terrified by it. Analysts go there, look at the breakneck development and wonder, if this is what one Chinese city can be like, what will it mean for the world when many Chinese cities are like it? The world looks on and sees an emerging new world order. Hong Kong looks on and sees its own emerging irrelevance. And what should that other billion-plus country, India, make of Shanghai?

From the vantage point of The Bund, Shanghai's famous riverside promenade, Shanghai today looks very much like Hong Kong, with neon-sign-topped skyscrapers on both sides of the wide Huangpu River. The Huangpu has become to Shanghai what the harbor has to Hong Kong. Except that Shanghai now is bigger, much bigger. The Bund remains charming with its historic buildings but what has grown up around it is astonishing.

The arguments for a big and powerful Shanghai are impressive. Some 200 million people live within a three-hour drive of the city. Historically, it has been China's most outward-looking, cosmopolitan and sophisticated city. It has long been richer than anywhere else in China. And that remains the case. One estimate is that by 2010, Shanghai will be the first area in China to reach a per capita income of US$10,000.

Today, Shanghai benefits by being overseen by one powerful government. The central government largely stays out of the way. Accordingly, the number of levels of officials who can obstruct, intervene or simply put out their hand is reduced. Shanghai has also benefited from being the home town of some of China's most powerful politicians, including former Premier Zhu Rongji. He served as Shanghai's mayor and has been credited with reducing the amount of red tape in the city's administration. Anecdotally, Shanghai's police and other officials are less corrupt than officials elsewhere in China. Indeed, the development in Shanghai and the speed with which it has occurred suggest that corruption and bureaucracy are not serious obstacles, which marks Shanghai out as almost unique in China.

And so today Shanghai astonishes. Utterly. Pudong, on the opposite side of the Huangpu River to The Bund, was swampy marshland in 1990. Now it is home to something that verges on Manhattan.

The Jin Mao Tower dominates Pudong. It is China's tallest and the world's third tallest building (or it was when it was completed). It contains what is described as the world's highest hotel, a Grand Hyatt, which starts at the 54th floor. If you go to the 88th floor, in every direction you see literally hundreds of square kilometers of tall office and residential towers. In fact, Shanghai today is home to more than 4,000 buildings that are 18 storeys or more high, twice that of New York. The speed with which this has happened compounds the shock. More than three quarters of these towers have been built since 1994.

Shanghai's Pudong International Airport is world class. By 2010, it will have three runways and double its existing capacity. The expressway from Shanghai to the airport is wide and impressive and alongside it runs the extraordinary Maglev train. On one recent visit to Shanghai, I thought my taxi was travelling fast until that thing shot past. Simply, I have never seen anything like it. The German-designed, magnetically propelled train reaches speeds of 430 kilometers an hour and is the fastest commercial passenger train on earth. It can do the 30-kilometer journey to the airport in just eight minutes. No other city in the world has one, which of course was the point in having it. Shanghai wants to be like the Maglev – to have arrived and to have done it faster than anyone else.

The first ever Chinese Formula One Grand Prix was staged by Shanghai in September 2004 at a state-of-the-art track at Anting, 30 kilometers outside Shanghai. Shanghai International Circuit, the local promoter, is state connected and has agreed to pay around US$40 million in licensing fees each year until 2010 to the Formula One governing body.

The Shanghai city authorities are keen not to develop a city that is simply an efficient multi-plant factory turning out huge quantities of goods but is actually an attractive place to live in and to visit. Civilizing touches are being added that say a lot about the breadth of the priorities of city officials. Parks and gardens of a quality rarely seen elsewhere are being developed. The Shanghai Museum in Renmin Square is one of the best of its kind, with high-quality exhibits set in surroundings that can only be described as best practice as far as museums of art go. It's part of a cultural complex that includes the Grand Theatre and the Shanghai Art Museum. The three were completed in the 1990s at a cost of US$230 million.

The care and cost that has gone into preserving the spectacular lobby of the old Hong Kong and Shanghai Bank building at no. 12 on The Bund is further testament to city officials' civic pride. The Pudong Development Bank now occupies the building. The city administration made the bank restore the lobby and the building more generally to its former glory as a condition of occupation. The result is extraordinary.

In 2001, the local government commissioned consultants McKinsey & Co. to develop a plan for a shopping precinct modeled on the Champs Elysées in Paris and others like it.[1] McKinsey looked at nine such shopping precincts, including London's Oxford Street and Tokyo's Giza; what Shanghai now has is the Nanjing Donglu, a spectacular pedestrian shopping street that runs three kilometers from Chengdu Lu all the way to The Bund. Upmarket department stores and restaurants line both sides, and at night it is ablaze with a dazzling array of neon signs of the type for which Hong Kong used to be famous. Indeed, Nanjing Donglu surpasses the Champs Elysées, which has become tired and tatty as upmarket retail names have moved to more fashionable locations. And as for Mumbai, well, it has been left in the dust, literally, as a later chapter will show.

A perennial question mark hangs over Shanghai's property market. Shanghai experienced a severe property glut in the 1990s. Premium and grade A office space that had commanded US$73 per square meter in 1995 fetched less than US$18 by late 1998.[2] The market bounced back but much demand comes from foreign companies that are in China to seek profits rather than because they are profitable. Such demand can only be regarded as fickle.

Undoubtedly, more gluts will come. A glut was headed off in the early 2000s because of China's accession to the WTO. Successive liberalizations of entry into China's insurance, banking, oil exploration, logistics and services sectors under the WTO are seeing waves of foreign businesses in these areas set up offices in Shanghai, if for no other reason than simply to be around when their sector opens up. By 2004, international legal and accounting firms were driving big increases in demand for premium office space in Shanghai. In 2005, investment in China's banking system was freed up and this helped to drive another round of big foreign companies opening a representative office in Shanghai, if nothing else. Property professionals also point to Shanghai's staging of the World Expo in 2010 as another factor that should help to hold up property demand.

Some enormous projects are planned. The biggest is the 492-meter, 101-storey Shanghai World Financial Center. It is to be built adjacent to the Jin

Mao Tower and will be the world's tallest tower when completed. It is supposed to be completed in 2008 (a deadline that has been pushed out several times). It will add at least 335,420 square meters of premium office space to Pudong. By late 2005, none of its 70 floors of office space had been leased in advance, nor had rents been determined, but Park Hyatt had agreed to manage its 15-floor hotel.

Built by the Mori Building Corporation of Japan, it was to have a giant, open circle built into its apex, giving it the appearance of a giant bottle opener. The circle was supposed to represent the sky, and the tower, the earth. But as one Chinese said to me: "Many Chinese feel that this building will be a disgrace to all Chinese. The circle represents the Rising Sun. How can we allow this symbol of Japan to rise over all Shanghai?" He had a point. Many in China have not forgotten the barbarism with which the Japanese bombed and murdered their way through Shanghai in 1937, and the massacre at Nanjing that December when tens of thousands of Chinese Nationalist soldiers and civilians were killed, thousands of Chinese women were raped, prisoners were used for bayonet practice and the injured were buried in mass graves.[3] Mori was surprised by the uproar and modified the circle to become a square, which in any event designers said would be faster and cheaper to build.

Vehicle traffic is a growing headache. Road congestion at 6pm weekday evenings is intense. Huge overpasses and freeways have been constructed but traffic forecasts have been wildly wrong. Vehicle numbers forecast in 1990 by the government for 2020 were surpassed in late 2004. The municipal government has raised vehicle registration fees every year since 2000, so that they are now around US$4,600 per vehicle, way beyond the city's per capita income.[4] But many if not most Shanghai drivers get around this by registering their cars in cities elsewhere that have far lower registration fees. The practice is illegal but difficult to police.

But, as ever, when it comes to the economy, China and the foreign investors in it need to be reminded that physical infrastructure is only half the story. The other half is less visible. It's the soft infrastructure of which the most important is an enforced rule of law. The first half without the second half will lead inexorably to the first half being wasted. After all, any fool can invest. The cleverness comes in generating a commercial rate of return on that investment. But then being halfway there is better than not having started the journey.

Chapter 26

And Then There is Beijing

Beijing has long been the poor older brother of Shanghai, concerned with the high-minded pursuits of public service while younger brother Shanghai grubbied itself with commerce and got rich in the process. But Beijing is changing. Being awarded the 2008 Summer Olympics gave the city's administration the impetus to undertake civil improvements and so now millions are being spent on beautifying and perfecting it. And it's working. Beijing is becoming beautiful.

The city is large, mostly flat and frequently covered in oily air pollution that grimes the skin and clothes. But it is orderly, with wide boulevards of quietly flowing traffic and more public toilets per square kilometer than anywhere else on earth. (Although, this is partly because many older-style houses don't have their own toilets.) It has all the trappings of an administrative center – large government buildings, showcase monuments and public places such as Tiananmen Square. And among them, many blocks of traditional *hutongs*, the beautiful, well-maintained alleys lined with old-style courtyard houses and graceful weeping willows.

But as the city's purpose diversifies, the heart of the city – its center of focus – is shifting from Tiananmen and toward the fast developing shopping and commercial office district. No longer is the city drab. Shades of Hong Kong are creeping in all over the city. It is becoming its own microcosm, which is probably just as well, because as the provinces develop economically, they're becoming less reliant on Beijing for administrative and political direction. China stretches across four hours of time zones but the entire country keeps Beijing time. But this stamp of authority is becoming one of symbolism. Increasingly, directives from Beijing are given their own local interpretations or ignored altogether.

Wangfujing Dajie has emerged as Beijing's premier shopping street. It is a smaller, but nonetheless impressive version of Shanghai's Nanjing Donglu. It too has been transformed into a pedestrian mall and at night it also blazes with neon signs and buzzes with people who can sit at outdoor cafés and bars. It is filled with upmarket Hong Kong-style shopping malls that blast out ostensibly soothing Kenny Gee background music over their PA systems.

Hong Kong billionaire Li Ka Shing's massive office, hotel and retail complex Oriental Plaza is around the corner, along a road that empties into Tiananmen Square. But not before an extraordinarily beautiful park with waterways and sculptures is reached. Beijing is becoming a mix of imported convenience (fast-food chains, Starbucks) and traditional Chinese elegance (sculptured gardens, fountains). Like Shanghai, it is developing rapidly. Visitors who were last there five years ago are shocked by the city's progress today. Beijing is changing for the better.

Beijing's Bar Street offers another surprise. A dissecting street cuts it into a northern section and a southern section. The north side is rumored to be controlled by Chinese Mafia groups and largely attracts local Chinese drinkers. Tellingly, beggars congregate at the south end, the one that is favored by Western tourists and expatriates. The beggars leave the north side well alone. Drinkers sit at pavement chairs and tables during the summer months. Hustlers offer "lady bars" and pimps offer prostitutes. Others offer pirated CDs and DVDs that are sold from bags that they keep inside the bars. Pornography is on offer too. Pornographic movies are not called "blue" movies in China but "yellow" movies. (Anything contraband is referred to as "yellow", the imperial color of the emperors.)

The immediate impression of Beijing is that its people are polite and friendly, noticeably more so than in Shanghai. Beijing is an easy place for foreigners to be. No longer do Beijingers find Westerners worth a second glance, if they notice them at all. The city streets are clean, although the air can be heavy with pollution. Beijing traffic must be the most orderly in Asia. Motorists have a genuine respect and concern for pedestrians. Taxi drivers are nearly always polite, good-natured and almost never rip off their passengers. Beijingers are self-confident, curious and interested in culture and the arts. Parks and gardens are being developed in Beijing that are among the most stunning I've seen. They are well kept, extensive and bursting with flowers in bloom. Street crime is low to the point that rarely are bicycles chained up and women walk alone freely at night even in areas that are poorly lit. But of course there are negatives. The uniformed police and soldiers who are evident everywhere have arrogant demeanors, are unhelpful and are distrusted.

Alcohol abuse is evident, particularly in the narrow streets of the *hutong*, the traditional residential areas, where, by 11pm on any night of the week, Chinese men, so drunk they can barely walk, shuffle home in pairs or more commonly alone. Such brazen public drunkenness is something that China shares with that other post-Communist behemoth, Russia, where I've seen middle-aged women go about their shopping mid-morning, shopping bags in one hand and an open bottle of beer or vodka in the other.

Beijing is also a multicultural city. The most obvious minority are Chinese Muslims. There are plenty of Muslim stalls and restaurants owned by Chinese Muslims that serve halal food. And there are mosques.

But importantly, Beijing, like Shanghai, is a city where city officials are concerned with civic pride. Large amounts of public money are being invested in museums, gardens and pedestrian malls. China's premier cities are acquiring the accoutrements of civil society and that says a lot about where China is heading and where it wants to be. These sorts of signal should be as encouraging to foreign investors as investments in port facilities, roads and airports.

Emerging Freedoms and Unshackled Conversation

China's emperors imposed a ban on emigration in the eighteenth, and first half of the nineteenth, century. Those who flouted it faced execution. And during the Maoist era, ordinary Chinese were discouraged from having contact with foreigners. Those who did were likely to attract the attention of the police.

Times have changed. China's young generation are very outward-looking and nowhere more so than in Beijing. The internet has been very important. It allows young Chinese to access news and information that bypasses government censors. It also provides a means for them to contact one another and people outside China. The BBC World Service is another important source for information among the educated young. During the 1989 protests in Tiananmen Square, BBC radio was how many of them stayed informed about events.

Young people in China increasingly are happy to be engaged on almost any topic. I have had many conversations with young Chinese in Beijing, especially about the events in Tiananmen Square in 1989, official corruption in China, the quasi-cult Falun Gong or China's treatment of Tibet.

In short, each person in Beijing with whom I have discussed the Tiananmen Square protests has told me that they are very aware of what happened, although few have seen pictures of the demonstrations. Each one assured me that "hundreds" of students were killed by the army during the protest's aftermath and that most of the killings did not occur in the square but in the streets away from it.

Are Tiananmen-like protests likely to happen again? No, is the typical opinion. The government is more liberal. As one person said to me, "each leader chosen by China is softer than the last". And besides, university staff are now better paid and students receive better allowances than in 1989. (It was this issue that drove the protests more than anything else. The students had protested under the rubric of "democracy", but better living conditions for students and academics was their prime concern.)

Tibet is a non-issue among the young Chinese with whom I've spoken. Few understand the West's interest in Tibet and one young man described the Tibetans to me as "very aggressive" and deserving of the treatment meted out to them by China. I mentioned that one concern in the West, beyond basic human rights, is that Han Chinese culture appears to be swamping Tibetan culture. It was a point that he had not considered but understood right away.

Young Beijingers with whom I've spoken are united in their rejection of Falun Gong. The movement is secretive and well organized, like the Chinese Government, which of course is why the government saw it as such a threat. Ordinary Chinese appear to support the government's crackdown on the Falun Gong. The government has made effective propaganda use of the case of a promising young violinist and Falun Gong adherent who set herself alight in Tiananmen Square to protest at the crackdown. She did not die but was horribly disfigured. Not unreasonably, this has turned many in China against Falun Gong and so now the movement's influence within China is almost negligible.

The corruption of government officials is another topic that everyone seems prepared to discuss. Most assume that such corruption is an inevitable part of government in a developing country and therefore to be expected. One young man assured me that government officials in all countries are corrupt because people everywhere are essentially "the same". I asked him if corruption is pervasive in his everyday life. "Oh yes", he said. "All the time. It's everywhere." He gave two examples. When he was due to graduate from high school, he needed a good reference from the headmaster so that he would be allocated to a good company in the state sector. To ensure that, he was required to bribe his headmaster. Once he was allocated to a company, he visited the company supervisor's house one evening to pay him a bribe to ensure that he would be allocated a good job within the company. Payments such as these are "very common", he said.

Another young man told me how he was arrested soon after he first came to Beijing. He didn't have the necessary residency permit for Beijing – a common infringement. He was jailed for 10 days and kept in a cell that had no mattress but a bare timber floor. The floor was wet and so on the first night he stood up all night rather than sleep in the wet. On the second night, he again stood up all night. But by the third night, he was too tired to stand so resigned himself to sleeping on the floor. He was able to win his release by paying Y350, which enabled him to obtain a prison uniform that entitled him to do prison work. And after one week's work he'd earned his release. He sought the correct residency permit to avoid further problems. It simply required that he pay a bribe.

I asked one young Beijinger if he had been to see Mao's corpse in Tiananmen Square where it lies on display. With great certainty, he said:

> No. I will not go there. My parents' lives could have been so different if it was not for him. He did some good things for China. But the last years were a disaster. The Cultural Revolution was a disaster for China. He closed the schools. For ten years they were closed. How different my parents' lives could have been if they had received a good education. Because of him they received nothing.

The previous day I had joined the queue at Mao's tomb. The queue always looks prohibitively long but it moves quickly. Why do Chinese queue to see the body of the man who murdered so many and destroyed the intellectual and artistic life of China in the dark years of the Cultural Revolution? Perhaps for many domestic tourists the trip is made more out of curiosity than reverence, like a trip to the freak show at the circus.

For others, Mao has become godlike. I'd noticed that some taxi drivers keep little images of Mao, as if venerating a potentially helpful deity. As we went into the tomb, some in the queue (but by no means all) stopped to buy silk flowers at an official stall. Once inside, they held the flowers aloft in front of a large marble statue of the chairman, bowed deeply as if before an image in a temple and then deposited the flowers in a large trolley that presumably when full is dragged to the stall and the flower offerings are resold.

The large brass doors at the entrance of the tomb have been polished clean at arm level by hundreds of visiting Chinese who run their fingers over them as if visiting a religious site, in the hope that physical contact might impart some sort of beneficial energy. (I'd noticed Catholics running their hands over the interior of the grotto at the pilgrimage site at Lourdes in southern France. And then, of course, there is the bronze statue of St Peter in St Peter's Basilica in the Vatican. The caresses and kisses of pilgrims over the centuries have worn the toes of the statue's right foot away, giving it the appearance of a leper.)

Behind the statue is the room in which Mao's body lies in state. It's kept behind glass where it is joined by two soldiers who stand to attention behind it. The crowd is kept moving the whole time. Lingerers are pushed forward rudely by attendants. A middle-aged Chinese woman behind me stopped to stare at Mao's face. She was rooted to the spot and despite yells to keep moving, she just kept staring. She didn't seem to hear. I might have been wrong, but she looked very, very angry.

Chapter 27

THE DALAI LAMA EATS MEAT

It is often said that there are few genuinely Asian brands and those that do exist have had little success in expanding beyond Asia. But one brand has traveled well to the West. It has widespread brand name recognition, celebrity endorsement from the likes of actors Richard Gere, Goldie Hawn and Harrison Ford, generates millions of dollars quickly and in cash and is identifiably Asian. In fact, it is probably the most successful, truly Asian brand in the world today. It's both chic and cool, enjoys considerable loyalty and attracts millions of dollars in free advertising from newspapers that cover it as part of their regular news coverage. And its corporate colors are well known: purple and saffron, as is its mandala corporate insignia. The product is consistent, non-threatening (unless you happen to be the government of China) and enjoys a strong global reputation. The brand is the Dalai Lama.

But who is the man behind the brand? Tibetans believe that the Dalai Lama is a reincarnation of Chenrezi, the Tibetan deity that represents compassion. (The Dalai Lama prefers the word "manifestation" to "reincarnation".) His actual name is Tenzin Gyatso. But Tibetans call him Yeshi Norbu ("Precious Jewel"). His inner circle call him Kundun ("Presence"). To the outside world he is the Dalai Lama. Often the Western media writes him up as a god-king but that is not accurate. Technically, he is a Bodhisattva, a being that has reached enlightenment but nonetheless chooses to remain on earth to teach others.

The Dalai Lama is charming and engaging. He is not tainted by scandal, unlike many other leaders. But should being beyond reproach mean being beyond scrutiny? Rarely, if ever, do journalists subject him to rigorous examination. Most published interviews breeze on as airily as does the subject, for whom a good giggle and a quaint parable are substitutes for hard answers. That is a pity because beneath the saffron robes of a holy man is a politician and there is much on which this politician might be challenged.

For a start, and this surprises most people, the Dalai Lama, the world's most famous Buddhist, is not a vegetarian. He eats meat. He has done so since (he claims) a doctor advised him to after liver complications from hepatitis. I have checked with several doctors, but none agree that meat consumption is necessary or even desirable for a damaged liver.

The Money

The Dalai Lama has confirmed that he was on the CIA's payroll from the late 1950s until 1974. He is believed to have received US$15,000 each month (US$180,000 a year) from the CIA. The funds were paid to him personally but he used all or most of it for Tibetan government-in-exile activities, principally to fund offices in New York and Geneva and for international lobbying. The government-in-exile itself received another US$1.7 million each year.[1] The money was to pay for guerrilla operations against the Chinese, notwithstanding the Dalai Lama's public stance in support of non-violence, for which he was awarded the Nobel Prize for Peace in 1989.

The Tibetan government-in-exile is based in Dharamsala in the northern Indian state of Uttar Pradesh. Its administrative wing comprises seven "government" departments and several other special offices. In addition, there are charitable trusts and a publishing company, five hotels in India and Nepal and a handicrafts distribution company in the US and one in Australia. These are under the auspices of the Department of Finance. The government was involved in running 24 businesses in all, but decided in 2003 that it would withdraw from these because such commercial involvement was not appropriate.

Revenue comes from the Tibetan diaspora, the remaining enterprises, donations, money made by the Dalai Lama on his overseas visits and indirectly from the US State Department's Bureau for Refugee Programs. Each exiled Tibetan is able to make a voluntary annual contribution of 46 rupees (about US$1), plus 4% of their basic pay or 2% of their gross salary, whichever is higher.

Little is known about the government-in-exile's finances. I did contact its Department of Finance in Dharamsala with a series of questions about how it funds itself and its expenditure. I was sent a series of spreadsheets in reply.

The government-in-exile claims that its total budget for 2002–03 amounted to the equivalent of US$22.028 million. The budget was spent on various programs such as health, education, religion and culture. The biggest item was for "political-related expenditure" at US$7 million. The next biggest was administration, which runs to US$4.5 million. Around US$1.8 million was allocated to running the government-in-exile's offices of Tibet overseas.

For all that the government-in-exile claims to do, these sums appear too low. Nor is it clear how donations enter its budgeting. These are likely to run to many millions but there is no explicit acknowledgment of them or their sources.

Many donations are channeled through the New York-based Tibet Fund, set up in 1981 by several Tibetan refugees and US citizens. It has grown into a multimillion dollar organization that disburses some US$3 million each year to its various programs. Part of its funding comes from the US State Department's Bureau for Refugee Programs. Nonetheless, the fund works closely with the government-in-exile in determining how the funds are spent.

If rumor is to be believed, then the government-in-exile is not free of factionalism and corruption. The Tibet Fund itself was accused of being subject to corruption, leading to Samdhong Rinpoche, the exiles' prime minister, walking out of the government-in-exile's assembly in September 2003. He did not return until the accusations were withdrawn.[2] I have spoken with refugee Tibetans in Nepal, who claim that they are constantly asked to make donations to this or that Tibetan cause. Huge sums are raised, middlemen abound and there is little accountability. Critics also complain of excessive bureaucracy. Nor is the government-in-exile free of nepotism. On this the Dalai Lama leads the way.

The Family

The Dalai Lama's mother gave birth to 16 children but 9 died very young. Seven survived into adulthood. Each of them has been involved in the administration of the government-in-exile and so too have more distant relatives. In 1993, for example, three of the six members of the *Kashag* or cabinet, the highest executive branch of the Tibetan government-in-exile, were close relatives of the Dalai Lama: a brother, a sister and a sister-in-law.

Gyalo Thondup, an older brother, is a former chairman of the *Kashag* and Minister of Security. He headed the CIA-backed Tibetan contra movement in the 1960s. For a time, he lived in Hong Kong.

Lobsang Samten, another older brother, helped to establish the Tibetan Medical Center in Dharamsala. His widow, Namgyal Lhamo Taklha, is a former secretary of the government-in-exile's Planning Council and a former secretary of its Department of Health.

Jetsun Pema Gyalpo, a younger sister, served as president of the Tibetan Children's Villages in Dharamsala and is a former health and education minister. Her husband Tempa Tsering served as secretary of the government-in-exile's Department of Information and International Relations. Their daughter Tencho Gyalpo is a member of the Tibetan Parliament in exile.

Tendzin Choegyal, a younger brother, is a senior member of the Private Office of the Dalai Lama and an important adviser to the Dalai Lama. His wife Rinchen Khando Choegyal is president of the Tibetan Women's Association and a former education minister.

Tsering Dolma Takla, the Dalai Lama's oldest sister, helped to set up the Tibetan Children's Villages in Dharamsala before she died in 1964. Her husband Phuntsok Tashi Takla was appointed commander of the Dalai Lama's security guards in Tibet in 1957. Later, in exile, he was a member of several delegations sent to Beijing to negotiate on the Dalai Lama's behalf. He remarried in 1967 to Kesang Yangkyi. She was appointed the Dalai Lama's representative to London in 1989 and is the representative of the Tibetan government-in-exile for northern Europe. She has served also as secretary for international relations of the government-in-exile's Department of Information and International Relations.

Thubten Jigme Norbu, the oldest brother, lives in Indiana, in the US. A former professor at Indiana University, he is a founder of the Tibetan Cultural Center in Bloomington, Indiana. His wife Kunyang is the younger sister of the Sakya Dagchen, the head of the Sakya Sect of Tibetan Buddhism. The Sakya Dagchen is also in exile from Tibet. Kunyang operates Café Django, a Tibetan restaurant in Indiana. Jigme Norbu, one of their three sons and thus a nephew of the Dalai Lama, operates the Snow Lion Restaurant, another Tibetan restaurant in Indiana. He also serves as the executive director of the Tibetan Cultural Center.

In 1997, in a brilliant example of brand extension, Hollywood produced two movies with the cooperation of the government-in-exile: *Kundun* and *Seven Years in Tibet*. Life merged with art. Several of the Dalai Lama's relatives had starring roles.

The Dalai Lama's sister Jetsun Pema Gyalpo had an acting role in *Seven Years in Tibet* alongside Brad Pitt. Tenzin Tsarong, a nephew of Namgyal Lhamo Taklha, the Dalai Lama's sister-in-law, played the younger Dalai Lama in *Kundun*. Tencho Gyalpo, a niece of the Dalai Lama, also had a role, as did Tenzin Lodoe, a nephew.

Had the Dalai Lama remained in power in Tibet, he most probably would be a dictator ruling one of the world's few theocracies. In fact, since the demise of the Taliban in Afghanistan, probably Tibet would be the world's only theocracy. It would also be one of the world's more nepotistic regimes in which key office holders are family members.

The State Lottery

How did Tenzin Gyatso become the Dalai Lama? The Thirteenth Dalai Lama died in 1933. The royal court now had to find his successor. What follows is an abridged version of the official account of how they did that. The Thirteenth had made vague suggestions that his successor (who would be him, given that he was to be reincarnated) would be born in Tibet's northeast. (The current Dalai Lama already has said that his successor will be born in a free country, which seems to rule out Tibet and China.)

Also, the Thirteenth Dalai Lama is supposed to have died whilst in meditation. His body was left in that position while awaiting the funeral. Overnight, its head twisted around to face the northeast. And then other signs began to appear in the northeast: rainbows and clouds that resembled elephants. The evidence was stacking up. Next, a dragon flower appeared from the direction of the stairway on the northeast side of the main courtyard of the Potala Palace. And to really top it off, a fungus appeared on a wooden pillar on the northeast side of the chamber built in memory of the Thirteenth Dalai Lama. The fungus was in the shape of a star. Members of the royal court had to suppress their excitement.

The regent traveled to a lake famous for inducing helpful visions. In the waters of the lake, he saw a baby with its mother in a house that had blue gable ends. The baby was the new Dalai Lama. So a new Dalai Lama had been born. But how to find him? At least the court now had an idea of what his house would look like.

A search party set out with possessions of the Thirteenth Dalai Lama the following year. Its members headed to the northeast. For several weeks they trudged through snow. They met up with the Panchen Lama (Tibet's most important lama after the Dalai Lama). He gave them the names of three candidates that he had heard might be the new Dalai Lama. The first child on the list turned out to have died. And the second ran away crying on the approach of the party. The third lived in a remote village. The party now trekked to it. The child's house had blue gable ends, as in the regent's vision. When the child saw the head of the party, rather than run away, he ran toward him, shouting "lama, lama", even though the party's head was in disguise and that the word "lama" is actually "aga" in the local Amdo dialect, the dialect spoken by the parents of the child. Various possessions that had belonged to the Thirteenth Dalai Lama were mixed up with other items and shown to the child. The child selected the correct possessions and announced them to be his. Various other tests were conducted and passed and, to seal his fate, the child had a birthmark that was felt to be in the shape of a conch shell. (The conch shell is an auspicious symbol in Tibetan Buddhism.) At last Tibet had its Fourteenth Dalai Lama.[3] And so a peasant child and his impoverished family from a remote part of Tibet were plucked from obscurity. The boy was two years old. He'd been born in the Year of the Wood Pig (1935).

The search party had to pay the local Chinese governor an enormous bribe to secure the safe passage of the child. His family also accompanied him. They were resettled in the Potala Palace in Lhasa. Essentially, this one poor Tibetan family had won the state lottery. It was now considered the "royal" family and their son, the head of state. Palace life must have taken some getting used to. The Dalai Lama's mother gave his younger brother, Tendzin Choegyal, a .22 rifle that he used to shoot out the windows of a house that belonged to a Chinese family, not far from the palace. He also kept a miniature pony on the roof of the palace and a sister would tear around the palace courtyards on a motorbike.

Meanwhile, courtiers indulged in the usual intrigues that they do everywhere. One more progressive faction apparently planned a coup and, in 1946, the Dalai Lama's father died prematurely, possibly from drinking poison that had been intended for the regent.

The Dalai Lama famously fled from Tibet in 1959 amid heavy People's Liberation Army (PLA) shelling. He took with him as many treasures and other assets as his party could carry. Whether the assets were his to take is questionable, not that anyone does. The world's media routinely condemns other leaders who, when driven from office, cart off the accoutrements of office and anything else, but then maybe Bodhisattvas are special cases. In any event, niceties such as a separation between the state and its head were not a feature of successive Dalai Lama dictatorships in Tibet. The items were later sold and the proceeds used to help Tibetan refugees. In India, the Dalai Lama first stayed in a bungalow lent by India's wealthy industrialist Birla family that owns the Mumbai-based Birla Group. Eventually, the Indian Government allowed him and his followers to establish a community at what is now Dharamsala.

Not Black and White

The Dalai Lama said in his 1989 Nobel Peace Prize acceptance speech that Tibet's population is 6 million. China argues that it's 2 million. It all depends on where the borders are drawn. And that's one of the problems with the Dalai Lama's claims for Tibetan independence: the region's borders were never defined. In any event, the Dalai Lamas never conducted a census during their rule.

China argues that Tibet has been a part of China for centuries. It's one of China's few stances with which almost every prominent Chinese dissident agrees. The view of Wei Jingshen, arguably the most prominent, is typical. He is adamant that Tibet belongs within China.

But the residents of three provinces, U-Tsang, Kham and Amdo, appear to have recognized the spiritual and temporal authority of the Dalai Lamas. Many paid taxes to the central authority in Lhasa. But then so did people in Ladakh and even in parts of India. And then the current Dalai Lama himself was born in a region of Tibet where the local governor was not Tibetan but a Chinese Muslim.

Tibet made no effort to become a member of the UN, so that when the PLA entered Tibet in 1950 it was unable to take its claim directly to that body. Instead, it had to ask sympathetic member countries to make representations on its behalf, but few countries were interested in Tibet's plight at the time. Non-membership was a mistake that the Dalai Lama has rued ever since.

Of late, the government-in-exile has said that it is willing to concede that Tibet is a part of China in exchange for genuine autonomy for the whole of Tibet. But by the "whole of Tibet", the Dalai Lama means not just the present Tibet Autonomous Region but also parts of Sichuan, Gansu, Yunnan and Xinjiang (East Turkistan) provinces. This is something to which China will never agree. Maps produced by supporters of Tibet's cause divide China's existing borders between China, Inner Mongolia, Tibet and Xinjiang. The result is a Tibet that in size is almost as large as China.

China issued a new White Paper on Tibet in May 2004 in which it said that the Dalai Lama's proposal to give Tibet a high degree of autonomy along the lines enjoyed by Hong Kong and Macau was "totally untenable". Nonetheless, it did host visits by envoys of the Dalai Lama in 2002 and 2003.[4]

But then in early 2005, the Dalai Lama again appeared to have softened his position. In an interview with a Hong Kong newspaper, he said:

This is the message I wish to deliver to China. I am not in favor of separation … Tibet is a part of the People's Republic of China. It is an autonomous region of the People's Republic of China. Tibetan culture and Buddhism are part of Chinese culture. Many young Chinese like Tibetan culture as a tradition of China.[5]

The Dalai Lama also referred not to Tibet per se but to the Tibetan Autonomous Region, thus suggesting that he might now be prepared to agree with China's definition of which areas comprise Tibet and which do not.

For its part, China says that the Dalai Lama can visit Tibet at any time. To emphasize this point, his bed at the Potala Palace in Lhasa has been left untouched (it's a single bed with an iron frame) to symbolize that he is welcome back, although it's unlikely that he would be allowed to live permanently in Tibet.

Perhaps if Tibet wasn't a part of China, it is now. Lhasa and other Tibetan towns have been deluged with ethnic Han Chinese migrants, a great deal of local culture has been displaced by that of the migrants and China and Tibet are now more commercially linked than ever before. And in 2001, China embarked on a US$3.1 billion project to construct a 1,100 kilometer railway link between Lhasa and Golmud in Qinghai province. But Tibet is an issue about which China remains acutely sensitive. The Chinese Government held ceremonies in Lhasa in September 2005 to mark the fortieth anniversary of the founding of the Tibetan Autonomous Region in 1965. Orchestrated crowds appeared in the newly paved plaza in front of the Potala Palace to wave at the various senior Communist Party officials visiting from Beijing. But the festivities were invitation-only events. China's embassies stopped processing the special permits that foreigners need to visit Tibet until after 10 September, which effectively barred the presence of foreigners in Tibet during the course of the anniversary.

China is no longer greatly concerned by the Dalai Lama. He is an old man and, from China's perspective, he will soon be dead. And with him the Tibet movement will lose its figurehead, its rallying point and presumably its momentum, which has created a lot of noise and color but little by way of tangible progress. A new Dalai Lama will be found but first he must be reincarnated and that means for the next 18 years or so the movement will be effectively headed by a child, and children do not make good lobbyists or interesting interviewees on *Larry King*, toddlers even less so. A regent will be appointed. But he will lack the natural authority and prestige of a Dalai Lama.

And the Dalai Lama's legacy? He has masterfully dragged Tibet before the world's focus. Somehow, a backward, feudal culture in which the vast majority of its subjects were desperately poor, and little was done to alleviate that poverty, and in which nobles were allowed to ride roughshod over the common people, with the Dalai Lama at the head of the whole feudal hierarchy, has become synonymous with nirvana in the collective mind's eye of the West. It has been a marketing job like no other.

And yet despite the world media's love for black and white, there is a lot of grey. The Dalai Lama says that during the Cultural Revolution, the Chinese destroyed 6,000 monasteries and temples in Tibet. But the truth is that many were in great disrepair at the time of the PLA's invasion. And then many of Mao's Red Guards in Tibet were young Tibetans. Many Tibetans outside Tibet are unhappy with the Dalai Lama's insistence on non-violence. Dharamsala itself has spies in the pay of the Chinese Government. Not all Tibetans follow the Dalai Lama's school of Buddhism and so not all Tibetans see him as their leader, either spiritually or temporally. And the Dalai Lama himself seems to lack the political skills needed to negotiate with China effectively, and crucial errors have been made in terms of timing and strategy. But the Dalai Lama has excelled on the public relations side. It's not clear what practical benefit Tibetans in Tibet have received from the Dalai Lama's activities abroad, though. Arguably, they have made their plight worse. The Dalai Lama's main achievement has been to turn himself into an international celebrity, a status that ironically is dependent on the continued subjugation of Tibet.

Tibetan Entrepreneurs in Nepal

Expatriate Tibetans can be found everywhere. But outside India and the US, perhaps the biggest number is in Nepal. There they form a distinct ethnic group. The womenfolk wear traditional Tibetan costumes and hairstyles. The men are less identifiable. The precise number of Tibetans in Nepal is unknown. The border between Tibet and Nepal is poorly patrolled and Tibetans cross in and out of Nepal almost at will. The Nepal Government does though occasionally deport Tibetans who have entered illegally. Clipboards with forms are handed out on long-distance buses in Nepal on which passengers are required to write their names and the country which they are from, and I've been surprised when I've traveled on these buses by the number of my fellow passengers who self-identify as "Tibetan".

The Dalai Lama has never been welcome in Nepal, although that's largely on account of the delicate diplomatic game that Nepal's government has long had to play. It must be careful to offend neither of its two massive neighbors, China and India. And in December 2004, Nepal shut down the local office of the Tibetan government-in-exile that had been open in Kathmandu since 1959, saying simply that it had been operating without permission.

Like many migrant minorities everywhere, Nepal's Tibetans appear to have been disproportionately successful in commerce. Ordinary Nepalese see them as rich and good at business. The antiques trade has been one source of income. Tibetan antiques are smuggled across the border with ease and, accordingly, Kathmandu has become the international clearing house for Tibetan artifacts. Most antique shops and many gem dealers in Nepal are Tibetan and in Kathmandu most Tibetan artifact shops are actually owned by Tibetan Muslim families that originate from Lhasa. At the time of the Dalai Lama's departure from Tibet in 1959, there were between 300 and 500 Tibetan Muslim families in Lhasa. Almost all fled soon after, mostly to Kathmandu and Kashmir.

The dominance of Tibetan Muslims in this field in Kathmandu is reminiscent of other ethnic minorities who use their cross-border connections to locate and ship artifacts. Almost all of the dozens of shops that trade in antique silver in the London Silver Vaults that run beneath London's Chancery Lane are owned and managed by Jews, for example. And in Penang's Georgetown in Malaysia, Teochiu Chinese operate most of the antique and curio shops (when most Chinese on Penang are Hokkien). Parsis operate many of the antique shops in Mumbai. And Minangkabau people from west Sumatra operate most of the antique shops in Jakarta and at least one prominent shop in Kuala Lumpur.

Tibetans are particularly evident in the northern Nepalese town of Pokhara, close to the Annapurna mountain range. Several Tibetan refugee settlements are near Pokhara. Tibetan women prowl around the Pokhara lakeshore looking for tourists to buy their Tibetan handicrafts.

"What country are you from?" is their well-worn opening line. Tourists tell them and the response is, "I'm from Tibet. I haven't got a country." And so begins the mournful tale that invariably leads to the listener buying some cheap Tibetan handmade jewellery. The Tibetans' success in business provokes the inevitable ire of the local Nepalese, who view them as good but aggressive businesspeople who capture tourist dollars that they see as rightfully theirs.

I visited one refugee settlement, Tashipalkhel at Hyangja, about ten kilometers north of Pokhara, in late 2003. The settlement is enclosed by a large stone wall and built around a monastery. It really is like a small piece of Tibet. Tibetans fully prostrate themselves on the ground outside the monastery, monks and novices wander around and Tibetan women attempt to sell the inevitable trinkets and beads. The housing at Tashipalkhel, though, is of a standard higher than most Nepalese would enjoy.

Many Tibetans in Nepal do not have clear citizenship or residency status. This uncertainty has made them targets for Nepalese immigration officials seeking unofficial payments to regularize their status. It's a situation similar to that faced by many ethnic Chinese in Indonesia. But what the Tibetans in Nepal do have is access to a well-defined and well-organized international diaspora.

India's Tibet

India has its Tibet in the form of Sikkim, a region of around 540,000 people today. It annexed the small Himalayan kingdom in 1975. And still it remains accessible to India by only one main road. China persistently refused to accept Sikkim as part of India. Until its annexation, China had considered the Buddhist kingdom as part of its zone of influence. China threatened to give political asylum to Sikkim's dethroned ruler Palden Thondup Namgyl. He demanded a billion rupees compensation from India for the loss of his assets and filed a claim for the sum just before his death in 1982. His son Wangchuk Namgyl was crowned the thirteenth king soon after. He has pursued the claim and his lawyers have had several rounds of talks with senior Indian Government officials.

For its part, India has endowed Sikkim with special privileges. Most families have at least one member in what is considered to be a well-paid government job. And, uniquely in India, no-one in Sikkim is required to pay income tax to the central government. Of course, Sikkim remains poor. But with these concessions, it's actually less poor than many other parts of India.

Chapter 28

THE INDIAN WAY

There are three ways out of any problem: the right way, the wrong way and the Indian way.[1]

Everyone wants to invest in China. But relatively few foreign investors are interested in India. Both are big countries with billion-plus populations – indeed, India's population is expected to exceed China's a little before 2030. Both are riddled with corruption. Both have terrible legal systems. So why the difference? India is a democracy. China isn't. In China things happen because the government wants them to. In India people argue about what should happen and so often it doesn't. China is driven by results, while India has been obsessed by process. The mansion that housed the British viceroys in New Delhi became the residence of India's president. The 400 acres soon had 10,000 staff and other hangers-on. This when the office of president is purely ceremonial.[2] It says a lot.

So India is not one of the world's great foreign investment destinations. It hasn't welcomed FDI for a lot of the time. And even if it had, few investors wanted to invest there.

Cumulative foreign investment figures are notoriously unreliable but it has been estimated that the FDI stock in India by 2000 was just US$19 billion. Table 28.1 shows some useful comparisons.[3] There has been significant investment in India since then, but even so, compared with China, India has gone backwards in relative terms.

Despite its abundance of cheap labor, India still ranks low on the world relative competitiveness scale (50 on the World Competitive Index in 2005; in 2001 it was ranked at 41 and so its ranking has deteriorated in relative terms. In 2005, China wasn't much better. It was ranked at 49). Excessive bureaucracy, corruption, anti-business regulations and abysmal infrastructure account for this lack of competitiveness. Yet the paradox

Table 28.1 Foreign direct investment compared

Economy	FDI inflow (1995–2000 annual average US$ billion)	FDI stock (2000, US$ billion)
India	2.6	19.0
China	40.9	346.7
Indonesia	1.3	60.6
Brazil	21.4	197.7

remains that its neighbor China is a Communist country and attracts billions of dollars in investment, while India, a mildly socialist economy but one that is a democracy, attracts almost nothing.

Looking at foreign investment is like reading tea leaves but more reliable. It tells you something of the future. Investors invest on the basis of expected future returns. So foreign investors seem to be saying that they expect China to get its economic house in order and that India won't. They might be wrong but the beauty of foreign investors' opinions is that when they act on them, they can become self-fulfilling. Investors believe that a country will become developed and so they invest. And that investment helps to develop the country. It means that foreign investors have an edge over tea leaves.

Other indicators must be looked at. There is a lot of hype now about India. But much of it is overstated. India has its IT and back-office outsourcing sectors but they are not huge employers by Indian standards. The number of workers in all forms of IT-related jobs in India is less than a million: that's a quarter of 1% of the workforce.[4] Most Indians remain very poor. There is a growing middle class but it is small overall: just 22 million Indians are credit card users, for example. Less than 30 million Indians have the spending power to eat in formal restaurants and to fly. Investors need to remember with India that aspirations are one thing; actual demand is quite another.

A Bad Start

India's economy has long been a mess riven with red tape. At the time of independence, India decided on a state-led development approach, which, with the benefit of hindsight, is an oxymoron. But the authorities didn't realize that at the time. Heavy intervention, protection and "picking" industrial winners were all the rage among the industrializing world. Development was felt to be too important to be entrusted to the market. It was an awful mistake to make. Jawaharlal Nehru, India's first prime minister, wanted state-owned companies to turn India into an industrial powerhouse by controlling the "commanding heights" of the economy.[5] Instead, what India got was more than 250 companies owned by the central government that have become the essence of inefficiency, mismanagement and corruption.

India also got a complex system of industrial licensing, import and foreign investment controls, government ownership, price regulation and other interventionist measures. The dead hand of government was everywhere. The invisible hand of the market existed only in the black economy. As a result, millions of Indians since have been needlessly poor.

Reforms, Some Backsliding and Some Progress

By the early 1990s, India's economy was in a terrible state. Tax revenue had fallen short of sustained increases in government spending. Intractable structural budget deficits at both the central and state government levels were the consequence. The country's balance of payments had deteriorated significantly too. International lenders and investors steadily lost confidence in India's creditworthiness and an external debt crisis loomed. Had India's currency at the time floated freely, it would have been dumped and India almost certainly would have faced a meltdown similar to the Asian economic crisis that erupted elsewhere in the region seven years later. As it was, India had to pledge its gold reserves to the Bank of England and had to go cap in hand to the IMF. The country was so broke it had only enough reserves to pay for two weeks' imports.[6] It was an appalling humiliation.

A new central government was elected under P.V. Narasimha Rao in 1991. It took quick and strong steps to avert a crisis. These early 1990s' reforms focused on reducing the government's budget deficit, abolishing industrial licensing, liberalizing trade policies and floating the rupee. Suddenly, India was open for business and the economy received a significant boost from these measures.

But the pace of reform slowed again, as did economic growth. Major reforms that still need attending to include public sector debt, government structural deficits, infrastructure development, reforming bureaucratic procedures and cutting red tape, increasing labor market flexibility and reforming bankruptcy procedures. The government, however, did introduce new legislation, the Foreign Exchange Management Act, in mid-2000, that freed up foreign exchange and current account transactions and allowed more participants to make foreign exchange transactions. So liberalization does still occur but more often than not such steps are stalled, watered down or only ever talked about.

Big problems remain. The demand for better infrastructure continues to outstrip public investment in it, which was cut back in the early 1990s as the Rao Government fought to control government spending. Private investment in infrastructure has not met expectations, after several high-profile cases in which foreign private investors had their fingers burned over contract disputes.

While the Rao Government averted a crisis, it did not fix the government's fiscal problems for all time. By 2002, public sector finances were once more in disarray. Interest payments consume almost half of all tax revenue collected in India. And at the central government level, interest payments accounted for almost 70% of tax revenue.[7] Public sector debt by mid-2003 was around 11% of GDP, 40% of which was accounted for by state and territory borrowing.[8]

Chronic government budget deficits keep real interest rates in India high. This creates a serious constraint on new investment, economic growth and employment. It also hampers foreign competitiveness. Indian companies that borrow locally must do so at rates that generally far exceed those at which their foreign competitors are able to borrow. Real interest rates in 2002 were around 12% in India, for example. In the US they were 3–4%.

Widening the tax base would help. Most Indians pay no income tax. Simply raising compliance would generate big inflows for the government's coffers. And that means more computerization in tax collections and less corruption, whereby companies and wealthy individuals "negotiate" their tax with tax officials.

Government estimates reportedly put the loss to the central government caused by tax cheating at US$85 billion, or about 20% of India's GDP. Prosecutions of tax evaders have actually fallen and so too have tax-related raids. India's chief sales tax commissioner was arrested in 2001, though, after allegedly having received a one million-rupee bribe.[9]

But then this is India, so nothing is ever straightforward. Amid the apparent backsliding, India has hit some real runs of which it is justly proud. In mid-2003, the country not only became a net lender to the IMF, lending it US$300 million, but also forgiving US$21 million in debts owed to it by seven "poor" countries: Mozambique, Tanzania, Zambia, Guyana, Nicaragua, Ghana and Uganda. By 2004, foreign reserves stood at US$100 billion after having been as near to zero in 1991 as is possible.

And foreign debt was around US$90 billion but was stable.[10] On top of that, India's IT and IT-enabled services are snatching billions of dollars of business away from developed countries (the subject of Chapters 30 and 31). India's diamond processing business is the world's biggest. Its pharmaceutical industry has grown to be the fourth largest in the world in terms of volume. And India is starting to look different too. In 1990, there was not a single modern shopping mall in the entire country. By 2005, there were around 70 and, if current plans are realized, by 2008 there will be around 300.[11] The economy was growing at 7% a year after the world had long grown to expect little more than 2% from India. And remember, with a population that is growing at 1.5% a year, an economic growth figure less than this can be considered to be going backwards, as it would mean that Indians are growing poorer on a per capita basis. Significant sums were being spent on main roads and highways nation-wide, although investment in ports, power and airport facilities was still seriously lacking.

Nonetheless, India was still losing out in relative terms. If India was doing well, China was doing far better. "If the rates of growth of India and China continue to differ by the margins of the past 15 years, within the next 15 years the Chinese economy will be six times that of India", warned India's Privatization Minister Arun Shourie in 2003.[12] This when, in 15 years, India's economy will have almost reached that of China's, its population growth rate being almost double that of China's.

The Go-ahead States

Increasingly, India is dividing into two – the go-ahead states of Gujarat, Karnataka, Maharashtra and Tamil Nadu and the rest. These four have experienced rapid economic growth rates since the 1990s. The economies of the other states grew by very little. In 1997–98, average per capita income in India's richest state Maharashtra was almost four times that of the poorest, Bihar. Fifteen years earlier, it was just twice the amount.[13]

What has accounted for the differences in development? Historical advantages in the more progressive states is one factor. Others are better infrastructure, a more outward-looking disposition, reform-minded state administrations and a body of Indians overseas who are descended from these states who help to facilitate trade and investment flows between them and the rest of the world.

The four go-ahead states now receive about 70% of India's foreign direct approvals even though they account for only 35% of India's economy and a quarter of its population.[14] Being a source of émigrés is also a help. Remittances from Indians who work abroad play an important role in their economies. Around US$10 billion annually is remitted to India from Indians abroad, mostly from those who work in the Middle East.[15]

Indian Elephants

A large part of the Indian non-agrarian economy is accounted for by inefficient state-owned enterprises. Sprawling, family-owned and managed diversified conglomerates comprise a big part of the rest.

Companies that belong to just 20 families were estimated to account for around 15% of India's output by the mid-1990s. The three leading families – Tata (Tata Group), Ambani (Reliance Group) and Birla (Birla Group) – collectively have sales of more than US$20 billion a year. By Reliance Group's own estimates, its output accounts for 3% of India's GDP. The market capitalization of its listed arms accounts for around 15% of the 30-issue Bombay Stock Exchange Index.[16] And Reliance Industries was the first privately owned Indian concern to enter the Fortune 500.

Reliance Group, headed by Dhirubhai Ambani (who died in mid-2002), frequently was mentioned as having grown huge with the help of close connections to politicians and senior bureaucrats, by mistreating minority shareholders and encouraging officials to launch endless audits and inspections on rivals.[17] Reliance is a bellwether group for the Indian economy for all sorts of reasons.

Bureaucracy and More Bureaucracy

India is famous for its bureaucracy. So much so that it has become a cliché. But things are not getting any better. Attempts to cut away red tape fall victim to, well, red tape. Not just foreigners but Indians must overcome huge hurdles in much of the country simply to establish a business. Large numbers of approvals typically are required from a startling array of agencies. At every step there are officials whose palms need to be greased, not so much to break laws but to comply with them; they must be paid off simply to do their job and not be obstructionist. Several states have opened shop fronts and one-stop shops, but the anecdotal evidence is that these are just as prone to delay as the cumbersome procedures they are designed to replace. In 2005, the World Bank found that it takes 71 days to start a business in India, 48 days in China but 6 days in Singapore.[18]

Labor laws in India are notoriously inflexible. The Industrial Disputes Act restricts the ability of managers of firms with more than 100 employees to fire staff. Such firms require government approval before they can make dismissals. Typically, that permission is not forthcoming, and if it is, it must be paid for by paying off the appropriate officials. The direct financial cost may not be great, but the cost of the time spent negotiating often is. Usually, foreign firms are most troubled by the labor laws. They are the ones from which officials typically seek to extract the biggest payments, assuming that they have the deepest pockets. But they are also more constrained by various foreign corrupt practices acts back home. Indian firms are not as troubled by such laws. Ultimately, what typically happens is that firms must seek dismissals of their staff via voluntary redundancies. And these are achieved by offering sufficiently lucrative exit packages so that staff leave of their own accord. So whether officials or the unwanted staff get the cash, either way, getting rid of employees can be a costly business in India.

The Joint Hindu Family Firm

Cultural nuances are one reason for the excessive bureaucracy and regulation. The impact that India's unique culture has on business is exemplified best in the allowable forms that an enterprise may take.

Five types of company have legal standing in India: sole proprietorship, partnership firm, joint stock company, cooperative enterprise and joint Hindu family firm. It's this last one that is peculiarly Indian and which has its origin in the personal laws of the Hindus.

In this form of business ownership, all members of a Hindu undivided family do business jointly under the control of the head of the family who is known as the *Karta*. This person is normally the most senior male member or father. The *Karta* has full control over the affairs of the family business and serves as the custodian of the firm's assets. Other members of the entity cannot question his judgment if the *Karta* has acted in the name of the family and for its benefit. The only remedy available to them is to demand partition of the ancestral property. The general rules and traditional conventions of Hindu law determine the rights and liabilities of family members and thus the co-owners of the business entity. No registration of such businesses is necessary but statutory recognition is given to them in India's Income Tax Act.

The Sindhi Harilela family of Hong Kong, who own the 650-room Holiday Inn Golden Mile in Hong Kong and another nine hotels around the world, continue to follow the Hindu joint stock concept. The arrangement is even reflected in how the family lives. Around 40 members of the extended family live under one roof at their compound at 1 Durham Road, Kowloon. It has 70 bedrooms and three dining rooms. (The excess bedrooms are taken up by household staff.)

Bankruptcy

Bankruptcy and liquidation procedures in India are notoriously cumbersome. Even companies that have made losses for years must attempt remediation under the auspices of the Board for Industrial and Financial Reconstruction. And that is a problem because the board must have unanimity to proceed with closure and any stakeholder such as a creditor, union or owner can block restructuring plans or company closure. This means that winding up companies is difficult and costly.

More than 60% of liquidation cases before the High Courts had been in process for more than 10 years, according to one recent estimate.[19] So investors' capital and creditors' collateral can be tied up for years.

Officially, non-performing loans in India's banking system hover at around 10%. But using international standards, they're more like 20% or more.[20] The poor functioning of the bankruptcy courts is one reason why non-performing loans are relatively high. Calling in a loan is pointless when the law provides little or no backup.

Corruption

India's colonizers bequeathed India with good legal infrastructure, although laws have not kept apace of new circumstances and technology. So the principles are sound even if the specifics are not. Property rights are patchy, for example. Some estimates suggest that as much as 90% of land ownership in India is disputed.[21]

But, unfortunately, the law comprises more than a set of rules, for those rules must also be enforced. And it's in the area of enforcement that India so badly lets itself down.

Although the judiciary is relatively independent, it is underresourced. More than 20 million cases were waiting to be heard in lower courts by 2001 and more than five million awaited hearing in higher courts. Lengthy waiting times mean that India's courts are not a good place to solve commercial disputes. Most companies prefer arbitration if major contracts are involved.

Then there is corruption. Many police are corrupt. And so too are many of the officials charged with prosecuting the law. And it's getting worse by most accounts. In 2003, the annual survey of executives' perceptions of Asian countries by the Hong Kong-based Political and Economic Risk Consultancy rated India as even more corrupt than China and second only to Indonesia as Asia's most corrupt country. It's quite an achievement. Corruption in India has pervaded all aspects of life, from bribing administrators to get children into better schools, getting police to act when a complaint is filed with them, to giving payments to nurses and doctors to ensure better hospital care.[22] Rarely do prices equal costs.

Even Hindu temples, shrines and ashrams have become a means of laundering money. Donations are given to the temples, which in turn provide receipts for much larger sums so that these amounts can be written off on tax. Or temples and ashrams can be set up specifically through which money can be donated. It then becomes legitimate and is thus "laundered".

Although it is a race for which there are many starters, some argue that India's customs authority is the most corrupt institution in the country. It is famous for its nightmarish bureaucracy and the lack of consistency between ports. Different price and value rulings are often made for similar items imported by different importers, suggesting favoritism and corruption. Customs authorities have a tendency to classify industrial inputs as consumer goods, thus attracting higher tariffs. Of course, they might not do this. It all depends on the incentives they face. If part of an order is missing, duty is routinely charged, not on the physical goods but on the full value of the invoice. On top of this, regulations do not keep up with new technologies and new types of goods that are imported, leading to further opportunities for discretion and bribery on the part of officials.

But it's not just top-level corruption that's the problem. Petty corruption is a constant annoyance. A 2005 study backed by Transparency International estimated that Indians pay around US$4.6 billion each year to low-level officials. A survey of 14,000 people in 20 Indian states found that more than 80% of them had bribed a policeman in the last year, and a quarter had paid bribes in government hospitals in order to get better service.[23]

A Destination but Where's the Road?

India's then Finance Minister Jaswant Singh predicted in May 2003 that

India would join the ranks of the developed countries by 2020. He pointed to India's healthy foreign exchange reserves and the fact that the country had retired some foreign debt early. He ignored India's fractious political system, its infuriating bureaucracy and inept and underfunded legal system. India will not be a developed country by 2020 or any date near it. India simply faces too many challenges and too little is being done to address them. The level of poverty remains confounding. Illiteracy is a huge problem. But overriding everything is the problem of government in India. There's too much bickering and too much politicking. These are luxuries that rich countries can afford, but not India.

Chapter 29

THE WORLD'S BIGGEST DEMOCRACY

The ballot box is a good way for the electorate to communicate to its leaders its satisfaction with their performance. It's not simply a case of whether this or that politician is reelected, but by how much. But it also serves as the means by which sectional interests can hold nations hostage. The need to cobble together coalitions means that voices are given a say that otherwise would go unheard. But there is another, perhaps more pernicious aspect. Democracy allows an impoverished, uneducated majority to punish an educated minority. It allows the poor to inflict damage on the rich and force the introduction of policies that do not aid freedom, the market and the economy but are anti-market and ultimately add to poverty. So when education and wealth are concentrated in the hands of a few, democracy is not so much a means of empowerment as a tool for revenge. Political freedom in this case is often not compatible with economic freedom and good governance. And so it is in India.

India is a federation of 28 states and seven union territories. The central or union government has a bicameral (two chamber) Parliament based in New Delhi. It comprises the Lok Sabha (the lower house), with 543 members who are elected by the people for five-year terms and the Rajya Sabha (the upper house) with 245 seats. Members of the various state legislative assemblies indirectly elect 233 of these and the president of India nominates the remaining 12. The central government is the key economic policy-maker and it retains the right to approve state borrowing. In return, the states have jurisdiction over law and order, electricity production, industry policy, commerce and internal security.[1] The states are relatively powerful. Of late they have exerted that power, so that the old realities of Indian politics have been subverted and possibly changed forever.

The Congress party and the Bharatiya Janata Party (BJP) are the only two truly national parties. Congress is the party of the Nehru-Gandhi family: Jawaharlal Nehru, India's first prime minister, his daughter the assassinated Prime Minister Indira Gandhi and, lately, Sonia Gandhi, who served as opposition leader until the party's victory in the 2004 national elections. Sonia is the wife of the assassinated Prime Minister Rajiv Gandhi, Indira's son. She is of full Italian descent and was born near Turin in Italy. As her detractors in India like to say, had she not met Rajiv while he was studying in England, she might now be working as a secretary in Italy. Instead, she led Congress to victory in 2004 and had the possibility of being the next prime minister of the world's second largest country.

Ultimately, she chose not to become prime minister. Probably she genuinely didn't want the job – often her career in politics seems to have been borne of duty and obligation rather than genuine desire. But also because several of the smaller parties that Congress needed to form a coalition with to cement its victory were uncomfortable with a foreign-born, non-ethnic Indian as prime minister. Another factor still might have been the Bofors scandal. It has an Italian connection as its centerpiece. Ottavio Quattrocchi, head of the Italian firm Snam Progetti's Indian operations, has long been wanted by the Indian authorities in connection with the 1986 illegal payments that weapons company Bofors allegedly paid in relation to a US$1.2 billion defense contract. Quattrocchi, who fled to Malaysia, was a close friend of Sonia Gandhi.[2] In any event, that an ethnic northern Italian could have become prime minister of more than a billion Indians seems an unusual outcome, to say the least.

But beyond Congress, there is a myriad of minor parties at the state level. Most have emerged only recently. Many are caste-based, others are linguistically based, some simply regional and some built around local personalities. As a consequence, traditional channels of decision-making have been undermined and gutter politicking, intimidation and violence have replaced the "old boy" network of the Congress party. Congress had been the "natural" party of government. But it failed to respond adequately to the growing politicization of the regions and so, in 1998, the BJP came to power and remained so for the next six years.

For those six years, the Oxbridge-educated Brahmin ruling class, as exemplified by the Congress party, was removed from power. In its place was a collection that includes village headmen, religious zealots and others adept at appealing to the poorly educated masses. Criminal bosses too have found their way into Indian politics, particularly at the state level.

Corruption is ever present. Under the Congress party of old, a corrupt elite ruled India but with a certain elegance. But the "old boy" Oxbridge elegance has now largely gone. It has been replaced by crude politicking and cynicism, particularly at the state politics level.

Accompanying the power shift has been the rise of coalition politics. The BJP came to power in coalition with 23 other parties. A subsequent coalition government contained a similar number. The emergence of coalition politics has meant endless squabbling and negotiations: special favors and pork barreling are the glue that holds disparate coalitions together. And Congress returned to power in 2004 also in coalition with a bizarre mix of bedfellows, including an assortment of Communist parties.

To a large degree, the BJP lost the 2004 elections rather than Congress having won them. The Indian electorate is traditionally anti-incumbent and so the BJP was punished simply for being in government even though its record on economic management had been relatively good. Another constant feature of Indian politics is the desire for star candidates, often irrespective of their policies. This is how various Gandhi family members have attained office despite occasional indifferent quality. Rajiv Gandhi, for example, had shown aptitude for relatively little, but less than five years after joining the Congress party, he found himself prime minister. And in the 2004 election campaign, his daughter Priyanka, then aged 33, appeared on Congress-sponsored billboards across the country for no reason other than her family connection: she was not running for office. Her brother Rahul did contest a seat for the first time, which he won. Again, it was his surname that worked the magic. So far Rahul has had little to offer other than lofty pronouncements on his family's destiny to rule. "Four members of my family before me retained their freshness. Four members of my family before me have done a lot for this nation", he was quoted as saying.[3]

Toward the end of 2005, posters of Rahul had mysteriously appeared in many parts of New Delhi, calendars depicting his face had been hung in regional Congress offices and 300 youth members of Congress had ritually decided to have Rahul's name tattooed on their forearms. Meanwhile, the foreign-educated 35-year-old commenced trips around India to learn about village life, a strong sign of his grooming for greater things. Free time was spent go-karting with friends.[4]

But there has also been a growing criminality and resorting to violence in some sections of Indian politics. Old certainties have been eroded via the ballot box. Another feature of India and its democracy is lobbying and the role of special pleading by vested interests. This happens everywhere but in India is particularly highly developed. US brokerage firm Merrill

Lynch estimated in 2004 that there are at least 61,000 US dollar millionaires in India.[5] But what was more interesting was the claim that almost every one of them had at least one house in Delhi. Staying close to politicians and senior civil servants is such an essential part of doing business in India that it pays to maintain a house in the country's political capital.

Uttar Mess

It is true that the quality of government varies across India and some Indian politicians are very fine people who do their best, often in the face of some appalling obstacles. But perhaps the worst case has been the state government of Uttar Pradesh. It's the state that adjoins New Delhi and where the Taj Mahal is located. It is India's biggest state with a population of 170 million. If it were a country, it would be the world's sixth biggest. The state is also home to almost 10% of the world's poor. Uttar Pradesh is in the heart of India and is also a symbol of all that's wrong with Indian politics. The goings-on in the state assembly, in the capital Lucknow, have become an embarrassment to all of India.

The writer William Dalrymple described arriving in Lucknow in 1999 to find the local political scene in more upheaval than usual. The members of the state assembly had just

> attacked each other in the debating chamber with microphone stands, desks and broken bottles. There were heavy casualties, particularly among the BJP politicians who had come to the Assembly building marginally less well armed than their rivals: around thirty had ended up in hospital with severe injuries, and there was now much talk about possible revenge attacks.[6]

In 1985, 35 members of the state assembly had criminal cases registered against them. By 1989 the number had grown to 50. Two years later, the total more than doubled to 103. In the 1993 elections, no less than 150 Uttar Pradesh Members of the Legislative Assembly (MLAs) had criminal records.[7] And then, in the state elections held in 2002, a grand total of 910 candidates had criminal cases pending.[8] Unfortunately, the profile of the denizens of the state assembly is now akin to that of a jail, although getting elected to the former has become a means of avoiding the latter.

Mulayam Singh Yadav is a symbol of the new way of doing things in Indian politics, particularly in the north. A semi-literate village wrestler, he rose to be the chief minister of Uttar Pradesh. He first was elected to the Uttar Pradesh legislative assembly in 1967. It was not until 1992 that he

founded his own party, the Samajwadi (socialist) Party. It served his ambitions well. The following year he was made chief minister, a position he
served until 1995. He was returned to office as chief minister in 2003.
Prior to his elevation to high office, he had over two dozen criminal cases
registered against him, including charges of wrongful confinement,
rioting, provoking breaches of the peace and criminal intimidation.[9]

The Mulayam Youth League is an adjunct to his Samajwadi Party. It
does a lot of its dirty work. Routinely it is accused of harassment and
intimidation, particularly in relation to how it raises political funds.
Frequent claims are heard that stallholders must pay protection money and
are threatened with violence if they don't pay up. In March 2003, its leader
was arrested on charges of fueling communal tensions.[10]

The star recruit to the Samajwadi Party was Phoolan Devi, otherwise
known as the Bandit Queen. A peasant girl from the lower castes, she was
repeatedly raped by male members of the Thakur caste (an upper caste), as
a young woman. She joined a band of bandits, became their leader and
then led a revenge attack on a Thakur village in 1981 in which 22 Thakur
men were lined up and massacred. She was arrested and jailed in 1983.
She was released in 1994 and was elected to the Uttar Pradesh state
assembly as a Samajwadi Party MLA. In July 2001, she was shot and
killed outside her Lucknow residence. The circumstances are unclear but
the apparent ringleader of the assassins was a Thakur who claimed that he
believed the killing would bolster his political career in the Thakur
community. Rumors of corruption also circulated. Devi's personal bank
account was found to contain the equivalent of US$215,000. Her
supporters said that these represented earnings from royalties from books
and a film made about her life. She must have had a good agent.

Mulayam's first two terms as chief minister of Uttar Pradesh will not go
down in history as the herald of a glorious epoch. On one occasion, several
of his MLAs, supported by the Lucknow University Student's Union, in all
a group of around 200 people armed with home-made guns and grenades,
converged on the State Guest House where Mayawati, the leader of a rival
party, slept with her associates. The attempt to murder Mayawati was not
successful but the shoot-out between the two groups of politicians and the
police made fascinating viewing. It was all caught on film by a television
camera crew.[11] Mulayam's government was thrown out of office shortly
after. And so what became of Mulayam? He was made India's defense
minister, a position he held from 1996 to 1998. During this time, he was
very nearly elected prime minister.

Mayawati followed Mulayam as chief minister of Uttar Pradesh, thanks
to a coalition between her Dalit caste-based party, the Bahujan Samaj Party

(she herself is a Dalit or untouchable), and the BJP. The tenure was a brief one, lasting only a few months. She was back as chief minister in 1997, again for only a few months. And again in May 2002. She celebrated her first full year as chief minister the following May. This yo-yoing in and out of office suggests something else about Utter Pradesh politics – its instability.

Mulayam and Mayawati's mutual hatred became the single most important dynamic in Uttar Pradesh politics. But it is a case of six of one and half a dozen of the other. In March 2003, Mayawati was seen on video at a closed meeting demanding a share for party coffers of the government money that assembly men had allocated to them to use for local development work. The video was made and distributed by Mulayam's supporters. She also admitted dipping into a government contingency fund earmarked for emergency waterworks to help pay for her lavish birthday party held earlier that year in January.[12]

Mayawati's defense in relation to her birthday expenses was simply that others had done it so therefore she could too. And in relation to her asking for government funds for political party purposes, her rebuttal was that the opposition had made the recording and then doctored it. She hadn't said these things at all, or so she claimed. Criminal cases were then filed against Mulayam and other top leaders of his party for illegally recording the proceedings of a private function. And, for good measure, 178 cases were filed against Mulayam and several of his party colleagues in 40 districts over the alleged misuse of politicians' discretionary funds when he was chief minister – the same crime that Mayawati was recorded as demanding to be committed. Mayawati then sought to portray the accusations against her in caste terms. The Dalits, she said, were tired of being treated by the other orders in the Hindu hierarchy as second-class citizens and that she and other Dalits would convert to Buddhism if the discrimination did not end.[13]

Mayawati next came under attack for her "selective" use of anti-terrorism legislation.[14] A local warlord was locked up after a search of his compound yielded a huge quantity of illegal arms, but critics complained that the chief minister at the same time befriended criminals and thugs. Governance also had eroded with Mayawati's time in office. Senior bureaucrats were shunted around with astonishing speed, largely for reasons of political expediency.

And then in August 2003, Mayawati resigned amid a scandal in relation to her approval of a shopping mall to be built near to the Taj Mahal despite the mall contravening environmental and other regulations. Her party then split, paving the way for Mulayam Singh Yadav and his party to return to office. By this point, the political situation in Uttar Pradesh had become such a national farce that the federal government threatened to impose federal rule on the state and dissolve the state assembly. To help avert this, many key members of Mayawati's party joined Mulayam's party in an effort to bring at least the appearance of stability to the state's politics.

Unfettered democracy in India is destroying India's chances for sustained prosperity. The rise of caste-based parties is seeing the political process used not for progress but revenge and payback. Corruption is rife and ethics are barely apparent in some quarters of Indian politics. It is ruining governance. And it is making much of India a bad place in which to do business. Unfettered democracy is a wonderful thing. But only when the electorate is relatively homogeneous, when there is not such a divide between the haves and the have-nots. And that, at this time in history, is anything but a good description of India.

The Die is Caste

Caste is becoming more important in Indian politics, but how does the caste system operate? It remains the most important regulator for the majority of Indians, of whom 80% still reside in rural areas. It works against anarchy but it is also feudal, repressive, and ensures the absolute minimum of social progression. Indian politics might be messy but under-lying Indian Hindu society is a system of some 3,000 carefully graduated castes and subcastes. Every Indian Hindu is slotted in. Each has a distinct categorization, of which they are acutely aware but most outsiders are oblivious. Mahatma Gandhi was a Modh Bania, for example, a Hindu commercial caste based in the arid Saurashtra Peninsular of Gujarat state. So too was Dhirubhai Ambani, founder of the Reliance Group, one of India's top conglomerates.[15]

One's caste in this life is determined by one's behavior in the previous life. Behave well and accept your lot this time around and you improve your chances of a better caste next time. Play the game exceptionally well and you might eventually achieve moksha or nirvana and so escape the otherwise endless cycle of suffering and rebirth. The caste system means that everyone in Hindu India knows his or her place and what is expected. And for those who deviate, the pressure to conform is enormous. One's caste determines where you will live, what occupation you will enter and whom you will marry. The Brahmins are at the top. Hindu Brahmins are strict vegetarians. Devout Brahmins also avoid alcohol and onions, ginger and garlic that are thought to "heat" the blood and arouse passions. They are the elegant, high-minded keepers of the culture. They are also the caste that has the most to lose should the system break down, so are seen as the chief oppressors of the lower castes.

And at the bottom are the Dalits or the untouchables, of whom there are about 170 million in India, or about 16% of the population. The Dalits still typically live apart from the rest of the community in the more traditional interior states such as Rajasthan and Bihar. They are forbidden to draw water from village wells, use communal bathing areas, enter certain teahouses and food stalls and to enter temples. When the giant tsunami hit southern India's coastal regions in December 2004 causing almost 15,000 fatalities in India alone, it was the Dalits who were left to search for corpses. Such work was deemed too "dirty" for higher level castes.

Central government policies to help the lower castes are usually blocked or resisted by the upper castes, who do not want their positions and privileges eroded and they cloak their arguments with self-serving appeals to avoid upsetting the "cosmic balance" of things.[16]

Another problem is that government programs designed to help the Dalits tend to be commandeered by politically savvy members of the group who corner the benefits for themselves, their families and associates. Seats are reserved in the national parliament and state assemblies for Dalit politicians but this has made them targets for lobbying. Correspondingly, many have been enriched via the proceeds of corruption and bribery. Meanwhile, the bulk of the rest of the community remains as poor as ever.

The Brahmins who are the best educated ought to know better. But privilege tends to triumph over reason or at least the desire to protect it. Recently, I attended a dinner party in London. The lady opposite me was Indian but had been born in England. "Where is your family from?" I asked, meaning Gujarat or some other part of India. "We are Brahmins", she answered, as if it should have been obvious and as if her caste was the only important consideration.

Caste and ethnicity are important in India when it comes to hiring personnel. India's big family-owned companies tend to employ friends and relatives in senior management and invariably try to fill as many management positions as possible from within the ethnic and religious grouping of the owning family. Parsis have long filled senior management positions at the highly diversified Tata Group, for example. Even new economy companies are not immune. Brahmins fill many senior management spots at Infosys, one of India's biggest software companies. Five of the company's six founders are Brahmins, including its Chairman Narayana Murthy, who is a Kannadiga Brahmin.[17] The age-old Brahmanical interest in mathematics, astronomy and the esoteric has left the Brahmins well suited to the new economy age.

The caste system tends to be weak in overseas Indian communities, such as among the Indians of Singapore or Malaysia, for example. But only because of chain migration: immigrants to an area tended to be all of the same caste, and so these new communities had little or no stratification. Emigration thus meant the possibility of economic opportunity and effectively the means of breaking out of the caste system.

Nonetheless, credit must be given where it is due. India's diversity is one of its great strengths. And despite the often negative media attention that communalism in India often receives, India is relatively peaceful, given all its diversity. That is one of the successes of India's democracy: the ballot box does allow grievances to be expressed. Furthermore, Indians have shown a preparedness not only to recognize Indian minorities but to celebrate them. The wealthy Parsi minority in Mumbai is deeply respected by every other group. And following the 2004 national elections, India had a Sikh prime minister, a Sikh army chief and a Muslim president – this in a country that is 80% Hindu. And that was after a party led by an ethnic Italian had won the elections.

Chapter 30
Mumbai: India's Financial Capital

A cow was tethered to the front fence of the Bombay Stock Exchange on my last visit. Not a bear, not a bull, but a cow. It was symbolic really. There was a run on the ICICI Bank, the country's second largest, a few days later. Long queues formed at branches in Mumbai and Gujarat. Its cash machines had to be restocked many times in a day to cope with the withdrawals. And throughout the course of the year, seven bombs went off around the city with a cumulative death toll that ran into dozens. Mumbai perhaps more than any other is the city of the mixed message.

Mumbai is India's financial capital. And that is more a commentary on India than on Mumbai. It is a city that is interesting for what it should be but isn't. If this is a financial capital for a country of a billion people, it shows what a long road India has yet to travel. It is a messy, complex city; a city of medium-rise flats, too few signs of substantial commerce and hectares of slums – 3,500 hectares to be precise. It might be India's financial capital but it is a long way from being a world financial capital. All of India seems to have spilled out onto the seven islands that have been joined by bridges and causeways to produce one long, thin peninsular – hence there is no dominant language, culture or religion. Life in Mumbai is fraught and tense. And it's getting more so. Soon, the city will have a population greater than all of Australia. And by 2020, its population is forecast to be 28.5 million.[1] Much of this rapid growth is fueled by internal migration. The city's administration estimates that 1,500 migrant workers flood into Mumbai every single day. Most head to the slums.[2]

There are few historical monuments save for those on Elephanta Island, about ten kilometers offshore. The island is home to four rock-cut temples that are about 1,500 years old. No doubt they were spectacular once, but they were severely damaged by the Portuguese in the sixteenth century. The motor launch trip leaves from Apollo Bunder, by the basalt Gateway of India monument that stands in front of the five-star Taj Mahal Hotel, where I was accosted by a saffron-robed holy man who thrust a wilted marigold at me while he attempted to chant a prayer. It ploughs through calm water dotted with refuse thrown overboard by local day-trippers, and past what looks like a nuclear power plant.

Reports about Mumbai talk of glittering, new office towers. But they don't glitter. They, like everything, seem drab and covered in a film of dirt. Guidebooks sing the praises of Marine Drive which runs along the coast, by downtown Mumbai and past its financial district. It is the place for an evening promenade, a place where Indian families like to stroll as the sun sinks, they say. But where are the outdoor cafés and coffee shops? Where are the civilizing facilities that make this a place to which people might gravitate? On the occasions that I have walked along it, the locals comprised mostly the homeless, beggars who took time out to pick lice from each other's hair and Indian men who stopped their cars long enough to urinate from the rocks into the sea before driving off.

The city is prone to flooding too. It experienced one of its worst ever floods in August 2005 after almost unprecedented rainfall. More than 400 people drowned, were smothered in landslides or were killed in stampedes. The airport was closed for two days. The city's creaking infrastructure was tested and failed: eight days after the floods began, many areas remained under water – this when Mumbai is located by the sea, which presumably should aid rapid drainage. Many areas were without electricity for a week and mobile telephone and even landline coverage remained sporadic for much of that time.[3]

In 1996, the ruling Shiv Sena Party renamed the city Mumbai. Most residents appeared to support the move. Marathi is the dominant language in Maharashtra, the state in which Mumbai is located. But native Marathi speakers probably account for less than 40% of the city's population. So Mumbai is Bombay's name in Marathi. But Mumbai is multicultural – one of the city's great strengths. It draws on ethnic links across India and abroad. It is home to Muslims, Hindus, Sikhs, Christians, Jains, Jews and Parsis.

The blue and white Keneseth Eliyahoo Synagogue near Kaikhushroo Dubash Road is well maintained. In its lobby I noticed photographs of Israel's Shimon Peres who visited in 2000. Two attendants handed me a skull cap for my visit. They raised the blinds and switched on the ceiling fans. Revealed was a synagogue that is beautifully maintained and still functioning.

Mumbai is also home to a small but highly visible ethnic Chinese population. Many Chinese came to the city during the British colonial period. They stayed on. And so downtown Mumbai has restaurants with names like China Garden, Chinatown, Chopsticks, Kamling, Ling's Pavillion, Nanking, Mandarin and Ming Place. In fact, there are significant Chinese communities in many parts of India. Calcutta has a large population of Chinese who are ancestrally Hakka. They came to operate the tanneries, a niche left open due to Hindu prohibitions on handling dead cows.

There are many Sindhis too. They are the Hindu Indians who fled the province of Sind when it became part of the new Islamic nation of Pakistan. Surnames that have "ani" as a suffix, as in "Mirchandani" or "Tolani", are typical Sindhi names. Many older Sindhis bear painful emotional scars of their forced departures during the Partition and the loss of family homes and other assets. An elderly Sindhi man who had been a law lecturer made my acquaintance one evening in Mumbai. Over dinner he described his departure from his home town.

"The bodies!" he said. "I could never have imagined anything like it. There were just so many bodies. Everywhere. Whole families just cut down. I got to the train station to leave for India but was told to come back later. And when I did there were bodies everywhere. On the platform, in the carriages. Can you imagine the blood? What had happened in the time that I had been away? And when we finally got to India, we had nothing. My family had a beautiful house in my home town. I've been told that a Muslim family lives in it now. When we arrived here, we did so with many others. And it was years before I could get my papers and have my qualifications recognized. I don't blame India. It was a poor country and it had so much to do. But really life was so very hard."

"But is it hard now?"

"India does the best that she can. I know that life is better outside. But I haven't seen it. Maybe it's for the best. Imagine that! I am a law lecturer and I have never been outside India."

Deceiving Looks?

Mumbai is home to Asia's largest slums and to Kamathipura, one of Asia's most fetid red-light districts. It is a city of extremes. Modern London-style cafés exist such as the busy and hip Nosh in the Colaba district, with its minimalist décor that could be modeled on Granita in Islington's Upper Street in London. And then, just outside, shoeless beggars vie for pavement space with the *paan* (betel nut) sellers and *chai* dispensers. One day I took a taxi from the cool marble of the Taj Mahal Hotel to the Mahalaxmi dhobi ghat, a giant outdoor area where hundreds of people make a living by washing hotel linen and other laundry items, each in a rough cement open-air cubicle. Here they stand all day in soapy water while they thrash the dirt from sheets and towels. Such stark contrasts are never far away.

Mostly, however, Mumbai simply looks run-down, a legacy of rent controls which mean that building owners have little incentive to repair their buildings. Tenancy laws greatly favor tenants and evictions are almost impossible to obtain. Developers typically are required to provide free houses for tenants of sites that they acquire for redevelopment. And today, about 2.5 million people live in 19,000 buildings in Mumbai that officially are classed as "decrepit".[4]

Organized crime has become more a feature of this city. In 1998, a wave of murders and police shoot-outs rocked the city. Increasingly, underworld gangs and mafia elements control Mumbai. Nowhere is this more clear than in the harassment for protection money that small traders face.

Shopping centers and supermarkets barely exist, certainly not in downtown Mumbai. This adds to the city's run-down feel. It is a massive city of 14 million people but with the shopping facilities of a village. The rent controls are to blame again, and so too are property regulations, along with a distribution system that is so poor that high spoilage rates make supermarkets unviable in most Indian cities. Besides, most people who could afford to shop in a supermarket have household servants who do the shopping for them. And so the demand for pleasant surroundings in which to shop is not there. Slowly, though, shopping malls are being constructed, but in Mumbai the problem is finding the space.

Religious Tensions

The Shiv Sena Party had won the city's municipal elections in 1985. Communal tensions increased and the Shiv Sena fanned them. When the Babri Mosque was destroyed in Ayodhya, rioting in the Muslim part of the city claimed almost 800 lives in late 1992 and early 1993. Muslims started the rioting but it was the Hindus who finished it. Mostly, the victims were Muslims, killed by Hindu fanatics or simply by ordinary Hindus caught up in crowd behavior.

Muslims, of whom there are 120 million in India, have a difficult time. Stories of police raping Muslim women abound and in the cities some of the most densely populated and most run-down slums are reserved for Muslims. The Muslim area of Mumbai is an example. It is a chaotic mess, dusty but also thriving with commerce as myriad stallholders ply their trade. But entering the area is like crossing a border and going to another country. In this regard, Mumbai is not one city but two: an informal religious apartheid exists. Often Muslims are accused of not being good citizens – Hindus will claim that at cricket matches the local Muslims support Pakistan, for example.

And then on 12 March 1993, between 1.28pm and 3.35pm, a group of terrorists and gangsters trained in Pakistani camps set off a dozen bombs across the city. The first to explode was outside the 29-floor tower that houses the Bombay Stock Exchange. It set off a blaze on the trading floor. Other bombs exploded in crowded marketplaces, a double-decker bus, three hotels, offices and the airport. The ground floor of the Air India offices was blown out. At least 257 people were killed or missing and 714 were injured. The city of 14 million ground to a halt with fear. Riots followed, forcing many Muslim families to leave the city.

Ten years later, in 2003, two powerful bombs exploded in two parked taxis, one in the commercial Mumba Devi neighborhood of Mumbai and another in a small car park beside the Gateway of India monument. The two explosions, five minutes apart, killed more than 50 people and wounded around 135. Windows as high as the 12th floor of the Taj Mahal Hotel were shattered. The attacks were attributed to the Students' Islamic Movement of India and another militant Islamic group, Lashar-e-Toiba. Both are banned organizations in India. This time, Mumbai proved itself more resilient. There was no rioting. The city picked itself up, dusted itself down and got back to work.

So this is India's financial capital. The city lags far behind what it should be. In essence, Mumbai is as confusing as it is confused. It is tangled and its population is tangled. It is a city of furious activity but with too few signs of outward progress. It might be the financial capital of a country with a billion-plus population, but it's no Shanghai. It doesn't come anywhere near. And that is very telling. But there are some bright spots in the otherwise dull landscape that is India's economy. Two of them are the subjects of the next two chapters.

Chapter 31

INDIA'S GREAT SOFTWARE REVOLUTION

After decades of economic stagnation, India's economy has found a niche in which it is truly a world player: information technology (IT) and IT-enabled services. These are the twins of India's high-tech revolution. In 1990, India earned little from this sector. Ten years later and it was the economy's saving grace; a very bright star of competence amid a galaxy of inefficiency, corruption and mismanagement. But little credit should be given to the Indian Government, either at the central or state level. The sector has boomed because it's the one sector, with its trade in intangibles, with which government and corrupt officials find it difficult to tamper. And so investment and creativity have flooded into this sector. It is because so much of the rest of India's economy has been so bad for so long that this sector is so good.

By 2000, the IT sector accounted for around 2% of India's GDP. That made it bigger than each of India's mining, communications, railways, and hotels and restaurants sectors.[1] By 2006, it was even more significant, earning India around US$17 billion annually. Membership of the National Association of Software and Service Companies (Nasscom), India's main body for the software and IT services industry, has rocketed. In the late 1980s, 38 companies belonged. By 2006, more than 900 did so. They accounted for 95% of India's total software and IT services revenue.[2]

By 2006, India's software and IT-enabled industries directly employed perhaps 800,000 people, of whom perhaps 70% comprised employees in the software industry. The sector has become a huge foreign exchange earner for India. In the year to March 2002, India recorded its first current account surplus in 23 years. A big contributor to this turnaround was India's export of IT and IT-enabled services.

In fact, unusually for any economy, services dominate India's exports. India exported almost US$20 billion worth of services in 2000–01. Around half of this was attributable to exports of IT services. Services exports were more than double the next highest export earner, gems, at US$7.4 billion. Ten years earlier the services category earned India less than US$5 billion. Simply, India's exports of services have exploded, thanks largely to IT.[3] How did this happen? And why did this happen?

Hot Spots

India's IT take-off has been highly regionalized. Three main IT hubs exist today: Bangalore/Chennai/Hyderabad, the Mumbai/New Mumbai/Pune corridor and New Delhi/Noida/Gurgaon.

Bangalore is India's best-known IT city. It is in Karnataka state, one of the four go-ahead states identified earlier. Karnataka is perhaps the weakest of the four, particularly with regard to the condition of its general infrastructure. But Bangalore is recognized as India's science and technology capital. It has a disproportionate number of universities and other institutions of higher learning and it is these that account for Bangalore's success. After all, the new economy is less about physical capital such as roads and railways than it is about human capital.

Gurgaon is another success story. It's close to New Delhi (just 30 kilometers away) but cheaper and less congested. Many multinational companies that had their headquarters in New Delhi have relocated them to Gurgaon. Coca-Cola, Pepsi, Motorola, GE and Hughes Software Systems are among them. The city is beginning to earn the nickname the "Singapore of India".[4]

Pune is also an IT hot spot. It is among India's top five IT exporters. It is a popular destination for companies that wish to set up in either software or IT-enabled services. Pune is growing and property prices are booming. Some forecast that Mumbai and Pune will grow to the point where they will merge within 30 years and thereby create the biggest city in the world. (Pune's current population is about 2.7 million. Mumbai's is about 13 million.)

The Leaders

Whilst the sector is populated by hundreds of firms, there are some clear

Table 31.1 India's top 10 IT firms

Company	Head office location	Share of industry revenues (%)
Tata Consulting Services	Mumbai	8.3
Wipro	Bangalore	5.2
Infosys Technologies	Bangalore	4.9
HCL Technologies	Noida	3.4
Satyam Computer Services	Secunderabad	3.4
IBM India	Bangalore	2.2
Cognizant Technology Solutions	Chennai	1.9
NIIT	New Delhi	1.8
Silverline	Mumbai	1.7
Pentasoft Technologies	Chennai	1.7

market leaders. The ten biggest firms produced 35% of India's gross software revenues and 40% of its exports by 2001 (Table 31.1).

Tata Consulting Services (TCS) the biggest (and thus India's single largest exporter of software services), has 28,000 employees and was listed in July 2004. It was India's biggest ever IPO, although just 14% of the company was offered to the public. Much of the remainder is ultimately in the hands of a series of Parsi charitable trusts established by the Parsi Tata family. Shares rose 27% shortly after listing, giving TCS a total capitalization of almost US$11 billion.

For its part, Wipro stands for Western India Vegetable Products. It's not the sort of name you'd expect for one of the world's leading new economy companies. Azim Premji, a Bohra Muslim originally from Maharashtra state, inherited control of the company from his father in the 1960s. It was then a cooking oil producer. Next, it moved downstream into soap, then into lightbulbs and then printers, scanners and personal computers. And from computers it moved into software. It was never an IT start-up, but an old economy company that opportunistically morphed (just as mobile phone producer Nokia of Finland was once a lumber company, named after the small, industrial Finnish town of Nokia. Having been there, I can report that it is not a tourist destination). Wipro listed on the New York Stock Exchange in 2000 and for a brief period, at the height of the internet bubble, it was India's biggest listed company in terms of market capitalization.

Today, Premji holds 84% of the stock in Wipro – worth about US$13 billion in 2005 – making him India's richest man. The company's revenue in 2004 reached and passed US$1 billion.

Wipro's Bangalore offices are divided according to the contracts that it has. So part of a floor might be devoted to staff who work in tandem with UK-based staff of Thames Water, jointly solving that company's software problems. A whole floor might be devoted to US investment bank Lehman Brother's software issues. And another floor to Weyerhaeuser, a timber giant, or two to Thomas Cook. Wipro's Bangalore competitor Infosys has a similar set-up. Nordstrom, the leading fashion specialty retailers, and Belgacom, Belgium's telephone company, are among its clients. It had around 30,000 staff by early 2006. Satyam Computer Services is another giant. Australia's Telstra announced in early 2004 that it would begin subcontracting its IT work to Satyam.

Increasingly, however, foreign IT firms are setting up subsidiaries in India rather than contracting work out to local companies. By 2004, many of the world's most important IT powerhouses were represented in Bangalore. They included Lucent Technologies, Hughes Software Systems and Texas Instruments. Software design that Texas Instruments' Indian technicians did in Bangalore was the basis for several patents that the company applied for in the US.[5] Other big names in software products – Microsoft, Oracle, Adobe, SAP and Sun – all employ thousands of IT workers in India, either in subsidiaries of their own or via contractors. Dutch multinational Philips said that by 2003, 25% of the software that it uses worldwide was developed in Bangalore. It expected that proportion to increase.[6]

India is Intel's largest non-manufacturing site outside the US. The Intel India Development Center in Bangalore employs more than 1,500 engineers to develop software and chips.[7] IBM too has a presence, with about 5,000 engineers by 2001. Management consultants Accenture also had around 500 staff at their software development unit in Mumbai by the following year.[8] Principally, they were employed in code writing.

In late 2005, Dutch banking concern ABN Amro announced that it had contracted out its strategic banking platform to Tata Consulting Services, a deal worth US$200 million over five years and the biggest ever deal yet won by an Indian IT services company. At the same time, another ABN Amro outsourcing deal went to Infosys for US$140 million.[9]

Why India?

India's IT sector is a triumph for India. Or is it? The truth is that the IT sector is a triumph for Indians. Public administration in much of India is a disgrace. There are some good politicians and some excellent administrators, but all too often their efforts are swamped by an excessive focus on process and too little concern for outcomes. The IT sector thrives because it has minimal contact with and reliance on government and the public sector more generally.

Narayana Murthy, chairman of Infosys, and six colleagues quit their jobs at a Bombay software consultancy in 1981 to set up Infosys Technologies. It took them 18 months just to get a license to set up a company. The firm struggled for 10 years with similar bureaucratic obstacles. But in 1991, India's economic crisis saw the introduction of widespread reforms. From then on, Infosys and other companies like it began to thrive. Until then, it was easier to send employees overseas to work on clients' problems. But, with increasing liberalization, it became more cost-effective to do more work onshore.[10] The 1991 reforms also saw a software technology park established in Bangalore. It offered tax holidays and high-speed satellite links. For once, the government had set up some infrastructure (albeit limited) for business and then the government got out of the way. The effect was astonishing.

India's IT sector is not as hampered by the constraints that hamper India's goods producing sectors. The IT sector relies less on India's terrible infrastructure. For example, the product does not have to be physically shipped and so that means avoiding India's notoriously corrupt and inefficient ports. And although power is important to the sector, it is not a big consumer of it. It can be produced readily by the sector to make up for blackouts and shortages that beset the public grid. India's road and train systems are inefficient and broken down but, again, the IT sector is not reliant on these.

In fact, the IT sector's lack of reliance on conventional modes of transport either to exist generally or to "ship" product is suggested by Bangalore's location. It sits in the middle of the southern part of the Indian continent in Karnataka state, equidistant from the Arabian Sea on one side and the Andaman Sea on the other. It could hardly be further from the coast and its ports.

Narayana Murthy has said:

There is no comparison between a Shanghai and a Bangalore in terms of infrastructure. But we can't wait for the government. We have found solutions despite the government. We've shown we can succeed in spite of the environment ... Twice a day we have to transform ourselves from a Third World mindset to First World expectations ... No matter what the physical reality, we have to behave in step with world class, top companies.[11]

Sawti Piramal, chief scientific officer at Mumbai's high-end drug maker Nicholas Piramal, has expressed a similar view: for his company "the internet is more important than roads", he has said.[12]

The IT sector has other advantages over more traditional sectors. India has long had high real interest rates. The IT sector typically has smaller capital requirements than the goods sector and so again is less hampered by this constraint. Also, India's highly restrictive labor laws apply less to the sector, being more focused on lower end workers and workers in the industrial sector.

The IT sector is less hampered by intrusive regulation and harassment from bribe-seeking officials. The sector's product has no physical form and so is difficult to quantify and tax. It is not reliant on government processes, so again the opportunities to extract bribes and other inappropriate fees from the sector are far fewer than for the more visible goods sector.

Avoiding, rather than courting, government has been one of the reasons for the success of India's IT sector. Azim Premji, the low-key head of Wipro, famously guards his privacy. Perhaps it's a matter of personal style. Or maybe it's an attitude that's more cultivated. The bigger the target, the more likely that it will attract the attention of politicians and officials. So perhaps Premji's low-key approach is a deliberate strategy.

The government did establish a Ministry of Information Technology in 1999. The IT industry then waited for disaster to strike. But rather than seek to intervene in a sector that had done well without the government, the new ministry and its first minister actually helped the sector, becoming its advocate in cabinet. In the late 1990s, the government exempted the IT sector from the labor and bankruptcy law regimes. Also many Software Technology Parks of India (STPI) have now been established. They provide ready-made facilities tailored for IT companies so that they need not face the same infrastructure constraints faced by many other companies in India.

Another factor is India's skills base. India's software industry has been able to tap large numbers of low-cost, technically able employees. India's universities and other higher education institutions churn out up to 100,000 engineering and science graduates each year. Of these, about half are believed to find employment in the IT sector and related fields almost immediately.[13] There are also around 10,000 private IT training centers, although many do not train students to high levels of expertise. A lot of emphasis is placed on vendor certification. India has at least 80,000 trained Microsoft engineers, a number that is second in the world only to the US.[14] Skills are being formed, but are they being formed quickly enough?

Rising Costs and Rising Risks

Where will it all end? Will it end? Of course it must. All booms peter out and so will India's IT boom. India's software industry accounts for only 2% of the estimated US$400–500 billion global software market, and probably India has captured 20% of world exports in software.[15] Clearly, there is room for more growth. But how much will depend on the sector's continued cost competitiveness.

India has a significant pool of IT professionals but the pool will start to dry up as India attracts more and more business. India's educational institutions are not producing enough IT graduates to keep wages growth flat. Instead, wages have been growing at 20–30% each year. And remember that's compound growth. If this continues, India's competitiveness will quickly erode.

Retaining staff is a problem that's common among most software companies. Turnover is high as employees chase better offers. The average age of Wipro's Bangalore staff was 28 in 2003. Almost half of them had been with the company for less than two years.[16]

English-language skills also have been essential to India's software success. And although English functions as an India-wide language, the proportion of the population that can speak it fluently is actually quite small. For India to continue to grow as the world's low-cost software solutions provider, not only will there need to be greater investment in software and engineering skills development but also in English-language training.

There are other risks for the sector. One is a backlash against IT professionals overseas. Seen as ultra-competitive and troubleshooters who solve problems, take profits and then move on, it is inevitable that they will attract criticism. The boss of Indian software company i-flex's Dutch operations was arrested in London in March 2003 for alleged visa irregularities in Holland. The Indian media portrayed it as part of a worldwide campaign to harass Indian IT expatriates on account of their having been too successful. It followed the harassment of some Indian IT workers in Malaysia.[17]

Nasscom has estimated that India has captured just 0.2% of the US$180 billion global market for software products.[18] Another challenge for Indian IT companies is to develop branded software products. It's something that so far few of India's IT companies have managed to do successfully. One exception is FLEXCUBE, the world's best-selling banking software product. It was developed in Bangalore by i-flex, a local listed IT company. The package was released in 1998 and is now used by more than 120 banks and other financial institutions in over 50 countries.

Furthermore, there is a quality issue when it comes to India's graduates. Engineers from elite institutions such as the Indian Institutes of Technology can be regarded as world class but they make up only a small percentage of India's technical graduates. The rest tend to be trained in a rote-learning, inflexible environment and lack the skills and self-confidence that multi-nationals require.[19]

Companies like Infosys and Wipro have suggested that they need to move up the value chain if they are to remain competitive. Rather than being "techno-coolies", software fixers and guns for hire, they need to become business solution providers. But this is a competitive sector, already occupied by well-entrenched Western names such as Accenture. India's IT sector has done well by leveraging its comparative advantage which derives largely from skilled labor and low wages. Moving "up the value chain" might sound glamorous but if growth is to be maintained, then moving down it might be where India's IT future really lies. The IT sector might now employ as many as 400,000 workers but that's 400,000 out of a population of more than a billion. It's an exciting sector and one in which India is truly excelling. But its true importance to India, and more-over to India's population, is easily overstated.

Chapter 32

INDIA: BACK OFFICE TO THE WORLD

The growth in India's software sector has been spectacular. But that growth has been eclipsed. It is in India's potential to become the world's back office that the country's natural advantages really come into their own. What began as a trickle around 1994, when the American giant GE started to shift thousands of back office jobs from the US to India, has become a flood. India's software services industry has been growing at around 30% per annum. But its back office outsourcing sector has been rocketing, with 70% annual growth.[1]

Software firms such as Infosys, Wipro and HCL Technologies, which had wanted to move higher up the software ladder, are now also looking down the ladder at back office functions so they can capture some of this growth.

But what are back office functions? They include IT-enabled services such as international call centers, data entry, insurance processing and travel bookings. Call centers show a lot of promise. They are where calls are placed or received in high volumes for the purposes of customer service, technical support, ISP and computer product help desks and sales.

The rewards for India will be enormous. IT research specialists Gartner estimated that, in 2005, the worldwide back office outsourcing market was worth US$234 billion.[2] Companies are looking to achieve savings in their back office functions and many consulting firms have sprung up to help companies outsource these functions to low-cost locations. Invariably that means India.

India earned US$2.2 billion in 2002 from back office outsourcing exports. The figure is likely to be as much as US$24 billion by 2008.[3] The sector is believed to have employed more than 100,000 people in 2002.[4] Undoubtedly it is many more today. A McKinsey survey found that 203 Fortune 1000 companies had outsourced back office work to India by 2003.[5]

AT Kearney, the consulting arm of EDS Corp, polled 100 US financial services firms back in 2003 to get an idea of the likely growth in outsourcing from that sector. From that it estimated that, by 2008, US financial services firms intended to move more than 500,000 jobs – about 8% of their current workforce – offshore and mostly to India. Any function that does not require face-to-face contact has become a candidate for possible outsourcing. And why not? Indian back office workers earn as little as 10–20% of their US counterparts and deliver comparable services.[6]

UK call centers alone are being relocated to India at a startling rate. In 2002, there were almost 200,000 financial services call center workers in the UK and about 600,000 call center workers overall. Management consultants Accenture estimated that up to 70,000 call center jobs were likely to be relocated from the UK to cheaper locations such as India in the short to medium term.[7]

Anecdotally, UK-based trainers who provide call center staff with customer service training say that they are impressed by the eagerness of Indian staff to learn compared with UK-based employees. Partly the difference is accounted for by the sorts of employee who present themselves for call center jobs in the UK compared with India. In the UK, they are at the lower end of the job queue in terms of skills and experience. The job market in India is much softer and so the candidates are better qualified and more eager. I've been told by trainers that many of the participants in their programs in India are very interested to learn about culture and current affairs in the UK so that they can deal with UK-based callers more efficiently and appropriately.

Among the training that Indian staff receive is speech and accent coaching – some are actually taught to speak with American or English accents according to their clients – American and British history education and training on popular culture such as sports and popular Western television programs. The training for employees at one call center company in Bangalore even included watching episodes of *Baywatch* and *Friends*.[8]

So which companies have moved their back office operations to India? It's a rapidly growing list. GE was one of the first to relocate back office jobs to India and is now one of the biggest such employers, with at least 10,000 back office staff in India.[9]

British Airways also located there. It established World Network

Services in Mumbai but then sold a majority stake in the company so that it could offer its services to other airlines and insurance companies. The company employs around 1,500 staff and still earned about 80% of its revenue from British Airways in 2002.[10]

Standard Chartered, a listed UK bank, began to shift its back office operations to the southern Indian city of Chennai (formerly known as Madras) around 2001. The move involved transferring 23 processing units from 35 countries.[11] Citigroup was another early entrant. By mid-2003 it employed 3,000 staff in India doing back office functions. HSBC had moved 2,000 jobs to India.[12] Bank of America is following suit, as is British Telecom. It gave India's HCL Technologies a US$160 million contract to undertake telemarketing, billing and conferencing.[13]

Barclays, the UK's third biggest bank, moved 150 data processing jobs from the UK to India in 2003 in its business banking and credit card divisions. Lloyds TSB and Prudential also have shifted UK back office jobs to India. By mid-2003, Lloyds TSB had 30 people working for it in Bangalore and planned to increase that to 250. Aviva, the UK's second biggest insurer, was opening a 1,000-person call center and claims processing unit in India.[14]

Investment bank JP Morgan said in mid-2003 that it intended to set up an offshore research department in Mumbai to perform tasks like data collection and basic financial modeling.[15] P&O Nedlloyd, ABN Amro, ING, Agilent Technologies, Cap Gemini Ernst & Young and American Express also have back office facilities in India.[16]

Even the World Bank shifted most of its global accounting operations, including payroll processing, to Chennai in 2002.[17] By mid-2003, 100 staff were employed in its Chennai back office.[18]

Typically, the companies expect to save 40% on their back office operations by shifting them to India. That is a massive saving and it can be achieved almost overnight. The export of back office jobs and functions from higher cost countries to India is one of the most important and radical trends in the world of big business today. It is an upheaval of massive proportions. And all upheavals bring risks and malcontents.

Backlash!

For customers based in the UK, the US and other mature economies, dealing with an Indian-based call center is often not as satisfactory as dealing with one based in their own country. The voices at the other end often sound distant, accented and the service provided is often transparently the product of training and conditioning rather than what comes naturally. The question is how inadequate is it? Are these inconveniences minor or are they significant? Some companies will find that it is the latter. In late 2005, the UK's Abbey bank, for one, said that it was considering closing its call center operations in India. Abbey had certainly saved money by relocating call center work to India in 2003 but it found that its customers were less than satisfied. Many complained of poor call quality and language problems. Meanwhile, other UK banks began to advertise the fact that they didn't use offshore call centers, as a way to attract customers.

Other problems have come when it has been found that data and other private information held by some outsourcing companies in India have not been held securely. There have been significant breaches of confidentiality and several cases of serious fraud when Indian call center staff have illegally acquired information and used it to defraud their companies' European and US-based clients. Clients of Citibank, for example, were defrauded by Indian-based outsourcing staff in 2005, leading to several staff at the Indian outsourcing company MphasiS being jailed.[19]

The politics of shifting jobs from high-cost to low-cost centers have never been good either. The political backlash has begun. But at best it will only slow the shift. Several US states have considered introducing legislation to stop government IT contracts from being outsourced to other countries. The application of such laws would be broad but the target is specific: India. The US also tightened visa conditions, which had the effect of constraining the ability for Indian IT professionals to work in the US.

In Britain, the head of HSBC caused an outcry in 2002, when he extolled the virtues of outsourcing UK back office jobs to India.[20] However, the outcry had little effect. The following year, HSBC announced that it would be transferring another 4,000 back office jobs from the UK to India, Malaysia and China.[21] British insurers Aviva and Prudential, along with British Telecom, earned the ire of unions with their plans to open call centers in India, enabling them to shed jobs at home in 2002 and 2003.

The 850 jobs that Prudential announced in 2002 would be cut from its call center at Reading and transferred to Mumbai caused a public backlash from trade unions and the Reading community. The local media was vociferous in its attacks on the decision. The company agreed to stagger the cuts, which allowed Amicus, the relevant union, to claim victory, but from the company's point of view, it was a minor concession given to placate the opposition and allow the union to claim that it had won something for its members. The reality was that the jobs would still be transferred and the company would still achieve its costs savings, albeit over a longer time frame.

Moves like that of Prudential and others in exporting UK-based jobs to India is a replay of what happened 100 years earlier when textile jobs were lost from northern England to India. Unions and local authorities then, as now, tried to stop the inevitable.

And in Australia, the head of the Australian Government's Economic Analytical Unit caused a similar outcry in 2001 when she said that Australian companies could be more competitive if they relocated lower skilled back office jobs to India. That country's trade union-dominated opposition party issued press releases condemning her remarks. But there's little point in attempting to halt the tide. The savings that companies can make by outsourcing their call centers, accounting and other IT-enabled functions to India are simply too great.

The industry in India has fought back. In the US, for example, Nasscom hired the US public relations firm Hill & Knowlton to lobby and put forward its case in Washington.[22] The Indian Government too has made representations to foreign governments via its embassies and high commissions abroad and also during trade and investment missions abroad by Indian ministers.

Competitiveness and Competitors

As in India's software sector, wages and other costs in its IT-enabled sector can be expected to rise and erode its competitiveness. India's top 10 outsourcing firms informally agreed in mid-2003 not to poach each other's newly trained professionals.[23] It was a measure to stop rapid staff turnover but was likely to fail. The only way to prevent staff from leaving for higher paid jobs is to offer them even higher salaries. And inevitably that will see India's comparative advantage in IT-enabled services erode.

India can expect to face competition from other countries as they too put their hands out for a slice of the world outsourcing pie. The AT Kearney study referred to earlier, ranked 11 countries as potential offshore locations for US financial services' outsourced business processing operations. India was followed by Canada, Brazil, Mexico, the Philippines, Hungary, Ireland, the Czech Republic, Australia, Russia and China. The criteria included labor costs and political stability.[24] So in the area of financial services back office outsourcing, India leads but there are others. Here are two.

The Philippines and Malaysia

The US accounts for at least half the world's potential outsourcing business. This is good news for the Philippines. The Philippines, a former colony of the US, has a commercial code that is compatible with that of the US. Language is another advantage. Based on Tagalog, Pilipino is the first national language of the Philippines. The Philippines is home to 87 different indigenous languages but less than a quarter of Filipinos actually speak Pilipino. The true national language is English, which is spoken by 95% of its population. This means that the Philippines (and not India) is the second largest English-speaking country in the world after the US.

A high literacy rate (94%), a large pool of IT professionals and a telecommunications infrastructure that might be patchy but is cheap to use all suggest the Philippines' potential competitiveness. With around 85 million, its population base is not small. Nonetheless, wages in the Philippines, even at the level of back office services, are considerably higher than in India. But India's cost competitiveness will decline. And as it does so, the Philippines will look increasingly attractive as a place to locate back office operations.

By mid-2003, 37 mostly US-owned companies operated call centers from the Philippines, including America OnLine, the largest ISP in the US. Its center at Clark in Angeles City, north of Manila, was staffed by 600 workers.[25]

Among the multinationals to have back office work undertaken in the Philippines by 2004 were Procter & Gamble, Delta Airlines, American International Group (AIG) and Citibank. US engineering giant Flour Daniel was having much of its technical work undertaken in the Philippines by a team of 800 local engineers, architects and draughtsmen.[26] And AIG's Philippines business processing unit had more than 4,000 staff.[27]

Medical transcription is a big, emerging business for outsourcing companies. Almost 7,000 US hospitals are now required by federal regulations to convert medical records into data format. It's a US$15 billion market in the US. By mid-2003, 17 medical transcription companies employing 1,200 locals were operating in the Philippines.[28]

Scicom, a call center company set up in Kuala Lumpur by expatriate Sri Lankan entrepreneur Leo Ariyanayakam, further demonstrates how the outsourcing of business processing functions to lower cost countries is not going all India's way. The company uses BT's virtual private network and is BT's largest customer in the Asia-Pacific region. Its principal clients are Nokia and HP for whom it handles all the customer service inquiries for the Asia-Pacific region, including those that originate from Australia. The Nokia account alone accounts for around a fifth of Scicom's staff.

But why did Ariyanayakam choose Malaysia? An important reason was language. Call centers in India are adept at functioning in English and the various languages that are indigenous to India, but not much else.

Malaysia's multiethnic population means that five languages are spoken widely in Malaysia and spoken well (English, Malay, Tamil, Mandarin and Cantonese). Scicom has sought to offer call center services not so much to the US and the UK as to the Asia-Pacific market. By also hiring expatriate workers from within the region (specifically from Indonesia, Korea, Japan and the Philippines), it can offer support services in 14 Asian languages. The language advantage that Malaysia has over competitor countries mirrors that of Belgium in Europe. In the early days, many European companies outsourced their call center work to companies in Belgium on account of the various languages spoken by the locals.

Another advantage of Kuala Lumpur is that office space is high quality but cheaper than in most locations in India. This compensates for higher employment costs that run to monthly salaries of US$450–600 for Malaysian-sourced staff. Nonetheless, most of Scicom's staff are graduates, which allows the company to offer higher end, premium call center services.

Asia itself has yet to make great use of lower cost back office alternatives. The most obvious candidates for this sort of outsourcing are banks and other financial service companies in Singapore and also the public utilities, various ministries and other arms of the Singapore Government. (Singapore Airlines tendered out its call center operations to India in 2003, while Singapore Telecom already has a call center near the Malaysian city of Malacca with around 400 staff.) So Singaporean business processing jobs can be expected to disappear, along with similar jobs in Australia and perhaps Japan, as big companies follow the lead of their US and UK competitors in shifting such jobs to India and other cost-effective countries. Essentially, business processing jobs everywhere are under review. Not by choice but because the inexorable pressures brought by globalization demand it. Manufacturing jobs have long chased the low-cost centers, leaving hollowed out regional economies from northern England to Detroit. A new dynamic is underway, for now it is the turn of services.

Chapter 33

STUNNING KOREA

The film footage of the 1974 assassination attempt on South Korean President Park Chung-hee is the most dramatic I recall having seen. President Park is addressing a ceremony in Seoul to mark the liberation of the country from the Japanese. He stands at the lectern, stern and deep-voiced. Suddenly, as he makes a point, shots ring out, in mid-sentence. The gunman is in the audience, handgun aloft and aimed at Park. The bullets miss. But a scream comes from behind. It is Park's wife. She had been seated on the stage with other dignitaries. She has been shot. Pandemonium breaks out. Men overpower the gunman, wrestle him to the ground and drag him outside. On stage, Park's wife is picked up and rushed out for treatment. But her injuries are serious. Later, she dies. Meanwhile Park remains on stage. He looks around, his eyes now acutely alert, his face more fierce. He can see that the assailant has been overwhelmed and the fracas behind him has quietened down. He returns to the microphone, straightens up and glares into the audience. "I shall now resume my speech", he announces. And with that he does.

Park was tough to the point of barely being human. He was utterly ruthless and instilled in Koreans the need for sacrifice. Wages were suppressed, trade unions were outlawed and the development of heavy industry was made the priority above all else. He was respected but not liked. Human rights were ignored. Opponents were jailed and sometimes killed. Park himself survived many assassination attempts before being killed in 1979 by his own security chief.

Park's single-mindedness and focus provides an analogy for all Koreans in how they faced the country's economic crisis in 1997–98. The fast-moving, "take-no-prisoners" vehicle that was the South Korean economy had careered into a brick wall. One massive Korean conglomerate *(chaebol)* after another went to the brink of collapse, the economy shrank by an extraordinary 6.7% in a single year, and the country's foreign reserves evaporated overnight. In a matter of months, Korea, one of the richest economies in Asia, was reduced to begging for help. It had little choice but to sign a stand-by arrangement with the IMF for credit, which it did on 3 December 1997, for US$57 billion. The bailout came with plenty of strings attached. For the time being no longer would the government decide economic policy alone but in conjunction with the IMF. It was an appalling humiliation for the country and its citizens. Unemployment reached 7% within a year and so, at an individual level, an even greater humiliation visited many Korean households, for there is nothing worse for a Korean man than not to be working and to be housebound. Korea's reversal of fortune was the most dramatic among all the economies affected by the Asian economic crisis. And yet among all the nations affected, it accepted its plight with the most grace. There was little time to indulge in the blame game. There was an economy to rebuild.

How has Korea fared since? The recovery was astonishing. Korea's foreign reserves hit US$141.5 billion in September 2003, the highest level ever and the fourth highest in the world. (They had been practically zero five years earlier.) The following month, Korea registered US$19.04 billion in exports for the month, its highest ever result. (This when the value of Korea's exports for *all* of 1965 was just US$200,000.) Real per capita income was almost 50% higher than it had been five years earlier, while unemployment for the year was down to 3%, a rate that is consistent with full employment.

Simply, Korea had put in an incredible economic performance. Again. The broad national consensus was not simply for recovery but on how to achieve it. It was a different story elsewhere. Indonesia's response to the region-wide crisis was to erupt into rioting. Many senior members of its business community fled to Singapore. Malaysia got on with the task of reform but not before its leader blamed the West, Jews, banks and specula-tors for the mess his country was in. Meanwhile, Koreans cashed in private stocks of gold and stopped buying imported goods to help with the effort, trade unions held back on industrial action and most *chaebol* owners accepted at least some of the reforms that had been needed for a long time.

This is not to say that all the reforms that needed to be made have been made. Many have not. Many others have been watered down. But there has been real progress. A significant number of *chaebol* executives and founding family members have been charged with corporate misdeeds. Laws have been passed to enhance the rights of minority shareholders, and foreign investment laws have been greatly relaxed. And in 2005, a law was passed limiting *chaebol* with assets of more than US$6 billion from holding stakes in other companies worth more than 25% of their net assets.

By early 2006, growth forecasts were being trimmed and South Korea was obviously losing its competitiveness compared with China's exporters. It was also suffering due to high world oil prices. But then as the world's 10th largest economy and with a per capita income to match, South Korea can no longer rely on manufacturing and the export of goods. It, like all other rich countries, must come to terms with the need to restructure away from manufacturing and in favor of services to become a more knowledge-based economy.

The Korean Paradox

So this is Korea's story. It is a fascinating one and it has a fascinating economy. But that is where the paradox lies, because who really knows anything much about Korea? Who's actually been there? Who knows much about Korean food? Korean history? Everyone seemingly wants to learn to speak Japanese or Chinese but who outside Korea is actually studying to speak Korean? Or to read it? There are countless academics and think tanks specializing in Japan and China but there are few specializing in Korea. Most people have clear perceptions of China, Japan and Hong Kong, but Korea registers a few vague notions, at best. It is a country with a name but no brand and little image. And yet Korean companies have become some of the best-known Asian brand names around the world. *Chaebol* such as LG, Samsung and Hyundai have spent millions to develop their brands, corporate logos and colors. Paradoxically, such companies have the imaging and branding of a clarity that their country lacks. (It's also the country that gave the world the Reverend Sun Myung-moon and his "Moonies" cult. He understood the value of brand building.)

Despite its economy, people are not drawn to Korea as they are to other Asian countries and cultures. This has left Korea underresearched and underrecognized for what it is. And what it is, is rich. Its people have a per capita spending power that nears that of the UK. And at 48 million people, its population is not that far off the UK's 60 million.

Cultural Nuances

What values do Koreans have? Here there are more contradictions. The legacy of the Park years is that if South Korea is known for anything, it is for authoritarian leaders and a remarkable sense of national purpose. The way in which ordinary citizens took ownership of the 1997–98 economic crisis, and saw it as their problem along with the government, and the national consensus to pull together to get the country out of the pit into which it had fallen, was unique among affected Asian countries. The preparedness to accept guidance from strong leaders suggests that Korea is the epitome of Confucianism. Well, yes and no.

For a start, South Koreans are highly Christianized: 47% of Koreans claim to be Buddhist but 49% profess to being Christians. This mix is reflected in the country's presidents. Park Chung-hee did not align himself with any particular religion. Chun Doo-wan was a Buddhist. Roh Tae-woo is a Buddhist. Kim Young-sam is Protestant. Kim Dae-jung is Catholic. And Roh Moo-hyun is Catholic. There are many elements of Christianity that do not marry well with Confucianism. Perhaps this schism might explain the apparent contradictions in the Korean national psyche.

The main contradiction is that there is both a Confucian desire for strong, all-knowing and remote leadership at the top in Korea, but also a view that everyone has a right to assert their views and be treated with respect.[1] What this means is that predicting Korea can be difficult: you never know which of these two opposing notions will override the other. Thus, Koreans are capable of admiring and even desiring strong-arm political leadership, whilst also forming themselves into Asia's most aggressive and strident trade unions to challenge authority, for example. Korean society is at times authoritarian and at other times plural.

Another paradox comes from there being a strong Korean state and yet Koreans are wary of the leaders they elect. Regular corruption scandals have undermined the legitimacy of successive governments and presidents. Accordingly, Koreans tend to be excessively cynical. And voter turnout at elections is falling.

Public displays of anger are quite acceptable (as opposed to Southeast Asian cultures where they are not.) In fact, not only are they acceptable but they seem to be a measure of Korean machismo and manliness. Among expatriates in Southeast Asia, those who are most intensely disliked by local employees are Korean managers, for whom aggression and humiliation are common management tools.

Koreans also have a culture of high risk taking. The boldness and audacity of what many prominent Koreans are willing to do frequently surprises. In decision-making, Koreans often plunge ahead with little anxiety and regard for the risks and possible consequences. The phenomenal amount of debt that most *chaebol* took on board perhaps derives from this. How those debts accrued is described next.

How the Mess Happened

Debt sank Korea in 1997. The value of the won collapsed. The size of *chaebol* foreign currency debts ballooned and one by one they fell. The solution was not simply IMF credit but to fix the structural problems that allowed such indebtedness to accrue. Checks, balances and transparency were needed. The *chaebol* had to be reformed.

That the state had played an intrusive role in Korea's economic build-up is an understatement. It interfered with microeconomic decisions in an extraordinarily systematic and vociferous fashion. The Japanese who colonized the Korean peninsular between 1910 and 1945 started the system, but it was President Park who pushed the development of the *chaebol* in the 1960s and 70s.

Park came to power in 1961 via a military coup. He was dictatorial but benevolent in terms of having a clear view of the need to develop the country's economy. And that became his foremost priority. Korean law restricts any individual shareholder (apart from the government) from amassing more than just a modicum of any bank's total equity. On the face of it, this was a very sound policy and one that all economies ultimately should adopt. It helps to make banks independent of non-bank interests and more likely to lend prudently. Although Korea's banks were independent of the *chaebol*, they were not independent of Park's government.

Credit was cheap and free-flowing if the *chaebol* did it the government's way and the government backed up its demands by telling the banks where to lend. The *chaebol* were told in which sectors to invest, where to put their plants, where to invest overseas and in what. If the *chaebol* consented, they were the recipients of a flood of easy credit. Object and they were shunted aside. Often the credit was so cheap that it was actually provided at negative real rates of interest. Government contracts were also awarded to favored companies. In return, the *chaebol* went into areas such as shipbuilding, steel and petrochemicals as demanded by Park. Later, the deal included that they provide huge political donations to Park's successors. The measure of success for Park was the rate of annual economic growth. Meanwhile, the *chaebol* had no concern with rates of return but only with market share. With such concessional financing and guarantees of future massive loans, profitability was largely an irrelevance.

The *chaebol* quickly grew into massive multibillion dollar concerns. But they also carried billion dollar debts. Samsung, for example, entered 1998 carrying US$23.4 billion in debt – about the same amount as the foreign debt of the entire Venezuelan economy. And Samsung was by no means unique. The *chaebol* did not evolve through a process of natural selection. They grew because the government had selected them and then puffed them up with cheap loans, like quails stuffed to be the size of turkeys. And as the saying goes, "in a strong wind, even turkeys can fly". And fly they did.

The degree of concentration of commercial power that Korea's big business groups had achieved by the 1997 meltdown was unrivalled anywhere else in the region. The top five *chaebol* – Hyundai, Samsung, LG, Daewoo and Sunkyong (SK) – accounted for around half the country's gross national product. And the top 300 groups accounted for almost 90%. Most of the groups had barely existed 20 years earlier. Daewoo, for example, started out in 1967 as a textile company with US$10,000 in capital. By 1997, it was a massive conglomerate, with ship-building, motor vehicle, electronics and textiles arms and combined sales of more than US$70 billion. Such diversity was typical. Beer, cement, cars and computer chips all were products typically produced by each of the major top five or so *chaebol* ("from chips to ships" once was the proud boast.)

Most *chaebol* were family-owned and managed. As many as a third of senior executives among the biggest *chaebol* had family relations with the owner. Chung Ju-yung, for example, the founder of Hyundai group, moved all seven of his sons into management positions in the group and at relatively young ages. The families ensured both family control and professional management by sending their children overseas for tertiary education. But even laggard family members must be found jobs.

Sometimes, new subsidiaries were set up simply to give family members something to do. It meant that even the dimmest siblings were put in charge of something and, for the sake of the face of the family, a range of cross-subsidies and other related transactions were used to prop up badly managed companies. This way the true degree of incompetence of individual family members was not revealed to the outside world or even to themselves.

Most *chaebol* comprised a large number of relatively small companies across a wide spectrum of activities. They had a mixture of listed and privately held companies that engaged in a complex web of related-party transactions. And they featured centralized decision-making and authoritarian management. The other common feature was an utter disregard for transparency, so much so that it is doubtful that even the *chaebol* owners knew the precise state of overall profitability or, sometimes, even solvency. As always, market share was their main indicator of success.

The *chaebol* were given definition by being grouped under one or a few holding companies but more often by sharing directors or drawing on the one family for directors, or via cross-shareholdings. Rarely was financial information published and, when it was, it was usually incomplete or suspect. The lack of transparency kept the *chaebol* together. After all, who would want to buy into something so ill-defined or attempt to take over a component and not know where they sat in the web of conflicts of interest that each *chaebol* was?

The *chaebol* rush to outdo each other to grow and keep growing, so that they would become too big to be "allowed" to fail, increased the risk that ultimately they would. The need to get big so that they would be guaranteed a government-assisted bailout should things go wrong encouraged Korea's *chaebol* into ever-more speculative and imprudent fields. Banks too accepted the line that size equated with creditworthiness. Accordingly, it became accepted wisdom that there was no great need for close credit analysis when it came to lending to a major *chaebol*, because there was an implicit, if unstated, sovereign guarantee.

The families that owned the *chaebol* used complex pyramid structures to control the hundreds of subsidiaries that many such groups typically had. Even after (some) reform, a study found that, in 2004, the founding families of the top 55 chaebol and their 968 affiliates owned on average just 5% of the shares but exercised 51.2% of the voting rights.[2]

They also tended to treat their business empires as a single entity. The boundaries between subsidiaries were porous, especially when the flow of funds was concerned. The *chaebol* often were built around one or a handful of highly profitable companies. These became the cash machines for the entire group, providing it with credit, loans and loan guarantees. Samsung Electronics, the world's largest manufacturer of memory chips, routinely was used to supply loan guarantees to other Samsung group companies – much to the irritation of Samsung Electronics' other shareholders. In 1997, it guaranteed hundreds of millions of dollars in loans for Samsung's fledgling auto division. Some minority shareholders believed that some US$136 million in guarantees were not even declared.[3] But then contingent liabilities often don't make it onto balance sheets.

The government's allocation of credit on the basis of who was in favor and who was not was complemented by a comprehensive system of bribe

taking and campaign donations. The *chaebol* bribed politicians, bank officials, or both, to ensure that their access to cheap credit was not obstructed
and that prudential safeguards (small though they were) would be ignored.
Hanbo Group is a case in point. It was Korea's 14th largest *chaebol* at the
time of the 1997 meltdown.

Chung Tai-soo founded Hanbo in 1974. How he had accumulated the
capital to found the group was a matter of open speculation. He had,
though, been a government worker in the Office of Tax Administration for
the previous 23 years.[4] Hanbo grew quickly off the back of billions of
dollars in loans. It grew too quickly and ventured into unprofitable areas.
Debts outstripped profits and the group eventually collapsed in early 1997
with debts that were 16 times its total equity. How did Chung amass such
loans? He bribed bank officials, something for which he later received
almost 17 years in jail. Billions were lost. But the case was hardly unique.
Hanbo Iron & Steel was finally sold in early 2003, after a six-year effort
by creditors to sell the company. At US$377 million, they received just a
fifth of their original asking price.[5]

The shipbuilding and car components Halla Group provides another
example of the poor corporate governance of the time. It had only
one really profitable subsidiary, the car components producer Mando
Machinery. But that company sold most of its output to just one customer,
Hyundai, Korea's largest car manufacturer. And yet Mando was the cash
cow for Halla and was expected to subsidise 14 other affiliates. Halla
collapsed in 1997.

Among the collapses, however, Daewoo's was the most spectacular. At
its peak, Daewoo employed 320,000 people and its sales were equivalent
to almost 10% of the Korean economy. As it expanded and diversified, so
too did its debts. Founder Kim Woo-choong directed senior managers to
inflate asset values by US$33 billion during his final months at the helm. It
all culminated in the group's collapse in 1999, creditor banks being left
with US$55 billion of almost worthless Daewoo bonds and Kim fleeing
Korea to avoid arrest. In a 19-month period, he was allegedly seen in
Morocco, North Korea, Sudan, Germany, Florida and the south of France.
Kim had built Daewoo up over 30 years. He'd worked tirelessly, rarely
sleeping more than four hours a night and not taking a single day off in 18
years, other than when he was hospitalized for five days with internal
bleeding. And even then he postponed an operation for 30 minutes so that
he could participate in a conference call.[6] Kim's superhuman efforts led to
a huge conglomerate. But not a profitable one. Kim did finally return to
South Korea in 2005. He was arrested as he returned.

The Grand Conspiracy

What Korea's economy lacked were checks and balances. And, ultimately, Korea paid for that. Corruption and nepotism are pervasive in Korea. Transparency International's corruption perception index routinely finds South Korea to be perceived as one of the most corrupt economies among those that have successfully recently industrialized. But these practices do not carry with them the connotations they do in the West. They are seen more as meeting one's social and family obligations, helping out and sharing one's good fortune. In this way, some practices that are seen as negative elsewhere are seen as virtuous in Korea. In many respects, Korea was one grand conspiracy: all potentially alternative voices were coopted into a single vision. Dissenters were jailed, exiled or, more usually, paid off.

In the 1980s, the government even organized "opposition" parties to give the government legitimacy. The leaders of these parties understood that they were to provide "loyal" opposition to the government as opposed to actual opposition. As Lucian Pye has politely remarked, the country was "saddled with party leaders, who to put it graciously, [had] obligations to the government".[7] The reality is that they were on the government's payroll. As were the *chaebol* through soft loans and other concessions. And in turn, the *chaebol* paid off the politicians.

Chun Doo-wan (president 1980–88) is estimated to have collected W220.5 billion in bribes from the *chaebol*. His successor Roh Tae-woo (1988–92) is believed to have collected W268.2 billion. Both were subsequently jailed for corruption and treason during the presidency of Kim Young-sam. Several *chaebol* heads were also jailed. Kim's own son was sentenced to a prison term for corruption. And the son of Kim's successor Kim Dae-jung was also convicted of corruption.[8]

Korea watchers have learned to look for hints of corruption and collusion everywhere. Kim Dae-jung won a Nobel Peace Prize in 2001. During a 2002 visit to Stockholm, I'd seen the pieces of toilet paper that Kim had used as writing paper whilst he was a political prisoner facing the death sentence. They were on display at a museum dedicated to the Nobel Prizes in that city's Gamla Stan district. Kim's prize was awarded in part for his efforts in brokering a summit with North Korea earlier that year. But money changed hands even for this. It transpired that US$500 million was secretly transferred by Hyundai Group to North Korea ahead of the summit.

But what about the media's role? Traditionally, the press in Korea has been weak (often newspapers and other media outlets are owned by the very *chaebol* they should be scrutinizing and about whom they should be reporting). Newspaper editors were expected to play a "constructive" role in the country's development (which really means not subjecting the country's leaders to criticism and scrutiny). Academics were also coopted into the government's national agenda rather than being a source of separate opinion or ideas.

The Clean-up

The Korean economy was indeed a miracle. But the real miracle was that it took as long as it did to collapse. The Korean Government was forced to spend more than US$130 billion of public funds to clean up the financial sector in the wake of the 1997–98 economic crisis. The way forward for the *chaebol* has been a matter of debate within government since. The pro-reform Fair Trade Commission has battled with the Ministry of Finance and Economy, which still views the *chaebol* as deliverers of substantial benefit to the Korean economy. The Federation of Korean Industries provides another voice, it being the principal *chaebol* lobby group. Another voice is the Commission on Anti-Corruption that was established during the term of President Kim Dae-jung. The reformers generally have been winning since 1997 but the direction has not been all one way.

An early reform was the government's demand that the top *chaebol* lower their debts to be no more than twice their equity by the end of 1999. Most of the top *chaebol* succeeded in doing this but did so in part by quietly shuffling off debt to subsidiaries and affiliates. This allowed Hyundai, for example, to claim that it had come in under the government's target, with debts at 181% of equity. Samsung's debt to equity ratio was 166%, LG's was 184% and SK Group's was 161%. New accounting rules were introduced that took greater account of debts attributed to affiliates and subsidiaries, and the *chaebol* were asked to recalculate the figures. The top four *chaebol* that had claimed to have met the government's debt to equity targets were then forced to admit that actually only one had done so. The revised figures showed that the ratio for Hyundai was 230%, 194% for Samsung, 273% for LG and 228% for SK Group. Overall, the 16 largest *chaebol* had US$192.5 billion in debts, which was significantly higher than twice their combined equity. Nor were they particularly profitable. The 16 had managed to make just US$6.7 billion profits off sales of US$279.3 billion, a margin of just 2.4%.[9]

Other reforms were structural and involved forcibly trimming the *chaebol* of excess divisions, reorganizing their internal structures to resemble pyramids rather than something more akin to a scrambled

omelette, and a clamp down on debt guarantees. LG Semicon, for
example, was merged into Hyundai Semicon to make Hynix. Hyundai
itself was broken up. LG Group unwound its cross-shareholdings, as the
means by which the group had definition, and group affiliates were
arranged under one of two holding companies: LG Chemical Investment
and LG Electronics Investment. Most *chaebol* are now trimmer and better
organized. The job is far from over but a good start has been made.

There is now wider ownership of shares and foreigners hold more
equity than they did – more than 40% of all outstanding shares by 2004.
Samsung Electronics, for example, is now almost 50% owned by foreign
investors. General Motors led a US$400 million deal to acquire the assets
of Daewoo Motor in 2002. Tata Motors of India acquired its truck division
in 2004. Slightly more than half the shares in SK Corp, South Korea's
largest oil refiner, are now in foreign hands. A consortium led by American
International Group took a controlling stake in the country's second
biggest high-speed internet operator Hanaro Telecom for US$500 million.
The UK's Prudential bought all the equity in the Korean fund manager
Good Morning Investment Trust Management Co. in late 2002. Almost
80% of the shares in Kookmin Bank are held by foreigners; Standard
Chartered of the UK now controls Korea First Bank; KorAm Bank is
controlled by Citibank of the US; and the Korea Exchange Bank is
controlled by US investment fund Lone Star.

Another important driver of reform is the growing number of joint
ventures between foreign firms and *chaebol* units. Foreign partners are
another source of pressure for openness and transparency. Samsung and
LG particularly have many foreign partners in Korea.

The political desire for reform continues. In late 2002, Roh Moo-hyun
was elected president of South Korea on a platform that included further
reform for the *chaebol*. He pledged to maintain his predecessor Kim Dae-
jung's policies of restrictions on debt guarantees and mutual financial
assistance to affiliates, to further enhance corporate governance measures
and push through legislation that would allow class action suits by shareholders. Families would also be made to declare their total stakes in
companies and the stakes of each family member.

Roh's opponent Lee Hoi-chang ran on a platform of "rational reform",
as opposed to what he labeled as Roh's "radical reform". This meant
rolling back some of the restrictions on the *chaebol* and restoring their
position as pillars of Korea's economy. Lee lost the presidential election
but only by a narrow margin, so although many Koreans want to see
further sanctions against the *chaebol* continued, a great many do not.

Still, old habits die hard. In 2001, Samsung Electronics appointed its chairman's only son to a key management position in the face of fierce resistance from minority shareholders. The son had been on the company payroll for 10 years but had not held a key position in the company during that time.[10] SK Group, the third largest *chaebol*, and its Chairman Son Kil-sueng were embroiled in an illegal stock transaction scandal in March 2003.[11]

In August 2003, Chung Mong-hun, chairman of Hyundai Group and younger brother of Chung Mong-koo, chairman of Hyundai Automotive Group, leapt to his death from his 12th-floor office. He and two aides of former South Korean President Kim Dae-jung were charged in June that year with the illegal channeling of US$500 million to North Korea. Hyundai had become one of the largest investors in the north – Chung's late father and Hyundai Group founder was born in what is now North Korea.

Chung senior had made Chung Mong-hun and his elder brother Chung Mong-koo co-chairmen of Hyundai Group in 1998. (Their oldest brother and heir apparent died in a car crash in 1982. Another brother committed suicide in 1990.) The two squabbled constantly, to the point that they were no longer on speaking terms. After just a year, Mong-koo took control of Hyundai Motor and then split it from the rest of the family's interests, to form Hyundai Automotive Group. The group also controls Kia Motor and now ranks in its own right as South Korea's fourth largest *chaebol*.

Mong-hun was left with the rest of the group. But then he lost the shipbuilding division – the biggest in the world – when another brother engineered its departure from the group in 2001. Yet another division was lost when it fell into the hands of creditors. And so he was left only with the remnants of a once massive empire, but with billions of dollars in debts. Ostensibly, his suicide was due to his regret over the transfer of the funds to North Korea. But then it also provided a means of escape from the new realities of corporate Korea.

Business was now being done differently. A new order was being established and it seemed to be working. By 2004, Korea had the economic data – record foreign reserves and exports – to prove it. Korea's trillion dollar turnaround means that the country is richer than it was when it went into the 1997 economic crisis and its corporate structures are now more streamlined and transparent. Debts are still huge, corporate governance improvements still have a long way to go and, on the political front, the issue of North Korea looms like a dark cloud. But among the countries affected by the Asian economic crisis, Korea's reforms and progress were the most impressive.

Chapter 34

THE INSIDER

The two most embarrassing social faux pas of my life to date occurred in Asia. I still shudder when I think of them. The first occurred when I was at a dinner at the house of a Malaysian Government minister. Perhaps forty others were present. I was the only non-Muslim and all the other guests had just completed their prayers in the *surau*, or small mosque, on the grounds of the minister's Kuala Lumpur residence. We ate at a series of round tables under a verandah adjacent to the *surau*. Present were many of Malaysia's most prominent Malay businessmen.

I happened to be sitting at the minister's table, and he sat directly opposite me. To my right was a prominent local businessman and to my left was another businessman but even more prominent. At the end of the meal, I became conscious of a man standing behind me, on my left. His arm was outstretched. He seemed to want something. I decided that it was my plate. He must be one of the minister's household servants, I thought. So I handed it to him. Or at least I tried to hand it to him. He didn't seem to want to take it. So I held it up a little higher to make it easier for him. It was then that the man sitting on my left said to me something like, "Actually Michael, this is our custom. When each of us is to leave, once we have eaten after our prayers, we go to every table and shake the hands of each person present." And so the man to whom I'd tried to give my dirty plate was in fact another of Malaysia's biggest businessmen. I felt terrible. But no-one made a fuss, everyone reacted politely and I'm probably the only one who remembers it.

Malaysian writer Karim Raslan writes in his book *Ceritalah* about some of the confusion involved in attending post-Ramadan Hari Raya open houses in Kuala Lumpur. "The scruffy little man you asked to park your car – you mistook him for a valet – is, in fact, the richest, best-informed stockbroker in town."[1] So it seems I'm not the only one. Even locals can make these sorts of mistake.

My second great social faux pas occurred at a dinner that I attended at the Jakarta residence of Australia's ambassador to Indonesia. Before we sat down for the meal I stood chatting with the ambassador and another man to whom I hadn't been formally introduced. Somehow the three of us had fallen into conversation and it had reached the point when formal introductions now seemed inappropriate.

"You have a very strong Singaporean accent", I said to the other man. (It's an accent of which I'm quite fond.) "Have you spent much time in Singapore?"

Indeed, he had. "Actually, Michael", said the Australian ambassador, "this is the Singapore ambassador." They laughed. I laughed. But I felt foolish.

We all make mistakes. It's what you do about them that matters. Use them as an opportunity to learn more and they become very useful. In fact, all opportunities to learn should be seized because Asia is large and complex. Few rules apply equally across the entire region, so it's important to always be on the lookout for new scraps of information. I have many friends across Asia on whom I rely for small gems of information, glimpses into their lives to see how they function and live.

Ghosts and evil spirits are an important element of traditional Chinese culture. Once while leaving a hotel lobby with a Malaysian Chinese friend, I saw a large tropical butterfly clinging to a wall near the entrance. I plucked it from the wall and took it outside to free it. "We don't like to disturb them because we say that they are the souls of dead people", my friend said to me, half-seriously. A few days later, in London, an Indonesian Chinese friend told me how his uncle had died and a butterfly appeared in his mother's shop back in Indonesia three days later. "We knew it was him", he said.

On another occasion, I was chatting with a Singaporean friend who worked in one of the two office towers that rise above the massive Ngee Ann City shopping and office complex that sits midway along Singapore's Orchard Road and is built over an old Chinese cemetery. It is 55% owned by the Ngee Ann Kongsi, a Teochiu clan group, which has long owned the land on which the center is built, hence the cemetery. The architects had had a big job, said my friend: how to negate the bad feng shui that comes from building over former cemetery land? On the advice of feng shui experts, Ngee Ann City was built back from the road and designed to have the appearance of a massive Chinese grave. Its façade is covered with red-tinged granite. For auspicious reasons, there is a pond in front in the fore-court. It has large statues either side, and there are tall flagpoles at the front to represent the joss sticks that are burnt before Chinese graves. Each year, at the time of the Hungry Ghost Festival, Ngee Ann City's management sets up a massive Taoist paper kingdom in front of the shopping center which they then burn to appease the spirits of all the dead who were buried beneath. But how many Western tourists are aware of all this as they step around it to shop at the boutiques inside? How many hungry ghosts lurk in the Gucci boutique or in Cartier?

I'd also noticed that those among my Chinese friends who are more traditional and Chinese-educated often have difficulty in being precise when saying how old they are. I asked another of my friends in Asia, who is Chinese educated, why? Chinese, especially traditional Chinese, he told me, add one year to their ages to take account of the nine months that they are in the womb. The nine months tends to be rounded up to a year. Chinese babies thus are traditionally said to be aged one year at the time of their birth. And so among the older generation, milestone birthdays are held a year early.

For example, Lim Goh Tong, Malaysia's casino billionaire, held his 80th birthday celebrations in August 1997. Some 800 people attended the party in the grand ballroom at the Hotel Istana in Kuala Lumpur. But Lim had not turned 80 using a conventional calendar. He was in fact 79. He was born in 1918, and so would turn 80 in 1998. (This is a consideration worth keeping in mind for companies that wish to mark the birthday of an important traditional Chinese business partner or client. But then when Singapore's founding Prime Minister Lee Kuan Yew held his 80th birthday at Singapore's Shangri-la Hotel in September 2003, he actually was 80. Lee, though, is not from a traditional Chinese family background, as we saw in Chapter 11.)

Another example of the confusion with Chinese ages occurred with the death of the widow of China's Nationalist leader Chiang Kai-shek in New York in October 2003. Some media reports gave her age as 105, others as 106. The conflict arose from remarks by the Taipei Economic and Cultural Office in New York. It had announced Madame Chiang's age as 106. But that was her Chinese age. She was born on February 12, 1898 and died on October 23, 2003 and so, by conventional reckoning, was 105. Born Soong May-ling on China's southern Hainan island to very wealthy, West-ernized, Methodist parents, much of her formal education took place in the US. At the time of her death, she'd lived in New York almost thirty years. "The only thing Oriental about me is my face", she'd once said.[2] No doubt she would have said that she was 105.

It's the small stories, the anecdotes and seemingly trivial observations such as these that go toward making one an Insider. Separately, they are interesting and maybe not much else. But put them together and you can build a picture of Asia from the roots up. Maintain your curiosity, listen carefully and travel as often as you can. These are the things that are key to becoming an Asian Insider, whoever you might be, from the region or from outside it. Add them to headline issues such as South Korea's growth rates or China's bank reforms and you will have a complete picture.

And the learning about Asia need not be restricted to Asia. On a visit to Lourdes, the Catholic pilgrimage town in southern France, I noticed dozens of Indians at the grotto which has a spring that gushes water said to be holy. Many were filling up large plastic containers with spring water. But they weren't Catholic. All the women were dressed in saris. Many had *bindi* (colored dots) on their foreheads. What are Indian Hindus doing at Lourdes, I wondered? But then they too have an affinity with the idea of holy water, given the religious association of the Ganges River and immersion in it. Perhaps this was part of the reason.

I asked a Hindu friend of mine in London about the Indians at Lourdes. "Oh yes!" she said. "They believe in Mary."

"But they are Hindu", I said.

"Yes, But we all believe in Mary. And Jesus. They are just another manifestation of God. Here, look." She showed me a photograph of the shrine that she has in her family home. And there, among the cluttered array of Shiva, Krishna and other statues from the Hindu pantheon, was a large statue of Mary and a smaller one of Jesus. It was another scrap of information, another small piece of intelligence. But surely such scraps are cultural and have little to do with the realm of business? But what is an economy other than transactions between people. And nowhere is that more true than in Asia.

Chapter 2

1 Claessens, S., S. Djankov and L. Lang, *Who Controls East Asian Corporations?*, World Bank, Washington, February 1999.
2 *International Herald Tribune*, "The fatherly side of Genghis Khan", February 13, 2003.
3 Maclagan, M., *Lines of Succession*, Little Brown, 1999.
4 *International Herald Tribune*, "Saudi society confronts genetic ills arising from inbreeding", April 29, 2003.
5 *International Herald Tribune*, "'Cousin marriages' hinder US efforts in Iraq", September 29, 2003.
6 *Bangkok Post*, "One in every four has a minor wife", February 5, 2001.
7 Xinran, *The Good Women of China*, Chatto & Windus, 2002, p. 41.
8 Huang E. and L. Jeffrey, *Hong Kong: Portraits of Power*, Weidenfeld & Nicolson, 1995, p. 114.
9 Studwell, J., *The China Dream*, Profile Books, 2003, p. 305ff.
10 Backman, M. and C. Butler, *Big in Asia: 25 Strategies for Business Success*, Palgrave Macmillan, 2003.
11 Chan, K.B. and C. Chiang, *Stepping Out: The Making of Chinese Entrepreneurs*, Prentice Hall, 1994, p. 318; Yeap, J.K., *Far from Rangoon*, Lee Teng Lay Pte Ltd, 1994.
12 *Washington Post*, "Relative success story", September 11, 1994.
13 *Business Times*, "Singapore biscuit king Chew Choo Keng dies at 86", July 12, 2001.
14 A point first made in Backman, M. and C. Butler, op cit.

Chapter 3

1 *Asiamoney*, "Asia's investment failure", September 2005.
2 *International Herald Tribune*, "Weak market cited in China mutual funds loss", August 30, 2005.
3 As cited in *The Economist*, "Pigs, pay and power", June 28, 2003.
4 *The Economist*, "Pigs, pay and power", June 28, 2003.

5   Backman, M. and C. Butler, *Big in Asia: 25 Strategies for Success in Business*, Palgrave Macmillan, 2003, p. 57.
6   *The Sunday Times*, "Kevin Maxwell: don't ever work for a family business", April 1, 2001.

Chapter 4

1   Studwell, J., *The China Dream*, Profile Books, 2003, p. 300ff.
2   *The Age*, "Megawati ticket aims for Muslim vote", May 6, 2004.
3   Chua, A., *World on Fire: How Exporting Free Market Democracy Breeds Ethnic Hatred and Global Instability*, Doubleday, 2003, p. 78.
4   Ibid.
5   Ibid. p. 124.
6   Ibid. p. 6.
7   Ibid. p. 190.
8   Ibid. p. 14.
9   Ibid. p. 1.

Chapter 5

1   Agence France Presse, "Millionaire ministers run Asia's cleanest governments", August 18, 2002.
2   *Business Times*, "Pay cut? Ministers ready to learn by example: DPM", May 2, 2003.
3   *Business Times*, "Goh Chee Wee paid $1.43m last year", August 17, 2002.
4   *Business Times*, "Keppel last year paid Lim Chee Onn $3.75–$4m", May 9, 2003.
5   Backman, M., *Asian Eclipse: Exposing the Dark Side of Business in Asia*, John Wiley & Sons, 2001.
6   Ibid. Also, these remarks were reported in various publications including the *Jakarta Post* and *Inside Indonesia*.

Chapter 6

1   *Business Times*, "Corruption rife in Asian justice", June 3, 2003.
2   *Bangkok Post*, "Campaign backfires on taxi motorcyclists in city", July 12, 2003.
3   *Bangkok Post*, "State commitment to governance questioned", May 9, 2005.
4   *Bangkok Post*, "Murder lifts lid on realty scam", June 9, 2003.
5   *Bangkok Post*, "Retired envoy sacked from civil service", May 22, 2001.
6   *Bangkok Post*, "Out-of-court deal sought for party bill", December 29, 2000.
7   *Bangkok Post*, "Ex-Manila envoy to be investigated", August 29, 2003.
8   *Bangkok Post*, "TRT challenge to Asavahame influence," May 8, 2003.
9   *Bangkok Post*, "Inquiry into bribery claim", July 9, 2003.

Chapter 7

1   Studwell, J., *The China Dream*, Profile Books, 2003, p. 250.
2   *Wall Street Journal*, "In a land where bribes are commonplace, a Chinese millionaire pushed the envelope", November 23, 2001.
3   Amnesty International Report 2002.
4   *The Economist*, "Singapore, world execution capital", April 3–9, 1999.

5 *International Herald Tribune*, "Fewer marijuana bars", October 22, 2003.
6 *Bangkok Post*, "Lethal injections from October 19", September 8, 2003.
7 *The Straits Times*, "His job was to kill", October 2, 2003.
8 Information on Singh comes from *The Australian*, "Unmasked: the hangman who will send Aussie drug courier to 'a better place'", October 28, 2005.
9 *Jakarta Post*, "Chaubey's 10 years of legal struggle ends", August 6, 2004.
10 Lintner, B., *Blood Brothers: Crime, Business and Politics in Asia*, Allen & Unwin, 2002, p. 284.
11 As quoted in Lintner, B., ibid. p. 284.
12 *International Herald Tribune*, "The police state endures in China", November 27, 2002.
13 Amnesty International Report 2003.
14 Stewart, I., *The Mahathir Legacy: A Nation Divided, A Region at Risk*, Allen & Unwin, 2003, p. 146.
15 *The Age*, "Rio de Janeiro police kill 132 in one month", November 16, 2003.
16 *Jakarta Post*, "Alleged thieves mobbed to death", September 20, 2003.
17 *Bangkok Post*, "Pornthip raises suspicions", February 19, 2003.
18 *Bangkok Post*, "Slain parents 'not peddlers'", February 28, 2003.
19 *International Herald Tribune*, "Drug 'war' kills democracy, too", April 24, 2003.
20 *Bangkok Post*, "Foreign community to get 'the whole truth'", February 27, 2003.
21 *Bangkok Post*, "Two senior officers transferred", February 18, 2003.
22 *Bangkok Post*, "Innocent victims suffer in silence", February 17, 2003.
23 *International Herald Tribune*, "Drug 'war' kills democracy, too", April 24, 2003.

Chapter 8

1 *Business Times*, "Thai govt's investment data called into question again," November 5, 2002.
2 *Wall Street Journal*, "Philippines may have overstated current-account surplus numbers", January 13, 2003; *Wall Street Journal*, "Smaller trade-related surplus could hamper the Philippines", January 20, 2003.
3 *International Herald Tribune*, "Philippines punishes UBS over bond report", March 27, 2003.
4 *International Herald Tribune*, "In Myanmar, economy is shrouded in mystery", April 16, 2005.
5 *Euromoney*, July 1998.
6 *Business Times*, "Temasek takes 10% stake in Indian logistics company", November 24, 2004.
7 UNCTAD, World Investment Report, 2003.
8 *Business Times*, "S'pore perplexed by Jakarta accusation on trade data", June 14, 2003.
9 *New Straits Times*, "Navy holds log-laden boat linked to police", July 29, 2004.
10 Schwarz, A., *A Nation in Waiting: Indonesia in the 1990s*, Allen & Unwin, 1994, p. 28.
11 *Business Times*, "Jakarta reiterates request for full Singapore-Indon trade data", July 9, 2003.
12 *International Herald Tribune*, "Asia oil subsidies bring windfall to smugglers", September 27, 2005.
13 *Business Times*, "Bank Mandiri IPO 3 times oversubscribed", June 23, 2003.
14 *Business Times*, "Jakarta told to improve credibility", June 3, 2003.
15 Studwell, J., *The China Dream*, Profile Books, 2003, p. 232.
16 Rawski, T., "What's happening to China's GDP statistics?", mimeo, University of Pennsylvania, September 2001.
17 Tripathi, S., "Chinese puzzle", *Guardian*, December 23, 2005.
18 *Business Times*, "54% of Chinese firms misreported profits", January 9, 2003.
19 *Wall Street Journal*, "Jailing of AIDS activist shows Beijing's rigidity", September 9, 2002.
20 *International Herald Tribune*, "Yahoo helped Chinese to prosecute journalist", September 8, 2005.
21 *International Herald Tribune*, "China declassifies disaster death tolls", September 13, 2005.

Chapter 9

1 See *The Economist*, "An open letter to Silvio Berlusconi", August 2, 2003.

2 *Business Times*, "Thaksin's son is Thailand's richest shareholder", December 18, 2001.

3 *Bangkok Post*, "PM's son sells 367m shares to sister at 1 baht each", September 12, 2002.

4 *Bangkok Post*, "Panel weighs 'intentions' of PM's son", September 5, 2002.

5 *The Nation*, "Media giant TCH to focus on magazines", February 2, 2005.

6 *Bangkok Post*, "Controversy cuts print run", January 9, 2003.

7 *The Nation*, "Witness in ShinSat case shot dead in Chiang Rai", March 27, 2003.

8 *The Nation*, "PM denies murder link", March 28, 2003.

9 *Bangkok Post*, "Alongkorn threatens move to oust PM", December 9, 2001.

10 *Bangkok Post*, "Thaksin's class pals get boost", August 9, 2001.

11 *Bangkok Post*, "PM's relatives put in charge of military's weapons procurement", October 18, 2002.

12 *Bangkok Post*, "Chaisit tries to shed his Shinawatra skin", August 29, 2003.

13 *Bangkok Post*, "Chalerm eyes promotion to air force chief", July 24, 2003.

14 *Bangkok Post*, "Another job for a chum", March 27, 2003.

15 *Bangkok Post*, "Thaksin's classmates promoted", August 29, 2003.

16 *Bangkok Post*, "Priewphan gets assistant chief post", March 12, 2002.

17 *Bangkok Post*, "PM's former classmates to be promoted", August 30, 2003.

18 *Bangkok Post*, "Editorial: Don't be too quick to judge the judges", March 20, 2003.

19 *Bangkok Post*, "Purachai's head on the block", February 6, 2003.

20 *Bangkok Post*, "Govt taken to task for rights abuse," August 4, 2004.

Chapter 10

1 *Jakarta Post*, "75 million people in RI have no access to power", October 26, 2005.

2 Friend, T., *Indonesian Destinies*, Belknap Press, 2003.

3 *Business Times*, "Yudhoyono suspends governor in graft case", October 12, 2005.

4 *Business Times*, "Ex-chief of Bank Mandiri faces life sentence", October 12, 2005.

5 On the former Aceh governor: *Financial Times*, "Ex-Aceh governor gets 10-year jail term for corruption", April 4, 2005.

6 *International Herald Tribune*, a brief on Asia, September 30, 2004.

7 See www.transparency.org.

8 *Business Times*, "Indonesia still short of judges for anti-corruption court", January 10, 2005.

9 *Jakarta Post*, "Ten-year jail term sought for ex-minister over alleged graft", January 18, 2006.

10 *Business Times*, "Foreign lenders face US$180m loss after Indon court ruling", August 28, 2003.

11 *Financial Times*, "Prudential Indonesia in move to overturn bankruptcy ruling", April 29, 2004.

12 *Business Times*, "Indon court annuls firm's foreign debt", May 13, 2004.

13 Accounts of the murder and Adiguna's role were widely reported, including: *Australian Financial Review*, "Trials test Yudhoyono's resolve", March 16, 2005; Antara news agency report, "Prosecution demands life for Adiguna Sutowo", May 10, 2005; *Jakarta Post*, "Lawyers maintain Adiguna's innocence", June 3, 2005.

14 Backman, M., *Asian Eclipse: Exposing the Dark Side of Business in Asia*, John Wiley & Sons, 1999, pp. 95–9.

15 Backman, M., op. cit., pp. 95–9.

16 See Bresnan, J., *Managing Indonesia: The Modern Political Economy*, Columbia University Press, 1993, Chapter 7, "The Pertamina Crisis".

17 Backman, M., op cit., p. 33.

Chapter 11

1 Powell, R., *Living Legacy: Singapore's Architectural Heritage Renewed*, Singapore Heritage Society, 1994, p. 30.
2 Goh Chok Tong, "From the Valley to the Highlands", National Day address, Singapore, 2003.
3 Lee Kuan Yew, *The Singapore Story*, Times Editions, 1998, p. 35.
4 Ibid., p. 29.
5 Ibid., p. 95.
6 Lee Chin Koon, *Mrs Lee's Cookbook*, Eurasia Press, 1974.
7 Ibid.
8 Lam Peng Er and Kevin Tan, *Lee's Lieutenants*, Allen & Unwin, 1999, p. 27.
9 *Asian Wall Street Journal*, "Singapore Inc. puts a premium on deals to be a global player", July 18, 2001.
10 I first made this point in Backman, M., "Asians and Victorian Values", *Far Eastern Economic Review*, March 30, 2000.

Chapter 12

1 *The Star*, "Philips moves unit HQ to M'sia", October 16, 2001.
2 *Business Times*, "Honeywell dumps S'pore, moves regional HQ to Shanghai", June 18, 2003.
3 See Backman, M., "What next, Singapore?", *Today*, December 12, 2002.
4 *Business Times*, "Crazy Horse Paris rides into S'pore in December", May 19, 2005.
5 Backman, M., "China and a tale of two cities", *Today*, June 4, 2003.
6 See *Today*, March 24, 2003.
7 See *Today*, October 8, 2003
8 "Backman's got it wrong", letters, *Today*, October 13, 2003.
9 Lee Boon Yang, minister for information, communications and the arts, "Towards a Global Media City", speech to a Singapore press club luncheon, Raffles Hotel, Singapore, November 11, 2003.
10 *Wall Street Journal*, "Shhh! It's Singapore", editorial, November 19, 2003.
11 US Department of Justice records, provided under the US Foreign Agents Registrations Act.
12 *Straits Times*, "Govt offices looking like posh hotels", May 14, 2002.
13 Information provided by Amnesty International.
14 *Business Times*, "PM Goh: Ho Ching appointed for the 'larger good'", June 18, 2002.
15 *Business Times*, "Define 'political' clearly, govt urged", June 13, 2003.

Chapter 13

1 Covent Garden Soup is made by S. Daniels, a company that Singapore Food Industries (SFI) acquired in December 2002. SFI is controlled by Singapore Technologies and other GLCs and they are controlled by Temasek Holdings.
2 *Asia Times*, "Singapore's capitalism myth", November 7, 2002.
3 *The Star*, "Temasek gets new chief amid reshuffles", June 27, 2002.
4 *Business Times*, "GLCs shine – with or without privatisation", September 6, 2002.
5 See "Apology" published in both the *Business Times* and *Today* on November 22, 2002.
6 *The Economist*, "Whither Singapore Inc?", November 30, 2002.

7　*Business Times*, "Singtel chairman bought M1 shares", June 9, 2003.
8　See *Asian Wall Street Journal*, "Government-linked firms spark debate in Singapore", December 26, 2001.
9　*Business Times*, "Pillay urges GLCs to improve governance", January 16, 2003.
10　*Business Times*, "ST Telemedia to take control of Global Crossing", October 8, 2003.
11　*Asiamoney*, "China – sale of the century", September 2005.
12　*Asian Wall Street Journal*, "Singapore Inc. puts a premium on deals to be a global player", July 18, 2001.
13　*Business Times*, "ST Telemedia to take control of Global Crossing", October 8, 2003.
14　*Business Times*, "GIC arm takes 80% stake in Japan property fund", September 2, 2005.

Chapter 14

1　*Time*, "The Lion in Winter", June 30, 2003.
2　Brazil, D., *No Money, No Honey!*, Angsana Books, 1998, p. 9.
3　Ibid., p. 12.
4　*TTG Asia*, "Boutique hotel for Chinatown", March 13, 2003.
5　*The Star*, "Chow Kit's new lease of life", July 18, 2002.

Chapter 15

1　*New Straits Times*, "Indefatigably mamak!", December 6, 2000.
2　Herbert, B., "Ask Bechtel what war is good for", *International Herald Tribune*, April 22, 2003.
3　As reprinted in *Daim Speaks his Mind*, Pelanduk Publications, 1995.
4　Mahathir M., *The Malaysian Currency Crisis: How it Happened and Why*, Pelanduk Publications, 2000, p. 9.
5　East Asia Analytical Unit, *Asia's Financial Markets: Capitalising on Reform*, Commonwealth of Australia, Canberra, 1999, p. 197.
6　*The Star*, "Lower costs lift Pertamina 2002 earnings", August 27, 2003.
7　*Business Times*, "KL cabinet minister charged with cheating, corruption", February 13, 2004.
8　*Business Times*, "Isa's downfall strengthens Abdullah's hand", June 27, 2005.
9　*The Age*, "Malaysian MP jailed for bribery", August 23, 2005.

Chapter 16

1　Stewart, I., *The Mahathir Legacy: A Nation Divided, A Region at Risk*, Allen & Unwin, 2003, p. 44.
2　*International Herald Tribune*, "Gore's speech stuns Malaysia", November 17, 1998.

Chapter 17

1　*Far Eastern Economic Review*, "Syed Mokhtar's coming-out party", May 29, 2003.
2　*The Star*, "Will Syed Mokhtar succeed where other bumiputera businessmen have failed?" October 8, 2002.
3　*Business Times*, "Syed Mokhtar acquires 15% of rice importer", February 8, 2003.
4　*Far Eastern Economic Review*, "Syed Mokhtar's coming-out party", May 29, 2003.
5　*Business Times*, "Syed Mokhtar bags monorail deal", October 22, 2003.

Notes

311

6 The Star, "Project tie-up with Gamuda seen as boost to MMC", August 7, 2003; Business
Times, "Syed Mokhtar's latest coup: RM15b rail deal", October 17, 2003.
7 The Star, "Britain's Gearbulk Pool relocates from S'pore to Johor Port", June 6, 2003.
8 Business Times, "Port alliance? It's up to PTP, says KL minister", August 15, 2003.
9 Business Times, "Port magnate Syed Mokhtar eyeing dredging jobs: report", July 24, 2002.
10 Business Times, "Syed Mokhtar's finances healthy, associates claim", October 10, 2003.
11 Business Times, "Johor-Dubai link set to pressure S'pore port", April 22, 2003.
12 Smart Investor, "One fashionable sport", November 1, 2002.
13 Business Times, "Johor-Dubai link set to pressure S'pore port", April 22, 2003.
14 Business Times, "Malaysia to let in foreign Islamic banks", June 3, 2003.
15 The Star, "CAHB pact on Bank Muamalat stake sale", August 7, 2003.
16 Business Times, "Krishnan, Syed Mokhtar most charitable M'sians", September 16, 2005.

Chapter 18

1 Irwin, R., "Ramadan nights", London Review of Books, August 7, 2003.
2 Raban, J., "The greatest gulf", Guardian, April 19, 2003.
3 Jakarta Post, "Indonesian VP says govt has different view on terrorism", October 26, 2002.
4 International Herald Tribune, "Malaysians are hunted for new Bali bombings", October 4,
2005.
5 Stewart, I., The Mahathir Legacy: A Nation Divided, A Region at Risk, Allen & Unwin, 2003,
p. 223.
6 The Star, "Foreign link probe on KMM", August 10, 2001.
7 Bangkok Post, "Muslims seek swift inquiry into shooting," June 19, 2003.
8 Bowring, P., "Thailand only feeds Muslim discontent", International Herald Tribune, October
28, 2004.
9 The Star, "Zam Zam Cola gets strong response", June 18, 2003; Business Times, "Malaysia
takes a small sip of Iran's Zam Zam Cola", June 16, 2003.
10 The quote is from one such ad which appeared in the New Straits Times, July 28, 2004.

Chapter 19

1 Schwartz S., The Two Faces of Islam: The House of Sa'ud from Tradition to Terror, Doubleday,
2002, p. 17.
2 Bernstein, P., Against the Gods: The Remarkable Story of Risk, John Wiley & Sons, 1998, p. 33.
3 Irwin, R., "Ramadan nights", London Review of Books, August 7, 2003.
4 For more on this point, see Schwartz S., op. cit.
5 Irwin, R., op. cit.

Chapter 20

1 Washington Post, "Indonesia's radical Arabs raise suspicions of moderate countrymen,"
January 9, 2003.
2 International Herald Tribune, "High court to hear case of bin Laden's driver", November 8,
2005.
3 Ibid.
4 Dunlop, P., Street Names of Singapore, Who's Who Publishing, 2000, p. 173.
5 Powell, R., Living Legacy: Singapore's Architectural Heritage Renewed, Singapore Heritage
Society, 1994.

6 Ibid.

7 Ibid.

8 *Straits Times*, "The family behind Boon Lay", November 16, 2003.

9 Ameen Ali Talib, "Hadramis in Singapore", a paper prepared for the British-Yemeni Society, November 1995.

10 Harris, J., "The Persian connection: Four loanwords in Siamese", *Pasaa*, XVI(1), Chulalongkorn University Language Institute, June 1986.

Chapter 21

1 *International Herald Tribune*, "Malaysia works to sell Islam on trade benefits", June 23, 2005.

2 *Business Times*, "M'sia sees big jump in Arab tourists", May 10, 2004.

3 *The Star*, "Syrian sensations", July 16, 2002.

4 *New Straits Times*, "Proton factory in Iran to start running in August", July 23, 2002.

5 *The Star*, "Hicom ventures into Bahrain", August 8, 2002.

6 *The Star*, "UEM to sign US$238mil Qatar deal", October 23, 2003.

7 *The Star*, "Dian Kreatif to supply domes for Abu Dhabi mosque", December 9, 2004.

8 *Business Times*, "Malaysian-Saudi group bags US$2.5b power, water job", November 17, 2005.

9 *The Star*, "Bahrain fund ready to invest up to US$200mil in M'sia projects", June 28, 2003.

Chapter 22

1 *The Age*, "Rising sun benchmark below horizon", January 29, 2003.

2 *International Herald Tribune*, "Japan's expensive rice could cost it plenty more", August 8, 2003.

3 Asian Demographics Ltd, "The Year Total Population is Projected to Peak for Each Country in Asia", February 1, 2003.

4 *International Herald Tribune*, "Outsiders waiting to be insiders", July 24, 2003.

5 Asian Demographics Ltd, "The Changing Age Profile of Mothers in Japan: 1982 to 2022", March 8, 2003.

6 *Financial Times*, "Japan waits for its angels to deliver", June 11, 2004.

7 *The Economist*, "The incredible shrinking country", November 13, 2004.

8 *Bangkok Post*, "Japan's land prices continue to decline", March 25, 2003.

9 *Business Times*, "Fears of Japanese financial crisis grow on bank bailout", May 19, 2003.

Chapter 23

1 *This is London*, "'Snakehead' link to shooting," June 6, 2003.

2 *Wall Street Journal*, "In China, foundation is set for a banking crisis to erupt", August 7, 2002.

3 *The Star*, "China reports record tax takings in 2004", January 11, 2005.

4 Becker, J., "A legacy of corruption and bad debts", *International Herald Tribune*, November 11, 2002.

5 *Wall Street Journal*, "China targets local laws to meet its WTO pledges", November 27, 2001.

6 *International Herald Tribune*, "Chinese banker convicted", August 13, 2005.

7 *Wall Street Journal*, "Corruption wiped out 13% to 16% of China's GDP, researcher says", March 8, 2001.

8 *Australian Financial Review*, "China punished 175,000 corrupt officials", January 25, 2002.

9 Backman, M., *Asian Eclipse: Exposing the Dark Side of Business in Asia*, John Wiley & Sons, 2001.

10 *South China Morning Post*, "Lines drawn over retail invasion", April 9, 2003.
11 Associated Press wire report, "Chinese pirates work magic on Potter book", July 31, 2005.
12 *Wall Street Journal*, "Piracy remains rampant after China joined WTO", December 11, 2002.
13 Studwell, J., *The China Dream*, Profile Books, 2003, p. 195.
14 *Business Times*, "Lego wins copyright case in China", January 22, 2003.
15 *Financial Times*, "Heat turned up in fake goods crackdown", November 8, 2005.
16 Studwell, J., op. cit., p. 195.
17 Studwell, J., op. cit., pp. 184–5.
18 *The Age*, "For Mr Mo, court win can mean jail", January 20, 2003.
19 *International Herald Tribune*, "In China, a system designed to convict", November 12, 2005.
20 *Business Times*, "On the rise: China firms with bogus IPO plans", October 22, 2003.
21 *Business Times*, "China unveils independent director system," August 23, 2001.
22 *Business Times*, "China tightens rules for delisting of companies", February 26, 2002.
23 *Wall Street Journal*, "China issues arrest warrant for former head of Brilliance", October 23, 2002.
24 *Business Times*, "Ex-Everbright chief escapes death, gets jail", October 11, 2002.

Chapter 24

1 *The Star*, "Pepsi China sales up 26%", January 19, 2005.
2 Chee H. and C. West, *Myths about Doing Business in China*, Palgrave Macmillan, 2004, p. 6–7.
3 *International Herald Tribune*, "Sports firms set China as a goal", January 2005.
4 *Asian Wall Street Journal*, "US urges Chinese: save less, buy more", October 14, 2005.
5 *The Economist*, "China business survey", March 20, 2004.
6 *Wall Street Journal*, "Starbucks expands in China, in talks to tap India market," December 16, 2002.
7 *International Herald Tribune*, "For China, new malls jaw-dropping in size", May 25, 2005.
8 *International Herald Tribune*, "More US firms rush to invest in China malls", July 27, 2005.
9 *International Herald Tribune*, "China strains to join the plastic economy", May 24, 2005.
10 *International Herald Tribune*, "China's answer to Larry King?", February 7, 2005.
11 From www.chinaguide.org/guide/china-statistics.
12 *International Herald Tribune*, "Baidu turns up spotlight on Chinese Web stocks", August 8, 2005.
13 *International Herald Tribune*, "Yahoo dealing for a big move into Chinese e-commerce", August 9, 2005.
14 *Business Times*, "The Web fortune that Jack built", August 16, 2005.
15 Chee H. and C. West, op. cit., p. 31.
16 Kurt Salmon Associates, Consumer Outlook Survey for China, October 2004.
17 Knight Ridder wire service, "In China, some global brands assailed by consumers, media", August 31, 2005.
18 Bloomberg wire report, "Chinese retail group urges boycott of Japanese goods", April 5, 2005.
19 *International Herald Tribune*, "Dragon faux pas offends Chinese", October 4, 2004.
20 Chee H. and C. West, op. cit., p. 6.
21 *The Economist*, "Staying young", July 16, 2005.
22 *Financial Times*, "Business to be had beyond Beijing", November 8, 2005.
23 From www.chinaguide.org/guide/china-statistics.
24 Ibid.

25 Laidler, K., *The Last Empress: The She-Dragon of China*, Wiley, 2003.
26 *International Herald Tribune*, "Health care falls short, Chinese tell leaders", August 20, 2005.

Chapter 25

1 *Far Eastern Economic Review*, "Shanghai's Champs Elysées", September 13, 2001.
2 *Business Times*, "Developers dismiss Shanghai bubble fears", February 6, 2003.
3 Levy, A. and C. Scott-Clark, *The Stone of Heaven: The Secret History of Imperial Green Jade*, Phoenix, 2002, p. 252.
4 *International Herald Tribune*, "Shanghai suffers as car culture takes hold", July 12, 2005.

Chapter 27

1 *New York Times*, "Dalai Lama Group says it got money from CIA", October 2, 1998.
2 French, P., "The cuddly monk and Tibetan reality", *International Herald Tribune*, September 24, 2003.
3 The search is described in Hicks, R. and Ngakpa Chogyam, *Great Ocean: An Authorized Biography of the Dalai Lama*, Penguin, 1990.
4 As reported in the *Far Eastern Economic Review*, "Two-faced", July 22, 2004.
5 As reported in *The Age*, "Tibet part of China: Dalai Lama", March 15, 2005.

Chapter 28

1 A joke commonly heard in India and retold in Tripathi, S., "The right way and the Indian way", *The New Statesman*, July 17, 2003.
2 Pye, L., *Asian Power and Politics: The Cultural Dimensions of Authority*, Belknap Press, 1985, p. 146.
3 Economic Analytical Unit, *India: New Economy, Old Economy*, Department of Foreign Affairs and Trade, Commonwealth of Australia, 2001, p. 45.
4 Bardhan, P., "Giants unchained? Not so fast", *International Herald Tribune*, November 3, 2005.
5 *Far Eastern Economic Review*, "In small doses", July 20, 2000.
6 Tripathi, S., op. cit.
7 Economic Analytical Unit, op. cit., pp. 12–13.
8 *The Economist*, "Small savings, big headache," March 29, 2003.
9 *Business Times*, "India loses US$85b a year to tax dodgers", November 12, 2001.
10 Tripathi, S., op. cit.
11 *International Herald Tribune*, "India's malls pull in people who aren't buying", May 11, 2005.
12 *Business Times*, "Hasten reforms or lose to China: Indian minister", August 19, 2003.
13 Economic Analytical Unit, op. cit., p. 150.
14 Economic Analytical Unit, op. cit., p. 44.
15 Economic Analytical Unit, op. cit., p. 16.
16 *Wall Street Journal*, "Ambani, founder and chairman of Reliance Industries, dies at 69", July 6, 2002.
17 *Time*, "Prince of polyester", July 22, 2002.
18 Bardhan, P., op. cit.
19 Stern, N., "Building a climate for investment, growth, and poverty reduction in India", speech by Nicholas Stern, World Bank chief economist and senior vice president at EXIM Bank, Mumbai, India, March 22, 2001.

20 Economic Analytical Unit, op. cit., p. 115.
21 Economic Analytical Unit, op. cit., p. 55ff.
22 *Financial Times,* "Graft in Asia on rise, says business", March 13, 2003.
23 *Guardian,* "Corrupt practices cost ordinary citizens £2.7bn, says watchdog", July 2, 2005.

Chapter 29

1 Economic Analytical Unit, *India: New Economy, Old Economy,* Department of Foreign Affairs and Trade, Commonwealth of Australia, 2001, p. 22.
2 Agence France Presse report, "Malaysian court rules in favour of Italian in Bofors scandal", December 2, 2002.
3 *International Herald Tribune,* "Gandhi dynasty produces new stars", May 15–16, 2004.
4 *International Herald Tribune,* "For a Gandhi who waits tributes keep mounting", October 28, 2005.
5 As cited in *International Herald Tribune,* "India's rich but into lifestyle", September 23, 2004.
6 Dalrymple, W., *The Age of Kali,* Flamingo, 1999, p. 40.
7 Dalrymple, W., ibid., pp. 87–8.
8 *The Economist,* "Uttar nonsense", March 15, 2003.
9 Dalrymple, W., op. cit., pp. 87–8.
10 *The Hindu,* "Mulayam youth brigade leader arrested," March 18, 2003.
11 Dalrymple, W., op. cit., pp. 87–8.
12 *The Economist,* op. cit.
13 Indo-Asian News Service report, "Mayawati slaps cases against Mulayam, Amar Singh", April 14, 2003.
14 *The Economist,* op. cit.
15 *Time,* "Prince of polyester", July 22, 2002.
16 Dalrymple, W., op. cit., p. 115.
17 *India Today,* "Infosys: Money machine", November 8, 1999.

Chapter 30

1 BBC News, "Bombay faces population boom", December 30, 2000.
2 *The Nation,* "'Richest city' falling apart", January 10, 2006.
3 *The Economist,* "After the deluge", August 6, 2005.
4 *The Times of India,* "Tenants of old buildings resist developers' plot", April 10, 2003.

Chapter 31

1 Economic Analytical Unit, *India: New Economy, Old Economy,* Department of Foreign Affairs and Trade, Commonwealth of Australia, 2001, p. 100.
2 Economic Analytical Unit, ibid., p. 102.
3 Economic Analytical Unit, ibid., p. 30.
4 *Sunday Times of India,* "Hot new hubs," April 13, 2003.
5 *Far Eastern Economic Review,* "Building the new India", July 20, 2000.
6 *Business Times,* "Philips to increase Indian investment, staff", September 4, 2003.
7 *Business Times,* "India to get Intel's investment dollar", June 12, 2003.
8 *Business Times,* "Accenture to add 400 jobs to Mumbai software unit", December 5, 2001.
9 *Business Times,* "Infosys, Tata in US$400m outsourcing deals", September 2, 2005.

10 *Far Eastern Economic Review*, "Gates and Gandhi", August 24, 2000.
11 *Far Eastern Economic Review*, "Building the new India", July 20, 2000.
12 *Far Eastern Economic Review*, "New frontiers", July 20, 2000.
13 Economic Analytical Unit, op. cit., p. 104.
14 Economic Analytical Unit, op. cit., p. 104.
15 Economic Analytical Unit, op. cit., p. 102.
16 *The Economist*, "An American in Bangalore", February 8, 2003.
17 *The Economist*, "Techno-coolies no more", May 10, 2003.
18 Ibid.
19 Tripathi, S., "India's skill shortage", *Wall Street Journal Asia*, January 5, 2006.

Chapter 32

1 *The Star*, "India offers solution to cost cutting", April 21, 2002.
2 Ibid.
3 *Business Times*, "Relocation game: India will win big," May 3, 2003; *Business Times*, "Barclays shifts data processing jobs to India," June 6, 2003.
4 *Business Times*, "Indian outsourcing firms' no-poach code", June 16, 2003.
5 *The Economic Times Mumbai*, "Outsourcing to create 40 lakh jobs in India", April 13, 2003.
6 *Business Times*, "Relocation game: India will win big," May 3, 2003.
7 *The Telegraph*, "Pru union fears call-centre's passage to India", September 30, 2002.
8 *The Star*, "Call centres boom in Asia", September 2, 2003.
9 *The Star*, op. cit.
10 *The Star*, op. cit.
11 *The Economic Times Mumbai*, op. cit.
12 *The Economic Times Mumbai*, op. cit.
13 *Business Times*, "India turning into world's back office", May 12, 2003.
14 *Business Times*, "Barclays shifts data processing jobs to India", June 6, 2003.
15 *Business Times*, "India aims to become world's back office", May 1, 2003.
16 *The Star*, op. cit.
17 *The Star*, op. cit.
18 *Business Times*, "India aims to become world's back office", May 1, 2003.
19 *International Herald Tribune*, "Indian outsourcers move to fix security", June 17, 2005.
20 *The Economic Times Mumbai*, op. cit.
21 *Financial Times*, "HSBC to cut 4,000 jobs in switch to Asia", October 17, 2003.
22 *Business Today*, "Backlash", April 13, 2003.
23 *Business Times*, "Indian outsourcing firms' no-poach code", June 16, 2003.
24 *Business Times*, "Relocation game: India will win big", May 3, 2003.
25 *Business Times*, "Manila guns for bigger slice of outsourcing pie," June 16, 2003.
26 *Business Times*, ibid.
27 *Business Today*, "Backlash", April 13, 2003.
28 *Business Times*, "Manila guns for bigger slice of outsourcing pie," June 16, 2003.

Chapter 33

1 Pye, L. *Asian Power and Politics: The Cultural Dimensions of Authority*, Belknap Press, 1985.
2 *International Herald Tribune*, "Seoul targets corporate cronyism", August 18, 2004.
3 *Asian Wall Street Journal*, "Halting pace of Korea Inc. reforms is highlighted", March 30, 1998.

4 *Far Eastern Economic Review*, "House of debt", 14 March 1991.

5 *International Herald Tribune*, "Hanbo sold for $377 million", February 13, 2002.

6 *The Age*, "Epic fall of a South Korean colossus", May 8, 2001; *International Herald Tribune*, "South Korean banking bailout will cost $126 billion", July 21, 2000.

7 Pye, L. op. cit., p. 222.

8 Lim Gill-Chin, "Sustainable governance for sustainable development", in *Trust and Anti-Trust in Asian Business Alliances: Historical Roots and Current Practices*, J. Kidd and F. Richter (eds), Palgrave Macmillan, 2004.

9 *Wall Street Journal*, "South Korea's chaebol's lose ground on debt reduction, accounts show", August 2, 2000.

10 *Wall Street Journal*, "Roh promises swift moves to revamp economy", December 23, 2002.

11 *The Star*, "S. Korea's 3rd-largest business group chairman questioned", March 5, 2003.

Chapter 34

1 Raslan, K., *Ceritalah: Malaysia in Transition*, Times Books International, 2000, p. 38.

2 Associated Press report, "Madame Chiang Kai-shek dies in NYC at 105", October 24, 2003; *The Age*, "Chiang Kai-shek's widow dies at 106", October 24, 2003.

BIBLIOGRAPHY

Ameen Ali Talib, "Hadramis in Singapore", a paper prepared for the British-Yemeni Society, November 1995.

Amnesty International Report 2002.

Asian Demographics Ltd, "The year total population is projected to peak for each country in Asia", mimeo, February 1, 2003.

Asian Demographics Ltd, "The changing age profile of mothers in Japan: 1982 to 2022", mimeo, March 8, 2003.

Backman, M., *Asian Eclipse: Exposing the Dark Side of Business in Asia*, John Wiley & Sons, 1999.

Backman, M., "Asians and Victorian values", *Far Eastern Economic Review*, March 30, 2000.

Backman, M., *Asian Eclipse: Exposing the Dark Side of Business in Asia*, rev. edn, John Wiley & Sons, 2001.

Backman, M., "What next, Singapore?", *Today*, December 12, 2002.

Backman, M., "China and a tale of two cities", *Today*, June 4, 2003.

Backman, M., *Inside Knowledge: Streetwise in Asia*, Palgrave Macmillan, 2005.

Backman, M. and C. Butler, *Big in Asia: 25 Strategies for Business Success*, Palgrave Macmillan, 2003.

Barber, R. (ed.) *Aceh: The Untold Story*, Asian Forum for Human Rights and Development, 2000.

Bardhan, P., "Giants unchained? Not so fast", *International Herald Tribune*, November 3, 2005.

Becker, J., "A legacy of corruption and bad debts", *International Herald Tribune*, November 11, 2002.

Bernstein, P., *Against the Gods: The Remarkable Story of Risk*, John Wiley & Sons, 1998.

Bowring, P., "Thailand only feeds Muslim discontent", *International Herald Tribune*, October 28, 2004.

Brazil, D., *No Money, No Honey!*, Angsana Books, 1998.

Bresnan, J., *Managing Indonesia: The Modern Political Economy*, Columbia University Press, 1993.

Chan, K.B. and C. Chiang, *Stepping Out: The Making of Chinese Entrepreneurs*, Prentice Hall, 1994.

Chee, H. and C. West, *Myths about Doing Business in China*, Palgrave Macmillan, 2004.

Chua, A., *World on Fire: How Exporting Free Market Democracy Breeds Ethnic Hatred and Global Instability*, Doubleday, 2003.

CIA, *CIA Factbook*, 2004.

Claessens, S., S. Djankov and L. Lang, "Who controls East Asian corporations?", World Bank, Washington, February 1999.

Daim Zainuddin, *Daim Speaks his Mind*, Pelanduk Publications, 1995.

Dalrymple, W., *The Age of Kali*, Flamingo, 1999.

Dunlop, P., *Street Names of Singapore*, Who's Who Publishing, 2000, p. 173.

East Asia Analytical Unit, *Overseas Chinese Business Networks in Asia*, Department of Foreign Affairs and Trade, Commonwealth of Australia, 1995.

East Asia Analytical Unit, *Asia's Financial Markets: Capitalising on Reform*, Department of Foreign Affairs and Trade, Commonwealth of Australia, 1999.

Economic Analytical Unit, *India: New Economy, Old Economy*, Department of Foreign Affairs and Trade, Commonwealth of Australia, 2001.

French, P., "The cuddly monk and Tibetan reality", *International Herald Tribune*, September 24, 2003.

Friend, T., *Indonesian Destinies*, Belknap Press, 2003.

Goh Chok Tong, "From the Valley to the Highlands", National Day Address, Singapore, 2003.

Harris, J., "The Persian connection: Four loanwords in Siamese", *Pasaa*, Vol. XVI, No. 1, Chulalongkorn University Language Institute, June 1986.

Herbert, B., "Ask Bechtel what war is good for", *International Herald Tribune*, April 22, 2003.

Hicks, R. and Ngakpa Chogyam, *Great Ocean: An Authorized Biography of the Dalai Lama*, Penguin, 1990.

Hu Jintao, speech to the Australian Parliament, October 23, 2003.

Huang E. and L. Jeffrey, *Hong Kong: Portraits of Power*, Weidenfeld & Nicolson, London, 1995.

Irwin, R., "Ramadan nights", *London Review of Books*, August 7, 2003.

Jones, S., "Corruption blocks Aceh peace", *Straits Times*, July 24, 2002.

Khoo Su Nin, *Streets of Georgetown, Penang*, Janus Print & Resources, 1994.

Laidler, K., *The Last Empress: The She-Dragon of China*, Wiley, 2003.

Lam Peng Er and Kevin Tan, *Lee's Lieutenants*, Allen & Unwin, 1999.

Lee Chin Koon, *Mrs Lee's Cookbook*, Eurasia Press, 1974.

Lee Kuan Yew, *The Singapore Story*, Times Editions, 1998.

Levy, A. and C. Scott-Clark, *The Stone of Heaven: The Secret History of Imperial Green Jade*, Phoenix, 2002, p. 252.

Lim Gill-Chin, "Sustainable governance for sustainable development", in *Trust and Anti-Trust in Asian Business Alliances: Historical Roots and Current Practices*, J. Kidd and F. Richter (eds), Palgrave Macmillan, 2004.

Lintner, B., *Blood Brothers: Crime Business and Politics in Asia*, Allen & Unwin, 2002.

Maclagan, M., *Lines of Succession*, Little Brown, 1999.

Mahathir Mohamad, *The Malay Dilemma*, Times Books International, 1970.

Mahathir Mohamad, *The Malaysian Currency Crisis: How it Happened and Why*, Pelanduk Publications, 2000.

Powell, R., *Living Legacy: Singapore's Architectural Heritage Renewed*, Singapore Heritage Society, 1994.

Pye, L., *Asian Power and Politics: The Cultural Dimensions of Authority*, Belknap Press, 1985.

Raban, J., "The greatest gulf", *Guardian*, April 19, 2003.

Raslan, K., *Ceritalah: Malaysia in Transition*, Times Books International, 2000.

Rawski, T., "What's happening to China's GDP statistics?", mimeo, University of Pennsylvania, September 2001.

Reid, A., *Southeast Asia in the Age of Commerce 1450–1680*, vol. one, Silkworm Books, 1988.

Schwarz, A., *A Nation in Waiting: Indonesia in the 1990s*, Allen & Unwin, 1994, p. 28.

Schwartz S., *The Two Faces of Islam: The House of Sa'ud from Tradition to Terror*, Doubleday, 2002.

Stern, N., "Building a climate for investment, growth, and poverty reduction in India", speech by Nicholas Stern, World Bank chief economist and senior vice president, at EXIM Bank, Mumbai, India, March 22, 2001.

Stewart, I., *The Mahathir Legacy: A Nation Divided, A Region at Risk*, Allen & Unwin, 2003.

Studwell, J., *The China Dream*, Profile Books, 2003.

Tripathi, S., "The right way and the Indian way", *The New Statesman*, July 17, 2003.

UNCTAD, *World Investment Report, 2003*.

Xinran, *The Good Women of China*, Chatto & Windus, 2002.

Yeap, J.K., *Far from Rangoon*, Lee Teng Lay Pte Ltd, 1994.

Journals, Periodicals, Newspapers and Press Agencies

Agence France Presse
Asia Inc.
Asian Wall Street Journal
Associated Press
Australian Financial
  Review
Bangkok Post
Business Times
Euromoney
Far Eastern Economic
  Review
Financial Times
Guardian
India Today
Inside Indonesia

Institutional Investor
International Herald
  Tribune
Jakarta Post
New Straits Times
Reuters
Smart Investor
South China Morning
  Post
Straits Times
Streats
Sunday Times of India
The Age
The Economic Times
  Mumbai

The Economist
The Hindu
The Nation
The New Light of
  Myanmar
The Star
The Times of India
This is London
Time
Time Asia
Today
TTG Asia
Wall Street Journal
Washington Post

INDEX